THE OXFORD HISTORY OF

BYZANTIUM

THE OXFORD HISTORY OF

BYZANTIUM

EDITED BY

Cyril Mango

OXFORD

UNIVERSITY PRESS

OXFORD

UNIVERSITY PRESS

Great Clarendon Street, Oxford OX2 6DP

Oxford University Press is a department of the University of Oxford.
It furthers the University's objective of excellence in research, scholarship,
and education by publishing worldwide in

Oxford New York

Auckland Bangkok Buenos Aires Cape Town Chennai
Dar es Salaam Delhi Hong Kong Istanbul Karachi Kolkata
Kuala Lumpur Madrid Melbourne Mexico City Mumbai Nairobi
São Paulo Shanghai Singapore Taipei Tokyo Toronto

Oxford is a registered trade mark of Oxford University Press
in the UK and in certain other countries

Published in the United States
by Oxford University Press Inc., New York

British Library Cataloguing in Publication Data

Data available

Library of Congress Cataloging in Publication Data

Data available

ISBN 0-19-814098-3

10 9 8 7 6 5 4 3 2 1

Printed in Great Britain
on acid-free paper by
Butler & Tanner Ltd., Frome, Somerset

Preface

I shall not repeat the adage that Byzantium has been and continues to be unduly neglected. That may have been true a hundred, even fifty years ago: it is certainly not the case today. The contemptuous abuse that was heaped on Byzantium by the likes of Montesquieu and Edward Gibbon kept some of its malignity into the Victorian era, but was generally dismissed well before the end of the nineteenth century in favour of a more positive assessment. The exclusion of Byzantium from the academic curriculum has been rectified, if not as fully as some may desire. At present Byzantine studies are taught at a great many universities in Europe and the USA; well over a dozen international journals are devoted exclusively to Byzantine material; the volume of relevant bibliography has risen at an alarming rate; the number of conferences, symposia, round tables, and 'workshops' has passed all count, and the same may be said of exhibitions of Byzantine artefacts. The last International Congress of Byzantine Studies (Paris, 2001) had an attendance of one thousand.

The rehabilitation of Byzantium forms an interesting chapter in the development of European historical thought and aesthetic trends in the nineteenth and twentieth centuries. What had been seen as a monotonous tale of decadence, intrigue, and moral turpitude has been transformed into a stirring and colourful epic; what was regarded by Gibbon as superstition has emerged as spirituality; an art that had been ridiculed for its clumsiness and lifelessness became in the early twentieth century a source of inspiration in the campaign against dead academic classicism. Have these changes occurred because we are better informed than our great-grandfathers? There has certainly been since about 1850 an enormous enlargement of our knowledge of Byzantine 'material culture', but the same does not apply to the written word. Practically all the Byzantine texts we read today were available in 1850 if anyone cared to consult them. Byzantium has not changed: our attitudes have, and will doubtless change again in the future.

Byzantium needs no apologia. Its crucial role in European and Near Eastern history is a matter of record. Its literature (if one may use this term for the entire corpus of writing) is very extensive and has suffered few significant losses. Its legacy in stone, paint, and other media is more lacunose, but sufficiently representative of what no longer exists. On this basis it is possible—not that everyone will agree on the result—to pass an informed judgement on the Byzantine achievement compared with other contemporary civilizations, notably that of the medieval West and that of Islam. Such comparisons have seldom been made.

The urge to reinterpret, to question accepted opinions has affected Byzantine history no less than that of other periods. On many issues of broad importance there is no longer a scholarly consensus. I have not tried, therefore, to impose either my own views or mutual consistency on the contributors to this volume.

C. M.

Acknowledgements

The editor should like to thank Marlia Mundell Mango for planning the illustration of this volume and the following persons and institutions for supplying or helping to obtain individual photographs and drawings:

M. Achimastou-Potamianou (Athens)
S. Assersohn (OUP)
J. Balty (Brussels)
L. Brubaker (Birmingham)
St Catherine's Monastery, Mount Sinai
A. Ertuğ (Istanbul)
A. Guillou (Paris)
R. Hoyland (Oxford)
C. Lightfoot (New York)
J. McKenzie (Oxford)
Ch. Pennas (Athens)
Y. Petsopoulos (London)
M. Piccirillo (Madaba)

N. Pollard (Oxford)
J. Raby (Oxford)
L. Schachner (Oxford)
I. Ševčenko (Cambridge, MA)
J. Shepard (Oxford)
R. R. R. Smith (Oxford)
A.-M. Talbot, for the Dumbarton Oaks Library and Collection (Washington, DC)
N. Thierry (Étampes)
S. Tipping (OUP)
L. Treadwell (Oxford)

Index compiled by Meg Davies

Contents

List of Special Features

List of Colour Plates

List of Maps and Figures

List of Contributors

CLIVE FOSS is Professor of History, University of Massachusetts, Boston. Author of *Byzantine and Turkish Sardis* (1976); *Ephesus after Antiquity* (1979).

ROBERT HOYLAND is Leverhulme Research Fellow attached to the Oriental Institute, University of Oxford. Author of *Seeing Islam as Others Saw It* (1997); *Arabia and the Arabs from the Bronze Age to the Coming of Islam* (2001).

ELIZABETH JEFFREYS is Bywater and Sotheby Professor of Byzantine and Modern Greek Language and Literature, University of Oxford and Fellow of Exeter College. Author of (with others) *Studies in John Malalas* (1990); *The War of Troy* (1996); *Digenis Akritis* (1998).

PATRICIA KARLIN-HAYTER has taught at the Universities of Birmingham and Belfast. Author of *Vita Euthymii Patriarchae Constantinopolitani* (1970); *Studies in Byzantine Political History* (1981).

PAUL MAGDALINO is Professor of Byzantine History, University of St Andrews. Author of *The Empire of Manuel I Komnenos* (1993); *Constantinople médiévale* (1996).

CYRIL MANGO is Bywater and Sotheby Professor Emeritus, University of Oxford. Author of *Byzantium: The Empire of New Rome* (1980); *Le Développement urbain de Constantinople, IVe–VIIe siècles* (1985); (with R. Scott), *The Chronicle of Theophanes Confessor* (1997).

MARLIA MUNDELL MANGO is University Lecturer in Byzantine Archaeology and Art, University of Oxford and Fellow of St John's College. Author of *Silver from Early Byzantium: The Kaper Koraon and Related Treasures* (1986); (with A. Bennett), *The Sevso Treasure. Part I* (1994).

STEPHEN W. REINERT is Associate Professor in Byzantine and Early Turkic Studies at Rutgers University. Author of numerous articles and principal editor of *To Hellenikon: Studies in Honor of Speros Vryonis, Jr.* (1993).

PETER SARRIS is University Lecturer in Medieval History, University of Cambridge and Fellow of Trinity College. Author of *Economy and Society in the Age of Justinian: The Oxford History of Medieval Europe, 500–700* (forthcoming).

IHOR ŠEVČENKO is Dumbarton Oaks Professor of Byzantine History Emeritus, Harvard University. Author of *La Vie intellectuelle et politique à Byzance sous les premiers Paléologues* (1962); *Byzantium and the Slavs in Letters and Culture* (1991).

JONATHAN SHEPARD was until recently University Lecturer in Russian History, University of Cambridge. Co-editor of *Byzantine Diplomacy* (1992); co-author (with S. Franklin) of *The Emergence of Rus, 750–1200* (1996).

WARREN TREADGOLD is Professor of Late Ancient and Byzantine History, Saint Louis University. Author of *Byzantium and its Army* (1995); *A History of the Byzantine State and Society* (1997).

Introduction

CYRIL MANGO

Byzantion, Latinized to Byzantium, was the name of a Greek colony at the mouth of the Thracian Bosphorus—a situation of striking natural beauty as well as great strategic importance. About a thousand years after its foundation Byzantium was chosen by Constantine the Great as his imperial residence (AD 324) and renamed *Constantinopolis nova* (or *altera*) *Roma*. That was not an unprecedented step at the time: Constantine's great predecessor, Diocletian (284–305), had already established his seat at nearby Nicomedia (now İzmit) and strove 'to make it the equal of Rome'. But whereas Nicomedia and a number of other transient capitals soon lost their status, Constantinople proved a lasting success and was to remain 'the Reigning City' for the next eleven centuries, not counting another five under the Ottoman sultans.

In the long perspective of history Constantine's inspired action took on the appearance of what it was not in reality, namely a *translatio imperii*, a new beginning in a new place under the auspices of a new religion—a renovation, however, that did not entail a break with the past. The New Rome encapsulated the Old. It was even rumoured that Constantine secretly removed from Rome the Palladium of Troy and buried it under his great column of porphyry at Constantinople—a column, incidentally, that has stood until today against all odds. Anthusa, the mystic Tyche to whom Constantinople was dedicated, was a replica of Rome's Flora.

Constantine's successors continued to regard themselves as the legitimate emperors of Rome, just as their subjects called themselves Romaioi long after they had forgotten the Latin tongue. They did not claim for themselves any other ancestry. To take one example at random, the eleventh-century polymath Michael Psellos, when called upon to produce an elementary history book for the instruction of his imperial pupil, Michael VII, started his narrative with Romulus and Remus, skipped quickly over the kings and consuls, then came to dwell in more detail on the succession of emperors who formed a single line from Julius Caesar, founder of the monarchy, to Basil II and Constantine VIII. Augustus, more than Constantine, was the key figure, for his reign had coincided with the Incarnation of Our Lord, the central event of universal history. Christianity and the Roman monarchy had virtually the same birthdate.

The pretence of Romanity began to wear thin only in the age of the Crusades when the eastern empire and the West were increasingly forced into a loveless embrace. From a western perspective the kingdom of Constantinople looked decidedly Greek in addition to being schismatic. For their part, some Greek intellectuals reacted by claiming for themselves the glories of ancient Hellas (see Chapter 11). It would be a mistake to say, however, that 'ethnic identity' attracted much attention at the time. The big issue, on which oceans of ink were spilt, was that of religion—of obedience to the Pope, the procession of the Holy Ghost, purgatory, clerical celibacy, leavened or unleavened bread in the eucharist. Those were the questions that separated the Greeks from the Latins. If only they could be resolved, Christendom would be reunited in a new Romanity under the Pope.

Sir John Mandeville in the mid-fourteenth century could still speak of 'the emperor of Grece', but such a designation was no longer appropriate in the more scholarly climate of the Renaissance. Greece had come to mean ancient Greece or its territory, now occupied by the Turks. The kingdom of Constantinople, which had become extinct in 1453, needed a distinctive name, and that is how the adjective *byzantinus* came into being. It was less cumbersome than *Constantinopolitanus* and had a pleasantly 'classical' ring. One could now speak of *scriptores byzantini*, *historia byzantina*, *imperium byzantinum*, although the earliest large-scale treatment of 'Byzantine' history, by one Louis Cousin (1672–4), was entitled *Histoire de Constantinople*. The first book in English to use the word 'Byzantine' in its title was, if I am not mistaken, George Finlay's *History of the Byzantine Empire from 716 to 1057* (1853). The substantive Byzantium, meaning the empire, not the city, did not become common in English until the twentieth century, though used earlier in French, German, and Russian.

Byzantium, then, is a term of convenience when it is not a term of inconvenience. On any reasonable definition Byzantium must be seen as the direct continuation of the Roman empire in the eastern half of the Mediterranean basin, i.e. of that part of the Roman empire that was Hellenistic in its culture and language. Being a continuation, it had no beginning, although a number of symbolic dates have been advanced as marking that elusive birthday: the accession of Diocletian (AD 284), the foundation of Constantinople (324) or its ceremonial inauguration (330), the adoption of Christianity as the all but exclusive religion of the empire (c.380), the division of the empire into separately ruled eastern and western halves (395), the abolition of the western empire (476), even the accession of Leo III (716), the last being still enshrined in *The Cambridge Medieval History*. To all of these dates more or less

cogent objections have been raised. That, however, does not solve a problem that probably owes more to feeling than to the kind of 'objective' criteria that are supposed to underpin historical periodization. For us, Rome, the fountainhead of our civilization, belongs by definition to the classical world. We commune with the spirit of Rome as we gaze at the Ara Pacis, or the reliefs of Trajan's column or the equestrian statue of Marcus Aurelius. But when we contemplate the famous mosaic depicting Justinian in the church of San Vitale, Ravenna, we find ourselves in a different world. It is no longer a naturalistic representation of a ritual act (the offering of a chalice), but an icon. Justinian wears a halo. He and all the members of his suite face us frontally against a gold background. We do not immediately understand that the artist intended to represent a procession moving to the right, which is why the figures, in spite of their frontality, appear to be stepping on each other's toes. To our eyes, Justinian in San Vitale looks fully Byzantine; yet the real Justinian, a native Latin speaker, conqueror of Italy and North Africa, the greatest codifier of Roman law, considered himself a quintessentially Roman emperor and was so seen by posterity.

Where, then, do we draw the line? If we abandon the fruitless quest for a precise occasion when Rome was transformed into Byzantium and seek a broader period or periods that witnessed a profound shift, two such dividing bands suggest themselves. The first may be placed in the fourth century, the second roughly between 575 and 650. The two were not of the same charac-

The emperor Augustus, whom the Byzantines regarded as the founder of their monarchy, performing a ritual act. Relief of Ara Pacis, Rome, 9 BC.

3

MAXIMIANVS

Successor of Augustus, Justinian presenting a paten to the church of San Vitale, Ravenna. He is preceded by bishop Maximian and two deacons. The identity of the other personages has been much debated. The bearded man to Justinian's left may be the general Belisarius. Mosaic c. AD 545.

ter. The first mutation was more cultural than political and was associated with the adoption of Christianity as the official ideology of the state. That is not to deny that other, more tangible changes occurred roughly at the same time: a thorough overhaul of the state's apparatus—administrative, military, and financial (already under Diocletian), the growth of a centralized bureaucracy, the move of the main imperial residence to Constantinople, the emergence of a new elite based on imperial service. Yet, when seen from a distance, what stands out is not the multiplication of provincial units or the introduction of a tax census or the reform of the coinage, but rather the imposition of a new ideology on all the empire's subjects and the suppression of dissent.

The second *coupure* was more palpable and painful. It was marked not only by vast territorial losses in both the Balkans and the Near East, but also by the collapse of the urban life that had been the chief feature of antiquity (see Chapter 2). Many cities vanished off the map; others shrank to a defensible citadel or moved to a nearby hilltop. The elites that had been the mainstay of provincial governance as well as of polite letters disappeared. Life became ruralized and militarized.

Between the two bands we have indicated lies the period we have learned to call Late Antiquity. Its distinctiveness has been recognized only in the past fifty years, during which time it has become a major academic industry. True, the chronological boundaries of Late Antiquity are themselves a little blurred: some scholars see its beginning in about AD 200, others make it extend to the year 1000. More usually, however, it is limited to AD 284–602, as in A. H. M. Jones's monumental *Later Roman Empire*, or 284–641, as in the equally indispensable *Prosopography of the Later Roman Empire*. Such a definition fits very well into a Byzantine perspective.

Late Antiquity embraces the whole Roman world, Latin and Greek. It includes Rome, Milan, Trier, Ravenna, and Carthage no less than Constantinople, Antioch, Alexandria, and Ephesus. It is represented by St Augustine as well as Gregory Nazianzen, by Ambrose as well as John Chrysostom, by Ammianus as well as Procopius. Apart from the difference of language, the cultural climate of Late Antiquity was reasonably uniform. It is true that the linguistic divide among members of the elite was a little deeper than it had been in the days of Cicero (Augustine knew little Greek, while few orientals ever stooped to learning any Latin), but a measure of cultural communication was maintained, elite education was based on the same principles and translations were made both ways. Ammianus, a Greek, chose to write in Latin. In the East knowledge of Latin was required for legal studies and service in some branches of the central administration down to the second half of the sixth century. The most authoritative handbook of Latin grammar, Priscian's *Institutiones*, was composed at Constantinople. So were the Theodosian and Justinianic Codes.

Late Antiquity provided the cultural soil out of which grew both the medieval West and the medieval East. The question to be asked is why they developed so differently or, to put it another way, why Byzantium, which was unquestionably a part of Europe, diverged from what we regard, rightly or wrongly, as the main avenue of European progress. That is not a question that will be directly addressed in this book, but one that the thoughtful reader may wish to keep at the back of his mind.

There has been little debate about the terminal date of Byzantium, which is unanimously placed on 29 May 1453, a Tuesday. The curtain comes down as the Janissaries clamber over the breach in the thousand-year-old Theodosian walls and a supernatural light rises heavenwards from the dome of St Sophia. If we regard Byzantium primarily as a state, i.e. as an independent political entity, 1453 does indeed provide an obligatory and suitably dramatic finale. If, however, we follow Arnold Toynbee and define Byzantium as a civilization rather than a state, the story does not end at that point. It expands geographically to include all the countries of the Orthodox faith—Russia,

Romania, Bulgaria, Serbia, as well as the subjugated Greeks—and extends in time if not to the present, at any rate until about 1800, when the spread of the European Enlightenment and European-inspired nationalism finally undermined what was still a recognizably Byzantine way of life. The story of *Byzance après Byzance*, to quote the well-known title of a book by Nicolae Iorga (1935), remains to be written in all of its regional complexity.

If we are able to tell the story of Byzantium, that is because there existed a more or less continuous tradition of Byzantine historiography, sketchy for some periods, much fuller for others. The nature of that historiography and its preservation or loss naturally determine the extent of our knowledge. As to its nature, it assumed three basic forms: the classicizing history (ultimately descended from ancient models such as Thucydides and Polybius), the chronicle, and the eccclesiastical history. The 'history' aimed at giving a reasoned and polished account of events, which, ideally, the author had himself witnessed, hence was limited to a fairly short timespan. The chronicle, which had a much wider readership, went to the opposite extreme: written in everyday language, it was meant to provide an overview of everything that had happened since the Creation of the world down to the compiler's lifetime. Its entries, arranged chronologically, tended to be brief and did not present events in a causal nexus. The chronicle was considered an edifying rather than a literary work, which meant that it was progressively updated and re-edited, while older versions were often discarded. The ecclesiastical history, invented by Eusebius of Caesarea in about the year 300, was concerned with episcopal succession and especially doctrinal disputes, while including some secular material. It had the unique feature of quoting original documents, which made it the most scholarly kind of historiography on offer. Unfortunately, the ecclesiastical history in the Greek language died in about the year 600. The Byzantine world produced practically no local or monastic chronicles such as were very common in the West.

The thousand years of Byzantium are very unevenly covered in surviving historiography. Some periods, like the brief reign of Julian (361–3) or the long one of Justinian (527–65), are brightly illuminated, others are quite obscure. Strangely enough, the fourth and fifth centuries, including even the reign of Constantine, are very poor in extant narrative sources other than the ecclesiastical histories. The seventh and eighth centuries are notoriously dark and even the ninth, when the empire was beginning to recover from its troubles, is narrated in texts composed a hundred years after the events in question. The record becomes a little fuller from about the middle of the tenth century onwards and is fullest for the Palaiologan period, which happens to be the least important segment of Byzantine history.

Apart from unevenness of treatment, one finds in the narrative sources a good deal of deliberate distortion both for theological and dynastic reasons. Heretical emperors are routinely denigrated as in the case of the Monothelite Constans II (641–68) and that of the Iconoclastic emperors, who in fact struggled valiantly and successfully for the preservation of the empire, while the far from brilliant reign of Irene (780–802) is presented in glowing colours because she presided over the restoration of 'orthodoxy'. Nikephoros I (802–11), an astute reformer, is painted black because he toppled Irene. Michael III (842–67) in particular is made into another Nero, a drunkard and debauchee, to justify his murder by Basil I, founder of the long-lasting 'Macedonian' dynasty. In all these cases the rewriting has been so thorough that we shall probably never know the true facts.

All branches of Byzantine historical writing are largely concerned with the deeds of emperors and rebels, the conduct of wars, court gossip, and divisions among bishops. Inevitably, that remains the stuff of Byzantine history as it is written today. Of course, there are other sources that supply occasional bits of information: imperial decrees, Lives of saints (a very prolific if highly stylized and often mendacious genre), collections of letters, conciliar acts, polemical treatises, rhetorical declamations, poems, not to speak of historiography in languages other than Greek—Latin, Arabic, Syriac, Armenian. Yet, even after making allowance for this miscellaneous input, it is the story of emperors, intrigues, and battles that remains in the forefront. That kind of narrative still appeals to many readers, but most professional historians, whatever their individual interests, would prefer to tell it differently by uncovering the hidden mechanisms—economic, social, and demographic—that underlay the *histoire événementielle* that is alone visible. Rather than enquiring whether Michael III was or was not a drunken sot, it would be more instructive to explain what factors determined the revival of the empire in the ninth century.

If in this respect Byzantine historiography appears the most backward sector of medieval studies, the fault does not lie with its practitioners. Our minute knowledge of the society and economy of western Europe is largely based on documents that have survived by the thousand—charters, parish records, tax registers, testaments, contracts, etc. For Byzantium we have only small pockets of documentary material, setting aside the plentiful but arcane evidence provided by Egyptian papyri down to the Arab conquest. When we come down to the Middle Ages, we have only some monastic archives relating to landholding (notably for Mount Athos, southern Italy, Chios, Patmos, and a few from Asia Minor), a small number of monastic founders' charters (*typika*), Italian documents relating to the Levant trade, a register of the patriarchal tribunal for the years 1315–1402, and a few other bits and pieces.

There is little hope that this meagre and haphazard body of material will ever be increased, nor can we remedy the near absence of inscriptions on stone, which for classical antiquity provide such a rich source of information for society, institutions, and religion.

If there are few documents left, we have a considerable number of lead seals (roughly 50,000) that were once attached to documents and these are being slowly published and exploited as a historical source. The information they yield is largely limited to names and titles, but occasionally we gain a glimpse into other domains, e.g. trade, as with the seals of the *commerciarii*, assuming these were customs officials (for a different view see below, p. 146). Numismatics, too, have been put to excellent use. The metallic purity of the coinage, the near disappearance of small change during the Dark Age (see p. 147), the geographical distribution and composition of coin hoards and the incidence of Byzantine coin finds beyond the borders of the empire are data that the historian of Byzantium is learning to exploit.

Finally, there is archaeology, perhaps the most promising avenue for the eventual enlargement of our knowledge. Thanks to archaeology we have already gained what may be called a visual apprehension of urban life during Late Antiquity in many centres of the eastern empire—some major, like Ephesus, others of the middle rank, like Stobi in Macedonia or Scythopolis in Palestine, others fairly minor, like Anemurium in Isauria. The cities in question had a classical past and the primary aim of excavating them has been to uncover antique monuments, whether Greek, Hellenistic, or imperial Roman. In many cases, however, the imperial Roman phase has been found to continue into Late Antiquity, the temples and gymnasia being abandoned or converted to other uses, churches and episcopal palaces being built, baths and theatres continuing to function. What today's visitor sees at Ephesus is the city as it was in the reign of Justinian. We know less about villages, although those of northern Syria, which were built as durably as cities and have remained standing to this day, have attracted a fair amount of attention from archaeologists.

By contrast, the archaeology of medieval Byzantium is still largely a blank. Of the four cities we have mentioned by way of example, Stobi and Anemurium had no medieval phase, while Scythopolis passed, of course, under Arab rule. Only Ephesus survived as a Byzantine town, but it is almost impossible to visualize, except for its reduced walls and shrunken cathedral. It incorporated many standing ruins and its houses appear to have been mean and poorly built. We expect to find a scattering of small churches and monasteries, but only a couple are discernible. We do not even know how much of the defended area was built over. For a somewhat fuller picture of a Byzantine town we have to go to Corinth and Athens, even Cherson in the Crimea, but we are still a long way from a comprehensive overview. Lack of monumentality and poor masonry do not preclude a lively economic activity, although undoubtedly they do not stimulate the archaeologist's attention. We can only hope that one day the reality of medieval Byzantium will be more fully revealed by the spade instead of being mediated only by the written word.

'Great Byzantium . . . where nothing changes,' wrote Yeats. That is an illusion that professional historians have been trying to disprove for a long time. Of course, there is no denying that Byzantium did change—socially, economically, militarily, both through an internal dynamic and in response to ever-shifting realities beyond its borders. It is no easy matter, however, to correctly describe and understand the nature of those changes. We used to be told, for example, that the empire's 'healthy' condition in the ninth–tenth centuries was due to the prevalence of agricultural smallholding, with sturdy yeoman *stratiotai* defending their country when they were not tilling their fields, and that this excellent system was subverted by the greed of land-hungry magnates, thus leading to a loss of morale and general decline in the eleventh century. It is true that the emperors of the tenth century did attempt by their legislation to limit the encroachment of 'the powerful' on village communes, but how widespread and economically important was smallholding? How is it that in *c*.860 the widow Danelis could be said to own 'no small part of the Peloponnese', including many hundreds of slaves? Why is it that there was demonstrably more intense economic activity and greater wealth in the eleventh–twelfth centuries than there had been previously? Did the Byzantines commit economic suicide by surrendering international shipping to the Italian republics or did they profit from this arrangement? Given the nature of our documentation, there is no clear answer to such questions and discussion of them will doubtless continue for a long time. We can only hope that one day we shall have a proper economic history of the empire in which both written and archaeological evidence will be given due weight.

In a given sense, however, Yeats was right. The empire, no matter how much it changed below the surface, did present a façade of studied immutability, which was an essential part of its mystique. It was the emperor's duty, stated the historian Zonaras in the period of the Komnenoi, 'to preserve the ancient customs of the state'. If one lived, say, in the ninth or tenth century, one did not have to be a scholar to know that the past—not the pagan past of long ago, but the Christian past of Late Antiquity—had been greater than the present. One had only to look at St Sophia to understand that such a stupendous technological achievement could never be duplicated, and that if Justinian managed to put it up, that was due to supernatural help. The past validated the present and had to be repeatedly dusted off through a process called restoration, renewal, or rejuvenation, as distinct from innovation (*kainotomia, neoterismos*), which was subversive and dangerous. That is why on state occasions the emperor dined in a hall that had allegedly been built by Constantine the Great, reclining on a couch as no one had done since antiquity, and watched on the Kalends of January a performance of dancing 'Goths', although no Goths had been in evidence for as long as anyone could remember. That is why medieval court dignitaries bore Roman titles like consul, patrician, magister, quaestor and received as their insignia such outdated objects as fibulas, ivory tablets, and gold torques of a type worn by army officers in Late Antiquity; why on coinage barely intelligible Latin inscriptions were maintained long after that language had gone out of use.

The feigned immutability of the empire was matched by its extraordinary longevity. Indeed, Byzantium was the only organized state this side of China that survived without interruption from antiquity until the dawn of the modern age. Its longevity is, indeed, its most conspicuous feature. True, it might easily have collapsed on several occasions—notably in 626, when Constantinople nearly fell to the Avars and Persians; in 717–18, when a massive Arab expedition against the city failed because, it seems, of an unusually severe winter and help from the Bulgars; in 1090–1, when the nomadic Cumans unexpectedly stepped in to avert a deadly threat from the Pechenegs and the Turks. Even earlier, in the course of the fifth century, the eastern empire might well have passed, like the western, under the control of German war lords with consequences that cannot now be estimated. It is also true that the convention of speaking of the Byzantine empire down to 1453 masks the obvious fact that its imperial phase had ended in 1204 or rather a couple of decades before that fateful date. But even if the empire lasted nine centuries instead of eleven, that is still a remarkable achievement, which shows that it commanded the loyalty or acquiescence of its inhabitants, who were willing to pay their taxes, serve in the army (at any rate until the eleventh century) and respect the emperor's authority.

It is perhaps even more remarkable that down to the end of the twelfth century the empire did not suffer any fragmentation, as happened, for example, to its neighbour, the Abbasid caliphate. There were, of course, many rebellions, but they were aimed at capturing the throne, not at detaching a particular piece of territory. No enterprising *strategos* ever thought of declaring an independent Cappadocia. It is only under the Komnenoi that we witness the first separatist movements as the idea of a unitary state is progressively eroded by a policy of distributing the empire's lands to members of the ruling clan as well as to foreign condottieri. Greatly accelerated as it was by the Fourth Crusade, fragmentation had actually begun earlier.

The cohesion of the empire down to the twelfth century is all the more difficult to explain in view of its ethnic diversity. Of the make-up and geographical distribution of its constituent population groups it is only possible to speak in very approximate terms, but there can be no doubt that next to old native stock there were great numbers of Slavs (throughout the Balkan peninsula), Caucasians (Armenians, Georgians, and Laz) and various other orientals, mainly Syrians, Turks, and Christian Arabs. Smaller groups included Jews, Gypsies, nomadic Vlachs, and western traders and adventurers. The long-standing imperial policy of transplanting whole populations to make up a demographic deficit in this or that area (e.g. in the Peloponnese in *c.*800) further complicated the picture. Of the ethnic groups, the Slavs, probably the most numerous, made the least impact on the composition of the elite, whereas the Caucasians were so prominently represented as to have almost taken over the empire for the duration of its medieval greatness, providing emperors and empresses (Leo V, Theophilos' wife Theodora and her powerful clan, Basil I and his descendants, Romanos I, John I Tzimiskes), influential ministers like Stylianos Zaoutzes under Leo VI, a plethora of military commanders and many of the great landowning magnates bearing the family names of Phokas (at least in part), Skleros, Kourkouas, Krinites, Mousele, Bourtzes, Taronites, Tornikios, etc.

General considerations will not help us understand why this mishmash of nationalities identified themselves with the empire. A couple of concrete cases may be more illuminating. Here is Kekaumenos, a retired military man of Armeno-Georgian descent bearing what looks like an impeccably Greek name ('the burnt one'). His ancestors had served the empire, not always faithfully, for at least four generations. Moderately educated, he wrote his famous *Admonitions* in the 1070s, one of the most self-revealing texts of the Byzantine period. Kekaumenos has much to say about loyalty to the emperor, which he recommends. 'No one', he writes, 'has ever dared to mount a rebellion against the emperor and the Roman country in an attempt to subvert the peace who has not himself been destroyed. For this reason I entreat you, my beloved children, to remain on the side of the emperor and in servitude to him; for the emperor who sits at Constantinople always wins.' Loyalty, in other words, was dictated by prudence: rebellion was too risky. Yet Kekaumenos was not entirely committed to the imperial ideal, nor did he wish the empire to expand at the expense of others. In addressing 'toparchs' (rulers of independent principalities on the empire's periphery), he urges them to keep their distance, otherwise the emperor will grab their lands and give no thanks in return.

A few years after Kekaumenos, another Georgian condottiere, Gregory Pakourianos, who had likewise served the empire faithfully, had risen to the much more exalted post of 'Grand Domestic of the West' and been rewarded with immense landholdings, founded the monastery of Bačkovo in present-day Bulgaria (1083). While professing his unflinching adherence to the religion of the Greeks, he formally forbids any Greek monks or priests to be enrolled in his monastery because Greeks are grasping and unreliable. Pakourianos died fighting for the empire, but never learnt to sign his name in Greek characters (he did so in Armenian).

We may imagine that the two examples we have given were not entirely untypical. Kekaumenos was largely assimilated, though well aware of his origins, whereas Pakourianos was as yet unassimilated, a foreigner among Greeks, whom he profoundly distrusted. If those two proved loyal, it is clear that many Armenian nobles resettled in Cappadocia after the absorption of their kingdom into the empire (1045) harboured a deep resentment against Byzantium, like the deposed king Gagik II, who ordered the execution of the Greek metropolitan of Caesarea after the latter had had the temerity to call his dog Armen. It is probably to their disaffection that we may attribute the incredibly swift loss of most of Asia Minor to the Seljuk Turks, who achieved in ten years what the Arabs had been unable to do in the course of two centuries. By 1071 Süleyman ibn-Kutlumush was installed in Nicaea and raiding the coasts of the Bosporus. The general whom Alexios I sent to oppose him, a certain Tatikios, was also a Turk.

In a wider perspective the latter part of the eleventh century proved for Byzantium a crucial turning-point. If we look to the West, we find that the period in question leads up to what has been called the Renaissance of the twelfth century—the age of the first Gothic cathedrals, of the universities, of scholastic logic and the revival of legal studies, of vernacular poetry, and much else besides. It is clear that in Byzantium, too, similar trends were beginning to surface: merchants were joining the ruling class (what was called rather vaguely the Senate), legal studies were temporarily encouraged, poetry in the vernacular was making a timid appearance, Aristotelian philosophy was taught at Constantinople by an Italian (John Italos), and a new lay spirit was being manifested by intellectuals like Michael Psellos and the civil servant-cum-poet Christopher of Mitylene (who even made fun of the collecting of dubious relics of saints). It was a promising beginning, but it came to very little. Why? Was it because of incompetent government, collapse of central authority, and military disaster, which required all the energy and ingenuity of Alexios I Komnenos to repair—and that only in part? Or (as argued by the late Paul Lemerle) was Alexios himself the culprit—a 'false saviour', who downgraded the nascent bourgeoisie, parcelled out the empire's best lands to his relatives and cronies, surrendered long-distance trade and shipping to the Venetians, shut down the teaching of Aristotelian logic, entrusted education to an obscurantist Church, and burnt heretics? Whichever explanation one adopts, Byzantium failed to experience the cultural flowering that occurred in the West and progressively fell further and further behind.

Fifty years ago it was still customary to claim that the political achievement of Byzantium had been the defence of Europe (or of Christendom) against continuous Asiatic aggression, but such a judgement is no longer considered acceptable. Today we are more likely to praise Byzantium, not for smiting Asiatics, but rather for having been multi-ethnic and multicultural. Multi-ethnic it certainly was, as we have seen; as for being multicultural, that was more from necessity than design. In matters of religious belief and observance variations were not tolerated except when uniformity could not be imposed. Even the Jews, a licit sect under the Roman empire, were repeatedly pressured to convert. It was only because all such attempts failed that the Jews, who were valuable economically, were left to their ways while being treated with contempt. Muslim merchants and prisoners of war were allowed their places of worship because denying them would have led to reprisals. Byzantium was less tolerant than Islam and marginally more tolerant than western Christendom.

The cultural legacy of Byzantium cannot be summed up by evoking names of great thinkers, poets, or artists. There was no Byzantine Abelard or Thomas Aquinas, no Chrétien de Troyes or Dante, no Nicola Pisano or Giotto. The few Byzantine intellectuals who rise above the average, like Photios in the ninth century, Psellos in the eleventh, Planudes or Gregoras in the thirteenth–fourteenth, do so not so much by their originality, but as polymaths and voluminous authors. Byzantine art is anonymous. In the domain of letters the biography of authors, even in summary form, ceased to be of interest after the sixth century and they came to be distinguished from one another, if at all, by their titles, civil or ecclesiastical—deacon, *skevophylax* (sacristan), logothete, magister, or whatever. In many cases we are still unable to sort out all the Georges, Gregorys, Symeons, etc. and assign even approximate dates to them.

Lacking in individualism, Byzantine culture may be seen as a tightly knit body of thought expressed in the institutions of government, Church, and monasticism and reflected in the domains of writing and art. In the formulation of the nineteenth-century Russian thinker K. Leont'ev, Byzantinism meant monarchy, Christianity of a particular kind, a low estimation of all earthly things, and a denial of the possibility of universal well-being. That is fairly close to the mark, but calls for a little adjustment and elaboration. Christianity should be placed first, its distinguishing feature being that it was a static system of doctrine as expounded by the Fathers and defined by the seven ecumenical councils. Being perfect, it admitted of no further development. Of all the major Christian denominations, Byzantine Christianity may be called the most authentic in the sense that it is closest to the dogma of the Patristic age, but in denying any development after 787 it placed itself in an illogical stance, besides leaving the Holy Spirit with little to do.

Monarchy may be placed next because its necessity followed from religion. The governance of the earth being a reflection of that of heaven, no other system was pleasing to God or even worth discussing. The last Byzantine treatise on political philosophy was written in the early sixth century and remained unread. By contrast, the Mirror of Princes by the deacon Agapetos of the same period, which defined in simple terms the qualities of the ideal emperor while admitting his God-given status, proved a lasting success. It was taken for granted that the emperor was chosen by God, to whom alone he was accountable, and that his responsibility encompassed both the spiritual and physical welfare of his subjects, the spiritual being by far the more important.

The Byzantine doctrine of monarchy entailed a number of paradoxes, which cannot be said to have been adequately addressed. In the first place, the emperor was theoretically ruler of all human beings or, at any rate, of all Christians. That was demonstrably not the case. To take account of the existence of independent Christian states, the fiction of 'the family of princes' was put into circulation: the emperor was represented as the paterfamilias, other rulers being his children or nephews. Second, if the emperor was chosen by God, why was he occasionally a wicked man (e.g. Phokas) or a pagan (Julian) or a heretic (Constantius II, Valens, etc.) or, under the Ottoman sultans, a Muslim? Simple answer: to punish Christians for their sins. Was such an emperor to be obeyed? Yes (read Romans 13: 1–4: 'the powers that be are ordained of God', etc.), although under Iconoclasm the option of subversion was considered in extremist circles (see Chapter 6).

A more difficult question concerned the status of the Church, of *sacerdotium* versus *imperium*. No matter how long one dances round the topic of Byzantine 'caesaropapism', the fact remains that the emperor, starting with Constantine, had effective control of the Church, that he alone convoked general councils and presided over them, issued binding dogmatic pronouncements (like Zeno's *Henotikon* or the *Ekthesis* of Heraclius), appointed patriarchs and metropolitan bishops, was allowed privileged entry into the presbytery, even preached sermons if he so wished (as did Leo VI), although he could not celebrate the liturgy. The emperor routinely legislated on matters that ought to have been the exclusive concern of the Church (e.g. on clerical marriage, private chaplains, the minimum age of entry into a monastery, etc.) just as canon law impinged on the daily conduct of laymen without any clear distinction between their respective spheres. One can cite, of course,

Left: An elaborate scroll border, enclosing grotesque heads, animals and fruit, surrounds the mosaic pavement of the Great Palace, Constantinople. Archaeological evidence indicates a date not earlier than the middle of the sixth century.

Below: The imperial palace of Ravenna. This mosaic in the church of Sant'Apollinare Nuovo was executed in the reign of the Ostrogothic king Theoderic (493–526) who was an Arian heretic. The personages represented under the arches were rather clumsily excised after the Byzantine reconquest of the city.

PALA·TIVM

examples when churchmen stood up against the emperor over matters of doctrine or morals (and were promptly ejected for insubordination) and, in the Palaiologan period, the inability of successive emperors to impose union with Rome in the face of public hostility. There is even the isolated case of (probably) the patriarch Photios inserting in a lawbook a statement resembling the western doctrine of the 'two powers', but the lawbook in question, called *Eisagoge*, was not applied in practice. The exceptions do not invalidate the rule: Church and State were indissolubly wedded, thus depriving Byzantium of that tension between the spiritual and the secular that did so much to shape the conscience of western Europe. In modern times Orthodox churches have followed the same path of subservience, whether under the Ottoman sultans, the Russian tsars or Soviet communism.

Nor did monasticism, which enjoyed an extraordinary diffusion in the Byzantine world, provide the necessary counterweight. An isolated attempt to create a monastic pressure group that would influence imperial policy and act as arbiter in the realms of morals and doctrine was, indeed, made by St Theodore Studite in the face of what he regarded as the culpable softness of the secular Church with regard to the 'adulterous' marriage of Constantine VI (795) and, later, the revival of Iconoclasm (815). Theodore, a man of dogged determination and great organizational skill, was able to capitalize on the increased prestige of monasticism after the lamentable performance of the episcopate during the first phase of Iconoclasm: at the Second Council of Nicaea (787) abbots of monasteries were for the first time admitted to the governing body of the Church. Theodore's initiative was, however, lost. Although monks continued to be held in high esteem and several emperors made a point of cultivating them, we do not find that either individually or collectively they won the kind of influence that Theodore had fought for. The scandalous conduct of Michael III (if we are to trust our sources) was not reproved by monks, nor the murder that placed Basil I on the throne. The fourth marriage of Leo VI shocked the ecclesiastical establishment, but Leo's spiritual director, who was a monk of great sanctity (Euthymios), took his master's side. And so it continued. Several reasons may be suggested why an effective 'monkish' party failed to materialize. The institution was too fragmented to have been welded into a coherent force. There were no monastic orders, as in the West, possessing a unified organization and specific aims. Monasteries were beholden to a variety of patrons. Some were classed as imperial (i.e. were in the emperor's gift), others as episcopal, many were administered for profit by laymen, but the trend, as the Middle Ages advanced, was towards independence (called *autexousion* or *autodespoton*) as a hedge against exploitation by outside bodies. Increasingly, Byzantine monasteries evolved into landholding corporations intent, above all, on maintaining and

Facing: The church of San Vitale, Ravenna, was started under Ostrogothic rule by bishop Ecclesius (522–32) and completed after the Byzantine reconquest by bishop Maximian in c.546. Its presbytery, with its marble, stucco, and mosaics, offers the most complete visual impression of a church interior of that period.

enlarging their endowment, which is why some of them have survived to this day. Their services to other causes, such as education, have been greatly exaggerated. Even on Mount Athos, which is a 'republic' of twenty monasteries, some of them quite rich, a school was set up for the first time in 1753 and closed permanently eight years later. The school only caused trouble and was an impediment to the pursuit of the 'angelic life'.

If one were to identify a single principle that underlay the Byzantine conception of the virtuous life, it would be that of order (*taxis*). Supremely manifested in the heavenly court, it permeated the whole world. Absence of order (*ataxia*), i.e. randomness or turbulence, was characteristic of barbarians and demons. In human affairs order entailed the observance of established principles. What we call the *Book of Ceremonies* of Constantine VII Porphyrogenitus is described as an 'Exposition of imperial order' and in its one-page Preface the word *taxis* and its derivatives occur eight times. Disregard of precedent, we are assured, would make the imperial institution unsightly and in no way different from the uncultivated regimen of ordinary people. If the quality of *taxis* was more essential to the conduct of the emperor than to that of ordinary individuals, the latter, too, were subject to its discipline, especially through their attendance at church. The revolution of the liturgical year with its fixed and mobile feasts and fasts, its daily commemoration of saints, its appointed lections, hymns, and processions, was for every Christian the supreme manifestation of the harmonious and orderly relation between man and God.

Byzantinism, as Leont'ev was right in stressing, showed little concern for human prosperity and, in particular, had no programme for the future. There was no expectation of a millennium on earth, of any physical or spiritual betterment. All one could look forward to were the final convulsions of a tired and sinful world, followed by the Second Coming. The Judge's verdict would be final. By denying the doctrine of Purgatory (admittedly a late invention), the Byzantines affirmed that in the next world as in this one there would be no development.

Faces of Constantine

CYRIL MANGO

Gold medallion of Constantine coupled with the Sun god. Mint of Trier, AD 313.

Colossal marble head of Constantine, now in the Capitoline Museum, Rome. The nose is original.

The Tetrarchic emperors cultivated a deliberately brutal, Mussolini-like type of portraiture, marked by a thick neck, stubble beard, and grim expression indicative of military hardship and determination. Constantine preferrred to appear as the 'founder of peace' (*fundator quietis*) ever-youthful and clean-shaven in the manner of Augustus. His colossal marble head from the Basilica Nova in Rome (*c.*315), eight times lifesize, with its aquiline nose, jutting chin, and enlarged eyes may or may not represent his true features, but does convey the calm majesty expected of a cult statue. His identifi-

cation with the deity, initially Apollo-Helios, was expressed on his coins by his bust overlapping that of Sol Invictus, and after 324 less overtly by a heavenward gazing head reminiscent of that of Alexander the Great.

Constantine became a Christian saint, indeed 'the equal of the Apostles' (*isapostolos*), the only emperor to have been so honoured, and made the subject of several hagiographic Lives that bear little relation to reality. Yet he killed both his wife and his eldest son, was baptized by a heretic, and, after his death, was accorded a pagan

deification. In the forum that bore his name at Constantinople his statue, once more in the guise of Helios, set up on his porphyry column, was the object of a public cult. No wonder that his personality has been variously interpreted. Was he a thug and an opportunist or 'a sincere man who sought the truth on the threshold of a dark century' (A. Piganiol)?

As a saint, Constantine appears regularly in Byzantine church decoration. In the tenth-century mosaic of St Sophia in Constantinople, he is shown dedicating to the Mother of God a model of the city he had founded. He is still beardless, perhaps in deference to the antiquarian spirit of the times, but long-haired, haloed, and attired in the ceremonial dress of a Byzantine emperor. Normally, however, in the medieval period he is portrayed bearded, as every grown man had to be, accompanied by his mother St Helena, both of them grasping the True Cross, which she had discovered.

Sts Constantine and Helena, wall painting in the church of Asinou at Nikitari, Cyprus, AD 1106.

Mosaic of Constantine in the south-west vestibule of St Sophia, Constantinople.

1 The Eastern Roman Empire from Constantine to Heraclius (306–641)

PETER SARRIS

'Licinius was thus besieged by Constantine in Nicomedia, whereupon he gave up hope, realizing he did not have sufficient men for a battle. Going out of the city, therefore, he threw himself before Constantine as a suppliant, and bringing him the purple, acclaimed him as emperor and lord . . . Constantine sent Licinius to Thessalonica as if to live there in security, but not long after broke his oath, as was his custom, and had him hanged. The whole empire now devolved on Constantine alone.' Thus did the pagan historian Zosimus, writing around the year 500, record the final victory in the year 324 of the Roman emperor Constantine over the last of his imperial rivals. This victory gave Constantine undisputed mastery over the eastern provinces of the Roman empire, the wealthiest and most densely populated region of the entire Roman world.

These prized territories Constantine added to the western provinces of which he had gained control during the course of a prolonged period of uncertainty and strife within the empire that dated back to the year 306. Although at times presented in the Christian sources as the result of some sort of divinely inspired mission, Constantine's ascendancy, as Zosimus reminds us, can only be understood in the context of the brutal and opportunistic manoeuvring of ambitious men which characterized the politics of the later Roman empire.

The detailed narrative of this power struggle is difficult to reconstruct with any certainty, although its broad outline can be traced. From 293 to 305, under an arrangement introduced by the emperor Diocletian, and known to historians as the 'Tetrarchy' ('the rule of four'), the Roman empire had been governed by two emperors, each bearing the title of Augustus. The senior of these was based in the East, the other in the West. Each Augustus had serving under him a Caesar, a deputy who in turn was expected to succeed as Augustus in his own right. In 305 the apparently ailing eastern Augustus,

The Tetrarchs (Diocletian and his colleagues). Statues of Egyptian porphyry originally attached to columns, these were brought to Venice after the sack of Constantinople in 1204 and remain displayed in the square in front of St Mark's.

Diocletian, and his western counterpart, Maximian, had abdicated. Accordingly, they were succeeded by their respective Caesars: Galerius in the East, and Constantius in the West. Galerius appointed as Caesar in the East his eldest nephew, Maximin. In the West, he foisted upon Constantius as Caesar an officer of his own entourage by the name of Severus.

In 306, Constantius died at York, on his way to campaign against the Picts. In spite of the superior claims of Severus, Constantius' army in Britain acclaimed as ruler Constantius' son—Constantine. This act of usurpation incited others to follow suit, and the army in Rome acclaimed as Augustus a certain Maxentius, son of the former western emperor Maximian, who went on to gain effective control over both Italy and Africa.

As senior Augustus, Galerius tried in vain to reassert control of the situation. Ignoring the reality of Maxentius' power in the central Mediterranean, he appointed another western emperor, a former military colleague of his by the name of Licinius, after he had withdrawn his support from Severus. There were now five Augusti: Galerius and Maximin in the East, Licinius, Constantine, and the usurper Maxentius in the West. The constitutional and political arrangement introduced by the emperor Diocletian less than twenty years earlier lay in ruins.

In 310, in a final attempt to salvage something from the wreckage, Galerius sought to prise Rome from the control of Maxentius, in a military campaign that ended in ignominious failure. In 311 Galerius died, his power in Asia Minor and the East devolving fully upon Maximin, though with Licinius exercising control over the European provinces that had formerly been under the sway of the eastern Augustus. The death of Galerius set the scene for the process whereby the remaining Augusti sought to liquidate one another once and for all.

In 312 Constantine achieved the success that had evaded Galerius, and defeated his major western rival, the usurper Maxentius, at the battle of the Milvian bridge. This stunning victory granted Constantine control of Rome. Constantine later ascribed his triumph to the fact that, prior to the battle, he had abandoned the religion of his ancestors and adopted Christianity. Certainly, from 312 onwards, one finds Constantine publicly declaring his support for the Christian Church, and favouring it with ever greater largesse. In 313, in a parallel move, Licinius defeated Maximin in Thrace and went on to establish himself as ruler in the East. There followed a series of military clashes between the two remaining Augusti. It was not, however, until 323 that Constantine took war to Licinius in a concerted fashion, defeating him first at Adrianople, then in 324 at Chrysopolis near Nicomedia.

In recognition of his victory, Constantine ordered that the ancient Greek settlement of Byzantium, located on the European shore of the Bosphorus and in the near vicinity of Nicomedia, be rededicated in his honour under the name of Constantinople. He further decreed that the city be adorned with the civic splendour befitting an imperial foundation. Within five years or so, much of the initial phase of this work was deemed to be satisfactorily complete, and 'the city of Constantine' was formally consecrated on 11 May 330. Constantine established a senate there and remained in the city for much of the time until his death in 337.

The history of the civilization we call Byzantine is inextricably bound up with the figure of the emperor Constantine. It was Constantine's city that was to serve as the capital and bastion of the medieval Byzantine empire. It was Constantine's conversion to Christianity, his establishment of his new faith as the favoured religion of the Roman state, and the extension of his rule over the culturally Greek-dominated eastern half of the Roman world, that permitted the fusing of Christian religion, Roman imperial tradition, and Hellenic intellectual culture that was to characterize the emergent Byzantine thought-world.

Yet it is worth pausing at the very outset to remember that Constantine did not regard himself as having founded a new empire, let alone a new civilization. Constantine was a Latin-speaker, who came to the east as an outsider. He restored, he did not fracture, the unity of a Roman empire ruled by one man as *dominus orbis terrarum*—the 'lord of the world'. Upon his conversion to Christianity, Constantine would appear to have had only a dim intimation of

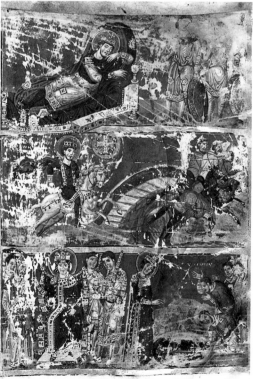

The legend of St Constantine is illustrated here in three episodes: Constantine's dream; the battle of the Milvian bridge with the appearance in the sky of the victorious sign of the cross; the invention of the True Cross by the empress Helena.

the nature of the faith. Initially at least, in his public imagery and propaganda, Constantine continued to use forms, expressions, and motifs which, whilst not exclusively pagan, nevertheless could appeal to a pagan audience. As late as 323, Constantine's officials were still minting coins dedicated to the pagan cult figure of the *Sol Invictus*—the 'Unconquered Sun'. Constantine was careful not to offend the powerful pagan elements within the ruling class of his empire, whose co-operation and support he needed.

In spite of this, it is not unreasonable to begin the history of Byzantium with Constantine's victory over Licinius. For not only did Constantine's military prowess create the cultural and ideological prerequisites for the emergence of the Byzantine world, but the establishment of his authority in the East further helped to catalyse a series of social processes which were to lead to the emergence of a very new type of society.

From 324, Constantine ruled over an empire that stretched from Mesopotamia, Syria, and Egypt in the east to the province of Britannia in the west, from North Africa in the south to the rivers Danube and Rhine in the north. Along these northern and southern frontiers, the empire faced tribes of generally quite primitive peoples, such as the various Germanic groupings beyond the Rhine, and the Berbers and Arabs of North Africa and Arabia respectively. To the east, the empire was confronted by the rather more formidable power of the ancient civilization of Persia. In essence, this was true in the fourth century as it had been in the second. Yet, in terms of underlying structure, the empire of Constantine was very different from that of his second-century forebears. Rather, this Roman world had recently undergone a period of marked transformation.

The Roman empire of the first and second centuries was city-based. That is to say, the regional elites of the empire lived in monumental urban centres termed *civitates* in Latin, or *poleis* in Greek. There, they were organized into civic councils styled *curiae* or *boulai*. It was primarily through these civic councils that the emperor ruled—his will being mediated to the councillors via imperially appointed governors, who, in turn, reported back to the emperor and senate of Rome on the condition of the provinces. Such a relatively devolved system facilitated rule over so wide an area. If, at a provincial level, communities enjoyed a high degree of autonomy, the highest offices of state were essentially the preserve of a markedly conservative, Italian-rooted, senatorial order focused on Rome.

This inherited system had come under great pressure in the mid- to late third century. Economic and cultural contact between Rome and the various barbarian peoples beyond the Rhine and the Danube had undermined these peoples' native, somewhat egalitarian, social institutions, and led to the emergence amongst them of ever larger tribes and confederations. Whereas hitherto the military threat posed to Rome by the northern tribes had been relatively atomized, by the third century, more formidable groupings had come into being.

Concurrently, the closing years of the second century had seen the Roman empire extend its eastern frontier at the expense of the Persians. This defeat at the hands of Rome led to the downfall of the ruling Parthian dynasty, and a struggle whereby different aristocratic interests vied for ascendancy. In AD 205–6, there occurred a major revolt led by an aristocrat by the name of Papak. Papak died some time around 208, but by 224 his son, Ardashir, had established leadership of the Persian world as a whole. In September of 226, at the palace of Ctesiphon, Ardashir was crowned the first shah of the Sasanian dynasty. Ardashir soon sought to unite the aristocracy of Persia behind him by launching a series of prestige-garnering offensives against the Romans. This policy of aggression was followed by his son and successor Shapur I, who, in 260, launched a daring campaign into northern Syria, sacking Antioch, and capturing and humiliating the emperor Valerian.

It was the supreme misfortune of the Roman empire that the period of maximum Persian aggression coincided with a series of large-scale incursions into Roman territory by the northern barbarians. This was a situation for which neither the military, the emperor, nor the Roman senate had been prepared, and with which they seemed incapable of dealing. The inability of successive emperors to address this military crisis had led to political instability, as one ineffectual emperor after another was deposed and murdered by his own soldiers. Local society came increasingly to rely on its own resources, leading to the emergence of a series of separate (although not necessarily separatist) regimes—the empire of the Gauls in the west between 258 and 274, that of Palmyra and the east for a few years up to 272.

In response to this crisis, a social revolution took place. The emperor, hitherto appointed by the senate, came increasingly to be appointed by the army, and the army was appointing men from its own ranks. The result was a series of military emperors of humble origin, absolutely committed to the ideology of empire, but impatient of failure. This process culminated in 284 with the figure of Diocletian, who overcame his rivals, established himself as emperor, and waged a series of successful campaigns against foes internal and external alike.

The peace that Diocletian had restored to the empire gave him the opportunity to consolidate a series of administrative reforms. The creation of the 'Tetrarchy'—the system of multiple rulers encountered earlier—gave the empire more devolved leadership, closer to the likely trouble spots. The Augusti and their Caesars resided in imperial capitals nearer the frontiers of the empire, such as Trier in the West, or Antioch in the East. At the same time,

Facing: Statues of magistrates continued to be erected in eastern cities until the sixth century and are often marked by a grim expression denoting determined probity. Here the governor Palmatus at Aphrodisias in Caria (western Asia Minor), late fifth or early sixth century.

the administrative and fiscal system was restructured to facilitate greater imperial control of provincial life. Military and civilian commands in the provinces were separated, and the size of the army increased. The provinces were reduced in size and increased in number so as to tighten central supervision of the city councils. As a result of the expansion of the army and an enlargement of the overarching imperial bureaucracy, the number of high-ranking military and civilian officials directly employed by the central imperial authorities would appear to have more than doubled. These posts were primarily filled by members of the dominant social stratum within the provincial city councils. To these officials access to the senatorial order was increasingly opened up. A new imperial aristocracy of service thus emerged.

Constantine was keen to further these developments. The process of elite formation in particular was given added impetus in the eastern Mediterranean by the emperor's foundation of a senate in Constantinople. In order to consolidate his political position in the eastern provinces, it was vital that Constantine establish a personal connection and following amongst the leading administrators of the eastern bureaucracy and the dominant members of the civic councils. This he sought to do by showering upon them flattery, favours, and prestige. Constantine was fully aware that friends not only could be, but had to be, bought. Granting entry to his new senatorial order was a good means of achieving this.

In order to draw men of influence to Constantinople, the emperor made grants of land to those building private residences in the city. In 332 Constantine instituted there a regular distribution of bread rations derived from the rich corn-supply of Egypt. The foundation of Constantinople and the creation of its senate represented more than mere self-glorification on Constantine's part—they were carefully calculated acts of *Realpolitik*. The long-term consequence of these policies was to draw together the aristocracy of service of the eastern Mediterranean into a single political community, giving a sense of common interest and common identity to the ruling classes of the eastern provinces. This common identity—focused on Constantinople—led to the emergence of that senatorial elite which was to bind together the early Byzantine world.

Constantine was no less sensitive to the extent to which material incentives could advance the cause of his new religion. In 312 he declared that those joining the Christian clergy were to be excused their responsibilities to their native town councils—a policy that appears to have led to a rapid influx into the Church of men of standing. State subsidies to the Church were sanctioned. After defeating Licinius, Constantine authorized the leaders of the Christian communities to draw from imperial coffers whatever sums they needed to expand, embellish, or construct places of worship. At the same time, the Holy Land was monumentally re-appropriated on behalf of God's new chosen people—with the construction of the Church of the Holy Sepulchre in Jerusalem, and that of the Holy Nativity in Bethlehem.

If Constantine's understanding of Christianity appears to have been somewhat limited, one should not judge him too harshly. Many of the basic doctrines of the religion were yet to be formulated; even the corpus of Holy Scripture had not been finally defined. Constantine's adoption of Christianity did, however, mark a major turning point in the ongoing definition of the faith. For the emperor's conversion meant that the coercive powers of the Roman state could now be deployed in favour of whatever theological or ecclesiastical faction could catch his ear. Churchmen who had deplored their own persecution at the hands of pagan emperors were now more than willing to use that self-same brutal authority against their Christian rivals. Thus, in 325, the emperor presided over a council of the Church held at Nicaea, convened primarily to debate the relationship of God the Son to God the Father. If the line that Constantine appears to have supported at Nicaea came ultimately to be regarded as heretical by future emperors and councils, that is less significant than the occasion itself. The decrees of such 'ecumenical councils' were to carry the standing of imperial law. To gainsay them was to resist not only the will of God, but also the will of the emperor.

These policies undoubtedly did much to promote the cause of Christianity. Arguably, however, the interests of the religion were more definitively advanced by its association with an emperor who, by the time of his death in 337, had restored peace and unity to the Roman world and, in the eastern Mediterranean, had set about creating a political community of author-

ity and influence whose members had good reason to celebrate his memory. In terms of allegiance to Constantine, his policies, and his dynasty, success in arms and liberality of patronage mattered more than questions of faith.

This attachment to the memory of Constantine soon found violent expression in the aftermath of his death. Constantine appears to have envisaged dividing the empire after him between his three sons: Constantine II, Constantius II, and Constans, along with the grandsons of his stepmother Theodora. For three months after Constantine's death, there followed an uneasy interregnum until, in September of 337, Constantine's sons declared themselves Augusti. This act was preceded by an uprising of the army in Constantinople. The soldiers demanded that they be ruled over by 'none other than the sons of Constantine', and Theodora's grandsons, along with a host of their relatives and supporters, were massacred. Amongst the few survivors were Gallus and Julian, the two youngest sons of Constantine's slaughtered half-brother, Julius Constantius. Julian was thought to be too young to kill, while his half-brother Gallus was believed to be sufficiently ill to render his murder unnecessary.

In the autumn of 337, Constantine's sons met in Pannonia in the Balkans to divide the empire between them. Constantius, the middle brother, took control of the eastern provinces along with Thrace. Constans took what remained of the Balkans, along with Italy and Africa, whilst the eldest, but probably illegitimate, son, Constantine, was allotted Britain, Gaul, and Spain. Clearly not content with this, Constantine II led an unsuccessful campaign into Italy in 340 that culminated in his death near Aquilea, his former dominions devolving upon his youngest brother. To the east, the Persian shah Shapur II sought to take advantage of the political dislocation so often associated with a transition of power to launch a series of assaults on the Roman frontier city of Nisibis. The first of these took place perhaps as early

Gold medallion of Constantius II, mint of Nicomedia, c. AD 355. On the reverse a personification of Constantinople placing her foot on the prow of a ship.

as the summer of 337, with the Persians making two further incursions in 346 and 350. These Constantius II resisted doggedly, and successfully, from his base at Antioch.

Constantius was a suspicious man and a Christian rather less pragmatic than his father. His military acuity, combined with his conscientiousness as a ruler, nevertheless won him the admiration of many of his eastern subjects. Even the pagan historian Ammianus Marcellinus, whose narrative covers the later part of his reign, was obliged to admit as much. Once again, the key to Constantius II's success appears to have lain in a combination of military prowess and the careful deployment of patronage. Under Constantius, the city of Constantinople was further embellished and its senate considerably enlarged. The senators of Constantinople were honoured as equal to their counterparts in Rome.

Whereas Constantius II can be said to have built upon his father's achievements, in the West, his brother Constans managed affairs rather less wisely. He was accused of keeping ill counsel, and his court drew censure for its excess. In spite of the fact that Constans is known to have legislated against homosexual acts, he is reported by later sources to have maintained a sort of male *harem* of barbarian prisoners-of-war. In 350, he was overthrown in a palace coup and replaced by a military officer of Germanic origin by the name of Magnentius. This act inevitably incited the wrath of Constantius, who, in 351, pursued the usurper's army first from the Balkans, then into Italy, and ultimately into Gaul, where, in 353, Magnentius was finally defeated.

Constantius' sojourn in the West had necessarily raised the question of who was to supervise the East, where the Persians remained an ever-present threat. Childless as he was, Constantius had been obliged to look to the princely survivors of the massacre of 337, and in 351 had appointed Gallus as Caesar. Gallus' period of rule in the East appears to have been characterized primarily by his penchant for unnecessary violence. As Ammianus puts it, 'going beyond the limits of the authority granted him . . . (he caused) . . . universal mischief by his excessive harshness'. Constantius could not afford to see the East alienated, and, in 354, with characteristic forthrightness, he summoned Gallus to him and had him executed. Constantius now busied himself with fighting a number of campaigns against barbarian insurgents on the Rhine. In 355, he appointed as Caesar Gallus' half-brother, Julian, whom he left to oversee events in Gaul as he himself moved on to campaign on the Danubian front.

Constantius must have realized that Julian had little reason to love him. The emperor was, after all, implicated in the death of nearly all of Julian's closest family. Between 342 and 348, Julian and Gallus had effectively been kept in a state of imprisonment in a palace in Cappadocia. Since 348, however, Julian had been permitted some relief from this closed world, and had been allowed to travel first to Constantinople, and thence to Nicomedia, Ephesus, and briefly, Athens, where he had busied himself with acquiring a liberal education. This bookish young man of 24 can hardly have seemed a threat to so hardened a soldier as Constantius, secure as he was in the affection of his army.

In 359, the Persians captured the important Roman frontier post of Amida, and the following year two other Roman outposts fell. Constantius was obliged to return to Antioch and prepare for war. Since 357, and Constantius' march on the Danube, Julian had effectively been the sole representative of imperial authority in the western provinces, a responsibility to which he adapted himself with remarkable *élan*. In an impressive series of campaigns, Julian had driven the marauding barbarians from northern Gaul, and shown the strength of Roman arms beyond the Rhine. At the same time, he had reorganized the collection of taxes in Gaul to the benefit of both fisc and subjects alike. Julian was proving himself to be not only a brave general, but an efficient and equitable administrator.

Julian's success in Gaul appears to have caused Constantius some consternation. Accordingly, in early 360, the emperor sent orders that a considerable portion of Julian's army be moved eastwards for the purposes of the Persian war. To Julian this must have seemed like a deliberate attempt to undermine his position. Julian's army was soon to head east in numbers that Constantius may not initially have expected. For, in February 360, Julian's troops proclaimed him Augustus. Constantius refused to countenance any diminution of his own authority, and in 361 Julian and his army began the long march east to settle the question of the imperial title by force of arms. Constantius in turn withdrew from Antioch, 'eager as always', Ammianus records, 'to meet the challenge of civil war head on'. As he and his army advanced through Cilicia, however, Constantius fell victim to a fever that claimed his life. The late emperor's advisers agreed to acknowledge Julian as supreme lord of the Roman world, and two officers set off to invite him 'to come without delay and take possession of the East, which was ready to obey him'. Julian hastened to Constantinople.

Julian's reign was to last little more than eighteen months. Yet, to contemporaries, as to modern scholars, his period of rule was to be of lasting fascination. On the death of his uncle he chose to reveal publicly what had long been known to a circle of close intimates, namely that, during his studies first in Nicomedia in 351, and subsequently at Ephesus, he had cast aside the God

Julian the Apostate, the last pagan emperor, had himself portrayed on his coins with a philosopher's beard, for which he was much ridiculed. The bull on the reverse remains an enigma. According to one interpretation it is the sacred bull Apis. Copper coin, mint of Constantinople, AD 361–3.

of Constantine, and instead embraced the mysteries of Neoplatonic paganism. Once in Constantinople, Julian declared religious toleration, removed the privileges enjoyed by the Christian Church and clergy, and ordered a revival of worship at the pagan temples of the cities of the empire.

Julian sought to present this declaration as restoring to the Roman world the publicly sanctioned worship of the gods who had granted Rome her past success. Yet it is important to realize the extent to which, even to many non-Christians, Julian's paganism seemed a strange and possibly alienating amalgam. Julian had been raised a Christian: his paganism had something of the quality of a foreign tongue, one eagerly acquired, but alien to the ear of a native speaker. Julian was a devotee of a highly intellectualized form of paganism that took a metaphorical approach to the myths and legends of Graeco-Roman tradition. Whilst the cults of individual deities were to be nurtured, the ultimate purpose of these cults was to lead one to a clearer appreciation of the single divine principle embodied in what Julian described as 'the creator . . . the common father and king of all peoples'.

This intellectualism, infused with a monotheistic tendency that had long been evident within late paganism, might well have appealed to members of the empire's educated elite. Yet Julian's high-mindedness went hand-in-hand with a taste for the spectacular, the sacrificial, and the magical, a taste which many members of this self-same elite would have regarded as rather vulgar. Thus Ammianus remarks that Julian was 'superstitious rather than genuinely observant of the rites of religion, and he sacrificed innumerable victims

Julian in imperial costume watches the sacrificial slaughter of a bull. To the right, a flaming altar stands within a niche topped by three pagan idols.

29

regardless of expense'. It was not just the accession of Christian emperors that had led provincial pagans to allow the civic temples and their associated cults to fall into desuetude. It was also, to some extent, the result of a lack of interest in overtly public and highly costly displays of pagan religiosity on the part of well-born pagans themselves.

If Julian's religious inclinations ran counter to much contemporary feeling, so too did certain of his secular aims. In essence, Julian's policies reveal a determination to roll back the Diocletianic and Constantinian revolution. The court was reduced both in scale and splendour. The emperor was to revert to the role of chief magistrate, rather than overlord, of the Roman world. The central government was gradually to be retrenched, and the administration of the empire was once more to devolve upon the self-governance of the city councils. Such conservative ambitions may have seemed praiseworthy to some. But the chance to escape burdensome civic duties, to advance oneself through the offices of central government, to experience and partake in the extravagance of the court, had opened up opportunities to members of the new imperial aristocracy which they would have been loath to lose.

It is thus perhaps no surprise that, as Julian headed off from Constantinople to Antioch in 362, he found himself distinctly underwhelmed by the enthusiasm his secular and religious policies were eliciting amongst the cities through which he passed. This was to culminate with Julian's spectacular falling out with the citizenry of Antioch. There, Julian's lavish sacrifices to mark the feast of Adonis at a time when the city was suffering from a food shortage, combined with the emperor's own botched attempts to relieve the city's hunger, annoyed Christian and pagan alike. This left the emperor vulnerable to a public lampooning that made a deep impression on him. Upon his return to the region, Julian declared, he would make Tarsus, not Antioch, his home.

Julian's journey east in 362, however, suggests that he was aware of the difficulties he faced in realizing his ambitions. For his aim appears to have been to do what Roman emperors had long done to unite the Greek-speaking cities of the East behind them: to launch a campaign against the Hellenic world's traditional enemy—the empire of Persia. In 363, with an army of 65,000 men, Julian crossed into Persian territory, and, in a series of spectacular victories recorded for us by the first-hand testimony of Ammianus Marcellinus, came within reach of the capital of the shahs at Ctesiphon. Within sight of the city's defenders, Julian presided over a set of athletic celebrations and games. A brilliant victory seemed within his grasp, one that would demonstrate the superiority of his religion. However, it soon dawned on Julian and his advisers that the city was, to all intents and purposes, impregnable. As the Christian Gregory of Nazianzus declared, 'from this point on, like sand slipping from beneath his feet, or a great storm bursting upon a ship, things began to go black for him'.

It was at this point that Julian made his fatal error. He decided that, rather than retreating the way he had come, he would burn the ships that his army had used to traverse the Euphrates and its tributaries, and instead strike further into Persian territory. As it did so, Julian's increasingly demoralized army found itself deprived of supplies and subjected to raids and ambushes. During one such attack, on 26 June, the emperor himself was struck down by a spear that passed through his ribs. Julian was carried to his tent where he died the same evening, professing satisfaction, according to Ammianus, that he had at least suffered a virtuous death in battle rather than 'through secret conspiracy'. Others were less sure: it was rumoured that the emperor had in fact been struck down by one of his own Christian troops.

Interior of the baptistery of Nisibis (Nusaybin in eastern Turkey), built by the bishop Volagesos in 359, four years before the city's surrender to the Persians following the failure of Julian's expedition.

It is easy for the historian to dismiss Julian as a hopeless idealist, whose policies were doomed to failure. Certainly, it is difficult to imagine how the emperor's secular policies could have succeeded. Yet, however eccentric Julian's paganism may have been, the goal of an empire in which Christianity was but one faith among many, tolerated but not privileged, was surely an achievable one, particularly had the pagan emperor shown himself as successful on the field in Persia as he had been in Gaul. As the reign of Constantine had demonstrated, what mattered most in securing the loyalty of his subjects was an emperor's success at arms, not his religious predilections. It is instructive that, upon Julian's death, his officers offered the crown first to an elderly pagan in their company by the name of Salutius. Only after Salutius had declined did the crown pass to the Christian officer Jovian, who negotiated his army's retreat from Persia in return for the surrender of the frontier city of Nisibis and a swathe of Roman territory. Never again was a pagan to rule over the Roman world. The Church was to make certain of that. In the late fourth century, the relative indifference to pagan survivals that had characterized the policies of the Christian emperors before Julian increasingly gave way to a grim determination fully to Christianize society and state, be it by consent or coercion.

Jovian led the dispirited Roman forces home through Antioch to Constantinople in the near vicinity of which, on 17 Februrary 364, he died. The crown now passed to the general Valentinian, who divided the empire with his brother Valens, the latter taking the East, Valentinian heading for the West, where the absence of Julian's army had led to a resurgence of barbarian raids across the Rhine and Danube. Valentinian spent much of the subsequent eleven years of his reign engaged in successful military campaigns. In the East, Valens was obliged to contend both with a revived Persian threat and a revolt on the part of Procopius, a relative and supporter of the deceased Julian. In addition to defeating Procopius, Valens took battle to the usurper's barbarian allies across the Danube, defeating them in 369.

Silver missorium depicting Theodosius I handing a codicil of appointment to an official. The senior emperor is flanked by the young Augusti Arcadius and Valentinian II. Below a personification of the bountiful Earth. AD 388.

In 375, whilst himself campaigning on the Danube, Valentinian died. He had intended his elder son, the 16-year-old Gratian, to succeed him as emperor, and had left the boy at Trier in northern Gaul. Indeed, in an unusual step, Gratian had been accorded the title of Augustus in 367. Rather than complying with these wishes, however, Valentinian's Danubian army acclaimed as emperor his 4-year-old son, Valentinian II, whose court was established in northern Italy, although the entourage around Gratian continued to exercise effective control in Gaul.

In 383, however, Gratian's regime was directly challenged by a revolt in Britain in favour of a general of Spanish origin by the name of Magnus Maximus, to whose colours Gratian's troops rapidly defected. This left Britain, Gaul, and Spain in the effective control of an usurper, and the court of Valentinian II isolated in Italy. Maximus appealed for recognition to the new eastern emperor, Theodosius I, who had succeeded Valens in 379. This recognition was withheld. In 387, Maximus crossed the Alps to take control of Italy and Africa, an act which, in 388, led Theodosius to invade the West in support of Valentinian. Maximus was defeated, captured, and

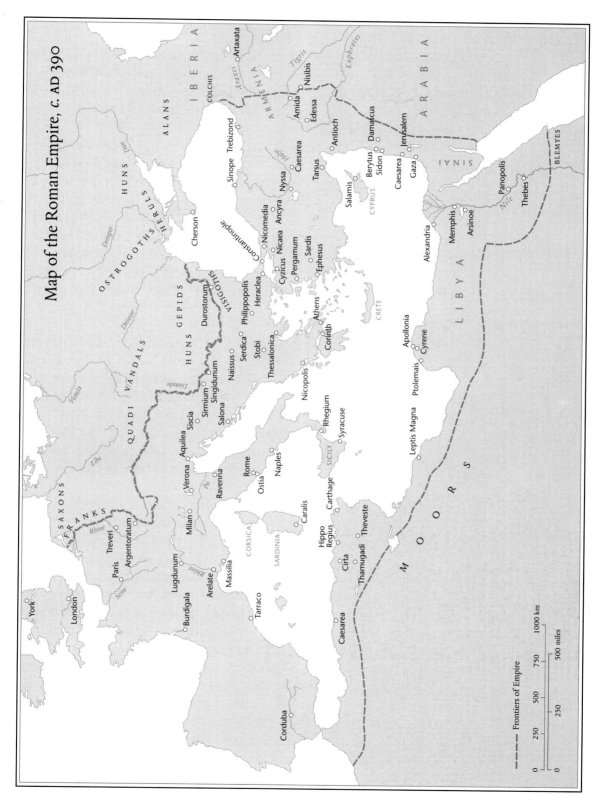

Map of the Roman Empire, c. AD 390

IBERIA

ALANS

ARMENIA

ARABIA

Araxes

Tigris

Euphrates

Artaxata

COLCHIS

Amida
Nisibis
Edessa
Antioch
Damascus
Berytus
Sidon
Jerusalem
Caesarea
Gaza

SINAI

BLEMYES

Panopolis
Thebes

Nile

Trebizond
Sinope

Caesarea

Nyssa

Tarsus

Salamis

CYPRUS

Memphis
Arsinoe

Alexandria

HUNS

HERULS

OSTROGOTHS

Don

Dnieper

Dniester

Cherson

Constantinople
Nicomedia
Nicaea
Ancyra

Cyzicus
Pergamum
Sardis
Ephesus

Heraclea
Philippopolis

VISIGOTHS

GEPIDS

Durostorum

Halys

LIBYA

QUADI

VANDALS

Vistula

Elbe

HUNS

Danube

Serdica
Stobi
Naissus

Thessalonica

Nicopolis

Athens
Corinth

Apollonia
Cyrene

Ptolemais

Sirmium
Singidunum
Salona

Siscia

Aquileia

Verona
Milan

Ravenna
Po

Rome
Naples

Rhegium
Syracuse

SICILY

Leptis Magna

M O O R S

SAXONS

FRANKS

Rhine

Treveri
Argentoratum

Paris
Seine

Lugdunum

Burdigala

Arelate
Massilia
Rhône

CORSICA

SARDINIA

Caralis

Ostia

Tarraco

Corduba

Carthage

Hippo
Regius
Cirta
Thamugadi
Theveste

Caesarea

CRETE

York

London

– – – Frontiers of Empire

| 0 | 250 | 500 | 750 | 1000 km |

| 0 | 250 | 500 miles |

33

Imperial group seated in their box (*kathisma*) in the hippodrome, receiving the tribute of kneeling barbarians. Pedestal of Egyptian obelisk in the Hippodrome of Constantinople. AD 390.

executed. Valentinian II was sent off to Gaul to establish his court at Vienne. There he remained a puppet of his eastern colleague, to whom he owed his throne.

In 392, evidently dispirited by his powerlessness, Valentinian II took his own life. This in turn led to another civil war, as Arbogast, commander of the western army, sought to place on the throne an ally of his by the name of Eugenius. Theodosius responded in 394 by leading yet another campaign westwards. The emperor was successful in defeating the usurper, but himself died in 395, dividing the empire between his two sons—Honorius in the West and Arcadius in the East.

The period between the death of Valentinian I and that of Theodosius I was in many ways a pivotal one for the evolving relationship between the eastern and western provinces of the Roman empire. Valentinian I's succession in the West by the ineffectual Gratian and Valentinian II, had meant that the governing classes of the western provinces, particularly in Britain and Gaul, had been left without a figure of sufficient personal authority or prestige to

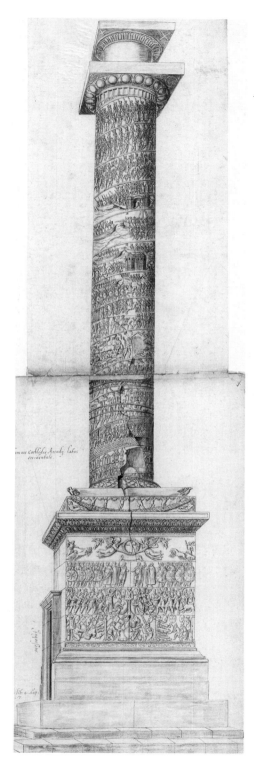

The column of Arcadius at Constantinople drawn in 1574. A close imitation of the 'historiated' columns of Trajan and Marcus Aurelius in Rome, this column celebrated the defeat of the rebellious Gothic general Gainas in 400. The shaft of the column was dismantled in the early eighteenth century. Only the pedestal remains today, bereft of its reliefs.

Marble head of the emperor Arcadius as a young man found near the Forum of Theodosius I at Constantinople, c. AD 395.

take effective charge of military affairs. The support given first to Maximus, and subsequently to Eugenius, demonstrated an increasing readiness on the part of the leaders of western society to follow usurpers, if those usurpers could offer them the leadership they required. This weakening of imperial government in the west was to become still more pronounced in the years that followed the division of the empire in 395, exacerbated as it was by two phenomena.

As has been seen, the military security of the Roman world was highly sensitive to developments amongst the various barbarian peoples to the north of the Rhine and Danube. These tribal groupings were themselves highly vulnerable to any threat from the world of the Eurasian steppe—the plains and grasslands that stretched from the east of the Pannonian plain, across the region to the north of the Black Sea, to the distant marchlands of China. Instability on the Eurasian steppe could lead to the westward migration of highly mobile nomadic groups, which might in turn either come to exercise mastery over the trans-Danubian world, or force the barbarians already resident there to seek to cross into Roman territory. In the course of the fourth century, groups of nomadic barbarians known to us as the Huns began just such a westward migration, one that was to cast into turmoil the world to the north of the Roman empire.

Some time before the mid-370s, the Huns appear to have established a power-base for themselves to the north of the Black Sea coast and to the east of the Carpathian mountains, first subduing the Alans, and subsequently coming into conflict with the Germanic Gothic tribes which had hitherto dominated the region. In 376 large numbers of Gothic refugees arrived on the northern bank of the river Danube. From there they sent requests to the emperor Valens, asking that they be permitted to settle within the Roman empire, offering their military service in return for land. Valens acceded to these petitions. The Gothic settlers were, however, mistreated by the Roman commanders in the region, leading in 378 to a large-scale uprising of the Visigoths under the leadership of a certain Fritigern. On 9 August, in a major engagement to the north of Adrianople, the Gothic host defeated a 40,000-strong Roman army. Two-thirds of the army was slaughtered, along with the emperor Valens himself. Although Theodosius was subsequently able to restore peace, settling the Visigoths in the western Balkans, the stand-off was an uneasy one.

Between 395 and 410 this situation again deteriorated. The death of Theodosius I vitiated relations in two key respects. First, Theodosius' appointed heir in the west, Honorius, was only 10 years old at the time of his accession. His court came to be dominated by the commander of the western army—a general of barbarian origin by the name of Stilicho, a man with a reputation

for hostility towards the Visigoths. Second, the demise of Theodosius presented the Visigoths, under their new leader Alaric, with the opportunity to attempt to secure ever better terms from the Romans. To this end they made periodic attacks on Roman positions in the Balkans and, increasingly, Italy. In Constantinople, the result was an anti-Gothic backlash, culminating in the year 400 with the massacre of the Gothic garrison in the city.

In the West, Stilicho responded to these attacks with a series of ultimately inconclusive campaigns. Eventually, in 407, he felt obliged to come to terms

Ivory diptych depicting Stilicho, general-in-chief and virtual ruler of the western empire, his wife Serena, and son Eucherius. The last, who was to be murdered in 408, is holding the codicils of his appointment to the honorific office of 'tribune and notary'.

with the Visigoths, offering them subsidies, payments, and honours. Here too, however, an anti-barbarian reaction appears to have taken place. In 408, Stilicho and his supporters were executed, bringing the continued existence of the western court's pact with the Visigoths into question. In order to apply pressure on the western regime, Alaric led his army into Italy. As negotiations floundered, in 410 he and his troops sacked the city of Rome. By virtue of Theodosius I's settlement of the Visigoths in the western Balkans, what had begun as a crisis for the empire in the East, was increasingly becoming a full-blown crisis in the West.

The Goths were not the only barbarian people to enter Roman territory at this time. By the early years of the fifth century, the Huns appear to have established themselves to the west of the Carpathian mountains, intensifying barbarian pressure, not least on the Rhine frontier. In 405 Radagaisus, the chief of yet another Gothic army, led his troops into Italy. On 31 December 406 the frozen river Rhine was traversed by a host of barbarian peoples including Vandals, Sueves, and Alans. Radagaisus was defeated and executed outside Florence in 406. But the raiders from across the Rhine extended their incursions until, by 409, they were able to strike into Spain. In 412, the Visigoths, under the leadership of Alaric's successor, Ataulf, crossed the Alps and established themselves in southern Gaul. By the second decade of the fifth century, much of the western empire was in the grip of a severe military paralysis. Barbarian armies were operative in Gaul and Spain and were heading towards Africa, which the Vandals were to conquer in 439. In 407 the mobile field army had been withdrawn from Britain, never to return.

What is perhaps most striking about this crisis is the inability of the Roman field armies successfully to meet the barbarian challenge. The presence of the Gothic host in Italy in the first decade of the fifth century necessarily meant that the imperial authorities were too preoccupied with events within the peninsula to concentrate effectively on the situation in Gaul. Since 395, the court had moved first to Milan, and subsequently, in 402, to Ravenna, so as better to address the Visigothic challenge. Accordingly, military commanders and imperial officials in the remaining western provinces were obliged to fall back upon their own resources. But the feebleness of the imperial response to military events in the west after 406 was a result of more than a mere distancing of imperial power. Rather, it is clear that the imperial army in the West did not possess the resources required to mount a sustained defence.

This was due to social and economic processes resultant from the emergence of the new aristocracy of service of the fourth century. As members of this new elite entrenched their social and political authority, so too did they expand their landed estates at the expense of lesser, more humble members of provincial society. This process is reflected in the fourth-century 'villa boom' which archaeologists have identified in the western provinces, as well as in what one scholar has described as the 'snowballing' of aristocratic fortunes attested in the sources. The same pattern is recorded in the East, where a series of surviving imperial laws dating from the fourth and fifth centuries attempted to limit the phenomenon. These laws are highly suggestive, for the imperial authorities claimed that wealthy landowners were using their influence and prestige to engage in large-scale tax evasion.

Diminishing tax revenues necessarily undermined the fiscal basis of the Roman state and, in particular, hamstrung the military, which was the main recipient of imperial expenditure. Due to this, the western imperial authorities in the early fifth century were increasingly incapable of raising the revenues required to support the standing army.

Paralysed both by the proximity of the barbarian threat and its inability to meet it, the western court became more and more of an irrelevance as the fifth century progressed. Imperial officials found themselves obliged to cut deals with the barbarians so as to have access to at least some sort of military force. Thus, for example, in 418 the Visigoths were settled in Aquitaine, establishing a kingdom at Toulouse. In return for this settlement they agreed to protect the region from the depredations of other barbarian groups. Accordingly, the courts of the barbarian leaders came to serve as the main focus for the political ambitions of the leading members of western provincial society. The imperial court at Ravenna receded from sight. By the mid-fifth century only Italy was under effective imperial control.

Yet even in Italy, the military situation was precarious. In 452 the leader of the Huns, the infamous Attila, led an army into the peninsula that was, to all intents and purposes, unopposed. In 455 Rome was sacked once more, this time by the Vandals. As the western court became increasingly emasculated, so too did the very concept of the western *imperium* come to seem expendable. In 467–8, when the western crown passed to an eastern placeman by the name of Anthemius, the

The colossus of Barletta, bronze statue probably of the emperor Leo I (457–74), taken from Constantinople after 1204 and shipwrecked on the coast of Barletta, where it has remained ever since. The arms and legs were added during the Renaissance.

imperial prefect in Gaul advised the Visigothic king Euric to reject the new emperor and divide Gaul between himself and the king of the Burgundians. Likewise, in a palace coup in the year 476, Romulus, the last of the Roman emperors in the West, was deposed by his barbarian general Odoacer. Odoacer set himself up as king in Italy and informed Constantinople that there was now no longer any need for a separate emperor in Ravenna. Titular authority in the region could pass to the eastern Augustus, a legal fiction that masked the emergence in the West of autonomous barbarian kingdoms which were now the successors to Rome.

If the fifth century proved to be a fatal one for the structures of imperial government in the western provinces of the Roman empire, the situation in the East was rather less cataclysmic. This fact was primarily due to the greater military security of the eastern empire at this time. The migration of the Visigoths, combined with the increasingly westward-looking nature of Hunnic military activity, meant that the barbarian question was of less urgency in fifth-century Constantinople than in Ravenna. Even so, there was little the imperial authorities could do to prevent Hun incursions into the Balkans. After the death of Attila in 453, and the subsequent collapse of Hunnic power, they were obliged to permit the settlement in the northern Balkans of a large and potentially dangerous Ostrogothic confederation made up of former subjects of the Huns. Eventually, in the year 489, the bulk of the Ostrogoths, under the leadership of Theoderic, were persuaded to march west to depose Odoacer from control in Italy. There, Theoderic set up a new regime, one which paid lip-service to imperial suzerainty, but little more.

Crucially, the fifth century saw a period of détente in Roman–Persian relations. Both settled empires were fully aware of the great threat posed to them by the disturbed nature of conditions on the Eurasian steppe. In such circumstances, co-operation was felt to be imperative. Nevertheless, it is important not to exaggerate the strength of the eastern empire in the fifth century and as it entered the sixth. The imperial authorities in the East were unable to make any substantial contribution to the defence of the West. The legal sources for the eastern empire, along with the surviving documentary evidence from Egypt, suggest that, as in the West, emperors in Constantinople were fighting a losing battle against the expansion of aristocratic estates and tax evasion on the part of their owners. Political conditions within Constantinople were periodically unstable, and the reign of the emperor Zeno (474–91) in particular was punctuated by a series of conspiracies and revolts.

This undermining of imperial authority was intensified by two further developments. First, ever since the Ecumenical Council of Chalcedon in 451, the Church in the East had found itself racked by disputes as to the nature of the relationship between the divine and the human within the person of Christ.

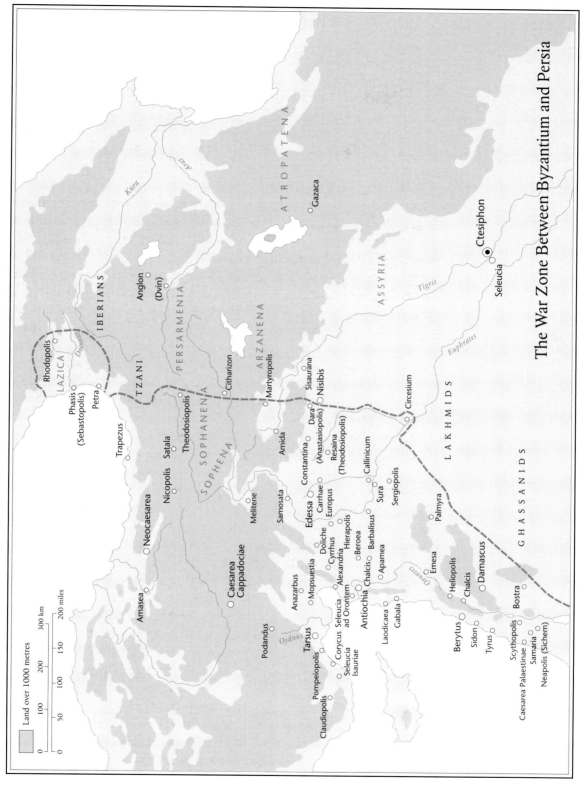

The War Zone Between Byzantium and Persia

Land over 1000 metres

Rhodopolis
LAZICA
Phasis
(Sebastopolis)
Petra
IBERIANS
Trapezus
TZANI
Anglon
(Dvin)
PERSARMENIA
Citharizon
ARZANENA
Martyropolis
ATROPATENA
Gazaca
ASSYRIA
Ctesiphon
Seleucia
Tigris
Sisaurana
Dara
(Anastasiopolis)
Nisibis
Resaina
(Theodosiopolis)
Circesium
Euphrates
LAKHMIDS
Satala
Nicopolis
Theodosiopolis
SOPHANENA
SOPHENA
Amida
Constantina
Carrhae
Edessa
Europus
Callinicum
Sura
Sergiopolis
Palmyra
Neocaesarea
Melitene
Samosata
Doliche
Cyrrhus
Hierapolis
Beroea
Barbalisus
Apamea
GHASSANIDS
Amasea
Caesarea
Cappadociae
Anazarbus
Mopsuestia
Alexandria
Chalcis
Emesa
Heliopolis
Chalcis
Damascus
Bostra
Podandus
Ojdnus
Tarsus
Seleucia
ad Orontem
Antiochia
Laodicaea
Gabala
Berytus
Sidon
Tyrus
Scythopolis
Samaria
Neapolis (Sichem)
Corycus
Seleucia
Isauriae
Pompeiopolis
Claudiopolis
Caesarea Palaestinae

Kura
Aras
Dacenia
Orontes

300 km
200 miles
0   50 100 150 200
0 100   200   300

41

The definition of this relationship established at the council met sustained resistance from the leaders of the Church in Egypt and Syria. The refusal of large sections of the Church in the East to accept the theological formula laid down at Chalcedon constituted a direct challenge to imperial power, a challenge to which emperors responded by means of limited persecution, cajoling, and attempted compromise, none of which had any lasting effect. The emperor Anastasius (491–518), who sympathized with anti-Chalcedonian sentiment, excited the hostility of the pro-Chalcedonian faction. The dispute appeared to be as intractable as it was debilitating.

Second, the early sixth century saw the return of the Persian menace. In 484 the Sasanian shah Peroz found himself humiliated at the hands of a group of Huns known as the 'Hephthalite' or 'White Huns', who defeated him in battle and made the Persian empire their tributary. In 502/3, the shah Kavad sought to restore the fortunes of his dynasty by once more waging war on Rome, seizing the frontier post of Amida. Whilst Anastasius was ultimately able to force back the Persian advance, the re-emergence of a bellicose enemy to the empire's east can only have revived insecurity.

Each and every one of these challenges to imperial authority elicited an energetic response during the early years of the reign of the emperor Justinian. His accession heralded the most determined period of rulership the Roman world had witnessed since the days of Diocletian. Between the years 527 and 541, he undertook no less a project than the complete reconstruction of the Roman state. Justinian came to the throne as sole emperor in August of 527, succeeding his elderly uncle Justin. Like his uncle, Justinian was a military man, who appears to have gained the throne primarily on the basis of military support and may thus have been viewed with some suspicion by aristocratic circles in Constantinople. It was therefore vital that the new emperor assert his authority as rapidly as possible.

The reforms initiated by Justinian in the period 527–41 should be viewed as a whole. Like the dome of his great monument in Constantinople, the Church of Holy Wisdom, or Hagia Sophia, the overarching concept of the reassertion of imperial dignity was dependent upon the supporting substructures of a disorientatingly diverse range of policies that encompassed religion, the law, provincial administration, fiscal policy, and imperial ideology.

Justinian's first priority was to reassert imperial control over the religious lives of his subjects. Amongst the first acts of the new emperor in the year 528–9 were measures instituting the concerted persecution of surviving pagans amongst the upper classes, as well as heretics and homosexuals. Likewise, the year 532 saw the first of Justinian's repeated efforts to reconcile the pro- and anti-Chalcedonian elements within the Church. This attempt combined an apparently genuine effort to establish a theological position with

which all could concur and a ruthless determination to punish and exclude those individual bishops who had led resistance to the imperial authorities. At the same time, the emperor sought to provide an ideological justification for the active part he was determined to play in the religious life of his subjects. More explicitly than any emperor before him, Justinian asserted that the authority of the emperor and the authority of the priesthood derived from a common divine source, and that it was the responsibility of the emperor alone to regulate priesthood and Church alike. Imperial ceremonial adopted an increasingly religious tone, emphasizing the unique place of the emperor at the intersection of the divine and earthly hierarchies of power.

This determined effort to reposition the emperor at the heart of the religious life of his subjects proceeded alongside an attempt to reassert imperial control over the secular structures of government. Between 528 and 534 Justinian's advisers reformed and codified the civil law of the empire. The inherited legal framework was remodelled to serve contemporary needs, and the emperor was established, for the first time in Roman tradition, as the one and only legitimate source of law. The person of the emperor was, Justinian decreed, 'the law animate'.

As the new legal framework of the empire took shape, so in 535 Justinian attempted to render recourse to the law more practicable for his subjects. Between 535 and 539 he legislated on the administrative and governmental structure of no fewer than seventeen provinces, in an attempt to make governors less prone to the corrupting blandishments offered by the patronage of aristocratic landowners, and to secure the collection of vital tax revenues. As Justinian declared in 539 in his edict on Egypt, tax evasion on the part of city councillors, landowners, and imperial officials threatened 'the very cohesion of our state itself'.

Such a concerted series of reforms was bound to elicit internal opposition, not least on the part of those aristocratic interests to whom active imperial rule was by no means an attractive option. The first and most dramatic expression of discontent erupted in the year 532, in what is known as the 'Nika' insurrection in Constantinople. Members of the senate took advantage of the discontent of the

Facing: Interior of St Sophia, Constantinople, built 532–7. Apart from the removal of the stepped seating in the apse, chancel screen, and pulpit, the interior is remarkably well preserved in spite of the many vicissitudes the building has undergone.

Marble head of an empress, often identified as Theodora. Another candidate is Licinia Eudoxia, daughter of Theodosius II, wife of the western emperor Valentinian III (437–55).

Facing: A pendant to the
Justinian panel in the
church of San Vitale,
Ravenna, the Theodora
panel shows the empress
presenting to the church a
jewelled gold chalice.
The theme of offering is
echoed by the representa-
tion of the Three Magi
embroidered on the hem
of her purple silk mantle.

Constantinopolitan mob to seek to dismiss Justinian's chief advisers and, ultimately, to attempt to replace the emperor himself. Justinian is reported to have considered taking flight, but was dissuaded by his wife, the indomitable empress Theodora, a former actress reviled in one contemporary account as a meddlesome whore. The revolt was crushed amidst a horrific bloodbath in the city's hippodrome. In the wake of the Nika riots, much of the monumental heart of Constantinople had to be rebuilt.

Justinian and his entourage did, nevertheless, attempt to appeal to conservative sentiment. However innovatory the reality of the emperor's legal project was, legal and provincial reforms were presented in antiquarian and conservative terms. The law was to be restored to its pristine glory. Changes in the administration of the provinces were justified in terms of ancient precedents. Moreover, Justinian took an aggressive stance towards the empire's rivals to the east, the north, and the west. In relation to Persia, he followed in the footsteps of his predecessors, Justin and Anastasius, in investing in the empire's defensive infrastructure along its Persian frontier. At the same time, he extended and entrenched the empire's position in the strategically vital region of the Transcaucasus, and fostered the Roman client chieftaincy of the Ghassan along the empire's Arabian flank.

Likewise, in the Balkans, the early years of Justinian's reign witnessed a major consolidation of the empire's position. Justinian engaged in a canny tribal policy amongst the barbarians beyond the Danube, setting one group against another. Within Roman territory, he provided the Balkan hinterland with a series of fortifications, walls, and rural redoubts, aimed at limiting the damage that barbarian raiders could inflict.

Militarily, the eastern and northern frontiers were Justinian's chief concerns. At almost no stage were their needs neglected. Nevertheless, in the 530s the emperor took advantage of political instability in the Vandal kingdom of North Africa and the Ostrogothic regime in Italy to attempt to restore direct Roman rule over these territories. In many respects, these were campaigns on the cheap: only some 15,000 men were sent to North Africa, and it is unlikely that there were ever more than 30,000 troops engaged in active service during the long-drawn-out Italian campaign. These western forays were, nevertheless, successful. North Africa fell in 533–4, and Italy was reduced between 535 and 553. In the early 550s, Justinian's armies were even able to establish a foothold in southern Spain. These victories did much to restore the empire to a position of political, ideological, and military dominance in the central and western Mediterranean.

From the beginning of the 540s, however, the mood of ambition and confidence that had characterized the first fourteen years of Justinian's reign, began to give way to a rather more sombre attitude. There appear to have

been a number of reasons for this. Men of a conservative frame of mind such as the historian Procopius, or another contemporary author, John the Lydian, began to feel that the price for the restoration of Rome's imperial glory, in terms of internal and fiscal reform, was a rather high one. Both authors, for example, take a distinctly negative view of the policies of Justinian's chief internal and financial minister, John the Cappadocian. It is perhaps no surprise that John fell from favour and was exiled in 541. Furthermore, in spite of Justinian's aggressive stance towards Persia, the Sasanians were still capable of breaching the empire's eastern defences. In 540, the Persian shah Khusro I bypassed Roman defences in Mesopotamia and sacked the city of Antioch— an event which left a deep impression on Procopius, who wrote that he 'became dizzy' when he attempted to report the calamity.

From the late 550s the imperial position in the Balkans was undermined by the arrival to the north of the Danube of yet another nomadic group fleeing the Eurasian steppe. Forced westwards by the expansion to the north of the Caucasus and the Black Sea of the western Turk empire, a

Facing: Exterior view of St Sophia, Constantinople (532–7) from the south. In the Byzantine period the view of the south façade was obstructed by the patriarchal palace, which reached up to gallery level. Today this space is occupied by the mausolea of Ottoman sultans.

The city-fortress of Dara (Anastasiopolis) was built on the Persian frontier close to Nisibis by the emperor Anastasius (505–7) and further strengthened by Justinian. It played thereafter a notable part in the wars between Byzantium and Persia. Portions of its walls, granaries, and cisterns still stand.

47

people known as the Avars came to establish themselves on the Pannonian plain. Although Justinian was initially able to incorporate the Avars into his tribal policy, their arrival was ominous.

Perhaps most crucially, Justinian's internal, fiscal, and religious policies themselves began to falter. It was becoming increasingly evident that the dispute over Chalcedon was essentially insoluble. In 553, at the Second Council of Constantinople, Justinian's theologians did in fact piece together a formula that ought to have addressed the concerns of all parties concerned. By this stage, however, the tradition of conflict over Chalcedon was so ingrained in the minds of the participants that few were interested in restoring peace to the Church. To do so would have been to show disrespect to the memory of the heroes of the previous generation whom each side revered.

Financially, the 540s saw the empire dealt a body blow by the advent of the bubonic plague, which, originating in central Africa, reached the empire for the first time via the Red Sea in the year 541. From Egypt, the plague soon spread to Constantinople, Palestine, Syria, Asia Minor, the Balkans, North Africa, and Italy. Both the cities of the empire and their rural hinterlands were severely affected by the initial impact of the disease and its subsequent recurrences, a fact attested by a wide range of contemporary eyewitness accounts. Thus Procopius, who was present at the arrival of the plague in Constantinople, describes how, at one point, it struck down 10,000 victims in the city in a single day. John of Ephesus witnessed 'villages whose inhabitants perished altogether'. The population of the empire may have been reduced by a third. Not only did this mean much human misery, it also dramatically diminished the number of taxpayers on whom the state could rely. The years after the advent of the plague saw the gold coinage of the empire repeatedly debased, as some attempt was made to stretch limited resources ever further.

At the same time, attempts to prevent the further expansion of aristocratic

Facing: Interior of the church of Sts Sergius and Bacchus, Constantinople, built by Justinian and Theodora between 531 and 536 for a community of Monophysite monks. The nave is octagonal in plan, covered by a huge dome. The dedicatory inscription is still preserved on the horizontal entablature.

Electrotype of lost gold medallion of Justinian, struck in 534 to commemorate the reconquest of Africa from the Vandals. The emperor is represented on both sides, nimbed and wearing an extraordinary helmet-cum-diadem surmounted by a tuft of peacock feathers.

The city of Zenobia, named after the third-century queen of Palmyra and situated on the Euphrates, was rebuilt by Justinian and given a permanent garrison. Its walls, which describe a triangle, are still standing. Here the military headquarters (*principia*) of the garrison.

Rusafa, burial place of St Sergius in the Syrian steppe, was an important centre of pilgrimage. Its walls—of which the highly ornate north gate is shown here—are ascribed to the emperor Justinian. Important remains of three large churches are still to be seen within the walls.

estates within the provinces and to curb the illicit patronage and tax evasion of great landowners appear to have been failing, thus further denying the state vital revenues. A number of Justinian's provincial reforms were reversed and legislative activity on the part of the emperor and his advisers diminished to a trickle.

In 565 Justinian died. As the court poet Corippus put it, 'the awesome death of the man showed by clear signs that he had conquered the world. He alone, amidst universal lamentations, seemed to rejoice in his pious countenance.' The memory of Justinian was to loom large in the minds of subsequent generations of emperors, just as the physical monuments built in Constantinople during his reign were long to dominate the medieval city. Nevertheless, in spite of the grandeur of Justinian's project, buffeted by plague, frustrated by deeply entrenched social and religious realities, a reign that had promised so much ultimately ended in disappointment. Justinian bequeathed to his successor, Justin II, an empire which, though larger, was nevertheless markedly fragile and fiscally unstable.

This fiscal instability in particular was to do much to undermine the reigns of Justinian's successors and limit their ability to meet ever more pressing military needs. Justin II declared upon his accession that he 'found the treasury burdened with many debts and reduced to utter exhaustion'. The emperor was consequently unwilling, or unable, to continue the subventions by which the empire had secured the support of the Ghassanids in Arabia, as well as, more recently, of the Avars in the Balkans.

The consolidation of Avar power to the north of the Danube rendered Justinian's policy of 'divide and rule' less and less effective. Both Slavs and Lombards attempted to flee Avar domination, entering imperial territory in the Balkans and Italy respectively. Between 568 and 572 much of northern Italy fell. In the 580s, a number of cities in the Balkans from Thessalonica to Athens suffered repeated Avar and Slav attacks, the Avars concentrating on the plains to the north, the Slavs taking advantage of mountainous highlands and forest cover to strike and settle ever further south. In the 590s, the emperor Maurice directed a series of successful military campaigns along and beyond the Danube, but these forays, impressive though they were, did little to remedy the situation elsewhere in the region. Economies were the order of the day. In 588, military pay was reduced by 25 per cent, leading to a major mutiny on the empire's eastern frontier.

Warfare with Persia continued intermittently during the late sixth century. In spite of a weakening of the Roman position in Arabia, the empire made significant advances at the expense of the Persians in Transcaucasia, when the emperor Maurice took advantage of a coup against the reigning shah Hormizd IV. In 591, Maurice helped to place on the Sasanian throne the

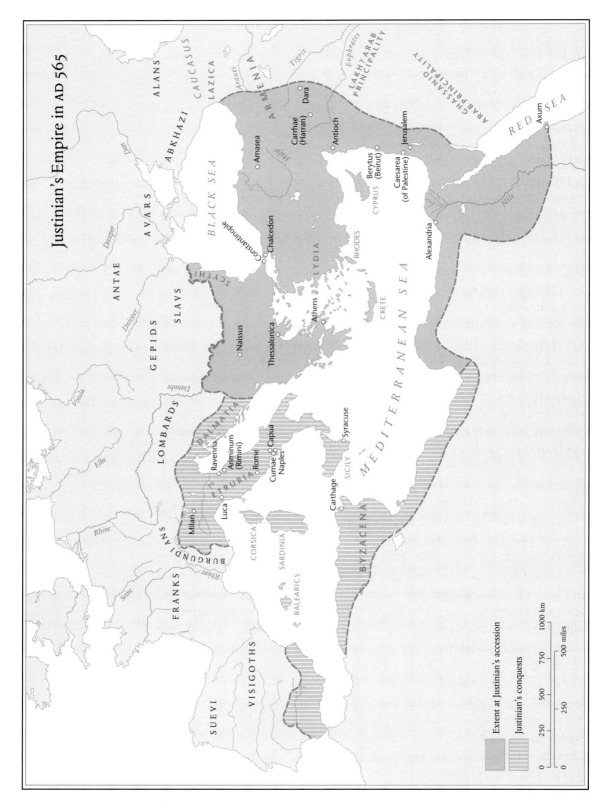

Justinian's Empire in AD 565

ALANS

CAUCASUS

LAZICA

ABKHAZI

ARMENIA

Araxes

Tigris

Euphrates

LAKHŽ ARAB PRINCIPALITY

GHASSANID ARAB PRINCIPALITY

Dara

Carrhae (Harran)

Amasea

Antioch

Halys

RED SEA

Jerusalem

Berytus (Beirut)

Caesarea (of Palestine)

Axum

CYPRUS

Nile

Alexandria

BLACK SEA

Dnieper

AVARS

Dniester

ANTAE

Chalcedon

Constantinople

SCYTHIA

LYDIA

RHODES

MEDITERRANEAN SEA

CRETE

Athens

SLAVS

GEPIDS

Naissus

Thessalonica

Dnieper

Danube

DALMATIA

LOMBARDS

Elbe

Vistula

Ariminum (Rimini)

Ravenna

Rome

ETRURIA

Capua

Cumae

Naples

Syracuse

SICILY

Milan

Luca

CORSICA

SARDINIA

BYZACENA

Carthage

Rhine

BURGUNDIANS

BALEARICS

Seine

FRANKS

SUEVI

VISIGOTHS

Extent at Justinian's accession

Justinian's conquests

0   250   500   750   1000 km

0   250   500 miles

52

shah's son, Khusro II, in return for major territorial concessions. This was a treaty that Khusro was bound to wish to reverse. Twelve years later, he was to have his chance.

In the year 602, imperial forces were campaigning against Slav tribes beyond the Danube. Maurice ordered that the troops continue the campaign into the winter. The emperor was already unpopular in military circles due to his economizing, and the Danubian army erupted into open revolt under the leadership of an officer by the name of Phokas. The army marched on Constantinople. On 23 August 602, Phokas was proclaimed Augustus. A few days later, Maurice was executed along with at least four of his five sons.

The fall of Maurice and the accession of Phokas saw the empire's descent into a protracted civil war. A seventh-century Armenian history, which appears well informed on imperial affairs, describes bloodletting throughout the provinces of the Roman world. Khusro II seized this opportunity to attempt to regain what he had been obliged to cede in 591. The weakness of the Roman resistance led to a dramatic escalation of the shah's ambitions. In the year 603, with the Roman army evidently in a state of some disarray, Khusro struck into the Roman frontier positions, seizing a series of cities and fortifications. By 609/10 the Persians had reached the Euphrates. This was followed by an extension of the campaign into Syria. In 611, the Persians advanced into Anatolia.

These dramatic Persian victories led to further political instability within the empire. In 608, the military governor of Carthage rebelled. In 609 his nephew, Nicetas, advanced into Egypt and seized control of Alexandria. On 3 October 610, the governor's son, Heraclius, arrived outside the imperial capital at the head of a fleet. Phokas' supporters deserted him. Two days later, Phokas was dead and Heraclius had replaced him as emperor.

Amongst Heraclius' first moves appear to have been a withdrawal of Roman troops from the Balkans in an attempt to concentrate resources on driving the Persians out of Anatolia. This Heraclius may have partly achieved in a successful engagement in 612, but in 613 his army suffered a major defeat in the vicinity of Antioch. The Persians now set about the reduction of what remained of Syria and Palestine. In 613 Damascus fell, whilst in 614 a victorious Persian army entered Jerusalem, where, amidst much slaughter, the remains of the True Cross were seized and sent off to Persia.

By 615, a cowed Constantinopolitan senate was willing to sue for peace. A high-ranking embassy was dispatched to Khusro II. The shah was addressed as 'supreme emperor', Heraclius was described as the shah's 'true son, one who is eager to perform the services of your serenity in all things'. The senate was willing to acknowledge the Persian empire as superior to that of Rome and the Roman empire as its tributary. Khusro's response was

forthright. The ambassadors were imprisoned. No mercy was to be shown. Persia was set to eliminate its ancient imperial rival.

The Persians were now ready to initiate the conquest of Egypt. In 619, Alexandria fell, and within the year the entire province appears to have been in Persian hands. All that now remained was for the Persians to resume the advance into Anatolia and make their way to Constantinople. In 622, the Persians struck to the north-west of the Anatolian plateau, where they met stiff Roman resistance led by the emperor himself. The Roman effort in Anatolia was, however, undermined by a crisis in the Balkans that necessitated the emperor's return to the capital. In 623 the city of Ancyra fell, whilst, that same year, the Persians launched a series of successful naval operations, seizing Rhodes and a number of other islands.

The Persians were applying inexorable pressure on what remained of the empire. Heraclius was faced with a stark choice: he could either wait for the Persian grip to tighten, fighting a series of rearguard actions which offered little chance of ultimate success, or he could throw caution to the wind and take battle to the enemy. He opted for the latter. Between 615 and 622 Heraclius instituted a series of crisis measures aimed at maximizing the resources at his disposal. Official salaries and military pay were halved, governmental structures overhauled. Churches were stripped of their gold ornaments and silver plate, the wealth of the cities was drained. These funds were used to attempt to buy peace with the Avars in the West, and to elicit the support of the Christian population of the Transcaucasus and the occupied territories. This effort was reinforced by a religious propaganda drive, emphasizing the horrors associated with the fall of Jerusalem, and playing upon the apocalyptic sensibilities that were a pronounced feature of the day. At the same time, the emperor set about organizing a sort of 'New Model Army'—an intensively trained infantry force versed in the tactics of guerrilla warfare and enthused with religious fervour. A concept of Christian 'holy war' against the Persian infidel came to be enunciated.

There was little point in Heraclius attempting to engage the superior Persian forces on open terrain. Rather, the emperor realized that his best hope would be to head north, to the highlands of Transcaucasia, where he would be able to request reinforcements from the Christian principalities of the region, and where a small, highly mobile army might yet outwit a numerically preponderant foe. On 25 March 624 Heraclius departed from Constantinople. Advancing up the Euphrates, the Romans marched into Persian Armenia, laying waste a number of cities as they went. The emperor then struck south into the Persian Caucasian territory of Atropatene, driving Khusro and his army from the city of Ganzak and destroying the premier fire-temple of the Zoroastrian religion at Takht-i-Sulaiman. Heraclius then headed north

Facing: The Monastery of St Catherine (originally of the Mother of God) on Mount Sinai was both a major centre of pilgrimage and a fortified military outpost. The still extant basilica, a somewhat rustic work, was built by the emperor Justinian between 548 and 565. The inscription over the outer entrance displaying the date 527 is a fake of the eighteenth century.

David and Goliath. Silver plate, AD 613–30. One of nine plates decorated with scenes of David's life, found with other silver objects and gold jewellery near Kyrenia, Cyprus. The iconography of the plate has been interpreted in the light of the war between Byzantium and Persia, which ended in 628.

once more, establishing his winter quarters in the principality of Albania. It is from here that the emperor is likely to have issued his summons to the Christian lords of the region, considerable numbers of whom appear to have flocked to his standard along with their men-at-arms. At the same time, an embassy was sent to the Turks to the north of the Caucasus, in an attempt to negotiate an alliance with the formidable steppe power.

In the spring of 625 three Persian armies were sent in pursuit of Heraclius. Outmanoeuvring and defeating each of these in turn, the emperor headed towards the Black Sea coast and the kingdom of Lazica. It was then that news reached him of disturbing developments back home. The Persians were once more mobilizing their troops for an assault not only on Anatolia, but on Constantinople itself, an attack which was to be co-ordinated with an Avar siege of the city's European defences. Heraclius gambled on his hope that the city would be able to hold out. Rather than rush back to his capital, he marched into Anatolia, from where he would be able to harry the advancing

Persian forces. This strategy appears to have been successful. The Persians could neither mount an effective naval assault on the city, nor convey their troops to the European shore so as to launch a land attack. At the same time, the 80,000-strong Avar host was unable to overcome Constantinople's formidable fortifications and soon melted away.

After a brief return to Constantinople, Heraclius hastened back to Lazica. It was now that he activated the alliance with the Turks that his ambassadors had successfully negotiated. In 627, a large Turkish army stormed the Persian defences between the Caucasus and the Caspian and struck deep into the Persian-held kingdom of Iberia. Outside the regional capital of Tiflis, the Turkish army met up with Heraclius and the Romans. In an impressive show of force, the joint Roman–Turkish army then headed south, through Atropatene, to the Zagros mountains. The Turks then returned north, but Heraclius marched still further south across the Zagros and, on 12 December 627, defeated a Persian army near the city of Nineveh. Advancing along the left bank of the Tigris, Heraclius bore down upon the Persian capital at Ctesiphon. It was at this point that he demonstrated the full extent of his military cunning. Rather than following in the footsteps of Julian and risking a frontal assault on the city, the emperor ravaged the cities and countryside to the north, intensifying the psychological pressure on the Persian high command.

Amongst military and court circles in Ctesiphon panic set in. A delegation was sent to Heraclius advising him of a conspiracy to depose Khusro, replace him with his son, Kavad-Shiroe, and initiate negotiations with the Romans. On 24 March 628 notice reached the emperor that Khusro II was dead and that the arrival of a peace delegation was imminent. The victory dispatch to Constantinople announced: 'fallen is the arrogant Khusro, the enemy of God. He is fallen and cast down to the depths of the earth, and his memory is utterly exterminated.'

Political conditions within Ctesiphon remained highly volatile. In October 628, Kavad-Shiroe died and was replaced by his son Ardashir. Ardashir was then overthrown by the commander of the Persian forces in the West, who in turn was deposed and replaced by a weak council of regency. As one regime succeeded another, Heraclius took advantage of the situation to extract ever more favourable terms. Eventually, it was agreed to return the Roman–Persian frontier to that established by Khusro II and Maurice in 591. On 21 March 630, Heraclius restored the True Cross to Jerusalem.

The eastern empire was thus restored, or at least, it was to some extent. The imperial concentration on the East had led to a further dramatic weakening of its position in the Balkans. Although the Avar confederacy lay in ruins in the aftermath of the defeat of 626, not only the highlands but, increasingly, the lowlands of the Balkans were coming to be settled by autonomous Slav tribes. The cities of Anatolia and Asia Minor had been exhausted by the financial exertions of warfare. Many of them stood in ruin as a result of Persian attack. In Syria, Palestine, and Egypt, the reassertion of imperial control at this point must have been largely nominal. Long-standing traditions of government had been dislocated and were yet to be restored. Before any such restoration could take place, the empire found itself faced with a new challenge from along its extended and largely undefended Arabian frontier.

The rivalry between Rome and Persia of the sixth and early seventh centuries had involved both empires in a series of military and diplomatic dealings with the Arabian tribes to their south. This involvement within the region on the part of the great powers appears to have sparked off what some historians have characterized as a 'nativist revolt' amongst elements within Arabian society. By the 620s, the tribes of Arabia had come to be united under the leadership of a religious leader originating from Mecca known as the Prophet Muhammad. Muhammad preached a rigorously monotheist doctrine, strongly influenced by apocalyptic trends within contemporary Christianity, and by Messianic fervour amongst the Jews of the region. Divine judgement was imminent, and all were to submit themselves to the will of the one God. In particular, all Arabs were to set aside their polytheist traditions and embrace the new faith. In return, Muhammad declared that, as descendants of Abraham's first-born son, Ishmael, whom Abraham had cast out into the desert, the Arabs would be granted mastery over the Holy Land which God had promised to Abraham and his seed for ever. Perhaps influenced by propaganda disseminated during the course of Heraclius' struggle against Khusro II, this return to the Holy Land was to be achieved by means of holy war.

Muhammad is said to have died around the year 632. His creed lived on. From 633/4, Roman Palestine suffered savage Arab incursions that combined the terrorizing and massacring of the rural population with assaults on towns and cities. Although the size of the Arab armies appears to have been relatively small, the imperial authorities were evidently in no position to offer effective resistance. Intelligence as to the nature of the Arab threat was limited, whilst the rapid advance of the Arab line of battle gave the imperial forces little time to regroup.

Faced with such a situation, a number of cities in the Transjordan, Palestine, and Syria simply capitulated. Damascus was taken in 635, whilst in 636 a large Roman army was decisively defeated near the river Yarmuk in northern Jordan. Thereafter, conquest was swift. Jerusalem fell in 638. The following year retreating Roman forces were pursued into Egypt. As with Khusro II's initial campaign of 603, the weakness of the Roman response to the Arabs led the invaders to campaign ever further afield. Similarly, only when they found themselves forced back into Asia Minor were the Roman commanders able to begin to stem the enemy advance. The civil strife of the early seventh century and the years of warfare with Persia had clearly inflicted lasting damage. When, in 641, Heraclius died, the empire was collapsing around him once more. The eastern Roman empire of Byzantium now faced its second great struggle for survival, one which was to dominate its early medieval history.

Status and its Symbols

MARLIA MUNDELL MANGO

Byzantine art had the aesthetic and material means to express imperial power—through images of hieratic authority, impressive trappings of office, and awe-inspiring settings. The emperor's image was displayed in sculpture and other monumental art. It was disseminated on coins, commemorative medallions, anniversary dishes, ivory plaques, weights, silver control stamps, and bullae. Costly materials such as silk, marbles, and mosaics enhanced prestige architecture. Byzantine imperial regalia were exclusive, yet bestowed to advantage on barbarian allies. As proof of their effectivenss, regalia and settings were imitated by barbarian rulers.

Imperial regalia are described in written sources and shown in portraits. Corippus describes how at the coronation of Justin II (AD 565) attendants carried the imperial robes, the belt studded with gems, the crown, and the brooch. So important were the imperial forms of adornment that Justinian reissued an earlier law that states: 'No one [but the emperor] shall hereafter be permitted to decorate the bridles and saddles of his horses, or his own belts with pearls, emeralds, or hyacinths.' The fine for infringement was 100 lb. of gold and capital punishment. Similar legislation applied to purple silk.

The imperial fibula, described by Procopius as a circular brooch with three pendant gems is shown worn by Theodosius I and Justinian. Justinian's bestowal of this fibula together with the right to wear red boots, on foreign powers, such as the five Armenian satraps, was regarded as an extraordinary concession. Later Byzantine emperors sent crowns 'as a claim to suzerainty' to the Khazars, the Hungarian Turks, the Russians, and other barbarian kings.

For documents of particular importance the emperor used a gold sealing (chrysobull), which gave its name to the document to which it was attached. The size of the gold bulla bearing his image sent to foreign powers, was regulated according to the importance of the addressee. In the mid-tenth century the heaviest bullae, of 4 *solidi* weight were destined for the caliph of Baghdad and the sultan of Egypt, the lightest, of 1 *solidus* weight were sent to the pope of Rome. Chrysobulls containing grants of real estate and privileges are still preserved in monastic archives on Mount Athos, Patmos (see special feature on Monasticism), and elsewhere. These are normally signed by the emperor in red ink.

Throughout its history, the Byzantine state was gov-

In the mosaic panel of San Vitale at Ravenna, Justinian is shown wearing the imperial fibula with three pendant gems, also worn by Theodosius on his missorium (p. 32). The person to his left wears a gold cross-bow fibula.

Notitia Dignitatum. At the top are four pairs of codices relating to four different *magistri*. The books are thought to contain mandates, orders issued by the emperor concerning each office. Below are four sets of scrolls, three books, and one writing tablet (in the lower right), also corresponding to the four *magistri*. The scrolls, perhaps of papyrus, represent documents.

erned by an extensive bureaucracy. Its personnel is recorded in documents such as the *Notitia Dignitatum* of the early period and the *taktika* of the middle and later periods. The elite of the Later Roman Empire was one of service, not birth, and all imperial service was designated as *militia*, whether it was military or civil. A more narrow distinction may be made, however, between the long-term *militia* appointments and the higher posts, the *dignitates* which carried honorific titles. The *Notitia Dignitatum* is a list of civil and military offices of the Roman Empire (drawn up *c.*400–29) which in its preserved copies illustrates the insignia and trappings of officials of the court (*comitatus*) and provincial government under the Praetorian Prefects. The *taktika* of the late ninth and tenth centuries list ranks of official posts and honorific titles. The *Kletorologion* of Philotheos of 899 gives 72 posts of seven ranks and 18 honorific titles for bearded officials and 8 for eunuchs. A continuous inflation of honorific titles resulted in the introduction of new ones, such as *proedros* in the tenth century and *sebastos* in the late eleventh. By the late twelfth, *sebastos* became *panhypersebastos* or *protosebastohypertatos*.

Among the offices listed in the *Notitia Dignitatum* is that of the *Magister scriniorum*, the Master of the Record Office, a member of the *comitatus*. The page devoted to this office in the *Notitia* has sets of codices and rolls corresponding to the *magistri* (*memoriae, epistolarum, libellorum*) charged with various legal and administrative duties, and to the *magister epistolarum graecarum* who wrote letters issued in Greek or translated into Greek

The protocol shown here, contemporary with Justinian's law of 537, is made out in the name of Fl. Strategius, Count of the Sacred Largesses (535–*c.*538), and was executed in the month of Phaophi, indiction 12 by the notary Aristomachus. Strategius was a member of the enormously wealthy Apion family and had served as governor of Alexandria.

those issued in Latin. The *scrinia* drafted responses to judicial and other petitions and issued letters of appointment (*probatoriae*) to civil servants. The various documents produced in the Record Office may be represented by the rolls shown lower on the page.

Other documents of the period, written on papyrus, survive in large numbers from Egypt. Although by Late Antiquity, literary and other texts were written in codices of parchment, papyrus was still used for documents. Our word 'protocol' comes from the papyrus roll and denotes the first sheet (*kollema*) that was gummed on to the others. Justinian's *Novel* 44 (AD 537) lays down that notarial acts written at Constantinople should bear on the *protocollum* the name of the Count of the Sacred Largesses in office at the time, the date and other appropriate details and that it should remain attached to the the rest of the document so as to avoid fraud. As a further precaution protocols were usually written in a special, stylized hand that proved very difficult to decipher.

While the *sacra scrinia* issued *probatoriae* to *militia* members, a codicil or document of appointment, signed by the emperor was presented to the new holder of a *dignitas*. This act is ceremoniously represented on the Theodosian missorium, while the young son of Stilicho, Eucherius, is shown holding his new codicil on an ivory diptych probably made to announce his appointment (see p. 37). For certain offices (Prefects, Masters of Soldiers or Offices, etc.) the codicil took the form of gilded ivory plaques, which were distinct in purpose from the ivory diptych of Eucherius and those issued by the consuls of Rome and Constantinople when they assumed office on 1 January. These diptychs, circulated to friends and senatorial colleagues, illustrate the trappings and activities of the consul (see p. 167).

Like the emperor, members of the bureaucratic hierarchy had a specific costume. The civil servant John Lydus, writing *c.* AD 550, describes in detail how the Praetorian Prefect of the East wore a purple tunic, a crimson hide belt fastened by a gold buckle, and a cloak (*chlamys*) with *tablia* (coloured patches) fastened at the right shoulder by a fibula or brooch. A contemporary lawyer, Agathias Scholastikos, wrote an epigram on a

Above: gold buckle with Greek monogram, possibly of one Baanes, on the right end. Probably early seventh century. From Crete.

Right: The gilded copper fibula with lateral pelta motifs is the type worn by Stilicho and his son on their ivory diptych. See p. 37. Fifth century.

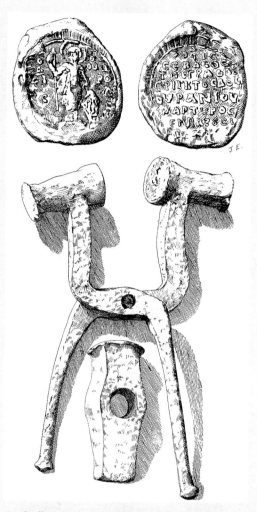

Five *boulloteria* survive. Every individual with a title—whether civil, military, or ecclesiastical—possessed this device and acquired a new one with every change of title. The example illustrated here (eleventh/twelfth-century) belonged to a Constantine *sebastos* whose name is engraved on one die, while the image of St Theodore is on the other.

portrait of the Master of Offices, Theodore, who was shown receiving his belt of office from an archangel. The phrase to 'lay aside the belt' signified resignation from office. The non-imperial fibula was cross-bow in shape and, like the buckle, made of gold, silver, gilded bronze, or bronze. According to Procopius, people were forced to wear gilded bronze copies of brooches and other jewellery as a safeguard against theft. The different types of fibulae as they evolved between the fourth and the sixth century appear in contemporary portraits and in those of military saints.

The bestowal of insignia on members of the court hierarchy, recalling those of Late Antiquity, continued into the early Middle Ages. The highest ranks received a purple, red, or white tunic, a mantle, and a belt: others were given ivory tablets, a gold collar, a gold whip, or a fibula. The practice may have ceased in the Komnenian period.

In the Byzantine period, from the sixth century onwards, lead sealings marked with the device and/or titles of the owner were used on documents and correspondence, where previously wax had been more convenient. The lead seal was produced by the massive iron *boulloterion*. Lead had been commonly used for sealing bales of merchandise in the Roman period, a practice apparently continued by Byzantine commercial agents (*kommerkiarioi*). About 50,000 Byzantine lead seals are known, most, it seems, discovered in Istanbul. They have made a significant contribution to our knowledge of Byzantine administration and prosopography.

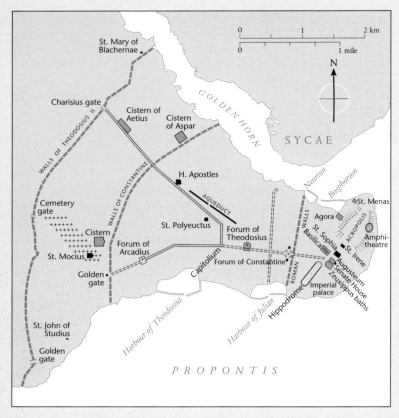

Plans of Constantinople, Antioch, and Alexandria drawn to the same scale. In terms of area Constantinople came closest to Alexandria, but the broad belt of land between the Constantinian and Theodosian walls was always sparsely populated.

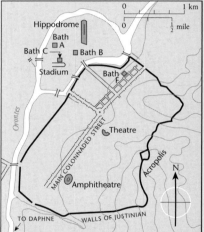

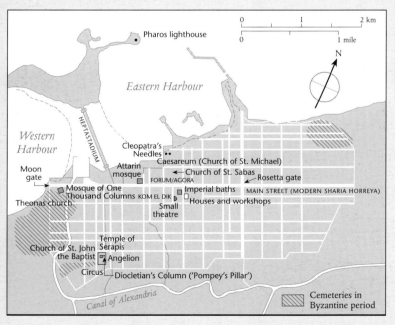

Constantinople

CYRIL MANGO

Although founded as the New Rome, Constantinople bore little physical resemblance to the city on the Tiber. Constantine's capital included six, not seven hills (a seventh was added under Theodosius II) and its basic feature of urban planning was the straight colonnaded street punctuated by squares and ornamental monuments, characteristic of the grander provincial cities of the Roman East, such as Palmyra, Antioch, and Apamea. Deliberate imitation of Rome is apparent only in the reign of Theodosius I, a Spaniard who claimed descent from the emperor Trajan. The Forum of Theodosius, of which only some bits survive, was a smaller replica of Trajan's famous forum in Rome, with a 'historiated' column copied from Trajan's, and a transverse basilica. A second historiated column of similar design adorned the forum of Theodosius' son Arcadius (see p. 35). The juxtaposition of imperial palace and hippodrome did, of course, mirror the coupling of Palatine hill and Circus Maximus in Rome, but had become a standard feature of Tetrarchic capitals even before Constantine.

Remains of the Forum of Theodosius I. The historiated column was pulled down in c.1500. Its spiral reliefs were broken up and built into the foundations of the Bayezid Bath, where some fragments may still be seen, like this group of Roman soldiers. The Forum had two monumental arches supported by clusters of four columns, bizarrely carved to resemble trimmed tree-trunks or possibly wooden clubs. The twin pedestals of one arch may still be seen.

Right: A somewhat fantastic view of the Hippodrome drawn in *c.*1480. On the right is Justinian's monumental column minus its statue. The church (centre foreground) is probably the Nea Ekklesia of Basil I (AD 880).

Below: Constantine's porphyry column as delineated in 1574 and as it looked in the 1950's. Constantine's statue as well as the capital were blown down in 1106 and replaced by a drum of masonry in the reign of Manuel I (1143–80). The stonework that conceals the pedestal and lowest drum of porphyry dates from 1779.

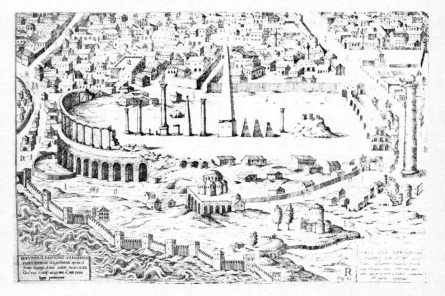

Why did Constantine choose the site of Byzantium for his new capital? Was it simply to commemorate his victory over Licinius at Chrysopolis (directly across the Bosphorus) in 324? Or was he swayed by its natural advantages, which so impress the visitor even today? The area of the straits (Bosphorus and Dardanelles) had indeed assumed growing importance in the third century, as emperors were obliged to cope both with a resurgent Persia on the borders of Syria and the barbarians north of the Danube. As the gateway to the Black Sea, Byzantium provided an excellent base of operations against the northern barbarians, who at the time were mainly the Goths. What Constantine did not foresee, but became evident after the disaster at Adrianople (378) was that once the barbarians had crossed the Danube, there was no natural barrier that would stop them from advancing on Constantinople. The vulnerability of Constantinople to attack from its European hinterland became a permanent feature of Byzantine history, whether the enemy were the Goths, the Huns, the Avars, the Bulgars, or the Pechenegs. The same scenario was repeated as the Ottoman empire declined in the eighteenth and nineteenth centuries.

To guard Constantinople from attack truly gigantic works of fortification had to be under-

Left: The Theodosian land walls, seen here before their recent restoration, consisted of an inner wall 11 m high with square or octagonal towers, a lower outer wall, and a moat.

Below: The Theodosian Gold Gate is built entirely of marble and had three arched openings flanked by massive square pylons. It was decorated with many statues, including a quadriga drawn by elephants. After 1453 the gate was incorporated into the star-shaped castle of the Seven Towers, which contained the treasury of Mehmed II.

taken. The triple Theodosian land walls (inner wall, outer wall, and moat) were built in 404–13 and continued to protect the city until 1453—eloquent testimony to the superiority of Roman engineering and the absence of technological advance until the invention of the cannon. But even that was not considered sufficient: a forward line of defence—the so-called Long or Anastasian walls—was constructed from the Black Sea to the Propontis along a length of 45 km, 65 km west of Constantinople. Some remains of them are still standing, but they did not prove particularly effective in the long run because of the difficulty of manning them adequately.

Coupled with the problem of defence, another serious consideration was the scarcity of water for drinking and bathing, which has plagued Constantinople from the time of Constantine until the present day. To remedy this deficiency, an enormous network of aqueducts ex-

Two extant statue bases erected in the Hippodrome in honour of the charioteer Porphyrius in the early sixth century carry epigrams that have been copied into the Palatine Anthology. Here Porphyrius, brandishing a crown, is seated in his chariot of four horses. The style of the reliefs is pretty deplorable.

The most spectacular of the underground cisterns of Constantinople is Justinian's Cisterna Basilica. It measures 138 x 65 m and was originally supported on 336 columns.

tending some 200 km to the west was constructed in the fourth century and remained permanently vulnerable to enemy attack, hence the provision of storage on a vast scale within the city. Of the scanty remains of Byzantine Constantinople, none is more striking than the proliferation of cisterns—three huge open-air ones that had a combined capacity of nearly 1 million cubic metres and the scores of covered ones like Justinian's Cisterna Basil-

Aerial view of Istanbul looking towards the Acropolis point. The mosque of Sultan Ahmed (centre) occupies a good part of Constantine's palace. In the lower left corner is the curved end of the Hippodrome.

ica or that of the Thousand and One Columns, as it is called by the Turks.

The peripatetic phase of Roman government, instituted under the Tetrarchy, ended in 380 when Theodosius I made his entrance into Constantinople. From then on emperors dwelt there more or less permanently as did the central ministers of the state with their staffs of bureaucrats. The provision of an adequate infrastructure in terms of defence, water supply, harbour installations, and storage of foodstuffs was completed by AD 500. In the absence of any population figures it is impossible to tell how big the city had grown. By the end of the fourth century it was said to have been bigger than Antioch, the latter having a population of c.200,000. It may have expanded to about 500,000 by the early years of Justinian's reign before contracting by at least a quarter as a result of the plague of 542. Thereafter things went downhill, with a low point of perhaps some 40,000 in the mid-eighth century. A slow recovery is discernible in c. AD 800, continuing until the twelfth century. Komnenian Constantinople was the biggest city of Christendom, but we have no means of estimating its population: Villehardouin's figure of 400,000 is certainly a gross exaggeration. Latin rule and Palaiologan misery reduced it again to some 50,000.

Justinian's ostentatious and over-ambitious building programme, of which the cathedral of St Sophia is the supreme creation, brings to a close what may be called the Roman phase of Constantinople. Building activity

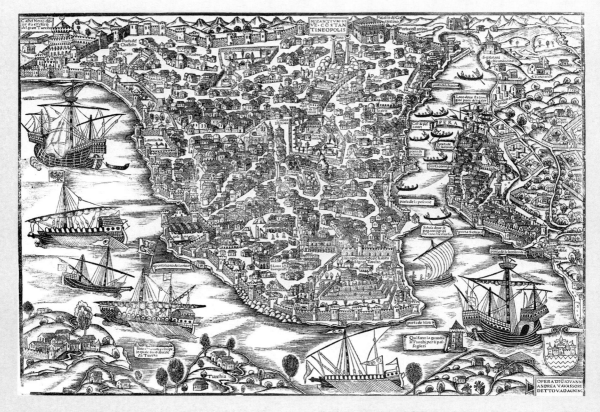

Bird's-eye view of Constantinople in *c.*1480. The original, perhaps by the painter Gentile Bellini, is lost. Of several published versions, this one by the Venetian engraver Andrea Vavassore is the earliest. It has been built up from a number of partial views, and some, though not all of the detail in authentic.

practically stopped in about AD 600, being confined to the strengthening of fortifications, repair of earthquake damage, and a partial patching up of the damaged system of aqueducts. Dark Age Constantinople was a ruin—its urban space invaded by orchards and cemeteries, its old public buildings abandoned or converted to artisanal activity.

When building resumes from about AD 800 onwards, it follows a different pattern from that of Late Antiquity in that it neglects all civic amenities, such as squares, markets, baths, and fountains—indeed, anything that may be described as a monument. Only two major projects can be identified: an extensive reconstruction of the maritime defences by the emperor Theophilos in the 830s and the reconditioning of some thirty parish churches that had fallen into disrepair by Basil I. Emper-

ors of the ninth and following centuries spent considerable sums on their own palaces and somewhat less on hospices and other welfare establishments, but if there is one trend that overshadowed all others and continued until the Turkish conquest, it was the setting up of family monasteries—essentially private foundations that split up the urban space into a multiplicity of walled cells, each endowed with commercial properties and estates in the provinces.

At the same time Constantinople was becoming more cosmopolitan following the establishment and growth from the tenth century onwards of Italian trading colonies. The merchants in question—mostly Venetians, Amalfitans, Pisans, and, lastly, Genoese—came to number a few thousand in the Komnenian period and were segregated in certain delimited neighbourhoods along the coast of the Golden Horn, but by the very nature of their business came into close contact with the natives. The Genoese colony of Galata (or Pera), set up in 1303, was a separate self-governing town. It retained its walls until 1864 and is still dominated by its massive Genoese tower.

2 Life in City and Country

CLIVE FOSS

Cities were the cornerstone of the Roman empire. They were centres of population, trade, manufacturing, and all forms of culture, as well as the basic building blocks of the administration. Virtually the entire empire was divided into the territories of cities, which maintained order locally and collected taxes. These tasks fell on the willing shoulders of a landowning aristocracy, whose members competed for the high municipal offices that would bring them distinction. As magistrates or members of the council that ran the city, they provided the public works and services characteristic of Roman urban life. In return for benefactions or constructions paid from their own pockets, they received honorific inscriptions or statues in a system that essentially put the burden of maintaining civic life on those who could best afford it. Cities also had endowments from legacies or investments, and managed the substantial funds that belonged to the local temples. The cities needed a great deal of money, since they had to maintain streets, markets, and other amenities, notably (and most expensive) the public baths. This voluntary and co-operative system functioned well for two hundred years, but began to break down in the crisis of the third century, when political chaos, invasions, civil war, and enormous financial demands put intolerable burdens on the local administrators and caused the former surplus of candidates for high office to dry up.

Late Antiquity maintained many elements of the Roman system, but with changes that gradually became more profound. First, the newly Christian government confiscated the property of the temples, then the endowments of the cities (though the latter were partially remitted). Local treasuries became notably poorer, but the same obligations still existed and people had to be found to meet them. The government typically resorted to compulsion. Councillors were obliged to pay in adequate sums when they assumed office to ensure continuation of public services, and the council as a whole had to make up any deficit in the tax collections. Members of the classes that normally provided the councillors, therefore, made every effort to evade their burdensome obligations. A favourite method was to gain some high rank, especially that of senator, that brought immunity from local burdens. Others joined the clergy, but that escape was soon closed. As a result, the poorer or weaker members of the local aristocracies were left to shoulder a burden that soon became unbearable. Consequently, the central government came to take an ever more active role. Its officials tended to take control, and the provincial governors constantly intervened. Eventually, by the sixth century, a regular system developed in which the governor, bishop, and great landowners took over the municipal administrations.

Officially, the local governments were run by the council and people, but the people had only an insignificant role to play in the autocratic system of Late Antiquity. Their formal role had long since disappeared (no elections were held), but they could make their opinions felt in very direct ways, peaceful or violent. Assembled in the theatre, the people could cheer or boo the governor or other officials. The cheering usually took the form of ritualized acclamations led by organized claques. The central government took note of these public reactions, which could play a role in the promotion or failure of high officials. Less formally, the people could and often would riot for or against an individual or policy. In the Christian empire, these often involved the partisans of the circus factions (the over-enthusiastic supporters of teams of chariot racers) or heresies who would demonstrate vociferously, and sometimes cause considerable damage, in support of their side. Local bishops could be a focus of disturbance, and even ecumenical councils were not immune. At the other extreme were the local landed aristocracies whose members, whatever office they held, exercised considerable influence on civic life and on the empire as a whole through their extensive networks of connections. These were often the people who had escaped municipal obligations and thus had wealth and leisure. Still pagan in the fourth century, most had converted to Christianity by the fifth.

Council and people alike lived in cities that preserved a basic Roman image and structure. Cities had a core of monumental public buildings—most of them dating to the first centuries of the empire—connected by paved streets and adorned with paintings, mosaics, statues, and monuments. If a Roman from the time of Hadrian could have seen a late antique city, it would have looked familiar, but with some notable differences, that mark the late antique city as the product of both continuity and change. These concern the city walls, new religious buildings, expanding small-scale commercial activity, and a new aesthetic that placed less emphasis on classical regularity.

Roman cities had normally been open; their defences were the legions of the frontier. In the crisis of the third century when no place was safe, cities began to be fortified, surrounded by high walls with towers and elaborate gates, taking on an appearance that was to be characteristic of urban life until modern times. Some of these were makeshift structures, slapped together from whatever materials were at hand. They normally incorporated the entire ancient urban area, often following an irregular trace to accommodate existing buildings or incorporate especially substantial ones into their circuit. Some, like the walls of Nicaea, were carefully designed along the most modern lines and so well built that they functioned for over a thousand years. Characteristically, when Diocletian established his new capital at Nicomedia, and Constantine his at Constantinople, powerful walls were considered a necessary element. The walls not only served for protection, but sharply segregated city and country and allowed greater control over the population by restricting entry and exit to a few well-defined points.

The rise of Christianity and its adoption by emperors brought another fundamental change. Ancient cities had been distinguished by their temples, some of them world-famous. They owned huge tracts of land and vast wealth. Their funds were confiscated early in the fourth century, and their structures soon succumbed. As the pagan cult was suppressed, its temples were largely abandoned or put to new uses. Those outside the city became quarries for stone, while those in the centre were often converted into churches. In some places, though, the pagan cult proved surprisingly resistant: the great temples of Athens, for example, were not converted to Christian use till the end of the period. Concurrently, the cities were adorned with churches, often displaying a magnificence appropriate to a triumphant religion. Although the majority were of the basilical plan, there was a striking variety of style throughout the eastern empire. Many churches grew up on early cult sites in cemeteries at the edge of the city, but soon most city centres also featured large churches, whether newly built or converted from pagan structures. This was especially the case of provincial capitals where the metropolitan bishop necessarily needed a large and impressive cathedral.

Cities of the East, the products of Greek or Hellenistic civilization, normally had a market place in the centre. It often served also as seat of the local administration, with civic buildings around the open market square. Market places continued to function, but were increasingly supplemented by rows of shops built along the major streets. Typically, the streets were lined with roofed colonnades for protection from the elements, paved with mosaics or cut marble. These opened to small shops which offered a great variety of products and normally consisted of two stories; the retail or manufacturing space below, and the residence of shopkeeper or artisan above. As commercial activity increased, the shops often expanded out into the street, a nuisance frequently denounced in imperial legislation. On a smaller scale, wooden booths or stalls would be set up on the pavement or between the

An entrance into a large walled space in the centre of Edessa, a provincial capital in Mesopotamia. The space, today the courtyard of the main mosque, may have been the principal market of the city. Fifth/sixth century.

columns that lined the streets. As time went on, the life of the street and market merged to produce something like an oriental bazaar.

Finally, the cities took on a new appearance as builders made increasing use of reused materials. Unlike the Romans who built as far as possible of solid stone or concrete, late antique builders employed rubble or stones abstracted from disused or ruined buildings (the wars of the third century and the demise of paganism produced them in abundance) and stuck them together with mortar. They often used courses of brick to level the material. This produced a rough, heterogeneous surface that needed to be covered. Layers of plaster disguised the new material and even imitated the old by being incised with rectangular lines to resemble ashlar masonry. More often, they were painted in bright colours and geometric patterns. Combined with the mosaics that lined the pavements these produced a bright and gaudy appearance that might have seemed alien to a classical Roman. Colonnades added to the effect, by employing marble columns of different colours, often of varying height, and levelled by higher or lower bases. Irregularity and colour came to mark the cities.

Literary sources and physical remains enable us to visualize the aspect of these cities. Although most written texts have little to say about an urban environment that was taken for granted, a curious saint's Life gives a living

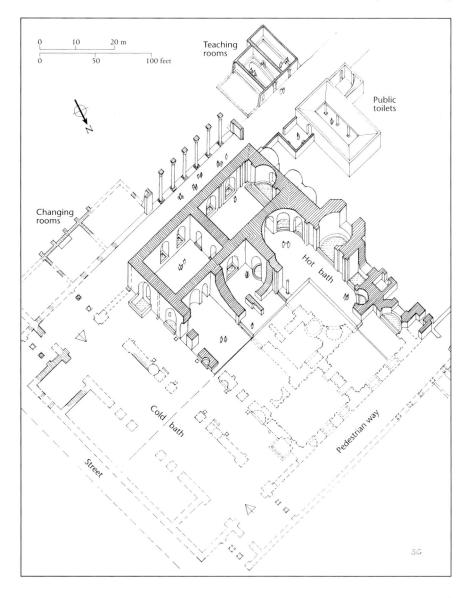

Changing rooms

Teaching rooms

Public toilets

Hot bath

Cold bath

Pedestrian way

Street

0   10   20 m
0   50   100 feet

N

S.G

Public baths at Alexandria. These large baths built on a symmetrical plan in imperial style have adjoining teaching rooms. The positioning of the pools in recesses rather than in the centre of the rooms is considered a late feature. An elevated cistern to the east of the baths provided the water. Second half of the sixth century AD.

picture, while the ruins of numerous sites put the texts into a real context and at the same time illustrate the striking similarities of urban life everywhere, despite notable regional variations.

The Life of Symeon the Fool is set in Syrian Emesa in the late sixth century. The saint, who feigned lunacy, wandered through the city. His Life mentions the buildings still considered essential for an urban existence: the walls, market place, theatre, baths, and colonnaded streets, as well as an innovation—the churches—and the mansions of the rich and shacks of the poor, with the shops, stalls, workshops, and cookshops so prevalent in these centuries. Outside the walls were tombs, places for washing clothes (Emesa is on a river), open space where children played, rubbish dumps, and the execution ground. The city was filled with people as well as buildings. Symeon met the full range, from local officials, large and small businessmen, and doctors to slaves, beggars, idlers, and whores. He dealt with teachers, sellers of food and drink, bakers, jugglers, musicians, fortune-tellers, lunatics, and churchmen. Emesa, like its counterparts in Greece, Anatolia, and the Levant, was a busy place full of life and every kind of activity.

Physical remains put such stories into a material context. The lands of the eastern empire preserve many large excavated sites that enable a way of life to be envisioned in some detail. Notable among them as representing two very different types of settlement are Ephesus in Asia Minor, a busy commercial city on major trade routes by land and sea, and Apamea in Syria, the home of a wealthy landed aristocracy. The evidence these places provide can be rounded out by casting a glance at other sites of Greece and the East.

Ephesus had all the elements of a Christian Roman city. Monumental public buildings, connected by richly decorated streets, dominated the centre, while the signs of the new religion were everywhere evident.

Most cities of the Greek East had a central agora or market place; Ephesus was so grand that it had two: the upper agora that functioned as the civic centre, and the lower agora, the main market. Both were products of the first century, and contain characteristic Roman buildings. The civic centre featured an open space for ceremonial, with a temple in the centre. Around it on the north were the council house (which resembled a small theatre), the town hall or prytaneum, and the temple of Rome and Caesar; on the east, a bath–gymnasium complex; on the south, a massive fountain where the waters of the aqueducts were gathered and distributed; a street lined with shops formed the west side. A long portico gave access to the buildings on the north side. The fountain represented one of the basic characteristics of both Roman and late antique cities: provision and maintenance of a dependable water supply, often brought from great distances by aqueducts, and distributed throughout the city in public fountains and the baths.

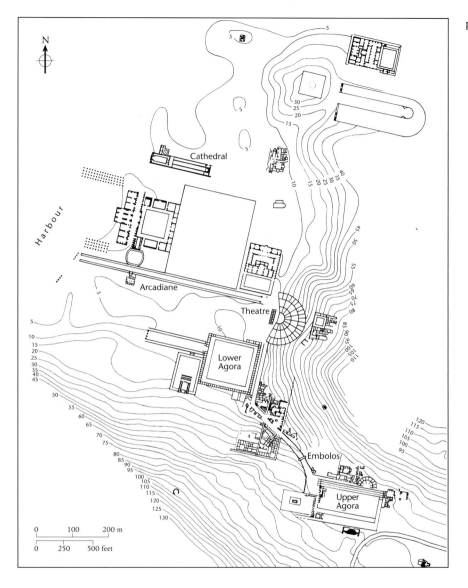

Plan of Ephesus.

In Late Antiquity, the specifically pagan aspects of this square disappeared or were transformed: the prytaneum, where the sacred fire of Vesta was kept burning, was closed, the temple of Rome and Caesar built over, the central temple demolished, and signs of the cross carved on statues of Livia and Augustus that stood in the portico, and over the entrance of the senate house that still functioned. Since demons were commonly believed to dwell in the fabric of ancient buildings or statues, the cross was a useful prophylactic. Thus, the ancient urban fabric was maintained, but Christianized. The new age made its presence felt in another way in the street west of the square,

77

where some of the shops added walls that extended out over the pavement, forcing the ancient classical regularity to yield to the unaesthetic demands of commerce.

The lower agora, a large open square lined with two-storey buildings built behind colonnades, maintained its shape and function. The square was used for markets, where goods could be brought by a street that led directly down to the harbour. Christianity did not affect business that continued unabated in this dynamic port city. On the other hand, the towering temple that rose on the slope above the market was transformed into a church, and the library of Celsus near the market's entrance, a benefaction of the first Greek who had entered the Roman senate, changed completely. Its interior was filled with rubble and its façade became the backdrop of a monumental fountain, a popular feature in this period. Not that the people of this age ceased reading or writing, but the entire harbour district had been devastated by a Gothic invasion in 262, and many buildings lay in ruins for a century or more. When the structure was eventually rebuilt, fashions or needs had changed.

Roman cities had a monumental core connected and adorned by an 'armature' of streets and squares. Late antique Ephesus was no exception, maintaining the principle but not the appearance. The most active street, the Embolos (the 'colonnaded street' *par excellence*), connected the two agoras. Colonnades, statues, old as well as new and transformed monuments, and lavish housing adorned it. Ephesus was so rich that its main streets were paved with marble, much of it abstracted from ruined—usually pagan— buildings. Typical of Roman cities, this was a pedestrian street, blocked to wheeled traffic by steps at its upper end. People walked, shopped, read inscriptions, scratched graffiti onto the marble, or simply loafed and played a game like *tavla* on the boards incised into the pavement. The colonnades, which often yielded to public buildings, were paved with mosaics, featured a mixture of reused columns of different coloured marbles, and had painted walls. Along their length were numerous statues of ancient and modern worthies, notably provincial governors honoured for their real or imagined benefactions. Monumental inscriptions contained the text of recent laws. Here, too, Christianity made its presence felt. A large cross bore an inscription celebrating the triumph of the cross over the 'demon' Artemis, while adjacent fountains (which replaced tombs of legendary heroes) were decorated with marble plaques with crosses in relief. On this street as elsewhere, fountains were a prominent element of the urban landscape.

Strollers along the Embolos could buy food in the restaurants that occupied part of the ground floor of a massive block of elegant dwellings, an *insula* flanked by streets that turned into steps as they climbed the slopes above

This silver gilt paten was presented by the bishop Eutychianus to the church of Sion built in rural Lycia in the mid-sixth century. The paten, 60.50 cm in diameter, is part of the largest known hoard of Byzantine church silver plate. It was discovered at modern Kumluca in Turkey.

The Second General Council (Constantinople, 381), presided over by the emperor Theodosius I, proclaimed the equal divinity of Father, Son, and Holy Spirit, while condemning both Arianism and the followers of the former bishop Macedonius. It is here shown in a miniature of cod. Paris. gr. 510 of c. AD 880.

the Embolos. This consisted of a series of houses, each of several elaborately decorated rooms. Reception rooms tended to have marble and mosaic on the floors and walls, while more private chambers were painted, often with landscapes or decoration that resembled marble. These were evidently the dwellings of the urban rich, occupying buildings in the centre of town that had seen relatively little change since they were first built in the early empire. Paintings and mosaics are so conventional that they are notoriously hard to date, for this civilization maintained a consistent style of decoration for centuries. Similar blocks, not yet excavated, lined the slopes in this part of the city. On the other hand—and this is true of all the great eastern cities—no one knows where the mass of the population lived. These rich houses hardly represent a typical urban life, and the people could not have lived in the monumental centre, for it was virtually filled with public buildings and spaces. They presumably dwelt in the outskirts, or in less substantial structures scattered around the centre, but their houses have not been discovered (though in St Symeon's Emesa they evidently lived within the walls). Consequently there is no way to calculate the population of such a city.

Much grander, and more formal, than the Embolos, was the Street of Arcadius which led in a straight line from the harbour to the square in front of the theatre, the very centre of the city. This boulevard, 11 metres wide and over 500 metres long, contained impressive monuments: a triumphal arch at the harbour, marking the entrance to the city, four huge columns in the middle that bore the statues of the four evangelists, powerful symbols of the triumph of Christianity. The colonnades, paved with mosaics, led to shops whose owners were obliged to maintain lamps to illuminate the street at night. Huge Roman bath–gymnasium complexes lined the north side of the street: the Harbour Baths, with their hot and cold baths and broad inner courtyard, damaged by the Goths and rebuilt in the mid-fourth century; a vast open exercise ground that was given up and built over in Late Antiquity, when the pressures of finance and space no longer allowed such an area to be maintained; and yet another gymnasium at the upper end of the street. Most cities had one or two of these complexes; Ephesus, a busy port thronged with visitors, had no fewer than five, all of monumental scale. These were all Roman constructions, but all were maintained in these centuries. Adjacent to one of them was a large public latrine. In addition, there was a smaller bath, without exercise ground, dedicated by a Christian lady on the Embolos. The fate of the nearby brothel, attested in a Roman inscription, is unknown, but texts that frequently mention whores in other large cities suggest that the profession was still active, especially in a busy port like Ephesus.

The Arcadian street led to the building that was usually the greatest in any city, the theatre. In this case, the vast semicircular open structure could

The street of Arcadius at Ephesus, named after the emperor, was 500 m long and was lit at night. It led from the harbour (now silted up) to the theatre (seen in the background). In the centre stands one of the four large columns that bore statues of the Evangelists.

accommodate some 25,000 people, but they did not come in this period to see classical drama. Performances featured singing and dancing and as often as not had a strong pornographic element. The theatres also served as the venue for public meetings, the only legitimate way the people could make their views known under despotism. Acclamations and riots that started in the theatre were frequent occurrences, especially during the two church councils held in Ephesus in 430 and 449, when mobs, stirred by speeches in the theatre, rushed through the streets in support of one faction or another. They were perhaps more concerned with the power and glory of their city than the abstruse theological doctrines involved. In any case, the theatre was such an essential building that it was constantly repaired and maintained, leaving its classical appearance unchanged.

Another venue of entertainment was the stadium, where athletic contests took place. It, too, kept its form and function, though the most popular activity, watching and supporting the teams of chariot races, could not have been accommodated in its narrow course. Graffiti on the public streets attest to Ephesian enthusiasm for the racing teams of Blues and Greens; their activity presumably took place outside the urban centre, perhaps in the open, for hippodromes were enormous buildings that few cities could afford. In the late antique East, hippodromes were built to adorn imperial residences like Antioch and Thessalonica, where they stood adjacent to palaces, following the models of Rome and Constantinople. Several other cities in Syria, Palestine, and Egypt, though, had older structures that were still kept in use.

Finally, Ephesus was a great centre of Christianity. The most important church within the city was dedicated to the Virgin Mary. This enormous basilica, 75 metres long, had an atrium and baptistery and adjoined the bishop's palace. All were accommodated in what had been one wing of the precinct of the grandiose temple of Hadrian. This was the site of two church councils. More revered, though, was the church of St John, on a hill a mile outside the city. Built over the Evangelist's tomb, it was famed throughout the empire for an annual miracle in which sacred dust, capable of healing all kinds of ills, issued forth from the tomb. The all-night service when this took place coincided with a fair that brought buyers and sellers from a wide region. Pilgrimage was a main factor in the fame and prosperity of the city.

The baths of Scholasticia at Ephesus bordered the Embolos leading from the lower to the upper agora. The baths were rebuilt at the end of the fourth century by a Christian woman of that name, whose statue was set up near the entrance.

Justinian rebuilt the church as a magnificent domed cruciform structure richly decorated with marble and mosaics and prominently displaying his name and that of his less than saintly consort Theodora. It significantly overlooked the ruins of what had been one of the seven wonders of the ancient world, the temple of Diana of the Ephesians. In Christian times, this became a major quarry, the source of the stones used in many public buildings. Its fate was typical of temples that lay outside cities.

Tradition made Ephesus the home of St John, St Timothy, Mary Magdalene, the Seven Sleepers, and many other holy figures. Their shrines, which became important centres of international pilgrimage and attracted huge throngs, lay outside the city. The Seven Sleepers, whose miraculous 200-year

Plan of the ground floor and reconstruction of a dyer's shop on the colonnaded street by the synagogue at Sardis. When the shops were destroyed by fire in *c.*616 the upper storey collapsed onto the lower and pinned down the contents (containers with dye, mortars, steelyards) as shown on the plan.

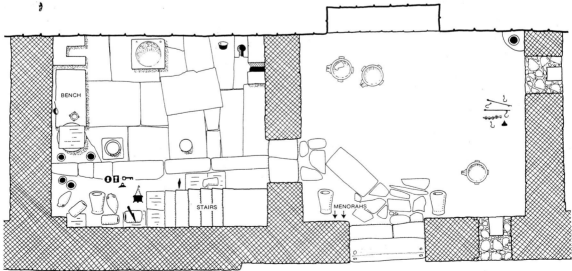

BENCH

STAIRS

MENORAHS

sleep ended in the fifth century, were eventually buried in a cave that had been part of the necropolis, for here as elsewhere, the city of the dead stretched outside the gates that separated it from the city of the living. This, too, became a site of great renown for pilgrims.

Ephesus illustrates urban life at its most prosperous, with a colourful environment that can easily be envisioned populated like St Symeon's Emesa. Other cities show the universality of such places, though usually on a smaller scale, but their remains often add variations that help to complete the picture. In Asia Minor Sardis, Aphrodisias, and Side present similar phenomena of a flourishing urban life, recognizably Roman yet Christianized. Sardis brings a new element: an important Jewish community. The massive bath–gymnasium complex at the west end of the city included two long structures that projected from the main façade. One of them became a synagogue in the third century and so remained throughout the period. In plan, it closely resembles a basilical church, with a typical rich decoration of marble and mosaics, and numerous inscriptions identifying the donors. It is much grander than the synagogues that formed an important element of the rural landscape in the Holy Land (though in many cities synagogues were converted into churches). Outside the complex, the wall is lined with shops whose Christian and Jewish owners dyed clothes and sold hardware as well as other goods. They did business primarily with copper coins, which have been found there in large numbers. The shops flank a colonnaded street whose mismatched columns and bases display a disregard for symmetry that was common in Late Antiquity.

Aphrodisias was originally a temple city built around the great shrine of Aphrodite. Under the Romans it acquired the usual complement of public buildings, richly decorated with the marble that was quarried nearby. They included the theatre, odeon, baths, monumental fountains, broad marble-paved porticoes, and a remarkable passageway dedicated to the imperial cult. At the edge of the city was a vast stadium, adjacent to the marble-faced walls of the fourth century. All these were put to use in Late Antiquity, with the usual transformations, but still leaving the city a more Roman appearance than most. Since the temple stood in the centre of the city, unlike those of Ephesus and Sardis that lay outside the walls, it was necessarily put to new use as the local cathedral, a conversion accomplished relatively late, in the fifth century. On either side were two extensive late antique villas with apsidal reception rooms, evidently the palaces of the governor and the bishop. In this case, religion and government symbolically dominated the central urban space.

At Side, the theatre and agora occupied the centre, connected by broad colonnaded streets to the city gate and to the harbour. One entire district was

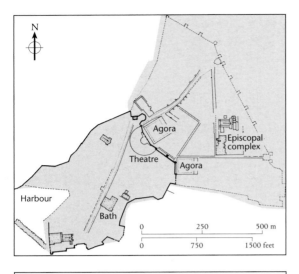

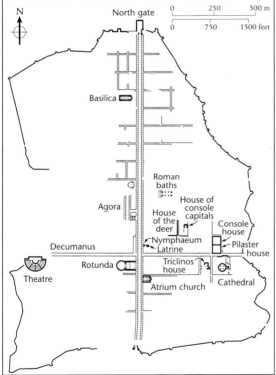

Above: Plan of Side.
Below: Plan of Apamea.

devoted to the cathedral and a vast complex of bishop's palace and related buildings. Another massive basilica towered over the harbour where it replaced two small temples dedicated to Apollo and Artemis. Inscriptions reveal that the city was divided into four districts, each named for a prominent monument, and each with its own council of elders. Inscriptions in the major cities of the East commonly name the provincial governor as a main benefactor. Governors, who served relatively short terms in a notoriously corrupt system, were anxious to leave monuments of their administration in order to win approval and gain ever-higher rank. Since they were in control of the civic revenues, they were in a position to become prime patrons in an age when the local councils were impoverished and the private benefaction of the Roman past had virtually died out. Governors carried out most of their activity in the cities where they resided. Consequently, places like Ephesus, Sardis, or Aphrodisias flourished while others enjoyed far less patronage. Laws actually admonished governors from taking stones or decorations from minor cities in order to adorn their capitals. Cities like Side, though, that were the seats of metropolitan archbishops, also shared in the government's generosity.

Other sites add other details or follow different developments. In Athens, for example, third-century invasions reduced the city to a small fraction of its ancient area. Eventually, it acquired buildings for its still-famed philosophical schools. Long a centre of paganism, its main temples were only converted into churches in the sixth century. Thessalonica, on the other hand, flourished thanks to its massive walls and its role as a regional capital. A whole district was given over to the palace of Galerius (305–11) and associated buildings, including a grand rotunda, a triumphal arch, and a hippodrome. Later, there was a burst of building activity when the city became the headquarters of the diocese of Illyricum in the mid-fifth century. This included rebuilding and expanding the walls and building two

large basilicas, one of which, dedicated to St Demetrius, became a major centre of pilgrimage. Philippi, likewise, was adorned with huge new basilicas, some of unusual plan. Its richly decorated octagonal cathedral, dedicated to the apostle Paul, became the centre of an ecclesiastical quarter, as at Side. In this case, ecclesiastical buildings were dominant; but in all regional capitals, church and government left a powerful mark on the urban landscape.

Apamea in Syria was a very different kind of city, dominated more by a rich aristocracy than by public life. This city had a more regular plan than

The north–south street (*cardo*) of Apamea in Syria was built in the course of the second century AD and was nearly 2 km long. Behind the colonnades were shops, some of which still exhibit painted inscriptions specifying prices of wine and other commodities.

85

86

most, with streets crossing each other at right angles to form regular blocks or *insulae*. A grand colonnaded street, two kilometres long and 20 metres wide, formed the axis of the city. Paved with limestone and decorated with mosaics in the colonnades, it provided access to the major public buildings: the agora, baths, a monumental fountain, a large latrine, and, via another broad intersecting boulevard, the theatre. Shops lined the two boulevards whose intersection was marked by a vast rotunda. With its rich decoration of cut marble, it appears to have been the shrine where Apamea's most sacred relic, a piece of the True Cross, was kept. Opposite was a large church, while nearby on the intersecting boulevard stood the cathedral, approached by a monumental staircase and a colonnaded courtyard. This massive domed tetraconch was the centre of a complex with numerous rooms, courts, and a bath, which appears to have been the bishop's palace. All three of these churches manifested novel plans and a rich sixth-century décor.

The remains that give Apamea its distinctive character are the enormous aristocratic mansions that fill much of its centre. Typically, they occupied entire blocks of some 55 by 110 metres. These were inward-looking structures, focused on internal courtyards; they presented blank walls to the streets, and their entrances gave little hint of what was inside. Apsidal reception and banquet rooms flanked the main colonnaded courtyards, reflecting the entertainment that was a central part of an aristocratic lifestyle. Smaller rooms on the ground floor were perhaps used for service and storage, but functional rooms like kitchens, baths, and toilets seem completely absent. The bedrooms were apparently on an upper floor. One large house, which has three apsidal halls and numerous smaller rooms, stood near the cathedral and may have been the palace of the governor.

Rare texts and abundant remains enable urban life to be visualized, and in one case inscriptions reveal the variegated life of the people. The necropolis of Corycus in southern Asia Minor contains nearly 400 epitaphs that name the occupations of the deceased. They reveal a vast range of occupations ranging from public and ecclesiastical officials to sausage-sellers, barbers, and dancers. Prominent among them are merchants and artisans (often overlapping categories). Manufactures included clothes, linen, leather, shoes, pottery, hardware, glass, and purple dye. People worked gold, stone, and marble and produced and sold many food products: fruit, vegetables, nuts, fish, bread, wine, oil, cakes, pastries, and drinks. Bankers, carpenters, architects, lawyers, tailors, cleaners, and keepers of shops, taverns, restaurants, and inns added to the complement of activities. All these need to be imagined in the context of such buildings and streets and harbours as those of Ephesus.

The cities were not static, but each followed its own and regional

Facing: Hunt mosaic which covered the floor of one of the three reception rooms of a large mansion at Apamea believed to have been the palace of the provincial governor. AD 539.

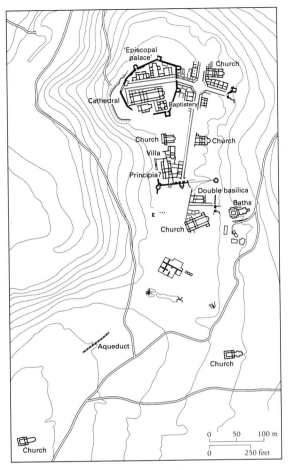

developments. Those of Asia Minor flourished throughout Late Antiquity, but in Syria, the great cities of Antioch and Apamea suffered severe disasters in the sixth century, while many places in Greece were devastated in the third and succumbed to further invasions in the late sixth. In most places, the heights of prosperity were reached in the late fifth and early sixth centuries; the work of Justinian was especially evident in many. Almost all, however, succumbed to the invasions and economic changes of the early seventh century to yield, in Greece and Asia Minor, to fortresses, and in Syria to the new centres of Islam.

Agriculture was the main occupation of the Roman empire, and villages, market towns, and scattered small settlements contained the vast majority of the population. Life in such places was very different from that of the cities, with few if any of the public works and services that characterized urban life; yet an active community life still flourished in highly varied settings. Texts and remains present a detailed image of this life, but focus on only a few regions. The most important texts are the Lives of two saints from sixth-century Asia Minor, Theodore of Sykeon and

Among Justinian's many building projects was the new city of Justiniana Prima erected in *c.*530 at his birthplace (modern Caričin Grad in Serbia). Although built on a small scale, it had traditional urban features including a forum, porticoed streets, shops, baths, an aqueduct as well as a cathedral, and a military *principia*.

Nicholas of Myra. Remains illustrate the environment of St Nicholas, as well as that of several marginal areas in Syria and Palestine. In these cases, remarkably well-preserved villages and towns reveal a high standard of living and an unexpected degree of wealth, even in remote areas. Nevertheless, they also show that rural life was far poorer than urban, both materially and culturally.

Theodore of Sykeon passed most of his life in the villages of Galatia in central Asia Minor, where the accounts of his miracles allow considerable insight into conditions of the time. They reveal the prevalence of religion and superstition, the problems that afflicted country life, the organization of a communal existence and its relations with the sometimes distant but always powerful government. The country contained a dense network of prosperous villages, with wheatfields and vineyards, cattle, mules, and oxen. Each had one or more churches or chapels and a population attentive to the teachings of a local holy man. The people, overwhelmingly farmers, also included smiths, lime-burners and builders as well as teachers, sorcerers, fortune-tellers, and real or quack doctors. Protection from disease and other afflictions was a constant need, for the countryside suffered from drought, floods, hail, locusts, worms, and beetles, while the people had a variety of ills of which the most feared was the plague. There were frequent cases of chronic or temporary madness, whose cause was believed to be demonic possession. Demons dwelt everywhere, notably in the ancient pagan ruins that abounded. They could only be driven out by the potent exorcism of a holy man, in a public ritual that stirred local emotions.

These villagers were free and evidently in possession of their land (little is heard of the tenants of the large estates that predominated in other areas). They had a local administration run by the landowners and elders, who assumed various titles. Normally they ran their own affairs, but the strong and usually brutal hand of the government would intervene to quell any serious disturbance or investigate violation of the laws, which included digging for buried treasure. News would reach the central authorities via the highways that intersected this countryside and formed a separate environment. The highways were part of the state. Armies, high officials, messengers passed along them, changing horse at the posting stations, sleeping in the inns and consorting with the prostitutes who often worked there. Like the great estates of the aristocracy that dotted the countryside, especially in the vicinity of the cities, they were more closely tied to the cities than to the countryside.

The Life of St Nicholas presents a similar situation in a different setting, the mountains instead of the plains. In addition to grain and wine, products include timber, so that wood and stone cutting are important local activities. Here, too, each village has its own church, and the villagers rely on the holy man to cure their ills and drive out evil spirits. In this more remote region, pagan practices survived longer, as they did in other mountainous parts of the country. Nevertheless, the Life makes it clear that the villages were closely connected with the city, and that trade was an essential element of their existence, allowing a high level of prosperity to be maintained. The prosperity is evident in the remains of numerous villages in the hills above Myra, where compact groups of fieldstone houses, many built on terraces, surrounded the local stone church, itself often elegantly built and decorated. Among them was the monastery of Holy Zion founded by St Nicholas himself. Its structure has survived, along with its spectacular treasure of silver plate that attests the surprising wealth of a remote church. The shrine evidently attracted pilgrims and rich patrons from the prosperous coastal cities, for Lycia included a shoreline full of small towns and villages that continued eastwards into Cilicia.

This maritime region formed another environment, prospering not so much from agriculture—many of its sites occupy rocky promontories or off-shore islands that could never have been self-sufficient—but from the trade that flourished in the entire eastern Mediterranean, especially districts on the coastal routes between Constantinople and the Near East. These coastlands contain extensive remains of stone houses and churches. They prospered while interior districts, particularly mountainous ones without fertile land or far from trade routes, were seriously afflicted by banditry or revolts that be-

Plan of Dar Qita, a village in the limestone hills of Syria.

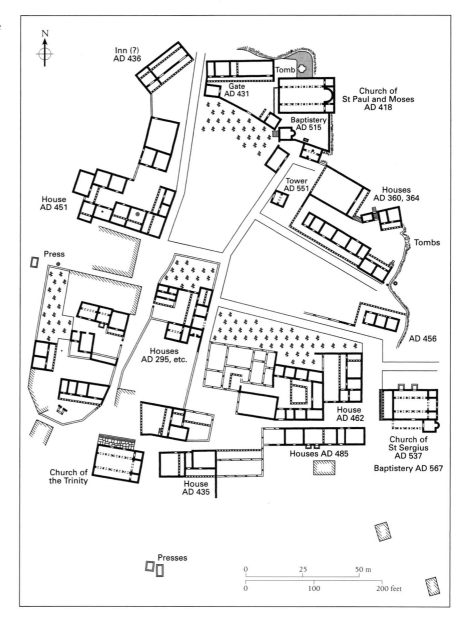

came especially acute in the sixth century. Rapacious governors and tax collectors were one affliction for the peasant; large landowners, who even kept private armies, and the military, who often succumbed to the temptation to loot, were another.

Syria contains the best preserved remains of villages in the eastern empire. A network of some 700 villages forms a spectacular landscape in the limestone hills above the Orontes river. Each usually contains between twenty and fifty stone houses and one or more churches. The houses, irregularly laid out along alleys or enclosures rather than streets, present blank walls to the outside and are often roughly clustered around the perimeter of the village to keep out marauders or wild animals. They are normally two-storey structures with open verandas overlooking inner courtyards, with the rooms (most commonly two to four, but with great variation) on the upper floor. The elegance of their stonework misled early investigators into thinking that they were the dwellings of a rural aristocracy, but there is nothing aristocratic or urban about these houses, for the people lived upstairs and the animals on

Two-storey houses at Serjilla in the limestone hills of Syria. The façade is enlivened by niches and well-carved mouldings surrounding the doors and windows. Sixth century.

Two public buildings at Serjilla. On the left is the bath built in 473 by Julianus and his wife Domna for the use of the village, as stated in a pavement inscription. The porticoed building to the right may be an inn.

the ground floor, while the courtyards were used for animals and domestic activities, not receptions or ceremonies. The houses rarely have latrines or separate rooms for kitchens, and no baths or running water. Among the 700 villages, there are only five public baths, and virtually no public buildings. The amenities of the city were alien to the countryside whose inhabitants had to travel far to enjoy them.

These villagers lived from growing olives, a major cash crop which they turned into oil in presses located, like other industrial activities, on the periphery of the villages. This was overwhelmingly the most important activity, supplemented by orchards and livestock. These products were sold to the neighbouring cities, but evidence for local trade is scarce: the villages contain no buildings that can be identified as shops or bazaars. Temporary stalls or local fairs were presumably the mechanisms of local exchange. In any case, oil, wheat, and wool provided the surplus which enabled the locals to build their stone houses—and frequently to add rooms to them—and to contribute to the churches, whose elegant, even grandiose buildings also contained treasures or gold coin or silver plate that evidently represented the accumulated capital of the countryside. They show that the demanding late antique government did not, as sometimes maintained, drain the wealth of the country for the benefit of itself or the cities, but allowed such regions as this to grow and prosper.

Left: The large church at Qalb Loseh in the limestone hills of Syria preserves part of its stone roofing. The side aisles have been opened up by the use of widely spaced piers supporting broad arches, instead of the traditional colonnade. Fifth century.

Below: Remains of a large village at Sha'ib Shahr south-east of Edessa in Mesopotamia. The stone masonry of the two-storey houses resembles that of the limestone hills in northern Syria.

Right: Aerial view of the bath built in *c.*558 at Androna in the Syrian steppe. Although identified as a village (*kome*), this large site has two sets of circuit walls, a barracks, a dozen churches, and large water reservoirs.

Below: Situated close to Androna is Qasr ibn Wardan, a 'desert estate' of the type found in the Umayyad period. It had a church, a barracks (561), and, here, a palace with a large triconch reception hall, built in 564.

Many regions also featured much larger settlements, which did not have the municipal status or bishops that defined cities, but were on a different scale from the villages. These contained a hundred or more houses (sometimes larger, though usually of the village type), numerous churches, open spaces perhaps used as markets, and even an occasional bath. Some of these are on the frontiers, where they also feature fortification walls, towers, barracks, and military headquarters. Most remarkable among them are the large settlements of the Negev in the desert of southern Palestine which could easily be mistaken for small cities, except that they lack the characteristic urban amenities. Among them in the arid countryside are the remains of much smaller scattered settlements, some apparently used by transhumants or nomads.

The greatest monument of the Syrian countryside is not a village or city but a monastery. The cruciform church of St Symeon was built in the fifth century around the pillar where the saint had dwelt. Its scale and lavish decoration suggest imperial patronage, and its location near a major highway allowed it to attract pilgrims from far and near. They were lodged in hostels in the town below the church and were evidently a major factor in the local economy, especially since their great feasts attracted a wide public who came for business as much as piety. These festivals usually included a regional trade fair that could bring people together from great distances and contributed seriously to the local economy. Such shrines existed throughout the empire, sometimes in cities (most notably Jerusalem, as well as Ephesus and Thessalonica) or not far from them (as the grand complex of St Thecla near Seleucia in Isauria), and rarely in the remote countryside, as Mount Sinai. These sites, usually the most renowned of their region, often included monasteries which formed an important element of both rural and urban environments. Monks performed works of piety and charity, but could also play a role in local manufacture. The monasteries, which ranged from small desert cells to grand urban or suburban complexes, appeared everywhere, but most commonly in or near cities. They employed an essentially domestic architecture for most of their buildings.

Cities, market towns, villages, and monasteries all formed part of an interdependent system connected by trade and reinforced by the political and ecclesiastical system. However Christianized, they maintained the fundamental structures of the Graeco-Roman world, with its prosperous cities embedded in the vast countryside on which they depended, as much as the villages depended on them. Although amenities and public works sharply differentiated the worlds of city and country, trade and the economy bound them together. When the cities declined or collapsed, a different world was created.

3 New Religion, Old Culture

CYRIL MANGO

At the time of Constantine's conversion (312) Christians made up a small minority of the empire's population, say 10 per cent, although that is only a guess. There were more of them in cities than in the countryside, more in the East than in the West. Originally recruited among the lower classes, they had been steadily climbing the social ladder.

Setting aside the Jews, who were not very numerous, and certain marginal sects, like the Manichaeans, the bulk of the population consisted of followers of traditional local religions whom we call pagans. Paganism was a welter of more or less compatible cults coexisting under a Graeco-Roman umbrella thanks to a process of mutual identification of deities.

To the ancient mind (and the same is still true of many parts of the globe today) *religio* was a body of ritual, a set of inherited prescriptions of great antiquity, which were performed both within the family and publicly so as to avert the anger of the gods and ensure the well-being of the community. As late as *c.* AD 500 the historian Zosimus, a pagan, could seriously state that the decline of the empire had been caused by Constantine's failure to celebrate the Secular Games, which fell due in 313 at the latest. Roman *religio* was civic rather than individual, which meant that it was run by the state. It had no sacred text, no professional priesthood, and no theology. It differed from *superstitio*, the latter being defined as an excessive or irrational awe of the gods. *Religio* was proper and gentlemanly. It did not concern itself with the Big Questions, such as the origin of the universe, the meaning of life, or ultimate ends. The few who were interested in such profundities turned to philosophy, which was seen as a different kind of activity. Several varieties of philosophy were on offer, all of Greek origin: Aristotelianism, Platonism (old, middle, and late), Stoicism, Pythagoreanism, Epicureanism, Cynicism, etc. Philosophy was based on human reason, not supernatural revelation, and the choice of a particular sect (*haeresis*) was not seen as being incompatible with the practice of traditional religion, although Epicureans (who held that the gods had no interest in human affairs) had a bit of a problem in that respect.

By and large, the distinction between religion and philosophy held good in the early centuries of our era when philosophies tended to move from rationalism to mysticism, whereas religion developed some theological content.

Was Christianity a *religio*, a *superstitio*, or a philosophy? By Roman standards it hardly qualified as a religion. Instead of being civic, it appeared as a kind of underground, cosmopolitan mafia. It did not entail anything that could be recognized as a cult, such as sacrifice offered to statues. It did have its rites, but these were performed behind closed doors. It is interesting to note in the light of future developments that early Christians, reacting to the ritualism of the Jews, laid little stress on the precise conduct and uniformity of observance. The apostles, they pointed out, had laid on them no other obligation than 'to abstain from meats offered to idols, and from blood, and from things strangled, and from fornication' (Acts 15: 29).

Another factor that told against Christianity was its recent origin, whereas respectable religions were ancient. In this regard the Egyptians and Chaldaeans had an unbeatable advantage, while the Jews could claim that Moses, their lawgiver, had lived a thousand years before the Trojan War—at any rate much earlier than the wise men of the Greeks. Traditional pagans, whose historical records went no further back than the sixth century BC, could nevertheless point to Orpheus and other semi-divine figures from a distant past. The Christians for their part could only say, 'We are of yesterday (*hesterni sumus*), but our scriptures are ancient'—a line of reasoning that required the questionable qualification, 'We have the same scriptures as the Jews, but they do not understand them properly, whereas we do.' Eventually, various

The Seven Sages with Socrates at the centre. Mosaic of the fourth century AD found under the floor of the cathedral of Apamea. It has been connected with the school of Neoplatonic philosophy known to have flourished in that city.

97

The superiority of religion over science. The astronomer Ptolemy, symbolized by the personification of Inquiry (*Skepsis*) behind him, is perplexed, while Hermes the Thrice-great sees the divine apparition, possibly of Christ, to whom the other personification points. Found in the sea off the coast of Gaza. Silver plate of the fifth century, 45 x 48 cm.

sophistries were devised to prove that Christianity was not only ancient, but, indeed, the oldest religion of all: for whereas Abraham was the founder of Judaism, the righteous patriarchs before him, being neither of the Jewish faith nor idolaters, could only be called proto-Christian. Thus Christianity could be shown to go back to the garden of Eden.

Actually, Christianity was even newer than it looked, for if its name originated in the reign of the emperor Tiberius, its doctrine had been thoroughly redesigned since the days of the apostles. It is not part of our story to describe the successive adjustments and elaborations that transformed a minor messianic movement into a Church of universal appeal, but it is important to point out that Christian teaching had not quite jelled at the time when Constantine stuck in his heavy boot with consequences that were to last throughout Byzantine history.

The polemicist Celsus (*c.* AD 180) was a little out of touch when he claimed that Christianity appealed only to women, children, and slaves, for at the very time when he was writing his diatribe Christian thinkers had embarked on the irreversible course of turning their religion into a philosophy, i.e. a coherent, total system, which may fairly be described as the greatest intellectual achievement of Late Antiquity. We are so familiar with the resultant synthesis that we tend to forget the enormous effort of scholarship and critical reflection that went to create it. Unlike traditional Greek philosophies, Christian philosophy was based on revelation contained in scripture whose every word counted. The bulk of that scripture (what now became the Old Testament), a mix of tribal history, ritual prescriptions, cosmology, prophecy, and inspirational musings, was both profoundly alien to Mediterranean peoples and accessible only through a translation into colloquial Greek (the Septuagint) whose accuracy could not be taken for granted. As a first step, therefore, the entire text of the Old Testament had to be checked against the Hebrew original; apocrypha had to be weeded out of the canon; each and every genuine book of the Bible needed to be expounded so as to bring out both its literal and its symbolic meaning; the parts that were no longer applicable, i.e. the ritual prescriptions, had to be identified. But that was only the beginning. Seeing that the Old Testament was largely a book of history concerned with the fortunes of a marginal nation, its narrative and chronology had to be integrated with the records (largely fictitious, but nevertheless accepted) of the Greeks, Romans, Egyptians, and Babylonians. The account of Creation in the book of Genesis had to be made credible in terms of contemporary cosmological thinking. It had to be explained why the Almighty had shown so much concern for the greater part of recorded history with the salvation of the Jews to the exclusion of all other nations and why the incarnation of Christ had occurred as late as it did. And then at the heart of the system was the insoluble conundrum of Christ the Logos, who had been 'with God' from the beginning, had created everything, and then, paradoxically and unacceptably to current pagan thinking, 'became flesh' and, indeed, suffered a humiliating death unworthy of a god. Was the Logos an emanation of the Father or a distinct person and, if the latter, was he self-existent or had he been created by the Father at some infinitely remote time, which would make him, so to speak, a divinity of the second degree?

Such were some of the inevitable problems consequent to the attempt of transforming Christianity into a philosophy, and their working out, especially as regards Christ the Logos, was to last for a good three centuries after Constantine. If, however, we go back to an earlier period, we discover that

not all committed Christians were keen on being taken down the path to philosophy, mindful as they were of St Paul's admonition, 'Beware lest any man spoil you through philosophy and vain deceit' (Coloss. 2: 8). On this topic there was a good deal of ambiguity. In one sense Christianity was the only 'sure and profitable' kind of philosophy as Justin Martyr put it; in another, Athens had nothing to do with Jerusalem, to recall Tertullian's famous dictum (*Quid ergo Athenis et Hierosolymis? quid academiae et ecclesiae? . . . Nostra institutio de porticu Solomonis est*[1]). Christians were not philosophers not only because philosophy was vain and provided no firm answers, but, more importantly, because philosophy was not efficacious, because it did not put demons to flight. Christianity did.

Tertullian was not speaking figuratively any more than the demons that sweep across the pages of the New Testament are to be understood as metaphors. Gentlemen like Marcus Aurelius could sneer at such childishness, but belief in the reality of demons was endemic in Late Antiquity. It should be explained that these were not the *daimones* (minor divinities) of Greek thought, but malevolent spirits, immortal and fast-moving, that preyed on human beings and even farm animals, causing derangement of the senses, many kinds of sickness, and, in humans, sinful desires. 'We wrestle', wrote St Paul, 'not against flesh and blood, but against principalities, against powers, against the rulers of the darkness of this world' (Eph. 6: 12). The rulers (*kosmokratores*) of darkness were the demonic powers that held sway in this nether world. The whole edifice of paganism could only be understood as a vast demonic machine, but its suppression did not entail the end of demonic activity. Ejected from the temples, where they had battened on the grease and smoke of burnt offerings, demons moved into the countryside, into tombs and solitary places, but were especially numerous in the agitated region of the upper air. From its inception Christianity had proved the most efficacious weapon against demons. Christ, himself

Pagan sages, here the 'Hellene' Pythagoras and 'Queen Sibyl', predict the advent of Christ. Wall painting representing the Tree of Jesse in the Moldavian monastery of Voroneţ, AD 1547.

---

[1] 'So what does Athens have to do with Jerusalem? What does the Academy have to do with the Church? . . . Our discipline comes from Solomon's Stoa.'

an exorcist, had explicitly promised to his disciples power over the demons, and it was thanks to that gift that Christianity had won its first converts— perhaps most of its early converts.

In the light of medieval European experience we tend to regard conversion to Christianity as a step up the ladder of culture and literacy. Undoubtedly it was so in the case of Saxons, Norsemen, Balts, and Slavs. But in the world of Late Antiquity conversion was often seen by cultivated people as a dumbing down. That is not to say that after the end of the second century Christianity could be described as anti-intellectual. On the contrary, it was becoming, as we have pointed out, distinctly erudite and was churning out copious treatises on 'theory' and apologetics heavily indebted to pagan philosophy. How many non-Christians read them is an open question, but if they had taken the trouble to do so, they would have found them as boring as the handbooks of Marxism-Leninism that used to be produced not so long ago in 'socialist' countries. And that is where the difficulty lay. For there existed at the time a highly sophisticated if thinly spread literary culture to which we must now turn our attention. It was based on a system of education that had remained virtually unchanged since the Hellenistic period and may be described as 'liberal' and non-technical. Boys of a certain social class, after learning in secondary school their classical poets (especially Homer and Hesiod) and a few tragedians (especially Euripides), went on to study eloquence as a general preparation to whatever profession they chose to follow, be it law, government or municipal service, teaching, or a life of cultivated leisure. Eloquence, for which Demosthenes and other Attic orators were proffered as models, meant the ability to speak and write in an approved style as laid down in dozens of textbooks, using an archaic idiom, namely Attic Greek, that in itself served as a class badge. While not deliberately ideological, this kind of education was permeated with pagan lore. Boys had to learn the myths and genealogies of the gods and the texts they absorbed were dominated by pagan values. Feeding into the practice of rhetoric, but also pursued on its own account, was a vast accumulation of erudition drawn from grammar, history, mythology, geography, astrology—the detritus of an old culture, collected from books, anthologized, paraded in after-dinner conversation.

It is difficult for us to appreciate the degree of enthusiasm which the practice of eloquence inspired throughout the Late Roman world. Professors of rhetoric (called rhetors or sophists) held endowed chairs in the main cities, attracted students from a wide catchment area, gave public performances before huge audiences, were sent on embassies to plead local causes, and were honoured with statues. Along with famous philosophers, they were the only class of people, apart from rulers, whose biographies were written down before the same privilege was extended to Christian saints. Above all, rhetoric served as a cultural glue that bound together the elites of the empire's far-flung cities. Not only were the students drawn from different areas; the professors themselves were increasingly international. Among those who won renown in the fourth century we find two Arabs, a Phoenician, a Mesopotamian from faraway Nisibis, and, amazingly, a Christian Armenian bearing the splendid name of Prohaeresius.

Let us take a concrete example, that of Libanius (314–93), who may be described as Mr Literature of the fourth century. His preserved works, largely unread today, fill eleven volumes in the standard edition and include 64 orations, 1,544 letters, 51 declamations, and a mass of school exercises. Libanius was a member of the landed gentry and occupied for half a century the chair of eloquence in his native Antioch. Born ten years before Constantine had made himself master of the East, a friend and admirer of the emperor Julian, he lived into the reign of the militantly Christian Theodosius I, who nevertheless conferred on him, a pagan, an honorary praetorship. Yet he tells us little about the momentous ideological changes he witnessed and is practically silent on the topic of Christianity. Not that he lived in an ivory tower. Nearly 200 of his students are known by name and he spared no effort to lobby on their behalf. They went on to become imperial officials, lawyers, teachers, members of municipal councils, thus creating a vast network of personal connections. Among them there were Christians, including (or so it was said) St John Chrysostom, St Gregory Nazianzen, and Theodore of Mopsuestia, a leading theologian of the Syrian Church. Libanius took up certain causes that affected him: he defended culture as he understood it; he railed against the 'technicians', who took up the study of law and shorthand to gain advancement in imperial service; he deplored the closure of temples. He was too famous to be censored or punished by a Christian government. But what was the secret of his success? Hardly his personality. In his autobiography he appears vain, neurotic, superstitious, and malicious, especially towards his competitors. We can only conclude that his reputation rested on his acknowledged literary gifts and public delivery, nor was the judgement of his contemporaries reversed by posterity. He remained a model of eloquence throughout the Byzantine period (hence the preservation of his works) and it was only in the nineteenth century that he began to sink into oblivion. Even today we still have to read him in Greek: only a small part of his vast output has been translated into a modern language.

How was the Church to react to the kind of culture exemplified by Libanius? Short of boycotting it altogether (the fundamentalist solution), it could either acquiesce in it or provide a curriculum of new, Christian classics suitable for schooling. Such a Christian literature, however, did not exist and the

Bible, though occasionally forceful, was widely regarded as barbarous in its language and style. The issue came up when Julian briefly banned Christian teachers from expounding pagan classics, i.e. deprived them of a livelihood. His measure was condemned on all sides. A few Christians rose to the challenge like the two Apollinarii (father and son) who turned the Old Testament into a poem using every kind of ancient Greek metre and the New Testament into a Platonic dialogue. Rather more significant is the case of Gregory Nazianzen, who composed not only highly rhetorical sermons, but also letters and poems with the express purpose of vying with the ancients. His efforts were rewarded in that he became in the Byzantine period a literary model and the most widely imitated Christian author. But that did not alter the perception that Christianity had no literary culture suitable for schooling. Secular education was, therefore, left in place, merely with a 'health warning': Christian boys were urged to disregard the immoral stories of the old gods and concentrate on what was good and useful. Besides, as the Church historian Socrates explained in the 440s, 'Hellenic' (i.e. pagan) education had been neither approved nor rejected by the Church, and that for good reason. For the scriptures do not teach logical argument and if Christians are to refute the enemies of truth, they should use the pagans' own weapons against them. What happened in effect was that Christian leaders who had themselves benefited from a rhetorical education introduced into their preaching and writing the precepts they had learnt in school, as is evident from the literary works not only of Gregory Nazianzen, but also of John Chrysostom, Gregory of Nyssa, Basil of Caesarea, and a host of others. None of them stooped to using ordinary speech so as to reach the masses.

Christianity became the religion of state only under Theodosius I in about AD 380. Constantine had proclaimed his personal attachment to it—not an unprecedented act among earlier Roman emperors. But he went further by actively promoting Christians in his service, showering enormous sums of money on the Church and building lavish houses of congregation and martyrs' shrines. Step by step, he found himself increasingly involved in ecclesiastical disputes as both umpire and enforcer. For the Church was deeply divided. Still bearing the scars of the Great Persecution (303–11), which had naturally bred deep resentment, suddenly flooded with new money and accorded undreamt-of privileges, the Church, governed by custom, lacked a coherent hierarchical structure that might have enabled it to settle its own affairs. The temptation to appeal to the saviour emperor proved too strong even in matters that should not have concerned him at all, as was the case of the Arian dispute that broke out at that time. The point at issue was purely philosophical. The presbyter Arius of Alexandria taught that Christ the Logos had been created by the Father at some infinitely remote juncture and

The earliest preserved representation of the Council of Nicaea is in a Carolingian manuscript. It shows an enthroned Constantine (already bearded), the assembled bishops, and, below, a bonfire being made of Arian writings.

was not, therefore, of the same essence as the Father. That view, stemming from the doctrine of the great theologian Origen, had considerable support among intellectuals, but the bishop of Alexandria, Alexander, was bitterly opposed to it. Invited to intervene, Constantine summoned an unprecedented throng of bishops, some 300 in all, to meet in May 325 in the sleepy lakeside city of Nicaea. The sessions took place in the imperial palace, hence on Constantine's own ground, and although by all accounts he behaved very correctly, he left no doubt that he was in charge. He did not pretend to understand the issues in dispute, but insisted that the bishops come to a consensus. Not surprisingly, he got his way: out of the 300 only five refused to sign on the dotted line, and three of those later changed their mind. Arius was exiled and his books were ordered to be burnt. Anyone concealing them was to suffer the death penalty, no less.

It is ironic to recall that a few months before the Council Constantine had written a joint letter to Alexander and Arius, telling them in no uncertain terms that their quarrel was altogether trivial and irrelevant to the worship of God. He urged them to follow the example of philosophers who agree to disagree on small points while preserving the unity of their doctrine. Why then did he get embroiled in a highly abstruse dispute in which he had no interest? Probably because he saw no other way of getting the squabbling bishops to make peace among themselves. He considered it his duty, as he put it on another occasion, to suppress dissension, 'because of which the Supreme Deity may perchance be moved not only against the human race, but also against me in whose care it has entrusted all earthly things'. A very Roman sentiment: as Pontifex Maximus, Constantine was responsible for the proper *cultus* or *veneratio* of the Deity, not for philosophical quibbling. Yet the legacy of Nicaea, the first universal council of the Church, was to bind the emperor to something that was not his concern, namely the definition and imposition of orthodoxy, if need be by force.

From that point onwards there was no turning back. Constantine's son Constantius II actively championed Arianism and even declared that his own opinion in such matters was to be 'the canon'. Valens followed the same line and is remembered for burning alive a party of his Nicaean opponents. Theodosius I made a complete U-turn and ordered all his subjects to follow the Nicaean formula: dissenters were denied the right of assembly and even threatened with the death penalty if they engaged in agitation. At the same time imperial legislation established long lists of heresies whose adherents were to be subjected to persecution, expelled from cities, forbidden to celebrate their rites. The Theodosian Code contains no fewer than sixty-five decrees directed against heretics. The state had become a theocracy.

Yet the appetite for deviant theological speculation was in no way diminished. Starting with Arianism, which took a good two centuries to suppress, Christianity went on a theological spree, which produced a rich harvest of heresies. If histories of the Byzantine empire devote so much space to this topic, that is partly due to the importance among available sources of the ecclesiastical history, a genre inaugurated by Eusebius of Caesarea and subsequently cultivated by Socrates, Sozomen, Theodoret, and others. As Socrates admits, ecclesiastical historians would have had nothing to write about if bishops did not quarrel concerning matters of doctrine. But even if we allow for an over-weighting of the phenomenon, the fact remains that different interpretations of Christian dogma, especially as affecting Christ's divinity, aroused a great deal of passion even among people who had no understanding of the issues involved. Arianism in its many manifestations was followed by Nestorianism, which was eventually driven out of the empire to become the dominant form of Christianity in Persia. Then came Monophysitism, which was never resolved and remained the prevalent faith of Syria, Egypt, and Armenia. It has never been satisfactorily explained why thousands of ordinary people were ready to suffer persecution, even death, for the proposition that the incarnate Christ was either in (*en*) or derived from (*ek*) two natures, but they were certainly convinced that their opponents were gravely in error in either dividing or confusing the person of the one Christ. Of course, the more the government persecuted dissidents, the more dissidents hardened their resolve. And then, just as mysteriously as theological fervour had started, so it died down. Or so it seems because no more ecclesiastical histories were written after the year 600. Monothelitism, which was but a pale continuation of Monophysitism inspired by political considerations, was laid to rest by the council of 680. That was the last of the 'noble' heresies. The issue of Iconoclasm, which was artificially inflated into a Christological heresy, was in reality concerned with observance, i.e. *cultus*, and that in itself was indicative of a new development: Byzantine Christianity had reverted to being a *religio* in the Roman sense.

The fuss over abstract theology diverted attention from the realities of piety and observance which, almost without comment, witnessed a profound change in the fourth and fifth centuries. By far the most important, which ended by transforming Christianity into something closely resembling polytheism, was the cult of the saints. It had started innocently enough. A persecuted sect, Christianity had honoured the memory of its 'witnesses' (martyrs). The date and manner of their death were recorded and commemorative meetings, including meals, held at their tombs. Constantine honoured them with huge covered shrines—St Peter's, S. Sebastiano, S. Lorenzo in Rome, Sts Mocius and Acacius at Constantinople. By the middle of the fourth century we find that the earthly remains of martyrs were not only honoured, but were working supernatural phenomena as a matter of everyday observation. In their presence, says St Hilary of Poitiers (*c*.360), demons bellowed, sicknesses were healed, bodies levitated, and women suspended by their feet—we are not told why they were so suspended—were not shamed by having their clothes fall over their faces. No wonder that possession of relics became an asset and the practice arose not only of shifting them

from place to place, but even cutting them up in contravention both of Roman law and deeply held feelings about the inviolability of tombs. The government—not the Church—reacted to no effect by prohibiting this abuse. A decree of 386 proclaims, 'Let no one divide or sell a martyr's body', just as the traffic in relics was assuming epidemic proportions. The possibilities of fraud were, indeed, obvious, not to speak of the unseemly character of the whole business. Yet, far from objecting to what strikes us as crass superstition, the most eminent churchmen rose to applaud it. Here is Theodoret of Cyrus

The martyrs, here Onesiphorus, companion of St Paul, and Porphyrius, in their heavenly abode. Part of a 'calendar' of saints in the Rotunda of Thessalonica, built as the mausoleum of the emperor Galerius. Mosaic, fifth/sixth century.

Above, left: Doric temple of Athena of the fifth century BC transformed into the cathedral of Syracuse.

Above, right: The Temple of Rome and Augustus at Ankara, famous for its bilingual inscription detailing the achievements (*res gestae*) of the emperor of AD 14, was transformed into a church in the sixth century. The added Christian choir is seen through the doorway.

in about 430: 'The glory of martyrs does not wither. Their bodies are not hidden singly, each in his own tomb, but have been divided among cities and villages, which regard them as the saviours of souls and bodies, as physicians and guardians. Using them as ambassadors to the universal Lord, they obtain through them divine gifts. Nay, when a body has been divided, its grace remains entire, so that a small part has the same potency as the whole body.' Once the logic of the argument is granted, it follows that there was an advantage in distributing relics as widely as possible: regions that had an excess could supply those that suffered a deficiency.

It is a matter of personal judgement whether one regards the cult of saints as a superstitious debasement of original Christianity or, on the contrary, as a beneficial development that gave comfort and confidence to many ordinary people. Besides, was pre-Constantinian Christianity as virginally pure as we imagine it to have been? The kind of circus described by St Hilary as occurring *quotidie* could not have started overnight. In theory it was all defensible: saints were human beings who had won God's friendship and with it the ability to hear prayers and intercede on behalf of their clients. As on earth, it was more efficacious to address a request to a patron who was influential at court rather than appealing directly to the emperor who was too busy to listen. For the mass of believers, however, saints were more than human beings: demigods might be a better description. And then there was the special case of the immensely popular St Michael, who was definitely not human.

The great club of saints in heaven was admitting new members at God's pleasure. Now that the path of martyrdom was closed or nearly so, asceticism became the preferred option. In a world that regarded the flesh as corrupt, mortification by abstinence or even self-mutilation (as in the case of Origen) offered a powerful appeal: not only was it good in itself, but by liberating the spirit, it facilitated the acquisition of those supernatural gifts which Christ had promised to his true followers—of healing, exorcizing demons, prophecy, and working 'signs', i.e. miracles. It was difficult, however, to be an ascetic amid the cares and obligations of everyday life: withdrawal (*anachoresis*) was the answer. And so in about 270 Christian monasticism was born in Egypt and spread like wildfire throughout the empire—to Palestine, Syria, Mesopotamia, and Asia Minor, reaching the West with only a slight delay. At first the

Byzantine magical amulets, worn for protection. The two on the left have the generic Holy Rider (good) spearing a demon (evil). The round amulets have other images (lions, snakes, etc.), incantations, magical signs, and a Medusa head that are considered uterine in nature. Fourth to eleventh century.

Facing, clockwise from top left:
The small Umayyad bath of Qusayr 'Amra, situated in the desert some 50 miles east of 'Amman, is famous for its extensive painted decoration featuring foreign rulers defeated by the forces of Islam, a Zodiac, musicians, animals, nude women, etc., no doubt executed by local painters (c. AD 715).

The ruined Umayyad palace of Khirbet al-Mafjar near Jericho (c. AD 743) contained a bath, a mosque, and several halls decorated with carved stucco and floor mosaics, mostly geometric, but also depicting a tree and wild animals.

Mosaic in the apse of the little church of the monastery tôn Latomôn (also known as Hosios David) at Thessalonica, depicting Christ seated on the rainbow, as seen by the prophets Ezekiel and Habakkuk (probably sixth century). The mosaic appears to have been deliberately concealed during the period of Iconoclasm.

Head of the archangel Gabriel flanking the Virgin and Child in the apse of St Sophia, Constantinople (reproduced on p. 44). The elongated face is freely modelled by means of colour without the linearity characteristic of later Byzantine painting.

government did not know what to make of monks, who did not fall into any established classification. They were not clergy, but simply committed Christians, something like the Cynic philosophers of former times. A decree of the year 390 barred them from municipalities, bidding them to inhabit 'desert places and desolate solitudes', but two years later that directive was revoked. Indeed, they were becoming an object of intense interest, even at court. Observers were sent to seek them out in their desolate solitudes and report on their superhuman regimen. Their sayings were recorded and circulated in special collections. Mortification became competitive: if father Paul could survive during the forty days of Lent on a small measure of lentils and one jug of water, one could always beat his record. As abstention became *vieux jeu*, more extreme forms were introduced: one could wear heavy chains or shut oneself up in a cage or take off one's clothes and graze like an animal in the countryside or stand on top of a pillar for many years. The last expedient, invented by Symeon Stylites (d. 459) and often imitated thereafter, drew maximum publicity.

Much ink has been spilt in recent years over 'the rise of the holy man', meaning specifically the wonder-working ascetic. Yet holy men were not a new phenomenon either inside or outside Christianity. Jesus was the archetypal holy man and the powers he vested in his disciples had been an integral part of the Church from its inception. The twelfth chapter of 1 Corinthians details, if rather obscurely to us, the various types of charismatics that were part of the Christian community. Itinerant 'prophets' were to be received with honour unless they happened to be frauds, as we learn from the second-century *Didache* (Teaching of the Apostles). The tradition of ecstatic prophecy, reflected in the *Shepherd* of Hermas, persisted in Phrygia. Gregory, bishop of Neocaesarea (modern Niksar in north-east Turkey), worked incredible miracles in the 240s, acquiring the title of Wonderworker. The question to be asked is why supernatural charismata were usurped by the monks and, by and large, departed from the established Church. The short answer seems to be that after the Constantinian settlement the Church lost its glamour. It became part of the civil administration responsible for ideology and welfare. Salaried bishops handled large sums of money, oversaw agricultural and commercial properties, sat on municipal councils and exercised judicial functions. Few of them captured the popular imagination. Monks were different. Independent of the ecclesiastical establishment, they appeared to incarnate Christ's persona. Even if they lived in the desert, they were not entirely cut off from society. A famous holy man would attract visitors who were willing to travel some distance so as to enjoy contact with him, receive healing or edifying advice. On occasion he would settle disputes, avert natural calamities, cause rain to fall or intervene with the authorities in a good

cause. Yet it is true to say of eastern monasticism that social action was not its avowed purpose. The monk's main goal was the attainment of personal perfection, which, as Justinian put it in his legislation, brought him close to God. Only on that condition could he confer benefit on the community through his prayers.

We have highlighted a number of developments that were to exert a lasting impact on the Byzantine world, namely the intimate interpenetration of State and Church; the creation of a total system of Christian 'philosophy'; an unresolved dichotomy between classical education and the radically different ideals of Christianity; the extraordinary diffusion of monasticism outside the established Church and the appropriation by it of charismatic powers. All these phenomena were rooted in the realities of the fourth century, yet survived nearly intact into a very different world. The one significant change, as we have pointed out, concerns the cessation of major theological disputes. After the Seventh Council (787) the Byzantine Church closed its books. It appeared that all the heresies had been annihilated. The approved body of doctrine was final and so perfectly formulated that nothing could henceforth be added to it and nothing taken away. As an archbishop of St Petersburg is quoted as declaring in the nineteenth century, 'Our Church knows no development.'

Old paganism disappeared even before the collapse of the Late Roman state in the East. We have ventured the guess that at the time of Constantine Christians made up 10 per cent of the population. Their number may have grown to 50 per cent by the end of the fourth century and to 90 per cent by the end of the fifth. Justinian ruthlessly mopped up the residue of pagans, who were obdurate academics at one end of the scale and illiterate peasants at the other. Conversion was thus fairly rapid and probably dictated more by expediency than conviction, leaving a substratum of 'superstitious' practices: recourse to magicians and diviners, public dances, the wearing of masks, the invocation of 'the detestable Dionysus' at vintage time, the lighting of fires to mark the new moon. The Quinisext Council (692) ruled that such 'Hellenic' practices were to be banned, but they surely continued. Magical amulets form an important part of the archaeological record even if the invocations they bear are increasingly addressed not to pagan gods, but to angels and Christian saints.

The artistic heritage of paganism had been comprehensively smashed by dint of Christian zeal. Starting in the late fourth century, statues of the gods were toppled from their pedestals, great temples demolished, others converted into churches after being stripped of their decoration. Of course, not everything could be destroyed without going to a great deal of trouble. In the Parthenon of Athens Christians defaced the carved metopes on three sides of

Facing: Interior of the Umayyad Dome of the Rock, built on the Temple Mount of Jerusalem (AD 691–2). With its octagonal plan, marble columns and revetments, and mosaics depicting acanthus scrolls, the Dome of the Rock provides the most complete visual analogue of a Byzantine martyrium of the early period.

Above: Aphrodite with Adonis, Hippolytus, and Phaedra. Mosaic of the mid-sixth century at Madaba, Jordan. The classical subject matter stands in strong contrast to the primitive style.

Right: Dionysiac procession. Detail of the Great Palace pavement, Constantinople, second half of the sixth century.

the temple, then gave up. The battered remains of pagan art, e.g. sculpted sarcophagi in cemeteries, acquired a sinister, demonic aura. It was best to give them a wide berth. Somewhat surprisingly, however, mythological subject matter lingered on in the private sphere of the well-to-do, especially in floor mosaics, silverware, and textiles, until as late as the seventh century. It is not likely that it held any religious significance. The Dionysiac procession in the pavement of the Imperial Palace of Constantinople (second half of the sixth century) is certainly not a sign of cryptopaganism, but a 'literary' reminiscence, one element amongst others of a pastoral setting.

The gap left by paganism was filled by the cult of saints on both a practical and an imaginative level. That is not to say that there was a simple substitution, that, for example, the sun god with his chariot (Helios) was replaced by the Prophet Elijah (Elias) who went up to heaven in a chariot, or that the Virgin Mary usurped the place of Athena or Cybele or Isis. What we observe is that certain practices were maintained under changed auspices, especially in the all-important domain of healing. Incubation (sleeping in) had been widely practised under paganism in temples of Asclepius, Isis, the Dioscuri, and other divinities. A patient would bed down in a sacred precinct, make the requisite offerings and await a visionary visitation that would bring about his or her recovery. Exactly the same procedure appears under Christianity, but the cures are now worked by St Michael, St Thecla, Sts Cyrus and John, Sts Cosmas and Damian. Christian incubation, similar in all respects to the pagan, flourished between the fifth and seventh centuries and subsisted until the end of the Byzantine period.

At the same time the cult of saints created a new mythology. Compared to pagan legends, the Christian ones were decidedly chaste, containing much violence, but no sex. They were also rather repetitive: all martyrs exhibited constancy, they never flinched, the only variable being the torments they endured—broken on the wheel, burnt in a fire, beheaded, frozen to death in a lake. The story of their sufferings was endlessly celebrated in sermons and depicted in painting and so became part of the mental baggage of the general public. Every inhabitant of Thessalonica knew that his patron saint, Demetrius, had been speared to death by order of the godless tyrant Maximianus and had a young companion, Nestor, who had killed a famous

Silver plate depicting a dancing Silenus and Maenad, dated 610–29 by its control stamps.

The sufferings of the martyrs, here the Forty Martyrs of Sebaste, who froze to death in a lake during the persecution of the emperor Licinius. Tenth-century ivory after an Early Christian original.

gladiator in single combat. It is pointless to ask whether this rather rudimentary story (there is not much more to it) has any foundation in fact. What is worth observing, however, is that nearly all the more popular saints in the Byzantine pantheon were fictitious figures from a distant past or so transformed as to have lost any historical dimension. Only by being stereotypes could they fulfil the role they were called upon to play.

Pilgrimage

MARLIA MUNDELL MANGO

An important phenomenon of Byzantine history was the development of pilgrimage centred, first of all, on sites in the Holy Land. This circuit was complemented by a series of memorial shrines commemorating Christianity's heroes, the holy men and women who bore witness to Christ's ministry, particularly those who gave their lives, the martyrs. A sacred landscape that stretched across the eastern parts of the empire was manifested by a network of impressive buildings between which pilgrim itineraries were established.

Both Jews and Christians considered Jerusalem the centre of the world. The city appears in a central position on a large map of the Holy Land laid as a tessellated pavement in the city of Madaba during the sixth century. In the fourth century Jerusalem had assumed a new spiritual status thanks to the interest of the emperor Constantine in the Holy Land. There he built large shrines at the Holy Sepulchre and the Mount of Olives at Jerusalem and at the cave of the Nativity at Bethlehem.

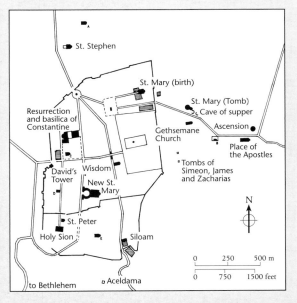

Plan of Jerusalem showing the principal stations in pilgrim itineraries as they had developed by the seventh century. The itineraries are known from the pilgrims' written accounts of their visits.

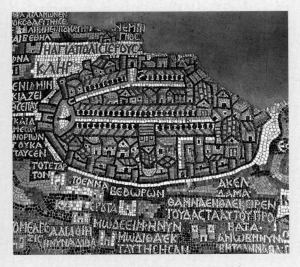

The city of Jerusalem, detail of a mosaic map at Madaba in Jordan. Recognizable features include the colonnades of the main north–south street (the *cardo*), a circular plaza with statue at the north gate (on left), the shrine of the Holy Sepulchre (lower centre), and the Nea church built by Justinian (upper right). Sixth century.

To reach the Holy Land most pilgrims travelled by ship, on foot, or by donkey. Many journeys were long, even within the Holy Land: the trip from Jerusalem to Mt. Sinai could last 13–15 days. The first pilgrim to leave a written account of his journey came from Bordeaux in 333. At Jerusalem he mentions only the two buildings put up by Constantine. Yet even without commemorative shrines a holy topography existed which already in the fourth century included 34 areas in the Holy Land. By the seventh century, the principal churches of interest at Jerusalem itself came to include the shrine of the Holy Sepulchre on Golgotha, the churches of Holy Sion (the Last Supper), of Holy Wisdom (where Christ was condemned and scourged), and at the Sheep's Pool (the Healing of the Paralytic and birth and childhood of Mary), and, in the Valley of Jehosaphat, at Gethsemane and the Mount of Olives (the Ascension). There followed trips to Bethany (the tomb of Lazarus) and Bethlehem. At Diocaesarea, pilgrims saw the chair of the

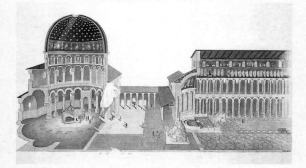

Reconstructed section of the shrine of the Holy Sepulchre as built by Constantine in the fourth century. On the left is the rotunda with the tomb of Christ in the middle. To the right in the open courtyard the site of Golgotha is enclosed by a small shrine seen in the lower right corner. To the right of the courtyard is the basilica where services were held.

Annunciation, at Cana were the jugs for water changed to wine, and at Nazareth the Christ child's first notebook.

The events commemorated at the shrines were illustrated on receptacles made to contain blessed substances relating to the Holy Land. Thus, a wooden box of *c.*600 preserved in the Vatican contains small parcels of soil, wood, and cloth labelled 'from the Mount of Olives', 'from Sion', etc. Its lid is reproduced below. Primary relics, such as the wood of the True Cross or bones of a martyr, were in limited supply, but secondary relics (called *brandea*), materials such as oil which came into contact with the primary relics, were in unlimited supply and could be put in containers for pilgrims, as in the decorated lead ampullae, inscribed 'Oil of the Wood of Life of the Holy Places of Christ' or similar text.

Left: Painted lid of a wooden box containing relics acquired in the Holy Land in *c.*600. The scenes depicted are major events of Christ's life: (starting in the lower left) Nativity, Baptism, Crucifixion, Resurrection, and Ascension. They incorporate 'modern' elements, such as grills under the manger and around Christ's tomb, which were visible to pilgrims at Bethlehem and in the Holy Sepulchre.

Below: Lead ampulla decorated with the same scenes as on the painted box lid as well as the Annunciation and Visitation. Such ampullae were used to carry blessed oil home from the Holy Land. This and other ampullae were probably presented to the Lombard queen Theodelinda in *c.*600.

The shrines prospered on the donations of pilgrims, including devout emperors, on sales of ex-voto offerings and souvenirs such as the ampullae and reliquaries, and on the sale or leasing of land. Many of the pilgrims who came wished to live and die in the Holy Land. They constructed hospices, churches, and monasteries for others and bought houses and built tombs for themselves. A law of 545 states that many who were 'attracted to Jerusalem through the desire of visiting the tomb of Our Lord wish to purchase buildings belonging to the Church with large sums of money'. The wealth generated by this buying and selling of property met the needs of the indigent and sick pilgrims who could become a burden on its charitable institutions. Another law of 535 described 'leasehold' sales of houses to provide the church with an income to meet its charitable obligations. Monasteries were founded to care for pilgrimage shrines and to provide lodgings for their visitors (see special feature on Monasticism).

Outside of the Holy Land, important shrines commemorated St Menas near Alexandria, St Sergius at

The remains of the column, originally 40 cubits high, on which sat the Elder St Symeon. From the surrounding, central octagon four basilicas radiate on a cruciform plan. The shrine, north-east of Antioch and now called Qal'at Seman ('Castle of Symeon'), was built c.490 some 30 years after the stylite's death. It had a large baptistery, an adjoining monastery, and, down the hill, further monasteries and inns built for pilgrims.

Rusafa, St Thomas at Edessa, St Thekla at Seleucia, the Apostle Philip at Hierapolis, St Theodore at Euchaita, St John the Evangelist at Ephesus, St Demetrius at Thessalonica, in addition to Sts Peter and Paul at Rome. Most of these saints dated from apostolic times or were martyred, particularly under Diocletian in the early fourth century. Later holy men to attract devotion were the stylites, the first of whom, Symeon, mounted his column (40 cubits high) north-east of Antioch in the fifth century. After his death in 459 a large cruciform monument was built around his column at Qal'at Seman where talismans were distributed to pilgrims. At Symeon's column these were clay tablets or tokens stamped with his

117

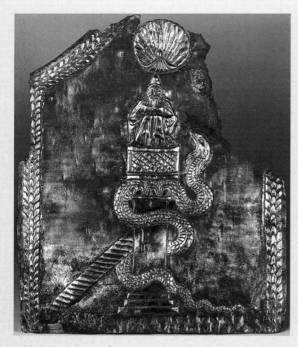

Gilded silver plaque of St Symeon the Stylite shown seated on his column. The inscription at the bottom, giving thanks to the saint for a favour granted, indicates that this was an ex-voto offering. The snake entwining the column may be that featured in the Life of either the Elder (d. 459) or the Younger (south-west of Antioch, d. 593) Symeon.

Clay ampulla decorated with the inscribed image of St Menas shown in the posture of prayer, flanked by camels. This type of flask was distributed at his shrine south-west of Alexandria. The contents may have been curative water or another substance. Sixth century.

image. Likewise, clay ampullae, similar to the lead ones from Jerusalem, were produced at the shrine of St Menas near Alexandria and elsewhere to hold holy substances (blessed oil, water, soil, etc.) for the pilgrims.

The geography of the holy suffered some dislocation when in 356–7 Emperor Constantius II translated the relics of Luke, Timothy, and Andrew to be placed in the church of the Holy Apostles in Constantinople. The practice quickly spread to the west where Ambrose, bishop of Milan, imported further apostolic relics. Eventually, important relics of the Passion were removed from the Holy Land and concentrated in Constantinople which became known as the New Jerusalem. The Arab conquest of the Levant by 640 did not completely disrupt international pilgrimage, but it became a less marked feature of Byzantine life. Byzantium's partial and temporary reconquest of the Levant in the tenth century led to the acquisition of further relics such as the *mandylion*, or sacred towel, sent by Christ to King Abgar

Upper half of a tenth-century icon showing King Abgar of Edessa receiving the holy towel (*mandylion*) with the imprint of Christ's face. The *mandylion* was removed from Edessa in 944 by the Byzantines following a siege of the city and taken to Constantinople. Mount Sinai, St Catherine's Monastery.

Above: Gold and cloisonné enamel pendant reliquary originally decorated on the front with a portrait of St. Demetrius, now lost. On the reverse side appears St George, often associated with Demetrius. Inside the recess for a relic is decorated with an image of the latter in his shrine at Thessalonica. Thirteenth century.

Left: Reliquary of the True Cross made of gilded silver encrusted with precious stones and numerous gold plaques of cloisonné enamel decorated on the lid (seen here) with the Deisis and saints. Inside are recesses for the cruciform case of the Cross and other relics. The raised inscription states that the reliquary was made for Basil the *proedros* (964–5). The reliquary was removed from Constantinople after the sack of 1204. Limburg an der Lahn, Cathedral Treasury.

of Edessa in Mesopotamia, as portrayed in a contemporary icon. During the Middle Period, relics of the Holy Cross assumed a universal popularity and the great majority of the reliquaries produced then held pieces of the True Cross or were at least cruciform in shape. St Demetrius, whose cult was based at Thessalonica, likewise remained the focus of devotion and reliquaries continued to be made with his image.

In 1204 the members of the Fourth Crusade removed prestigious relics from Constantinople to western Europe. In Paris, the Sainte Chapelle was built to house the most important of them, namely the Crown of Thorns and other relics of Christ's Passion. But the Byzantine reserves were replenished subsequently and continued to attract veneration by Russian pilgrims down to the fifteenth century.

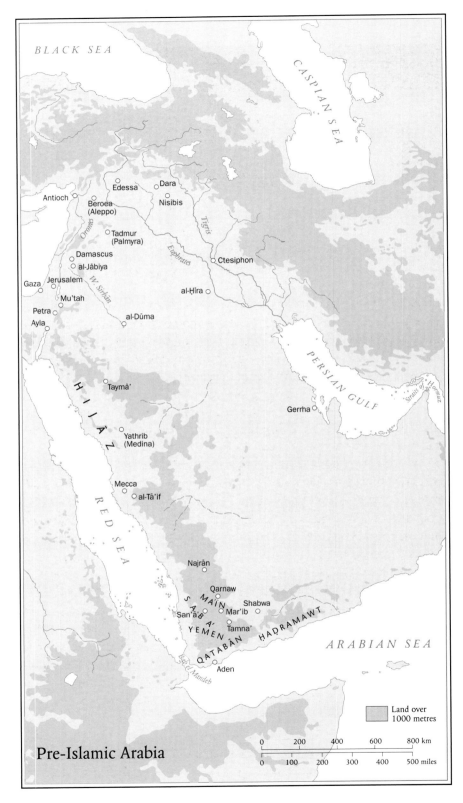

Pre-Islamic Arabia

BLACK SEA

CASPIAN SEA

Edessa
Dara
Antioch
Beroea
(Aleppo)
Nisibis
Tadmur
(Palmyra)
Damascus
al-Jābiya
Ctesiphon
Gaza
Jerusalem
Mu'tah
al-Ḥīra
Petra
Ayla
al-Dūma

PERSIAN GULF

Taymā'

Gerrha

Yathrib
(Medina)

H I J Ā Z

Mecca
al-Ṭā'if

RED SEA

Najrān

Qarnaw
MA'ĪN
Shabwa
San'ā'
Mar'ib
YEMEN
Tamna'
ḤAḌRAMAWT
QATABĀN

ARABIAN SEA

Aden

Land over
1000 metres

0   200   400   600   800 km
0   100   200   300   400   500 miles

120

4 The Rise of Islam

ROBERT HOYLAND

To describe the Arabs, the inhabitants of the Arabian peninsula and the Syrian desert, Byzantine writers used such expressions as 'rapacious kites', 'wolves', 'unreliable and fickle', 'a barbarous nation'. In part, this reflects the prejudice of a settled state towards the uncivilized tribal peoples on its periphery. The aridity of much of the Arabs' homeland meant that there were not the resources for complex social and political organization. Certainly there were some exceptions. Monsoon rains and spices allowed several kingdoms to develop in south Arabia, and statelets emerged in the Syrian desert when civilization showed itself willing to provide commercial revenues (thus the kingdoms of the Nabataeans and Palmyrenes) or imperial subsidies (thus the kingdoms of the Ghassanids and Lakhmids). But for most Arabs statelessness was the norm, and all Arabs, whether settled or nomadic, were organized in tribes, that is, descent groups based on self-help. In the absence of a law-enforcing agency, one had to seek justice for oneself and one's kin by one's own efforts—'with the sword will I wash my shame away', as one poet said. This uncouthness of the Arabs was coupled with another even more serious defect in the eyes of a Byzantine, namely their biblical ancestry; for as descendants of the slave-woman Hagar they were tarnished as religiously inferior, as 'the most despised and insignificant peoples of the earth'.

It was nevertheless from a remote corner of Arabia and at the hands of an Arab that Islam was to arise. At the same time that the armies of the Persian emperor Khusro II were sweeping through the Byzantine provinces of Syria and Palestine, a man named Muhammad, of the Arab tribe of Quraysh, began preaching in his native town of Mecca, on the north-west Arabian littoral. His message, the *Qur'an*, consisted of warnings about the impending day of reckoning, legal prescriptions, polemic against infidels, an outline of Judeo-Christian and Arab prophetic history and, in particular, exhortations to adhere to the One True God, associating none other with Him. For those willing to accept this counsel Muhammad outlined a programme of action. They were to form a community (*umma*) united in 'belief in God and the

Last Day', dissociate themselves from the unbelievers by making an exodus (*hijra*), and
finally make war (*jihād*) on those unbelievers in
order to convert them to the right belief or to
bring them to submission. This programme of
action was as effective as it was simple, and
within two decades Muhammad had won much
of northern Arabia over to his creed. His successors Abu Bakr (632–4) and 'Umar (634–44)
extended this success, first to the rest of Arabia,
then, in a series of lightning military campaigns, to the whole Middle East.

Mosaic inscription
naming 'Erethas [*sic*], son
of al-Arethas', the latter
being presumably al-Harit
ibn Jabala, king of the
Ghassanids, 529–69.
Church of St Sergius at
Nitl (Jordan).

How are we to explain this feat? To the Muslims the answer was easy: 'It
is a sign that God loves us and is pleased with our faith, that he gives us dominion over all religions and all peoples.' And indeed we must give credit to
the message which Muhammad imparted, its potency and simplicity guaran-
teeing its continual use by revolutionary and reformist Islamic groups until
today. But why were the seventh-century Arabs so receptive to this message?
Had something changed in Arabia that made its inhabitants particularly dis-
posed to Muhammad's teaching, or did he offer a new solution to some
perennial problem? The latter hypothesis cannot be excluded. As noted
above, tribes lack a coercive apparatus with the result that large-scale co-
ordinated activity is all but impossible for them. Muhammad overcame this
difficulty by giving the Arabs a sense of common purpose, one eminently
suited to a tribal environment, namely to advance God's cause through conquest (*jihād fī sabīl Allah*).

More commonly, however, it is argued that the novelty lay more in the circumstances than in the message. And it is certainly true that the Near East
underwent large-scale change in the century or so before the rise of Islam.
The loose-knit empires of the Romans and Parthians had given way to the
superpowers of Byzantium and Iran, and politics became increasingly polar-
ized as both powers courted neighbouring peoples for their allegiance and
support. The Arabs were both the beneficiaries and victims of this imperial
scramble for influence. They could extract subsidies and power, but at the
price of compromising their independence. Various Arab confederations
emerged, the best known being the Ghassanids and Lakhmids, allied to
the Byzantines and Persians respectively. We know very little about the
Lakhmids, but we can see that the Ghassanids had over the course of the
sixth century built up a considerable power base for themselves in Jordan and
southern Syria. This is illustrated by the buildings and inscriptions which
commemorate the names of their rulers, and by contemporary Syriac documents that speak of their patronage of and arbitration in matters of religion.

Facing: A small church-like
building situated at the
north gate of Rusafa (here
seen looking towards the
entrance) has been inter-
preted as the audience
chamber of al-Mundhir,
king of the Ghassanid
Arabs from 569. A carved
inscription in the apse
may be freely translated as
'Up with al-Mundhir!'.

Greek and Syriac texts mention them alongside Byzantine emperors as 'our most pious and Christ-loving kings', even speaking of their 'kingdom'. And in the verses of their poets there would seem to be none more powerful: 'Do you not see', wrote one to his Ghassanid master, 'that God has granted you such a degree of power that you will observe every king trembling at your feet; for you are the sun, the kings are stars, and when the sun rises, no star will be seen'. The elevation to power of these confederations meant that what had formerly been minor feuds between rival Arab tribes, in which 'only one or a few of them might be killed', now became significant confrontations. And it would seem that the Arab conquests began as a similar clash between the north-west Arabian and Ghassanid confederations, the former intending to usurp the latter's position.

The superpower conflict had ideological as well as political repercussions. Warfare assumed an increasingly religious character and religious difference frequently became equated with political dissidence. On the Arabian stage this was played out most dramatically in the south when the ruler of Ethiopia, an ally of Byzantium, invaded Yemen in response to reports about persecution of Christians and installed on the throne a Christian king. Fur-

Mosaic in the courtyard of the Umayyad mosque of Damascus, built by the caliph al-Walīd I (705–15) within the temenos enclosure of a pagan temple, itself transformed into a Christian church of St John. The courtyard mosaics depict landscapes and buildings in a 'Hellenistic' style, but have no living creatures in them.

thermore, traders turned missionaries, spreading Christianity, Judaism, and Manichaeism throughout the peninsula. Thus, by the time of Muhammad, monotheism had gained a firm hold in Arabia. What the relevance of this was for the rise of Islam is difficult to say, but at the very least it meant that Muhammad's audience was already acquainted with the concept.

Finally, the sixth and early seventh centuries were visited by recurrent bouts of bubonic plague, commencing in 542, by which 'nearly the whole world was eliminated', and by a series of clashes between the Byzantines and Persians, which culminated in the latter's annexation of many of the former's provinces. 'Nations have been wiped out,' wrote one Byzantine historian in 580, 'cities enslaved, populations uprooted and displaced, so that all mankind has been involved in the upheaval.' These events served to diminish the great coastal cities and to favour the smaller towns of the interior regions, where lesser population density mitigated the effects of the plague and distance from major thoroughfares spared them from pillage. The northwest Arabians participated in this efflorescence of the interior, trading especially with settlements in the Negev, Balqa', and Hawran.

In short, the century before Muhammad saw Arabia become increasingly integrated into the political, religious, and economic world of the superpowers of Byzantium and Iran. And yet the Arabs retained a distinctive

Decorated façade of the fortified palace of Mshatta (near 'Amman in Jordan) before its removal to Berlin. The date of Mshatta has been much discussed, but it is now accepted as an Umayyad structure, probably put up by the caliph Walid II in 743–4. Its over-rich carvings include figures of animals.

culture and sense of identity. This was partly because of the very different ecology of their homeland which ill supported state structures. But it was also because increased resources, especially imperial subsidies, allowed them now to give expression to this difference. Chiefs of client kingdoms began to designate themselves as 'king of all the Arabs' and had Arabic poetry composed in their honour and for their entertainment. It is they who gave impetus to the creation of an Arabic script to record their deeds, requests, and genealogies. And it was, therefore, natural that God chose to send down to Muhammad a 'recitation in Arabic' (*qur'an 'arabiyy*) in 'clear Arabic speech' (*lisān 'arabiyy mubīn*).

This sense of being different from the civilized peoples of the Near East was to stand the Arabs in good stead when they were their masters. Tribal peoples, because they were highly mobile and because their menfolk were all militarily active, were often successful at overrunning settled states, but being culturally inferior they would very quickly become assimilated to the culture of their subjects. The Arabs were able to resist this process, for they had brought their own religion and their own cultural heritage, each of which validated the other. Moreover, they initially kept apart in military camps rather than dispersing amongst the native population as landlords and farmers. Lands taken by force were appropriated by the state and the revenues therefrom were paid to the Muslim soldiers by the government as stipends in return for military service. There were, of course, disputes. The third caliph, 'Uthman (644–56), was murdered by veteran warriors angry at being shortchanged in favour of newcomers and at the nepotistic style of rule, and there ensued a civil war during which various factions struggled to assert their own view of government. But in the end the Arabs stuck together, many feeling that even an unjust ruler was preferable to loss of their unity (*jamā'a*).

The winners of this first Arab civil war were a dynasty called the Umayyads (661–750), who immediately set about laying the foundations of a new empire. They built administrative complexes, palaces, and mosques; they reclaimed marshlands and undertook irrigation projects, carried out land surveys and censuses. For such tasks competent managers were required and, since the Muslim rulers paid no heed to the birth or creed or rank of non-Arabs, there were great opportunities for advancement open to the able. Bashshar ibn Burd's grandfather, a native of Tukharistan, was captured and taken to Basra where he worked as a bricklayer; Bashshar himself became a famous court poet in a position to boast to his masters 'that I am a man of ancestry superior to any other man of ancestry'. Conversion was not essential—thus Athanasius bar Gumaye, a native of Edessa, made his fortune as right-hand man to 'Abd al-'Aziz, brother of the caliph 'Abd al-Malik (685–705) and governor of Egypt, while remaining a devout Christian. But

among prisoners-of-war or émigrés to Muslim cities, who would be spending all their time among Muslims, conversion was the norm, as was noted with much grief by their erstwhile co-religionaries: 'many people who were members of the Church will deny the true faith . . . without being subjected to any compulsion, lashings or blows.' The entry into the Islamic fold of such a diffuse mixture of people, from so many different races and of so many

The small town of Anjar, near Baalbek (Lebanon) has been attributed to the caliph al-Walīd I (705–15). It is built on an orthogonal plan in the Roman style, framing a square 175 m to the side.

The earliest Umayyad coins imitate the Byzantine issues of Heraclius with three standing emperors, even including the mint mark CONOB. Only the cross on steps is made into a staff. The imperial figures are then replaced by the caliph drawing his sword. Finally, a purely epigraphic design was introduced.

different religious and philosophical persuasions, lent a tremendous variety and vitality to the nascent Muslim world and meant that Byzantium came face to face with a new and virulent civilization taking shape within its own former provinces.

The confrontation of these two powers dominated their politics for centuries. Initially each strove totally to vanquish the other. However, 'Abd al-Malik's construction of the Dome of the Rock on the Temple Mount in Jerusalem, his minting of aniconic coins bearing the Muslim profession of faith, and his moves to institute Arabic as the official language of the new empire made it clear to all that the Muslim realm was to be no mere temporary phenomenon. Equally, the failure of the Muslims' great thrust to take Constantinople in the early eighth century demonstrated to them that the Byzantines were not so easily to be ousted. War in the field became often no more than a ritual display, and the battle turned rather to one of words. Amidst the vituperative polemic exchanged by both sides there were also, however, occasional fruitful exchanges and rare enlightened overtures, such as that made by the patriarch Nicholas to the caliph Muqtadir (908–32): 'The two powers of the whole universe, the power of the Saracens and that of the Romans, stand out and radiate as the two great luminaries in the firmament; for this reason alone we must live in common as brothers although we differ in customs, manners and religion.'

5 The Struggle for Survival (641–780)

WARREN TREADGOLD

These years can rightly be called the Dark Age of Byzantine history: a time of military reverses, political instability, economic regression, and declining education, which has left but a scanty record for modern historians. The evidence is so poor that we often have trouble not only reconstructing the course of events and evaluating the personalities of leading figures, but even discerning the broadest outlines of development. One of the harder questions to answer is how Byzantium managed to survive the Arabs' attacks at all.

To judge by the precedents for old empires attacked by vigorous peoples making their first bids for world power, Byzantium should have been doomed before the Arabs. It found itself in the role of the western Roman empire attacked by the Germans, Carthage attacked by the Romans, or the original Persian empire attacked by Alexander's Greeks. None of those ancient states had lasted as long as a hundred years after its first decisive defeat. By 641 the Sasanid Persian empire had already lost its heartland and its capital to the Arabs, and was to last only ten more years as an organized monarchy.

When Heraclius died, Byzantium also looked highly vulnerable. The Arabs had already despoiled it of Syria, Palestine, its part of Mesopotamia, and most of Egypt. Still exhausted by the ravages of the Persian war, which it had won only with agonizing difficulty, the empire was disorganized, impoverished, and almost bankrupt. It was also chaotically led, since Heraclius had divided the succession between his elder son Constantine III, who was dying from tuberculosis, and his younger son Heraklonas, who was dominated by his unpopular mother Martina. For three years the empire suffered from internal strife.

Constantine III died after reigning a mere three months, and Martina and the 15-year-old Heraklonas succeeded. But many of the people of Constantinople had always considered Martina's marriage to her uncle Heraclius

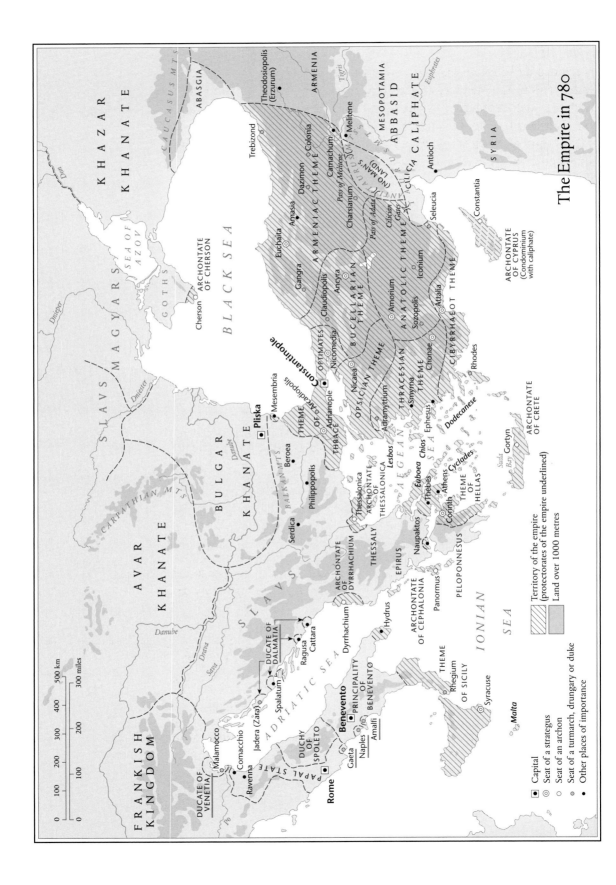

The Empire in 780

KHAZAR KHANATE

ABASGIA

ARMENIA

Theodosiopolis (Erzurum)

MESOPOTAMIA

ABBASID CALIPHATE

SYRIA

Tigris

Euphrates

CAUCASUS MTS

SEA OF AZOV

Don

GOTHS

MAGYARS

SLAVS

Dnieper

Dniester

BLACK SEA

Trebizond

Colonia

Dazimon

Amasia

ARMENIAC THEME

Camachum

Melitene

Pass of Melitene

Camachum

ANTI-TAURUS

Charsianum

NO MAN'S LAND

CILICIA

Gates

Antioch

Cherson

ARCHONTATE OF CHERSON

Euchaita

Gangra

Claudiopolis

Ancyra

BUCELLARIAN THEME

Amorium

Iconium

ANATOLIC THEME

Sozopolis

Attalia

Cilician Gates

Seleucia

Constantia

ARCHONTATE OF CYPRUS (Condominium with caliphate)

CARPATHIAN MTS

Danube

Drava

Sava

AVAR KHANATE

SLAVS

BULGAR KHANATE

Pliska

Mesembria

THEME OF THRACE

Adrianople

Arcadiopolis

OPTIMATES

Nicomedia

Nicaea

OPSICIAN THEME

THRACESIAN THEME

Chonae

CIBYRRHAEOT THEME

Rhodes

Constantinople

Beroea

Philippopolis

Serdica

BALKAN MTS

Adramyttium

Lesbos

Smyrna

Ephesus

Chios

AEGEAN SEA

Cyclades

Dodecanese

ARCHONTATE OF CRETE

Gortyn

Suda Bay

FRANKISH KINGDOM

Danube

SLAVS

Thessalonica

ARCHONTATE OF THESSALONICA

THESSALY

EPIRUS

Thebes

Athens

Corinth

THEME OF HELLAS

Naupaktos

PELOPONNESUS

Panormus

ARCHONTATE OF CEPHALONIA

IONIAN SEA

Po

Ravenna

Comacchio

Malamocco

DUCATE OF VENETIA

Jadera (Zara)

DUCATE OF DALMATIA

Ragusa

Cattara

Spalatum

ARCHONTATE OF DYRRHACHIUM

Dyrrhachium

Hydrus

ADRIATIC SEA

DUCHY OF SPOLETO

PAPAL STATE

Rome

Gaeta

Naples

Amalfi

Benevento

PRINCIPALITY OF BENEVENTO

THEME OF SICILY

Rhegium

Syracuse

Malta

Territory of the empire (protectorates of the empire underlined)

Land over 1000 metres

Capital

Seat of a strategus

Seat of an archon

Seat of a turmarch, drungary or duke

Other places of importance

0 100 200 300 400 500 km

0 100 200 300 miles

incestuous and invalid, and Heraklonas a bastard. In any case the usual Roman and Byzantine practice had been for the succession to pass not from brother to half-brother but from father to son; and Constantine had left a son, Constans II, who was not much younger than Heraklonas. Heraklonas and his mother clung to power for just six months before the chief army commander, the Armenian general Valentine, overthrew them with the help of a Constantinopolitan mob.

Rather than execute a woman and child, Valentine slit Martina's tongue and Heraklonas' nose to seal their deposition, using punishments previously imposed upon ordinary criminals. Then he proclaimed Constans II, married his daughter to the 11-year-old emperor, and became the power behind the throne. Meanwhile the Arabs finished conquering Egypt and raided Armenia and Anatolia. When Valentine tried to assume the title of emperor along with Constans, the mob, loyal to the legitimate heir, lynched the usurping general.

When Constans II finally became his own master at the tender age of 13, every part of the empire that remained was endangered. Anatolia and Armenia were under Arab attack, and Byzantine Africa and Italy were plagued by revolts and at best half-independent. All that slowed the Arabs a little was their need to round off and pacify their conquests, especially in Persia. No one could have had great confidence in young Constans, who seems actually to have begun to rule, no doubt relying heavily on his advisers and generals.

Having secured Armenia in 654, the Arabs started to invade Anatolia in earnest, sacking its main cities while looting Cyprus, Rhodes, and Crete with a powerful new fleet. Though the next year an Arab civil war gave Byzantium a respite, which led to a formal truce and even a payment of tribute by the Arabs, nothing suggested that the Byzantines could stop the Arab onslaught when the truce ended. The empire must have been desperately short of money after losing so much land and so many taxpayers, and especially its main granary in Egypt. Yet its defensive needs were greater than ever, and seemed to demand spending money that the empire could not raise.

At this point, our meagre sources begin to use Hellenized names for the empire's five main armies and the districts where they were stationed. Both the armies and their districts are called 'themes' (*themata*, apparently meaning 'emplacements'), and their commanders *strategoi* ('generals', except for the Count of the Opsician Theme). The origin of these themes is not in much doubt: they were evidently the field armies of the previous period. The large Opsician Theme combined what had been the two Praesental armies, while the Anatolic, Armeniac, and Thracesian themes were the former armies of the East, Armenia, and Thrace, which had retreated from their original positions to new stations in Anatolia. Only the origin of the Carabisian Theme is

Above: Inscription in honour of an emperor called Constantine—probably Constans II—following a victorious defence of Sardinia against the Lombards undertaken by the local duke, also called Constantine, c. AD 645 (?). Porto Torres, Sardinia.

Below: Acclamation in honour of Constans II or Constantine IV on the land walls of Constantinople. The erased fourth line probably associated the emperor with the Green or Blue circus faction.

doubtful; the best guess is probably that its men, who were marines, came from the former army of Illyricum.

What modern scholars chiefly dispute is how the new themes functioned. Our first clear evidence dates from the ninth and tenth centuries, when all our sources markedly improve. Then the soldiers of the themes were mainly supported and equipped not by their cash pay, as in the sixth century and before, but by land grants of specified minimum values located within their theme. The question is, did the themes have more or less their later form when they first appeared in the mid-seventh century, or did they only reach that state by some process of evolution?

No source mentions the distribution of military land grants at any date, and their minimum values are only noted in legal texts of the tenth century. On the other hand, the obvious reason for using land grants to support soldiers is to save money. The empire had no special need to economize in the ninth or tenth centuries, but its need was acute in the mid-seventh century. At that time the vast imperial estates known from the earlier period should still have been available for distribution. Strikingly, by the ninth century these estates had become insignificant, while the military lands had become extensive. Such considerations point to the conclusion that the imperial estates were distributed as military lands in the middle of the seventh century, most likely during the truce with the Arabs between 659 and 662.

Besides saving the government desperately needed cash, giving the soldiers land grants had other consequences, one advantageous and one not. The advantage was that, with themes now covering almost the whole empire, every important region had resident soldiers to defend it, who were strongly motivated to defend their own land. The disadvantage for the government was that, once the soldiers became mostly self-supporting, they had less reason to obey the emperor, and were easier to raise in rebellion against him. Though Constans II is unlikely to have anticipated either of these effects, he soon saw how both of them worked.

In 662 Constans embarked for the West with a large army. He left his adolescent son Constantine to govern at Constantinople, doubtless assuring the boy that his own duties at the same age had been even heavier. After visiting Pope Vitalian in Rome, Constans made Sicily his headquarters. He managed to stop the slide of Byzantine Africa and Italy towards independence, and may well have distributed land grants to the soldiers there. During his absence the Arabs, whose civil war had ended, returned to the attack. They met with stiffer Byzantine resistance than before, presumably from the themes. But in 668 the *strategos* of the Armeniac Theme proclaimed himself emperor, and the Count of the Opsician Theme, who was in Sicily with Constans, assassinated him and also claimed the throne.

Few historical figures of comparable importance are as poorly documented as Constans II, who lived thirty-seven years and reigned for twenty-seven of them. His reputation among orthodox Byzantines suffered because he refused to condemn Monotheletism and persecuted its opponents Pope Martin I and Maximus Confessor—though in fact he punished them for abetting rebellions in Italy and Africa. At the least, however, Constans successfully defended an empire that had seemed doomed when he took it over. If he was indeed the founder not merely of the themes but of the system of military land grants, he provided Byzantium with a flexible, affordable, and effective tool for the long struggle with the Arabs that stretched ahead.

The themes' penchant to rebel, while real enough, proved not to be disastrous in this case. The Armeniac Theme ended its revolt after its *strategos* died in a riding accident, and the expeditionary force in the West promptly arrested Constans' assassin. Constans' son Constantine IV, though barely 20, had taken to ruling as precociously as his father had, and had already been in power in the East for six years. He sailed to

Above: The last gold issues of Constantine IV (668–85) show a reversion to types of the sixth century and exceptionally high quality of execution, although the emperor's name is misspelt as *Constanus*.

Below: Justinian II introduced for the first time the bust of Christ with the legend *rex regnantium* on the obverse of his gold coinage, relegating his own effigy to the reverse.

Sicily, established his control of the West, and executed his father's assassin. Constantine returned to the East the next spring, bringing with him the eastern contingents of Constans' expedition.

The emperor was needed there, because the Arab threat had become more pressing. The Arabs had already taken advantage of the Armeniac Theme's revolt to seize some border territory, and they now began concerted land and sea attacks on Byzantine Africa, Sicily, and Anatolia. Worst of all, they began to make large-scale raids on the region around Constantinople itself. The raiders took as their base the nearby port of Cyzicus, where they first wintered in 670–1, and then returned in 674 for an indefinite stay. Though they had little chance of taking the strongly walled capital outright, their raids kept much of the Byzantine army pinned down. While the raiders from Cyzicus looted wherever they wished, other Arabs captured Cilicia and Rhodes, the Lombards conquered more of Byzantine Italy, and the Slavs besieged Thessalonica, by now the empire's second-largest city.

After three miserable years of this, Constantine decided to risk a battle with the raiders, especially because he had a new weapon. A Christian refugee from Syria had discovered a formula that we call Greek Fire, which burned on the surface of seawater and destroyed any ship in its path. In 677 the Byzantine fleet attacked the Arabs' ships, burned many of them with Greek Fire, and sent the raiders fleeing back towards the caliphate. A storm then wrecked most of what remained of the Arab fleet, as the Opsician, Anatolic, and Armeniac themes decimated the Arab army. The Byzantines had never won such signal victories against the Arabs before.

Having made a truce with the Arabs, recovered Rhodes, and defeated the Slavs near Thessalonica, Constantine tackled the question of Monotheletism, which his father had determinedly left open. That doctrine had long been detested in Africa and Italy, and since the loss of Armenia it had few remaining adherents even in the eastern parts of the empire. In 681 the emperor called an ecumenical council, the Third Council of Constantinople, which after a year of deliberations condemned Monothelitism, declaring that Christ, as fully human and fully divine, had two wills corresponding to his two natures. This definition resolved the last ambiguities in official church doctrine about Christ. In the future the Byzantine Church would quarrel about matters less central to the Christian faith.

Meanwhile many of the Turks known as Bulgars, whom their fellow Turks the Khazars had attacked from the east, crossed the Danube and migrated into Thrace. Though they were occupying land inhabited by Slavs and outside Byzantine control, Constantine realized that the Bulgars would make troublesome neighbours, and marched against them. At first he forced them back to the Danube delta. But when he withdrew from the campaign be-

Greatly eroded relief of a mounted figure followed by a dog on a vertical cliff face at Madara, near the Protobulgarian capital of Pliska. Next to the horseman are inscriptions in Greek in honour of the khans Tervel, Kormisos, and Omurtag. Early eighth to early ninth century.

cause of an attack of gout, his troops panicked and fled, and the Bulgars defeated them.

The Bulgars quickly established themselves in northern Thrace, taking a few coastal towns that had been Byzantine. Constantine agreed to a peace that recognized their new borders, and as a defence against them created a new Theme of Thrace from the territory of the Opsician Theme. He must have felt that one war of attrition was all the empire could handle at the time; he could hardly have foreseen that the Bulgars would outlast the Arabs as a danger.

Constantine soon made further gains against the Arabs, who were fighting amongst themselves in new civil wars. At the Armenians' request, he restored the Byzantine protectorate over much of Armenia, and retook Cilicia and the border regions that he had lost at the beginning of his reign. In 685, he concluded another truce with the Arabs, just before he died. A scarcely less shadowy figure than his father, he had had similar success, against similarly formidable opposition. While avoiding warfare when he could, he had handled the Arabs, the Bulgars, and his own subjects creditably. He died fairly young, but he died in bed, which was itself something of an accomplishment at the time.

Constantine's 16-year-old son Justinian II became the fourth emperor in a row to take power in his teens. Like his father and grandfather, he was capable, but with the Arab onslaught in abeyance he was more confident about the empire's future. He saw that it would survive as a great power, but he seems not to have seen that it was still far weaker than the caliphate.

Awareness of the vast achievements of his namesake Justinian I also appears to have made Justinian overly ambitious in his plans. Yet he is hard to judge, because our sources, though slightly more informative than before, are clearly unfair to him.

Without formally breaking his father's treaty with the squabbling Arabs, Justinian kept jockeying for advantage. He strengthened his control over Armenia. By agreement with the caliph, he received from Syria some Christian mountaineers known as Mardaïtes, who had long raided within the caliphate. Justinian now made them oarsmen for the Carabisian Theme, and probably also for a new Theme of Hellas that he created in Greece. He campaigned against the Slavs of Thrace, capturing a large number of them to enrol as soldiers in the Opsician Theme.

The emperor seems to have liked to resettle people, because he also deported much of the population of Cyprus to the devastated region around Cyzicus, which he refounded under the name of Justinianopolis. Then he provoked a war with the Arabs. In 691 he minted new coins marked with a bust of Christ, demanding that the Arabs use them to pay their tribute. With the Arab civil war dying down, the caliph refused to use the coins, invaded Anatolia, and defeated the Byzantine army when its unwilling Slavic recruits deserted to him. The Armenians submitted to the Arabs not long afterwards.

Justinian then decided to seek glory by other means than warfare. He held a church council, known as the Quinisext (Fifth–Sixth) because it was supposed to complete the preceding fifth and sixth ecumenical councils. Yet it included no western bishops, and offended his western subjects by mandating various eastern church customs that the West did not share. The emperor also began to add buildings to the imperial palace in Constantinople. Justinian's military campaigns had already led him to resort to rigorous taxation and even confiscation from his wealthier subjects, and his building programme caused further exactions.

In 695 some disgruntled aristocrats organized a conspiracy that overthrew Justinian, slit his nose, and replaced him with a general whom he had earlier disgraced, Leontius. The revolution was an inauspicious one. Although Justinian had sometimes been reckless, on the whole he had been competent, and his hereditary right to rule was clear. Leontius, while intelligent and vigorous, was only the second deposer of a legitimate emperor in Byzantine history, and the disastrous precedent was Phokas in 602. Without a strong hereditary ruler, the danger that the themes would rebel became much greater, at a time when the Arabs were resurgent.

The caliph soon struck at Byzantine Africa, where his troops seized Carthage in 697. Leontius promptly sent a naval expedition to recover the city, and it did so, but the next year the Arabs drove it out again. The defeated

Byzantine force sailed back to Crete, where, rather than face responsibility for its defeat, it proclaimed an officer of the Carabisian Theme as emperor. Then the rebels sailed to Constantinople, besieged the city, and forced their way in. They slit Leontius' nose and installed their candidate as Tiberius III.

With scarcely anything to justify his usurpation, Tiberius tried to win an easy victory by raiding Arab Syria. The caliph, who had finished taking Byzantine Africa, retaliated by attacking the empire's eastern frontier. In 702 the Armenians rebelled against the caliphate, but despite Tiberius' best efforts the Arabs soon conquered both Armenia and some adjacent Byzantine territory. Meanwhile the deposed Justinian II escaped from Byzantine Crimea, where he had been exiled, and made his way first to the Khazars and then to the Bulgars, where the Bulgar khan gave him an army to lead against Constantinople. Contriving to enter, Justinian captured Tiberius and reclaimed his throne.

Mutilation and exile had obviously not improved Justinian's temper, but he acted more prudently after his restoration than might have been expected. Though he executed both Tiberius and Leontius, his own example had shown that mutilation was not enough to keep an emperor deposed. He soon became embroiled in wars with the Arabs and his recent allies the Bulgars, but he held his own until his former place of exile in the Crimea revolted against him with help from the Khazars. A naval expedition that he sent against the Crimea, presumably involving the Carabisian Theme, joined the rebels in proclaiming a new emperor, Philippicus. In 711 Philippicus sailed to Constantinople and overthrew and beheaded Justinian.

The least impressive usurper to date, Philippicus tried to repudiate the anti-Monothelete Sixth Ecumenical Council, which was unpopular in his native Armenia. He fared poorly in wars with the Arabs and Bulgars, and after two years was blinded by the Count of the Opsician Theme. But the head of the imperial chancery outmanoeuvred the count, whom he blinded in his turn, taking the crown for himself. The new emperor, Anastasius II, was a man of marked ability, who could say that he was not a rebel and in fact had punished one. Nonetheless, after five rebellions, overthrowing emperors had almost become a custom.

By this time the caliph, seeing the Byzantines in such disarray, was planning an attempt to take Constantinople outright. The Arabs advanced along the coast and through the interior of Anatolia. Anastasius strengthened the fortifications of the capital, and sent an army to Rhodes to attack the Arabs in 715. Once arrived there, however, some soldiers from the Opsician Theme led a revolt against Anastasius, perhaps in revenge for his having blinded their count two years before.

The rebels returned, besieged Constantinople, and installed yet another emperor, the reluctant Theodosius III. Though Anastasius agreed to abdicate and become a monk, with the Arabs swarming over Anatolia the Anatolic and Armeniac themes refused to accept Theodosius. They proclaimed the Anatolic *strategos* emperor as Leo III. Amid mounting chaos, Theodosius too abdicated and became a cleric in 717, and Leo entered Constantinople, not very far ahead of the Arabs.

Leo III took over an empire shaken by seven violent revolutions in twenty-two years and a recent civil war, and facing the most formidable assault on its capital it had ever seen. He had only a few months to prepare before an immense Arab army and navy, reportedly of 120,000 men and 1,800 ships, arrived to put the city under siege. The Arabs built a fortified camp that extended the full distance of the land walls, and had the ships to blockade the city by sea as well. If the capital fell, the rest of Anatolia was likely to follow, and the rest of the empire not much later.

No sooner had the Arab fleet arrived, however, than the Byzantines attacked it with Greek Fire. The losses the Arabs suffered frightened them into keeping the rest of their ships in port, so that the Byzantines could resupply the city by sea. Leo had made an alliance with the Bulgar khan, who sent raiders to harry the foraging parties of the Arabs. It proved extremely difficult to supply the huge Arab army with food. The winter was unusually bitter, tormenting the Arabs in their camp with unaccustomed snow and cold. Many of the besiegers died.

In spring 718 the caliph sent a new army and fleet as reinforcements. But when the fleet arrived, many of its crewmen, who were Egyptian or African Christians, deserted to the emperor. Leo ambushed the reinforcing army as it approached Constantinople, and its survivors fled without ever crossing the Bosphorus. The remaining besiegers, suffering from hunger, disease, and Bulgar raids, raised their siege after thirteen months. Though their army evacuated Anatolia without opposition, most of their fleet succumbed to storms, Byzantine attacks, and a volcanic eruption in the Aegean Sea as the ships passed by. Duly impressed by their devastating failure, the Arabs never made a serious effort to take Constantinople again.

Even if Byzantium had survived the worst the Arabs could do, its troubles were far from over. The caliphate was still much stronger than the empire. Though Leo III plainly owed his victory not only to luck but to his talents and resolve, the very next year the deposed emperor Anastasius II tried to overthrow him with the support of the Opsician Theme and the Bulgars, and nearly succeeded. Byzantine Italy had rebelled during the siege, and some of it, including Sardinia, was lost for good. Byzantine attempts to regain some eastern border territory came to nothing, and the Arabs soon resumed raiding Anatolia as before.

Like many Byzantines, Leo seems to have attributed Byzantine failures since the rise of the Arabs to divine anger. But he was not quite sure in what respect the empire was displeasing God. First Leo tried forcing the empire's Jews to convert to Christianity. Probably in the spring of 726, he issued a short new law code, the *Ecloga*, full of such biblically inspired prescriptions as the death penalty for homosexual acts (Romans 1: 24–32) and bodily mutilation for many other crimes (Matthew 5: 29–30, Mark 9: 43–8). Leo also began to think that the Byzantines' habit of venerating religious pictures might break the biblical commandment against idolatry. When the volcano in the Aegean erupted again in the summer of 726, Leo ordered his soldiers to take down the icon of Christ over the palace gate (see Chapter 6).

Though apparently surprised that this act provoked a riot, the emperor seems to have issued an edict against icons the same year. In 727 the Carabisian Theme and the Theme of Hellas rebelled against him, possibly because of the edict; but he defeated them. In 730 he banned all icons. The patriarch Germanus abdicated in protest, and Pope Gregory III declared Iconoclasm a heresy, opening a schism with Byzantium and virtually declaring his independence. Leo sent a naval expedition against Rome that failed, but he deprived the papacy of jurisdiction over southern Italy and Greece, assigning them to the patriarchate of Constantinople. In political terms, Iconoclasm seemed a dead loss, though Leo chose to give it credit for a victory he won over Arab raiders in 740.

In 741 Leo managed to die of natural causes while still reigning, as his six predecessors had failed to do. He had certainly improved upon their record.

Inscription in the walls of Nicaea in the names of Leo III, Constantine V, and the curopalate Artabasdos commemmorating the deliverance of that city from the Arabs 'with divine help' in 727.

139

He had kept his nerve during the terrible Arab siege of Constantinople, and afterwards had slowly restored the empire's defences. A good ruler, if not a great one, he had shown enough moderation in his Iconoclasm to limit its ill effects. His reign had been the longest since that of Constans II, who had himself been assassinated, and he left a son, Constantine V, old enough to rule at age 22.

Leo had at least broken the cycle of revolutions that had encouraged the Arabs to think they could destroy the empire. Yet he had found no lasting solution to the problem of rebellious themes. Within a month of his death, his son and heir Constantine V was attacked by Artavasdos, Leo's son-in-law and Count of the Opsician Theme. Artavasdos defeated Constantine, seized Constantinople, and held it for two years before Constantine managed to starve him out, retake the city, and blind him in 743.

Not long after putting down the revolt, the emperor broke up Artavasdos' Opsician Theme, the empire's largest, which had rebelled so many times. He apparently reassigned more than half its men to six new units called *tagmata* ('regiments'). These were stationed in and around the capital, some on the territory of the Opsician Theme and Theme of Thrace. The three principal *tagmata* were the Scholae, the Excubitors, and the Watch, previously companies of guards that had long declined into unimportance. Their commanders, most of them styled domestics, were directly responsible to the emperor.

Even if Constantine V founded the *tagmata* primarily to weaken the Opsician Theme, as Constans II had founded the themes to save money, they turned out, like the themes, to have incidental military advantages. While tagmatic soldiers appear to have held military lands like those of thematic soldiers, they were more mobile troops, intended more for offensive campaigns than for garrison duty. Constantine seems to have used them for the first time to conquer land on the Thracian frontier from the Slavs, and then to capture Christian settlers in the Arab borderlands for resettlement in this new land in Thrace.

The creation of the *tagmata* and the successes he gained with them won Constantine the loyalty of most of his troops, but the policy of Iconoclasm he had inherited from his father made him unpopular with many people in the empire and almost everyone abroad. In 751 the Lombards took Ravenna and the tiny Exarchate around it. Byzantine rule in Italy lapsed outside the far south, which was already a separate Theme of Sicily, and a few practically independent enclaves, like Naples and Venetia. Iconoclasm had put Byzantium in schism not only with the whole western Church but with the orthodox patriarchates of the East. Nothing daunted, Constantine held a council in 754 that proclaimed venerating icons to be heretical.

Constantine's expansion in Thrace, though it came only at the expense of the Slavs, alarmed the nearby and much stronger Bulgars. They began to raid across the frontier. In 759 the emperor retaliated with a full-scale campaign, defeating the Bulgars in a bloody battle and forcing them to make a truce. When they repudiated this truce four years later, Constantine attacked again, and again won a hard-fought victory. He prepared a land and sea expedition against them once more in 766, only to have his fleet wrecked by a storm. Though undefeated in the war, he had lost a good many men for no particular advantage.

Returning to Constantinople, Constantine discovered a formidable iconophile conspiracy against him. Its ringleaders were some of his most powerful civil officials and military commanders, including the *strategoi* of the Opsician Theme and the Theme of Thrace and the Domestic of the Excubitors. He executed or blinded the lot of them, and executed the patriarch of Constantinople the next year for complicity in the plot. Appointing new and more loyal officers, Constantine intensified his persecution of iconophiles, and his favour to iconoclasts.

Though the Arabs were raiding Anatolia again, Constantine concentrated his efforts on the Bulgars. He defeated them once, in 774, but the next spring another storm damaged the fleet he was sending against them. Then the Bulgar khan tricked him into revealing the names of the Byzantine spies in Bulgaria, whom the Bulgars killed. Constantine led another expedition against them in the autumn, but before reaching Bulgar territory he suddenly fell ill and died.

An effective general but no diplomat, Constantine had won a generally good reputation among his soldiers and bitter hatred among iconophiles, who still appear to have been in the majority in the Church and the bureaucracy. Although his harsh enforcement of Iconoclasm and neglect of the West contributed to the empire's definitive loss of central Italy, his creation of the *tagmata* and military efforts had won some modest gains in Thrace from the Bulgars and allowed some easy raids on the territory of the squabbling Arabs. Of his two main legacies, the strength of the *tagmata* proved to be more lasting than the divisiveness of Iconoclasm.

For only the second time since 641, the succession was uneventful, as the crown passed to Constantine's oldest son Leo IV. Though his enemies gossiped that Constantine had homosexual tendencies, he had married three times and left five sons besides Leo. The year after his accession, Leo had to suppress a plot by his bodyguards to replace him with one of his brothers. The emperor tried to calm the passions aroused by his father's iconoclast measures by appointing monks and even some secret iconophiles as bishops. But in 780 Leo was enraged to discover that members of his household had supplied icons to his own wife Irene. Soon after punishing them and banishing her from his bed, he died under suspicious circumstances, leaving her to rule for their young son.

By 780 Byzantium had emerged from a horrendous period of military defeat and internal unrest to regain a measure of stability and security. Its losses to the Arabs had been catastrophic, and the Bulgars and especially the Arabs remained fearsome enemies. After so many examples of successful revolts, Byzantine emperors were in much greater danger of deposition than they had been before 602. Yet in the themes and the *tagmata* the emperors had found a means of defending most of their territory. Once divided into smaller units, the themes were less likely to rebel, or to prevail if they did. Although Byzantium could expect many trials to come, for the present it no longer had to struggle for bare survival. The immediate danger of collapse, anarchy, or complete conquest by enemies had passed. After so many perils, reaching this point of safety was no mean accomplishment.

The Transformation of Social Structures

Few states have long survived such devastating losses as Byzantium suffered at this time. The lost territories included Syria, Egypt, northern Mesopotamia, Armenia, North Africa, and most of Italy and the Balkans. Of its major regions, Byzantium kept only Anatolia entire; of its three largest cities, Constantinople, Antioch, and Alexandria, it kept only the first. Along with these lost territories, it lost almost all of its Monophysites and speakers of Latin, Syriac, and Coptic. Unlike the more diverse sixth-century empire, that of the eighth was overwhelmingly Chalcedonian Christian, Greek-speaking, and rural. Byzantium was also a good deal less prosperous, populous, and secure than it had been in the sixth century.

While these broad generalizations are reasonably certain, any more detailed description of this phase of Byzantine history must be partly speculative and more or less controversial. Our unsatisfactory written sources provide few descriptions of what Byzantium was like. The patchy coverage of Byzantine remains by archaeologists has left a more than usually ambiguous picture. Although some historians conclude that Byzantium weathered the seventh century as an organized state not fundamentally different from the earlier Roman empire, others maintain that Byzantium became a radically different and less organized society more like early medieval western Europe.

The worst problem is that, though this disagreement is essentially a matter of scale, we have only the scantiest statistical evidence. Archaeology seems to indicate that the inhabited area of most Byzantine cities fell by a little more than half between the sixth century and the eighth; but it is debatable which side of the argument this finding supports, especially because most Byzantine cities continued to exist. Those who believe in a thorough transformation cite the drastic falling off in coin finds at archaeological sites after the mid-seventh century; those who argue for more continuity note relatively high recorded figures for the army's size and payroll. Yet the significance and reliability of all this evidence is disputed.

Though a good case can be made that the truth lies somewhere in between the most extreme positions, such statistical evidence as we have supports the defenders of a measure of continuity. Their opponents are reduced to rejecting that evidence, and assuming that the tendency of several numbers from very different sources to agree is coincidental. As for the decrease in coin

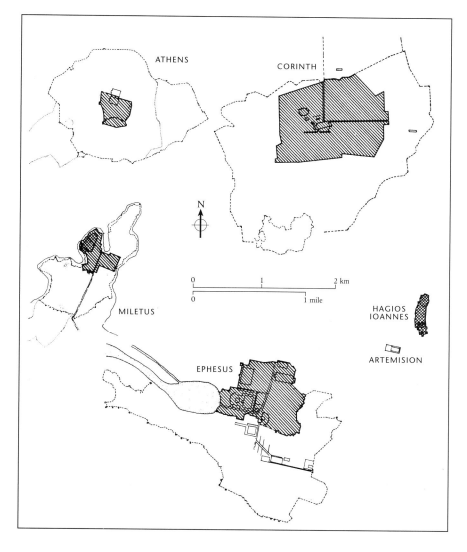

Plans of several cities drawn to the same scale, showing their contraction within their ancient walls and further reduction in the seventh/eighth centuries (cross-hatched).

143

Plan of Thessalonica. Only in a few cases, like Thessalonica and Constantinople, physical features and access to the sea did not allow a contraction of the fortified area, much of which was probably given over to orchards and fields.

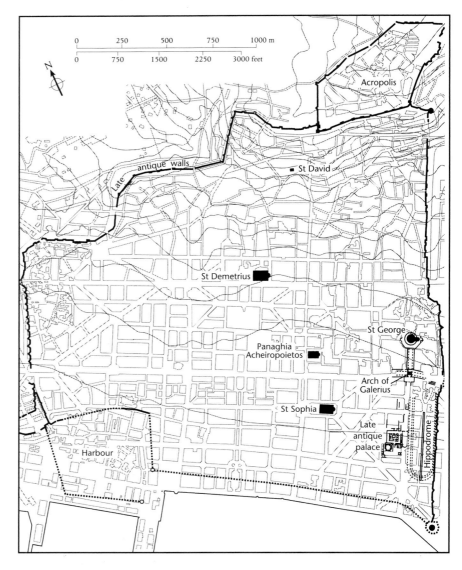

finds after 659, its abruptness seems to indicate not a gradual social evolution but a sudden administrative change, most likely the replacement of most of the army's pay with military land grants as suggested above.

Faced by a persistent military threat to the empire's existence, the government had to give priority to preserving and paying its army. Given its territorial losses, it succeeded remarkably well. In 565 the Byzantine army is fairly reliably recorded at 150,000 men. In 641 a payroll figure indicates that it still had about 109,000 men. This meant that Byzantium was supporting nearly three-quarters as many soldiers as in 565 with about half as much land. Moreover, in 773 the Byzantine army is said to have totalled 80,000 men.

This meant supporting more than half as many soldiers as in 565 with less than a third as much land. Although the total for 773 has been doubted, ninth-century figures closely corroborate it, and any number much lower would make Byzantium's surviving the Arab onslaught almost inexplicable.

The contrast between Byzantium's losses of land and much smaller losses of soldiers seems to show a well-executed strategy on the part of Heraclius and his successors to withdraw soldiers to safety rather than risk them in desperate attempts to defend the frontiers. It seems also to show a successful effort to maintain a large army without the help of tax revenues from many lost lands and subjects. Such maintenance was apparently the function not only of the soldiers' land grants but of another somewhat mysterious feature of the time: the provincial warehouses attested after 659 by hundreds of lead seals. These seals, originally attached to documents or goods, bear the names both of the warehouses and of the officials who ran them on government contracts, the *kommerkiarioi* (*commerciarii*).

While *kommerkiarioi* are known to have collected customs duties and dealt in silk, gold, and slaves, the proliferation of their seals at this date can hardly reflect an increase in commerce. The years beginning in 659 must have been a time of economic contraction in Byzantium, when people were becoming

In the Middle Ages the centre of Ephesus shifted from the harbour site to the nearby hill, now called Ayasuluk (Ayos Theologos) on which stood the great shrine of St John the Evangelist. The summit of the hill was later fortified as a separate citadel.

The so-called Gate of Persecution is made of ancient spolia and leads into the walled settlement of Ayasuluk. It may date from the eighth century.

poorer, trade routes less safe, cities smaller, and coins rarer. One clue to the mystery is that the most active *kommerkiarios* of the years from 659 to 668, Stephen the Patrician, who has left ten seals of five warehouses from at least three themes, also served as Military Logothete, the government minister responsible for paying the army. Probably the major function of these warehouses was to sell arms and uniforms to the soldiers, who, even if they were supposed to pay their own way, still needed reliable places to buy their equipment.

146

The militarization of society during this period was pervasive. The old provinces with their civilian governors were replaced by the themes, which the *strategoi* and their subordinates administered under what amounted to martial law. Soldiers took possession of a substantial portion of the land, in grants large enough that they must have had a number of relatives, tenants, or hired hands to farm for them. The military payroll, even paid at about a quarter of the old rate as it seems to have been, would still have dominated the state budget and monetary economy. In the chaotic period between 695 and 717, the army repeatedly made and unmade emperors. In contrast to the period between Theodosius I and Heraclius, most emperors were themselves generals, and often led armies against the enemy.

With the ascendancy of the army, the civil service became smaller and less influential. The time of the creation of the themes around 660 also saw a reduction and reorganization of the central bureaucracy. Most of the old ministers either disappeared, like the *Comes rei privatae* who had managed the vanished imperial estates, or became less important, like the *Magister officiorum* whose office became the honorary title of Magister. Now the chief ministers were three officials called logothetes: the Postal Logothete (*Logothetēs tou dromou*), who, besides the postal service, managed foreign relations and internal security, the General Logothete (*Logothetēs tou genikou*), in charge of taxation, and the Military Logothete (*Logothetēs tou stratiôtikou*), already mentioned as the army's paymaster. The entire central bureaucracy seems to have

In many excavated urban sites the number of stray coin finds in base metal drops to almost nil towards the end of the seventh century and shows slow recovery from the ninth onwards with a peak in the eleventh-twelfth. This pattern (which does not apply to either Constantinople or the village of Dehes in Syria where Byzantine coin circulated) has been viewed as showing a drastic decline of a monetary economy during the Dark Age.

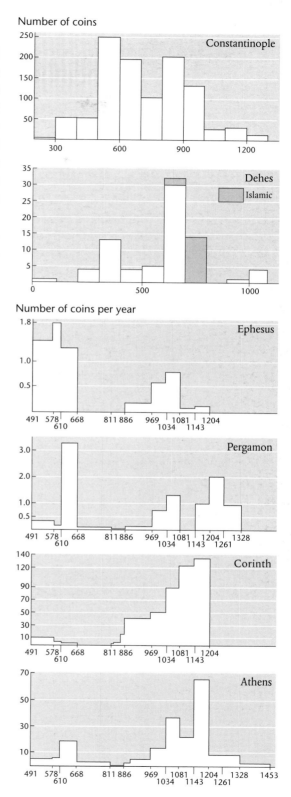

147

shrunk to about six hundred men. Scarcely any civil officials survived in the provinces except for tax collectors, including the *kommerkiarioi*.

Enemy invasions and the empire's need to defend itself against them had a profound effect on the life of its subjects, as appears clearly from excavations of towns. During the seventh century the Byzantines abandoned the Hellenistic and Roman fashion for monumental cities with a gridiron plan, wide streets, open squares, and large public buildings. Such cities had become an unaffordable luxury in a time of populations reduced by plague and sudden enemy invasions and sieges. Except for a few cities that already had strong fortifications, like Constantinople and Thessalonica, the inhabitants saved expense and effort by building walls only around the most defensible areas. They abandoned large parts of most cities, and even moved some cities from plains to more easily defended sites on hills.

The smaller and hillier sites of these new cities, most of which are better called towns, required that the streets be narrow and irregular and the size of squares and large buildings restricted. Except in Constantinople itself, townsmen had to do without hippodromes and theatres, and to make do with smaller churches and baths than before. Although the resulting towns were much less grand than those of the earlier Roman empire, they were hardly more cramped or untidy than those of classical Greece or of Renaissance Italy. Though the urban life of Byzantium in this period was far less vital than in either of those, the reasons had more to do with militarization and a general cultural and economic decline than with the towns' size or aspect.

One significant change was that the Byzantine towns had lost most of their administrative importance. They no longer had city councils responsible for governing and taxing the countryside. The decurions, prosperous landholders who had served on the councils, disappeared as a class, though some landholders must have continued to live in the towns, along with the bishops who still had jurisdiction over the surrounding regions. As trade declined along with the coinage, towns also lost some of their function as markets. The importance of their new role as places of refuge during enemy raids is evident from their often being called simply forts (*kastra*).

Another important change in the towns, evident even at Constantinople, was cultural decline. In the earlier Byzantine period, most of the better educated people had been senators, decurions, and civil servants, or teachers who trained them. These were the men who had written and read most secular literature, and their relatives became the ecclesiastics who wrote and read most religious literature of any sophistication. Now that the decurions had disappeared and the senators had merged with the civil service, which in turn had become smaller and less prestigious, education and literature inevitably suffered. Though practically all military officers and clerics were literate, they generally contented themselves with an elementary education.

Literature tended to become limited to sermons, hymns, hagiography, and some theology, all displaying few literary pretensions. Only enough history was recorded to leave us a bare account of the main sequence of events. The *Ecloga* of Leo III, in which the emperor complains of the ignorance of the lawyers of his time, is a pathetic document to set beside the *Justinian Code*. The Quinisext Council's strictures against those who destroyed or discarded religious books, saying nothing of secular ones, give a dismal picture of the decline of education. Yet the destruction of books cannot have been catastrophic, because in the subsequent period the Byzantines still possessed most of the literature that they had had in the sixth century.

The changes of the seventh century appear to have been somewhat less pronounced in the villages, where, as before, the bulk of the empire's population lived as farmers. In most of the countryside enemy raids would have occurred at least once a generation, but they were more frequent in regions easily accessible from the frontier. In the most exposed areas, the rich evidently weathered the insecurity better than the poor, so that the largest landholders were now to be found on the Anatolian plateau, where the Arabs raided most often. In the more secure coastal plains, large landholders apparently became quite rare, probably because a general decline in population had increased the value of labour and reduced that of land.

Demographic decline was probably the main reason for an economic contraction that affected both the towns and the country in this period. The bubonic plague that had first struck in the sixth century returned again and again. The epidemic in Constantinople from 747 to 748 caused so many deaths that Constantine V repopulated the city with settlers from Greece. The last recorded outbreak of the plague within the empire came in southern Italy as late as 767. Enemy raids also discouraged population growth, and the condition of the economy did nothing to encourage it.

The rarity of the gold coins used for large transactions, and the greater rarity of the copper coinage used for everyday buying and selling, would not so much have reflected a reduction in trade as caused one. The government minted coins not for the convenience of private citizens but for its own purposes, which meant primarily to pay and supply the army. When the state circulated fewer coins, private traders would have needed to resort to barter more often, putting up with the inconvenience of shipping and storing bulky and perishable goods instead of small and durable coins.

Because even the soldiers would have had less cash, the *kommerkiarioi* who ran the provincial warehouses probably accepted the products of the soldiers' farms as payment for their arms and armour. If so, the warehouses would have come to serve as trading posts for all sorts of goods, making up for some of the inefficiencies of barter and paying out coins when necessary, even if at a premium. Practically everyone still needed coins, if only to pay his taxes. In 767 our sources report a sort of monetary panic, in which farmers were forced to sell their goods at absurdly low prices to get the money to pay their taxes.

In comparison with earlier Byzantine times, the rich appear to have been poorer and the poor richer. The old senatorial class had vanished by the end of this period, having succumbed to too many political revolutions and too much demographic and economic change. The rural magnates of the Anatolian plateau came from fairly new families, many of them Armenian; they earned most of their income from ranching rather than rents, and aspired to careers in the army rather than the civil service. They became richer and more powerful than civil servants and merchants, who were themselves poorer than they had been in the sixth century.

Yet most peasants seem to have owned farms of sufficient size and fertility, and to have lived without worrying about exactions from anyone but tax collectors. When a peasant defaulted on his taxes, the other peasants of his village were expected to make up the difference, and usually they seem to have been able to do so. Bad weather was presumably as common as ever, and enemy raids were worse than before. But with enough land available for the reduced population, anyone who survived a bad year could mend his fortunes. Rural slaves and the urban poor had become insignificant groups.

The Dark Age of the seventh and eighth centuries left Byzantine society more primitive than before, but still recognizably the descendant of late Roman society. Unlike contemporary western Europe, Byzantium kept most of the superstructure of the Roman state, including its system of taxation, professional army, civil service, monetary economy, and secular schools. All of these were scaled back, often drastically, out of economic necessity, so that the public sector shrank more than the private sector. But the Byzantine state remained large enough to give its emperors greater powers than any king or emperor in the early medieval West, and to give Byzantium the ability to withstand the similarly organized caliphate.

Icons ⚬⚬⚬⚬⚬⚬⚬⚬⚬⚬⚬⚬⚬⚬⚬⚬⚬⚬⚬⚬⚬⚬⚬⚬⚬⚬⚬⚬⚬⚬⚬⚬⚬

CYRIL MANGO

The word icon is defined in the *Oxford English Dictionary* as a devotional painting usually on wood, of Christ or another holy figure, especially in the eastern Church. By so restricting its meaning, we are following Russian rather than Greek usage, for in Russian the term *ikona* is confined to religious representations, whereas Greek *eikon* means a likeness of any kind, both literally and metaphorically. We usually assume that the Orthodox icon was not meant to be a naturalistic portrait. While preserving the lineaments of the human figure, it trans-

Portraits on wooden panels, often highly naturalistic, were used in Egyptian mummy cases. Here that of a priest of the second century AD, excavated at Hawara.

Icon of Christ executed in the encaustic technique, probably sixth century. It has been cut down on both sides and partly repainted. Mount Sinai, monastery of St Catherine.

Commemorative mosaic depicting St Demetrius in his church at Thessalonica between two 'founders', probably of the middle of the seventh century. This work has often been quoted as an example of the 'abstract' style.

Icon of St. Nicholas of the eleventh century, now fully evolved as a devotional object, with greater emphasis placed on ornament than on the human figure. Mount Sinai, monastery of St Catherine.

poses them (or so it is said) to a higher, unearthly level of reality by observing a tradition established 'by the Fathers'.

It is certainly true that, after the Council of 787, Orthodox painters were not free to follow their fancy, but had to adhere to accepted formulas. St Nicholas, e.g. was always a man with a short, curly, grey beard, dressed in episcopal vestments and holding a gospel book. He could not be shown with a black beard, for then the worshipper would not recognize him as St Nicholas. The bishop with a black beard was St Basil. It is also the case that medieval and later icons tended towards abstraction, accentuated by a frontal pose and a plain gold background, although the degree of their lifelikeness varied somewhat with the style of the period.

There is nothing, however, in the Orthodox doctrine of sacred painting to say that icons had to be abstract and non-naturalistic; indeed, that doctrine assumes the opposite, while ignoring the finer issues posed by the problem of likeness. The earliest preserved icons—the best ones to have survived are in the monastery of St Catherine on Mt. Sinai and date from about the sixth century—are painted in a realistic style, which reminds us of the funerary portraits of the Roman period found in the cemeteries of Egypt. We know from literary sources that portraiture was very widespread in Late Antiquity—portable portraits were put up of emperors, dignitaries, living bishops, popular actors, and dancing girls—and there is no reason to think that saints were represented in a different style. The images which the iconoclasts sought to banish were not 'icons' as we conceive them today.

6 Iconoclasm

PATRICIA KARLIN-HAYTER

Iconoclasm, literally the smashing of images, is the term designating the movement that forbade the making or veneration of images, whether of God or of saints. The opposite position we usually call Iconoduly, although that word is not attested in Greek. Byzantine Iconoclasm was initiated in 726 or 730 by Leo III, reversed in 787 by the empress-regent Irene, restored in 815 by Leo V, and suppressed for good in 843 by another empress-regent, Theodora. Making allowance for the iconodule interlude, it is customary to speak of the First and the Second Iconoclasm.

No other topic of Byzantine history has received as much attention on the part of western scholars, chiefly because the Iconoclasm of the eighth and ninth centuries has been seen as the ancestor of similar initiatives stemming from the Reformation, starting with Calvin and going on to the Puritans and even the French revolutionaries of 1789. The iconoclasts, enemies of 'superstition', have generally enjoyed a sympathetic press.

It is difficult to give a balanced appraisal of Byzantine Iconoclasm. Few historians still hold it to have been the greatest issue of the period, with every Byzantine deeply involved except for a servile episcopate. One thing emerges clearly: the vast majority of the upper ranks took the change in either direction in their stride. Theoktistos had been Theophilos' trusted collaborator in enforcing Iconoclasm, but when the latter's widow decided to reverse the official line, he was no less hers in restoring veneration of images; nor was he an exception. The Church, whether bishops and priests or monks and holy men, did not react uniformly. Indeed, one may doubt whether militant support of Iconoduly, even by 'saints', necessarily stemmed from real commitment. Even St Theodore the Studite, the most redoubtable of iconodule apologists, could say of the iconoclast bishops reintegrated after the Council of 787 that 'their transgression had not been over essentials'. As for the masses, when Leo III first decreed Iconoclasm, it is likely they were convinced that this emperor, who had brought Constantinople through a terrifying Arab siege, enjoyed God's especial favour.

The two historians of the First Iconoclasm, namely Theophanes the

'Confessor' (d. 818) and the patriarch Nikephoros (in office 806–15), both suffered for the cause of images, yet their narrative is dominated by the Arab advance, plagues, famines, earthquakes, transfers of population, conflict with Bulgaria, and civil wars. Their iconophile slant is chiefly recognizable through the opprobrious epithets they bestow on the iconoclast emperors. Nikephoros' *Brief History* ends with the year 769. Theophanes carries on until 813. For the Second Iconoclasm all the available historical sources are iconophile and most of them were composed a full century after the relevant events, some of which, like the 'restoration of Orthodoxy' in 843, are presented in mutually contradictory versions. Outside the historians, our material consists almost exclusively in polemical literature of the winning side, Lives of 'martyrs' and 'confessors' (many of them of considerably later date and frequently commissioned by monasteries seeking to restore their reputation), Acts of iconodule councils, and, in particular, the correspondence of Theodore the Studite (d. 826), of whose 550 preserved letters at least 368 are concerned with the struggle against Iconoclasm. Obviously, the tale is going to be slanted.

Condemnation of holy images had been dominant in the early Church, due, in the first instance, to its Jewish roots, but theologians familiar with Greek philosophy, such as Origen or Clement of Alexandria, revoiced it in terms of that discipline, sometimes surprisingly parallel to those of pagan Neoplatonism. At no time had this condemnation disappeared. When Christian iconography was introduced, its use was at first justified by its didactic value ('the Bible of the illiterate'), but as we reach the second half of the sixth century, we find that images are attracting direct veneration and some of them are credited with the performance of miracles. They are increasingly seen as doubles of their sacred 'models', capable of speaking, exuding oil, and bleeding when stabbed. Canon law remained silent on the subject, except for the Quinisext Council (692), whose famous 82nd Canon recommended the representation of Christ in human form in preference to the

In several church pavements situated in Arab-held lands, especially in modern Jordan, human and animal figures have been excised and the spaces they had occupied patched up following an iconoclastic ordinance of caliph Yazid II (c. AD 721). Here the pavement at Umm el-Rasas, which was itself laid in 718.

symbolic figure of the Lamb, so as to give expression to the reality of the Incarnation. On the eastern borders of the empire, however, following the first wave of Arab conquests, Christians came under increasing accusations of idolatry, especially, it seems, on the part of Jews, and tried to justify themselves in a series of anti-Jewish dialogues. The debate attracted some attention within the empire. Before 726 the bishop of Claudiopolis (modern Bolu in Turkey) was a professed iconoclast.

Neither the exact date nor the manner of initiating imperial Iconoclasm is certain. Was the edict forbidding veneration of images issued in 726 or in 730 and was it preceded by public consultation? According to the Life of St Stephen the Younger, 'The wild beast [Leo III] summoned all his subjects to a rally and roared like a lion in their midst as he belched forth from his angry heart fire and sulphur (like Mount Etna), pronouncing these grievous words, "The making of icons is a craft of idolatry: they may not be worshipped".' Or did he begin not with words but with action, sending his dignitary Iouvinos to destroy the image of Christ above the gate of the imperial palace—an action which, unfortunately for the officer concerned, so irritated a group of pious females that they lynched him?

The patriarch Germanos (in office 715–30) was deposed for his opposition to Iconoclasm and consequently was made a saint. A eunuch, he is depicted beardless in this eleventh-century painting in the monastery of St Nicholas 'of the Roof' at Kakopetria, Cyprus.

What moved Leo III to forbid 'veneration'? The two historians nearest to the events, the patriarch Nikephoros and Theophanes, say that he took this measure in response to the eruption of the volcanic island of Thera in 726. To the medieval mind there was a direct correlation between unusual events and obedience or disobedience to God: catastrophes were His response to sin. After nearly a century of Muslim success and other disasters, He was now sending a final warning through this spectacular eruption. The emperor, a military man, Arab-speaking, born at Germanicea (now Maraş in eastern Turkey), certainly aware of the realities of the eastern frontier, knew he had to take appropriate action. He had earlier decreed compulsory baptism of Jews and Montanist heretics. This had not proved a success: 'The Jews washed off their baptism, ate before receiving the eucharist and defiled the faith. The Montanists set themselves a date, gathered in the house of their error and burnt themselves.' Leo endeavoured to face up to the eruption of Thera by forbidding the making and veneration of images.

Repeating Christ's suffering at the Crucifixion, the iconoclasts deface an icon of Christ by smearing it with whitewash. The sponge one of them is holding at the end of a stick repeats the sponge filled with vinegar that had been given to Christ. Miniature of the Khludov Psalter (ninth century).

The kind of veneration that was routinely addressed to icons—prostration, prayers, incense, the lighting of tapers (we even hear of an icon being made the godparent of a child)—may indeed have appeared excessive and going beyond the iconodule argument that it was directed not to the image, but to the person represented. Brushing aside the question of practice, iconodules annexed the whole issue to the domain of theology. Can God be represented? The answer had already been given by the Quinisext Council: in the 'new dispensation' (Christianity as distinct from Judaism) God incarnate can and ought to be depicted. Iconodule theologians reserved *latria* (worship) to God, allowing icons only *proskynesis*, here to be translated 'adoration'.

Theology in answer to Leo III's initiative begins with St John Damascene (*c.*675–*c.*749), safely ensconced in Palestine beyond the emperor's reach, who takes the step from affirmation of the legitimacy of icons to that of benefit derived from them: 'they reveal what is invisible or distant or to come', and also manifest the divine presence: 'Where Christ's symbol is, there He is also.' This approach, centred on the relationship between the image and its 'prototype', was to become the basis of the future theology of the conflict.

The emperor Leo had not made any theoretical contribution to the debate. Indeed, he does not appear to have regarded it in a theological light. What he saw was that the cult of icons practised by many of his subjects looked dangerously like 'falling down and worshipping images', which was forbidden by God (Deuteronomy 5: 9) as no one tried to deny. Nor does the evidence suggest that opposition to Iconoclasm was initially theological. The letters in defence of images of Germanos, patriarch of Constantinople, especially that addressed to Thomas, bishop of Claudiopolis (before 730), are practically unconcerned with either theology or idolatry. What worries Germanos is that the banning of images would only prove that the Church had been in error for a long time and so play into the hands of Jews and Muslims.

It was Constantine V at the Council of Hieria (754) who took the next decisive step: whereas Christ was composed of two natures, divine and human in perfect union, only his human ingredient could be delimited or circumscribed as was necessary for the act of painting him. By portraying Christ, therefore, one either divided the two natures or else circumscribed the divine as well. Both options were heretical. The uncircumscribability of the divine nature, more than any of the preceding arguments, turned mere error into heresy. Icons ceased to be a personal option: the very nature of the divine Economy was now in question.

Iconoclasm tends to be summed up as theology plus persecution, especially of monks. A critical review of the evidence hardly supports such a view. Persecution, when it occurred, appears to have been due more to political than to religious reasons. The best attested victim, St Stephen the

Iconoclastic cross replacing an image of a saint. The saint's name, written under the medallion, has been removed and the space filled in with gold tesserae. Mosaic in an annexe of the patriarchal palace, off the gallery of St Sophia, Constantinople.

Younger, had been implicated in a serious conspiracy against the emperor, in which a group of prominent military commanders and civil dignitaries had taken part. It was only then that Constantine V 'held up to public scorn and dishonour the monastic habit by ordering that each monk hold a woman by the hand and so process through the Hippodrome, while being spat upon and insulted by all the people'. There can be little doubt that prior to this monasteries had not been under attack—indeed, their rights are expressly respected in the law code known as the *Ecloga*, promulgated in the names of Leo III and Constantine, while the short list of monasteries said to have been desecrated by Constantine turns out on inspection to be highly dubious.

Under the Second Iconoclasm, communion with the patriarch was the test, and the operation was made as easy as possible: 'All we ask of you is to commune once with Theodotos [patriarch 815–21]. Then you will be free to go, each to his own monastery, keeping your own belief and opinions.' It is quite clear from the evidence of his own *Vita* that the austere Ignatios, the future patriarch, had been abbot of a monastery in communion with the official iconoclast Church. The correspondence of Theodore the Studite shows up a campaign of subversion. One of his letters, addressed to Pope Paschal, begs him to let the whole earth hear that 'those who have dared this have been synodically anathematized by you'. Pursuing papal excommunication of the emperor is an initiative whose implications may not be immediately obvious to a modern reader, but success would have been an encouraging signal to any potential usurper. Iconodule zeal manifested itself through lawbreaking up to and including treason. The patriarch Nikephoros actually deplores law-abiding under an iconoclast regime. Too many of the clergy, he says, 'go by political laws and recognize civil authorities. This is not Jacob's heritage, nor are such the ways of those whose dogma and thinking are ordered by piety'.

The popularity of the iconoclast emperors with the army and the masses cannot be doubted, nor can their deliberate pursuit of that popularity. Constantine V raised living standards at Constantinople for long after his death. The patriarch Nikephoros gives the reader the impression that his reign was remembered as one of plenty and cheap food: 'All their boasting about his time is nonsense'—in reality, he snorts, it was a time of 'plagues, earthquakes, shooting stars, famines

and civil wars', yet 'these utterly mindless lower animals brag and boast loudly about those happy days—of abundance, say they'. For Nikephoros the ultimate proof of Constantine's baseness lay in the lowly status of his supporters: 'I think this, too, worth mentioning, the kind of people they are, where they come from, how they live. Most of them don't even know the names of the letters of the alphabet and despise and abuse those who set store by education. The roughest and rudest of them are short even of the necessaries of life; they couldn't so much as feed themselves for a day, coming as they do from crossroads and alleys.'

The Life of St Stephen the Younger also gives the populace a prominent role. It is deliberately constructed, says its most recent editor, M.-F. Auzépy, 'to show that in his confrontation with Stephen, the emperor can do nothing without the backing of the masses, that he carries weight only in the territory of the common people in the street and the hippodrome'. Stephen was lynched to shouts of 'Punish him! Kill him!' for being the emperor's enemy.

Why did Iconoduly win in the end? Could it be because of the two female regents, Irene in 780, Theodora in 842? Not because, as women, they were particularly given to 'super-

Left: Detail of the Pala d'Oro on the high altar of St Mark's in Venice. On the left the Doge Ordelaffo Falier, who had the enamels of the Pala commissioned at Constantinople in 1105 (his head has been changed). On the right the empress Irene Doukaina, wife of Alexios I Komnenos.

Right: Mosaic (now destroyed) in the apse of the church of the Dormition at Nicaea (Iznik). The figure of the Virgin and Child, made in the ninth century, replaces an iconoclastic cross whose outline is clearly visible on the gold background. The cross, in turn, had been substituted for an earlier Virgin and Child dating probably from the late seventh century.

stitious' veneration of icons, but because they both loved power? Backed by power-groups condemned to stay in the background—carefully chosen civil servants, eunuchs ideally, or churchmen—they could hope to enjoy it. The alternative—entrusting their interests to a military commander—meant surrendering it completely. Neither empress has a dossier that suggests deep personal commitment to icons.

Irene ensured for herself the support of safe elements. The patriarch Paul, who had sworn an oath to maintain Iconoclasm, conveniently resigned or was made to resign (784) and was succeeded by Tarasios, who was head of the imperial chancery, hence a layman. It was decided to convoke an 'ecumenical' council, but it proved impossible to secure the presence of duly empowered legates of the eastern patriarchs (of Alexandria, Antioch, and Jerusalem), while the pope of Rome was represented by two relatively lowly priests. The council met at Constantinople in the church of the Holy Apostles (786) and was immediately dispersed by army units faithful to the heritage of Constantine V. After the necessary measures had been taken to neutralize opposition, the council reconvened a year later at Nicaea, evoking the memories of Constantine the Great and his condemnation of Arius; besides, Nicaea was easier to police. The resemblance of iconoclasts to Arians was made a theme of official propaganda.

Nicaea II obtained papal recognition and is regarded by the Orthodox Church as the Seventh and last Ecumenical Council, completing the dogmatic edifice erected by the six previous ones. It was attended by about 350 bishops and upwards of a hundred monks who, strictly speaking, had no business being there. Practically all the bishops in question had been ordained and had served under Iconoclasm. Ten of them, known to have been active iconoclasts, were forced to recant publicly. In the end everyone was reinstated in his post, and 'orthodoxy' prevailed until 815.

For Theodora, almost the only fact to emerge clearly from the confusion of the sources concerning the 'restoration of orthodoxy'—as the aftermath of Theophilos' death is termed—is the presence of potential male con-

Left: Iconoclastic cross in the apse of the church of St Irene, Constantinople. The church, which belonged to the episcopal complex, collapsed in the earthquake of 740 and was rebuilt in *c*.760.

The first gold coins struck after the restoration of images have the empress Theodora on the obverse and, on the reverse, figures of the young Michael III and his older sister Thekla. A bust of Christ, copied from that of Justinian II, was introduced a few years later.

The first major figural mosaic to have been put up in St Sophia after the restoration of images was the Virgin and Child in the apse (AD 867).

tenders who might have kept her on as nominal empress during what promised to be the long minority of her son, not yet three years old at the time. She therefore looked for support from men who could not mount the throne. If Irene's case is mainly one of deduction, Theodora's hagiographic Life states that as long as her husband lived, she 'dared not' let her Iconoduly be discernible. Naturally, when it became the official policy of the throne, the appropriate image of her was diffused. Some of this propaganda has come down to us and has coloured modern interpretations of the event.

The most direct consequence of the iconoclast affair concerned the development of Byzantine art. If Iconoclasm had won, church decoration would have been limited to the depiction of gardens and swirls of vegetation as in contemporary Umayyad mosques. Secular art would have gone on—indeed, Constantine V is censured for commissioning 'satanic' hippodrome scenes. The Umayyad caliphs likewise allowed and probably enjoyed non-religious pictures in their palaces and bath buildings. There was thus in the first half of the eighth century a temporary artistic convergence between the Byzantine and Arab realms, soon to be followed among Muslims by a complete ban on the depiction of all living creatures. Whether an iconoclast Byzantium would have gone down the same road is perhaps unlikely.

What happened in Byzantium as distinct from what might have happened is that Nicaea II not only 'restored' the cult of icons, but made it obligatory. The faithful were ordered to adore them. That was an infringement of individual conscience. It also forced artists to follow established, time-honoured formulas without deviation, for otherwise the icons they produced would not be 'true' icons.

Commerce

MARLIA MUNDELL MANGO

Merchants, bankers, and money-changers were generally held in low esteem and are sometimes represented suffering the torments of hell. To combat fraud the state kept a tight control of weights and measures, as stated in laws and in the tenth-century Book of the Prefect. Two types of weighing devices were used, the steelyard for relatively bulky items of low value, and the balance for lighter items, usually of high value (coin, spices). Steelyards had pendant weights often fashioned as an imperial bust, or as a bust of Athena/Minerva, a form inherited from the Roman period. Balances used copper-alloy flat weights marked either in pounds or ounces or in the equivalent number of gold coins indicated in Greek (*nomismata*) or Latin (*solidi*). Coin weights (*exagia*) are also made of glass and give the name of the Urban Prefect of Constantinople.

Shops and workshops in use in the early or medieval period have been excavated at Apamea, Ephesus, Justiniana Prima, Sardis, and Corinth (see Chapter 2). Most long-distance trade was conducted by ship. Navigation, confined to the fine season (April to October), was considered dangerous and did not lead to substantial profits. In Late Antiquity a major part of it, including the provisioning of the capital cities, was in the hands of the state, operating through hereditary guilds of subsidized shippers (*navicularii*) who were exempt from tolls or paid very low ones.

Even if private initiative was restricted, a lively inter-regional trade may be deduced from finds of transport amphorae. These were containers of commodities ranging from honey to fish-sauce, but were used especially for bulk transport of oil and wine by sea. Six main types of amphorae originated in the eastern Mediterranean. Their contents may be identified by stamps or inscriptions on the outside of the amphorae, or by carbonized remains within them. Early Byzantine amphorae have been found throughout the Mediterranean, in Britain, and along the Black, Red, and Arabian Seas. Their discovery on an archaeological site indicates trade with a particular area. Amphorae continued to be used in the medieval period. Specimens attributed to the eighth–tenth centuries have been found at Constantinople and

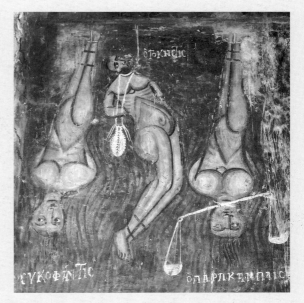

The dishonest merchant who cheated customers is shown suspended upside-down in a wall painting of the Last Judgement. His falsified weights and balance hang from his neck. Beside him dangle a usurer with a heavy purse and a false accuser. Thirteenth/fourteenth century.

Wooden boxes having compartments to hold a balance scale and a variety of weights have been found in Egypt. Sixth/seventh century.

Left: Inscription of *c.492* from Abydos on the Hellespont. The text which dates to the reign of Anastasius I refers to commodities (oil, wine, dry vegetables, bacon, wheat) shipped to Constantinople for distribution by the annona system. Ships from Cilicia are mentioned twice.

Below, top: The main types of transport amphorae from the late antique eastern Mediterranean probably originated in (1) northern Syria, (2) the Aegean, (3) western Asia Minor, (4) Gaza, (5) northern Palestine, and (6) Egypt. Type 1 is often said to have contained olive oil and Type 4, the well-known wine of Gaza.

Below, bottom: Several types of medieval transport amphorae have been identified. Types 1–3 of the ninth–eleventh centuries continue Types 1–3 of the earlier period. New types of amphorae with large handles appeared in the tenth/eleventh centuries (Type 4) and the twelfth/thirteenth (Type 5). Type 6 is a later version (twelfth–fourteenth centuries) of Type 2, and Type 7 dates to the thirteenth–fourteenth.

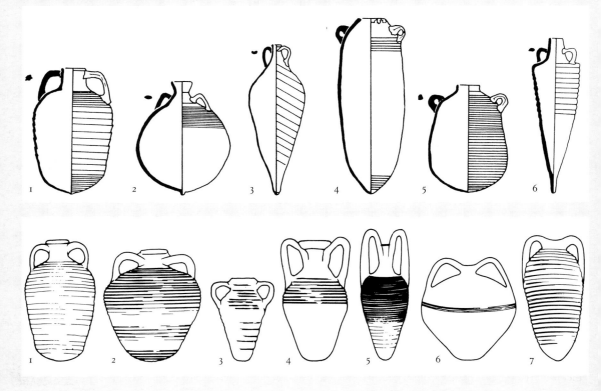

in the Black Sea area more than around the Mediterranean. From the eleventh century Byzantine amphorae are again found in large numbers throughout both seas. By the fourteenth century the use of clay amphorae had declined in favour of wooden barrels, due perhaps to the Italian monopoly of trade.

Table pottery was another staple of long-distance trade. Slipped red-bodied ceramic finewares with stamped or applied decoration were manufactured until the seventh century in North Africa, western Asia Minor, Cyprus, and Egypt, and enjoyed varying circulation in some cases throughout the Mediterranean. By the ninth century a dramatic technical shift occurred with the introduction of lead-glazed, white-bodied and then red-bodied finewares with painted, impressed, scratched, and excavated ornamentation. The white-bodied wares (ninth–eleventh centuries) may have been made at Constantinople, while at least some of the red-bodied wares (eleventh century onwards) were produced in factories excavated at Corinth. The later wares, of orientalizing decoration, enjoyed a wide circulation and have been recovered as cargoes from shipwrecks.

Marble likewise enjoyed a wide circulation in Byzantium. Marbles and other decorative stones were highly valued for statues, important monuments and in buildings, for columns, wall revetments, pavements, and furniture. Some of these marbles were quarried in Greece and Asia Minor (Bithynia, Phrygia). The island of Proconnesus in the Sea of Marmara produced much of the empire's standard architectural grey-white marble and was well placed for cheaper transportation by sea. A ship carrying marble from Proconnesus and quarries in Thessaly sank off the coast of Sicily in c.530. Its cargo included twenty-eight columns, bases, and capitals, slabs ornamented with crosses, and twelve colonnettes—all destined to serve as chancel screen, ambo, and altar in a church, perhaps in North Africa. Further documentation of the circulation of Byzantine Proconnesian marble has been established on the basis of several distinctive types of capital found dispersed around the Mediterranean.

When the Proconnesian quarries went out of production by the seventh century, they were eventually replaced by the abandoned ancient monuments in coastal cities which were quarried for their marble. In the medieval period, the ancient city of Cyzicus, situated on the Sea of Marmara, became a source of marble, both of pieces reused intact in nearby eighth-century monastery

Above: Marble capital with decorated cornucopias above a row of acanthus leaves. The *tabula* in the centre bears an inscription mentioning the emperor Heraclius, added during his reign. Similar capitals were used in the cathedral of Amorium and elsewhere. Sixth century.

Below: Marble cornice block decorated with a frieze of upright palmettes, carved in 907 for the church of Constantine Lips (today Fenari Isa Camii), Constantinople. The block is a reused funerary stele from Cyzicus.

buildings and recarved as new sculpture for buildings in Constantinople, such as the Lips monastery built in 907. Coloured marbles were also recycled as small pieces and as disks sliced from marble columns, both used in *opus sectile* pavements.

Other materials that were the object of international trade, as exports and/or imports, included metal, ivory, and silk. The empire produced high-quality silver plate in both the early period and the medieval. Its *cloisonné* enamels formed an important part of medieval ornament. Both silver and enamels were exported abroad (in trade, for diplomacy) or taken there by looting. Baser metal products formed the basis of a broader, more systematic export. These included bronze vessels in the early period and brass doors in the medieval.

Byzantine bronze basin with drop-handles and openwork base, excavated in an Anglo-Saxon tomb at Faversham in Kent, together with amethysts drilled in the Byzantine manner.

In the sixth–seventh centuries copper alloy objects produced in Byzantium were exported to western Europe, where about 120 have been found in burials. They include household items such as cast bronze drop-handle basins, washing sets, and hammered brass buckets, some decorated with hunting scenes and inscribed in Greek.

Panel of brass door at St Paul's Outside the Walls, Rome, made in 1070 at Constantinople. Between Christ and St Paul, the prostrate figure of the donor Pantaleon begs for mercy. The figures had silver inlaid faces, hands, and feet, now missing, while the inscriptions were inlaid with niello.

The latter have been found in Britain, Spain, the Levant, and Turkey. Comparable objects totalling 170 were found in burials in Nubia, south of Egypt. Fewer have been recovered within the empire, probably because they were not used as grave goods.

Another export industry is known in the eleventh century. Brass doors decorated with figures and scenes inlaid in niello and silver were manufactured in Constantinople for export to Italy. Their place of manufacture is clearly stated in inscriptions on the doors themselves which were acquired for churches in Amalfi, Venice, Rome, Monte Cassino, Salerno, and Monte S. Angelo, between 1060 and 1080 and in the twelfth century. None survives at Constantinople itself. The doors were imported into Italy by an Amalfitan family whose principal members, Pantaleon and Mauro, resided at Constantinople, had Byzantine honorific titles, and maintained commercial interests in Syria and Palestine. A bilingual Greek and Latin inscription on the Amalfi doors gives the name of the master craftsman as Symeon, while doors in St Paul's in Rome have bilingual Greek and Syriac inscriptions naming a Theodore and a Stavrakios. The Syriac inscription suggests an oriental link for this new industry at Constantinople.

Silk, spices, and ivory were important imports of international trade with the East, documented in part by Cosmas Indicopleustes, a merchant of Alexandria, scholar, astronomer, and theologian. His *Christian Topography* (536–47) included references to his trading experiences in the Mediterranean, the Red Sea, the Persian Gulf, and Sri Lanka. Byzantine commercial agents, *kommerkiarioi*, collected duty on imported goods; their lead seals give their names and locations. The medieval Book of the Prefect regulated foreign trade in Constantinople.

Ivory was imported from both Africa and India. The larger African tusks were probably used for plaques which measure up to 42 cm in height, while sections of the smaller Indian tusks could have been sliced for cylindrical caskets which are 8–10 cm in diameter. In contrast to these earlier caskets, most medieval oblong caskets had a wooden core to which thin plaques and strips were attached by pegs. As with the early plaques used for diptychs and the cylindrical caskets, there are signs of serial manufacture. Borders carved with rosettes were produced in long strips and cut as needed, while figural plaques appear repeatedly on different caskets. Medi-

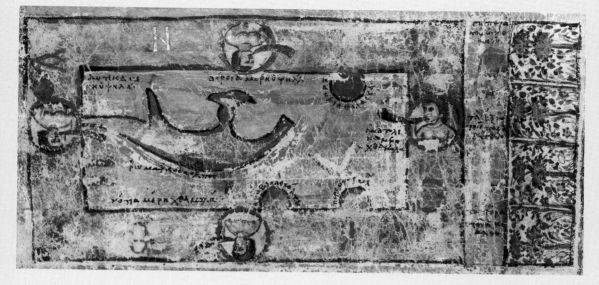

A map of the world illustrates the *Christian Topography* written in 536–47 by Cosmas Indocopleustes, a merchant of Alexandria. The ocean surrounds the earth and forms the Roman (Mediterranean) Sea, the Arab (Red) Sea, the Persian Gulf, and the Caspian Sea. Paradise lies along the right side. Eleventh-century manuscript. Mount Sinai, St Catherine's Monastery Library, cod. 1186.

eval ivory was supplemented by bone and some caskets were made entirely of bone, often skilfully carved.

Most numerous among early Byzantine ivories to survive are diptychs issued by the western and eastern consuls of the empire who changed every year, until 540 when the consulship was abolished. Although the surviving diptych plaques indicate mass production, their carving could be intricate and refined. The codicils of office, presented by the emperor, and tabellae shown in the *Notitia Dignitatum* were also of ivory. See p. 62.

Most medieval ivories are attributed to the tenth and eleventh centuries. Imperial plaques commemorate the coronations of the emperors Constantine VII Porphyrogenitus and Romanus II (pp. 222, 228). Religious ivory carvings include triptychs and caskets. Other caskets decorated with mythological, hunting, bucolic, or military subjects, constitute a relatively large body of secular art from the period. An outstanding example is the Veroli casket with mythological scenes (see p.228).

During the Byzantine period, silk was both imported and exported. Of the silk, flax, and wool textiles pro-

The ivory consular diptych of Areobindus (506) shows him seated on the consular lion-headed chair. Below are scenes of entertainments which he provided to the public during his year in office. The *tabulae ansatae* at the top of the leaves give his name (on the right) and titles (on the left) in Latin.

167

duced in Byzantium, silk was the most important commercially, and the Byzantine industry was renowned. Until the mid-sixth century raw silk was imported from the Far East into the Byzantine empire where it was woven into cloth. According to Procopius, Berytus and Tyre were the most important centres of the silk industry which was partly state monopoly, partly in the private sector. Imperial silk, reserved for the emperor, was tinted purple with murex shellfish dye at Tyre and Sidon. In 552 silkworms were brought into Byzantium, and by 568 mulberry plantations were established, apparently in Phoenicia. Although these factories were lost to the Arabs in the seventh century, Byzantium remained a major producer of silks. An imperial silk factory operated in the former Zeuxippos Baths in Constantinople and five silk guilds were regulated by the Book of the Prefect. Silkworms were cultivated in Byzantine south Italy, and both Thebes and Corinth in Greece were important centres of production. Two series of silks, with lions and with elephants, bear inscriptions stating that they were manufactured in the reigns of Leo VI (886–912), Romanus and Christopher (921–

3), Constantine VIII and Basil II (976–1025). Elaborate silks are depicted in imperial and other portraits. European churches preserve prestigious Byzantine silks woven from the eighth century on, for example in the tombs of Charlemagne at Aachen and S. Germain at Auxerre. Textiles in general formed an important part of domestic furnishings. Documents of the tenth–twelfth centuries preserved in the Cairo Geniza attest to the demand for Byzantine *mandils* (veils) and upholstery by brides in the Arab world.

The Islamic conquests of the seventh century diminished but did not completely disrupt the Mediterranean trade of Late Antiquity. Other factors at work were the decline of cities, now reduced to a level of self-sufficiency, the discontinuation of the state-sponsored provisioning of Constantinople, and the privatization of shipping. Conditions were beginning to improve by the tenth century, but the Byzantines, with their traditional anti-business ethos, did not profit greatly from the situation. Initiative passed instead to the Italian cities which gained trading concessions in the capital.

Silk compound twill decorated with roundels enclosing confronted elephants. An inscription woven into the silk states that it was made 'under Michael, *koitonites* and *eidikos*, and Peter, *archon* of the Zeuxippos', probably during the reign of Constantine VIII and Basil II. It was introduced into the tomb of Charlemagne by Otto III in 1000. Late tenth century.

7 The Medieval Empire (780–1204)

PAUL MAGDALINO

Byzantium in the Medieval World

The Byzantine empire in 780 was a territorial rump of its former self, confined to Asia Minor, the coastal fringe of the Balkans and the Crimea, the Greek islands, Sicily and the southern extremities of the Italian peninsula. In terms of Christian geography, it was co-terminous with only one of the five ancient patriarchates of the Church. The three eastern sees of Jerusalem, Antioch, and Alexandria had been under Arab domination for more than a century, along with the rich lands of Syria, Egypt, and Palestine which had been the economic and cultural power-house of the empire in the fourth to sixth centuries. The large Christian communities over which they had presided were diminished by conversion to Islam, and increasingly detached from Constantinople as Arabic replaced Greek in administration and intellectual discourse. In the West, much imperial territory in Europe—Sicily and those parts of mainland Italy and Greece which remained under imperial control—had formerly come under the see of Rome, but it was entirely characteristic of the new situation that ecclesiastical jurisdiction had been brought in line with political reality. The greater part of Latin Christendom had long fallen outside imperial control; from the mid-eighth century, Rome itself and the lands of the Roman Church in central Italy ceased effectively to belong to the empire of Constantinople. As a result of papal opposition to imperial Iconoclasm, but more particularly of the imperial failure to protect the papacy against the encroachment of a newly aggressive Lombard kingdom, the popes had invited the new Carolingian rulers of the Franks, Pepin and his son Charlemagne, to intervene in Italy. The papacy in theory resisted the substitution of one empire for another—it was at this time that the Roman Church invented the *Donation of Constantine* to claim that Constantine, in founding Constantinople, had relinquished imperial responsibility in Italy to the Pope. However, the practical outcome was that Charlemagne took over the Lombard kingdom of Italy as well as the emperor's role as protector of the Church.

After the death of Leo IV, his widow Irene, who took power for their young son Constantine VI, moved to end the empire's growing isolation from the rest of the Christian world. She renewed the negotiations for a marriage alliance with the Carolingians which had been cut short by the death of Pepin in 768, and preparations were made for Constantine to marry Charlemagne's daughter Rotrud. More cautiously, she worked to end the official policy of Iconoclasm in the Byzantine Church, and after the death of the patriarch Paul in 784 secured the election of a successor, Tarasios, who would co-operate with her to call an ecumenical council for the restoration of icons and Church unity. After an abortive meeting at Constantinople in 786, the council concluded its business at Nicaea the following year. By this time, however, Charlemagne had called off his daughter's betrothal and come into conflict with Byzantine interests in southern Italy and the Adriatic. In 788 the Franks defeated a Byzantine expeditionary force sent to restore the Lombard king Adelchis. In the circumstances, it is not surprising that Charlemagne refused to recognize the Council of Nicaea, on which he had not been consulted and which omitted all mention of him from its proceedings.

If the Byzantine government was hoping to divide Charlemagne from the papacy it was disappointed; their relationship remained close, and it culminated in the famous occasion on Christmas Day 800 when Pope Leo III crowned Charlemagne emperor. The question as to who took the initiative and who was doing the favour to whom has been open ever since, but there can be no question that Byzantium was seriously offended, or that even without the formality of the title Charles was imperial in ways that matched and surpassed the achievement of any contemporary Byzantine emperor. He chaired his own reforming Church council in 794. To the huge conglomeration of Germanic kingdoms which was his dynastic inheritance he added by consistent success in war. He all but terminated the political existence of two peoples who had caused the empire much grief: the Lombards, whose Italian kingdom he had annexed in 774, and the Avars, whose kingdom on the middle Danube he invaded in 791 and finished off in 795–6, thus winning for the Franks the fabulous treasures which the Avars had amassed from plunder and tribute, mainly at the expense of Byzantium. He exchanged embassies with the Abbasid caliph Harūn al-Rashid, who recognized him as the protector of the church of the Holy Sepulchre at Jerusalem: Charlemagne made conspicuous benefactions to the church of Jerusalem at a time when the Byzantine government was conspicuously unable to help.

The Carolingian empire was hardly the equal of the Abbasid caliphate in resources and sophistication, or in terms of the threat it posed to Byzantium. The Abbasid realm stretched from Tunisia to Central Asia, comprising all the ancient centres of civilization in the Near East, and dominating all the major trade routes between the Mediterranean and the Far East. It was one of the most bureaucratized and urbanized states in the world. It shared a long frontier with Byzantium from the Black Sea to the Mediterranean, and Islam confronted Orthodox Christianity with the challenge of an alternative monotheism which saw the conquest and conversion of the Christian world as one of its basic objectives, and preached the *jihād*, the struggle against non-Muslims, as a means to spiritual salvation. The Abbasids, with their capital at Baghdad and with a strong political orientation towards Iran, did not prioritize the conquest of Constantinople in the way their Umayyad predecessors had done, but they promoted the *jihād* all the more energetically, either leading campaigns in person or delegating them to the emirs of Syria and North Africa. This meant a constant pressure of annual raids into Asia Minor, the greater part of which remained a war zone, while on the maritime front the islands of the Mediterranean, all still Christian at the beginning of the ninth century, came under increasing attack. Thus in 827, the Aghlabids of al-Ifriqqiya (Tunisia) began the long conquest of Sicily, while a group of political exiles from Muslim Spain launched a successful invasion of Crete. Byzantium thus lost its two main island possessions in the central and western Mediterranean, with devastating consequences for the security of Italy, Greece, and the whole Aegean and Adriatic littoral.

The threat from the Carolingian empire was hardly of the same order. There are nevertheless parallels in the ways that both Abbasids and Carolingians challenged Byzantium over the legacy of Graeco-Roman antiquity. Both appropriated core areas of the Graeco-Roman world, but dominated them from power bases that were far from the Mediterranean and from cultural traditions that did not wholly identify with Rome. Both also appropriated enough of ancient culture for their propagandists to assert that the wisdom of the ancients, along with world domination, had deserted the Greeks and found a new home. The mutual recognition of Harūn al-Rashid and Charlemagne was thus significant for Byzantium. It signified that the continuation of the Roman empire in Constantinople was no longer the sole focus of the other great powers of the post-Roman world, but was fast becoming the smallest and weakest of the three. An observer of the world scene in 800 could well have concluded that if the end of the world was not imminent, the future of the western part of it lay with Latin Europe and Islam. It is no accident that both Harūn and Charlemagne were to become immortalized in literature and legend, whereas no contemporary Byzantine ruler left any reputation for greatness, apart from the partisan recognition that the empress Irene received for the restoration of icons. The empire in the decades around 800 was afflicted by humiliating military defeats, usurpations, and short reigns of emperors who all, apart from Irene, had bad relations with the Church. So bad had the situation become by 813 that a strong pressure group in Constantinople and in the army convinced the emperor Leo V that the solution lay in a return to the Iconoclasm that had seemingly guaranteed Leo III and Constantine V long reigns, a secure dynastic succession, and military success, above all against the Bulgars.

The empire's straitened circumstances derived not only from the constraints imposed by the superpowers to the east and west of it, but also, and more urgently, from the pressure of the medium-sized power to the north, with which it had to share domination of the Balkan peninsula. The greatest obstacle to the empire's revival was the presence to the south of the Danube of the Bulgar khaganate with its capital at Pliska and a southern frontier in the Hebros/Maritza valley only three days march from Constantinople. In 780 the Bulgar state had survived in close proximity to Byzantium for almost a century, taking advantage of the empire's internal problems and wars against the Arabs, and this survival had hardened it into an extremely tough political entity. Its Turkic ruling elite combined the military ferocity of the steppe people they had been with the agricultural resource base of the Slav peasantry they dominated, and with the skills of civilization acquired from Greek traders, captives, and defectors. The emperors Constantine V, Irene, and Nikephoros I all tried with some success to extend the area of imperial control in the frontier region of Thrace by fortification and resettlement, but their work was undone when Nikephoros I and his army were trapped by the Bulgar khan Krum in a valley near Sardica (modern Sofia) in 811. Nikephoros became the first emperor since Valens (378) to die in battle against a foreign enemy; Krum followed up his victory by terrorizing Thrace and threatening Constantinople. His sudden death from a stroke (814) gave Byzantium a reprieve, but the thirty-year peace concluded in 816 left the frontier where it had been in the mid-eighth century, and Krum's successors used the peace to expand northwestwards up the Danube and southwestwards towards the Adriatic.

The conversion of Bulgaria to Christianity was clearly inevitable; that Khan Boris (852–89, 893), baptized Michael in c.865, adopted the Christian religion

One of several boundary stones set up in the reign of King Symeon (AD 904) between Byzantium and Bulgaria. This one was found about 20 km north of Thessalonica.

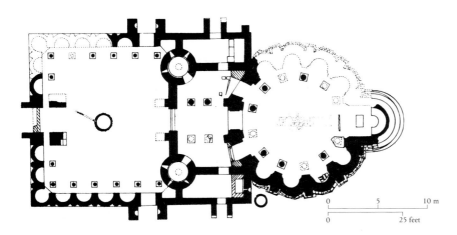

At the end of the ninth century Symeon of Bulgaria moved his seat to Preslav, which he adorned with many buildings, including churches. The Round Church, situated in the outer city, has no exact counterpart in contemporary Byzantine architecture.

in its Byzantine form, is seen as a triumph of Byzantine diplomacy. But it is questionable whether Byzantium would have undertaken the conversion if it had not been on the agenda of the Frankish Church and the papacy, or whether it was as advantageous to Byzantium as it was to Bulgaria. For all his deference to the emperor and patriarch of Constantinople, the convert-king used Christianity to define the separate identity of his kingdom, both culturally through the development of a Slavonic religious literature, and territorially through the establishment of new bishoprics under the jurisdiction of a semi-autonomous archbishop of Bulgaria. The new bishoprics were heavily concentrated in frontier areas, and thus served to define the partition

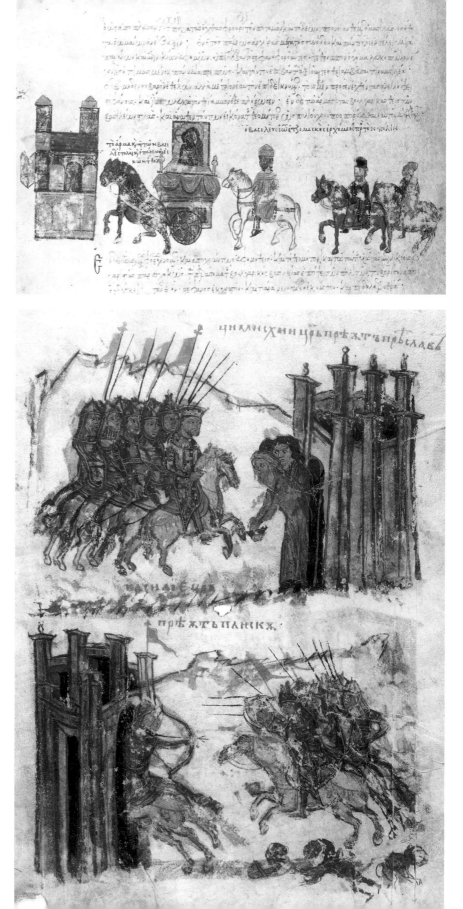

John Tzimiskes celebrates his triumphal return to Constantinople. In front of him an icon of the Virgin Mary is carried on a chariot. Miniature of the Chronicle of John Skylitzes, illustrated in southern Italy in the late twelfth century.

The emperor John Tzimiskes conquers Preslav in 972 (upper register). In the lower register Basil II captures Pliska in 1000. Miniatures illustrating the Bulgarian translation of the Byzantine chronicle of Constantine Manasses (fourteenth century).

of the Balkan peninsula to Bulgaria's advantage, as can be seen from the way the name Bulgaria came to apply to a vast swathe of territory stretching from what is now central Albania to the hinterland of Constantinople. Things did not improve for Byzantium when the convert-king was succeeded by a son who had been destined for the monastic life and educated in Constantinople. Perhaps because of this background, Symeon seems to have gone out of his way to demonstrate to those of his subjects with a nostalgia for paganism that he was no cloistered Byzantine puppet. The effect of seeing Byzantium from the inside was certainly to make him want the empire, or something very much like it, for himself. Though committed in principle to peaceful co-existence with Byzantium, he spent more than half of his thirty-three-year reign at war with its rulers in retaliation for being cheated out of what he considered to be his legitimate expectations. From 913, when the patriarch Nicholas Mystikos tried to appease him by performing some sort of corona-tion ritual on him outside the walls of Constantinople, he expected recogni-tion as emperor (*basileus* in Greek, *tsar* in Slavonic) and a marriage between his daughter and the young Constantine VII. His ultimate ambition eluded him, but in pursuing it he matched Byzantium in diplomacy and constantly outperformed it in battle. And he did not ruin his country in the process: it is apparent that his son Peter inherited a kingdom which was as coherent and viable a military power as any in tenth-century Europe. As the price of peace with Peter after Symeon's death in 927 the emperor Romanos I was prepared to give Peter his granddaughter in marriage, to recognize Peter as *basileus*, to pay an annual tribute, and to accord patriarchal status to the Bulgarian Church.

The peace established in 927 lasted forty years, by which time, a century after the baptism of Boris-Michael, Bulgaria was well on the way to becom-ing a permanent fixture among the states of Europe, at least as fixed as any of the Frankish kingdoms which remained from Charlemagne's empire. Yet Byzantium was fundamentally opposed to coexistence. After the overthrow of Romanos I in 944, Constantine VII denounced the marriage of Peter to Maria Lekapene as an anomaly. The view of Bulgaria in Constantine's trea-tise on foreign relations, the so-called *De administrando imperio*, is entirely consistent with that expressed some fifty years earlier by his father Leo VI in a survey of the military tactics of the empire's enemies: the Bulgar kingdom is pointedly left off the map, as a black hole at the centre of the empire's web of relationships in eastern Europe, neither Christian ally nor barbarian foe, but implicitly classed with the barbarian nations to the north of it, and iden-tified as a target for their attacks. Indeed, tenth-century Byzantine rulers had no scruples about inciting pagan peoples to attack Christian Bulgaria. The Magyars and the Pechenegs were used against Symeon; in 967, the emperor

Nikephoros II, deciding not to renew the treaty with Peter, engaged the Rus under Sviatoslav of Kiev. Sviatoslav greatly exceeded his brief by occupying Bulgaria and reducing it, under Peter's son Boris, to a protectorate of the vast East European empire that he now proposed to rule from the Danube. However, this Rus occupation made it possible for Nikephoros' successor, John I Tzimiskes, to subsume the liquidation of the Bulgarian kingdom in his victorious campaign against Sviatoslav in 971: the ceremony which stripped Boris of his royal insignia was a part of the triumph which Tzimiskes celebrated on his return to Constantinople. The Bulgarian capital, Preslav, was made the headquarters of a Byzantine military governor. However, the decapitation of the Bulgarian state left much of the organism intact, especially in the west. During the civil wars which followed Tzimiskes' death in 976, the Bulgarian elite rallied under the leadership of the sons of an Armenian official, one of whom, Samuel, made himself the ruler of a revived Bulgarian kingdom centred first on Prespa and then on Ochrid. It took Basil II (976–1025) the greater part of his reign to destroy Samuel's dynastic regime.

The conquest of Bulgaria brought much additional territory, removed a major threat to the hinterland of Constantinople, and restored overland communications between the Aegean and the Adriatic. The Balkan wars of John I and Basil II made the empire a superpower on two continents. Yet those wars were hard fought, and could not have been won if the empire had not, in the meantime, improved its position on other fronts, especially in the east, where the frontier with Islam had advanced significantly between 931 and 968. This was partly the result of a great increase in military efficiency, but it was also due to the political decline of the empire's great imperial neighbours. Whereas Byzantium in the year 1000 was clearly recognizable as the state it had been in 800, only bigger and stronger, the empires of Harūn al-Rashid and Charlemagne were looking somewhat altered and greatly the worse for wear. Both the Abbasid caliphate and the Carolingian empire had fractured into smaller units and the dynasties which had created them had lost effective power. Islam was being pulled apart by religious divisions, all expressed in dynastic terms, between the Sunnites and various groups of Shiites, by regionalism in Syria, Egypt, Iraq, and Iran, and by strong non-Arabic cultural traditions, notably in Iran and among the Turks whose role in the caliph's armies made them an increasing presence at the heart of the caliphate. Thus instead of a *jihād* financed and recruited from the whole Islamic world, Byzantium was now confronted on its eastern border by independent regional emirates, which however bellicose—like the Hamdanid emirate of Aleppo led by Sayf al-Dawla—could not prevail against the co-ordinated might of the empire's resources. In the West, Charlemagne's empire had crumbled under pressure from the inheritance demands of multiple

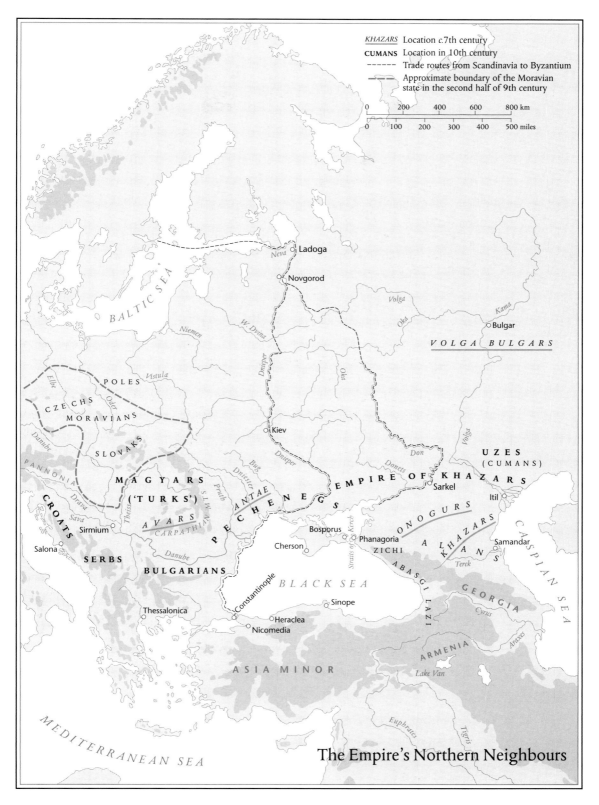

BALTIC SEA

Neva ○ Ladoga

○ Novgorod

Volga

Oka

Kama

○ Bulgar

VOLGA BULGARS

Niemen

W. Dvina

POLES

Vistula

CZECHS

MORAVIANS

Elbe

Oder

Dnieper

Oka

SLOVAKS

○ Kiev

Danube

PANNONIA

Drava

MAGYARS

('TURKS')

Theiss

AVARS

CARPATHIANS

Bug

Dniester

Prut

Dnieper

Don

Donets

Volga

UZES

(CUMANS)

E M P I R E   O F   K H A Z A R S

○ Sarkel

Itil ○

CROATS

Sirmium ○

Salona ○

SERBS

BULGARIANS

P E C H E N E G S

A N T A E

Bosporus ○

Cherson ○

Straits of Kerch

Phanagoria ○

ZICHI

O N O G U R S

A   K H A Z A R S

Samandar ○

Terek

ABASGI

LAZI

GEORGIA

CASPIAN SEA

Thessalonica ○

Constantinople ○

BLACK SEA

○ Sinope

Cyrus

Heraclea ○

Nicomedia ○

ASIA MINOR

Lake Van

ARMENIA

Araxes

MEDITERRANEAN SEA

Euphrates

Tigris

The Empire's Northern Neighbours

177

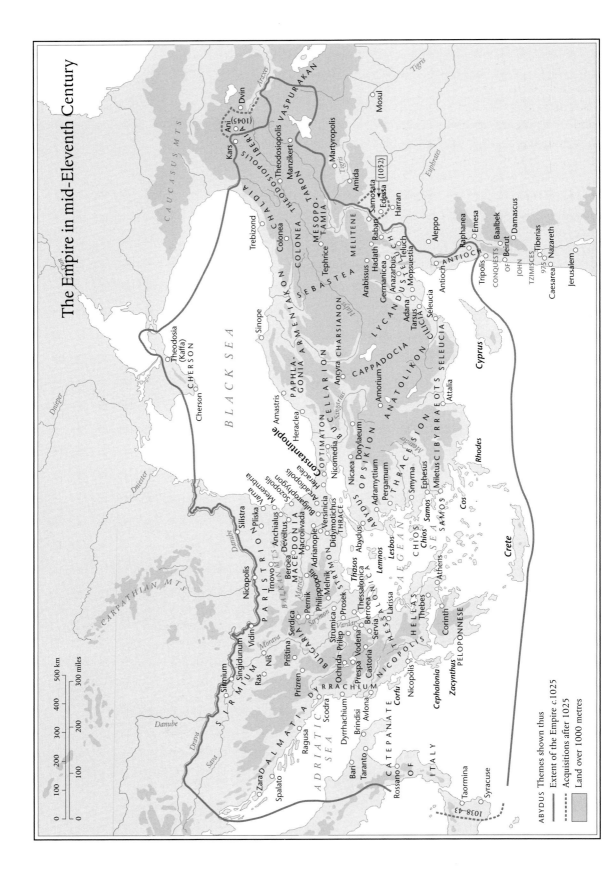

The Empire in mid-Eleventh Century

Tigris
Arctos

Dvin
Ani (1043)
Kars
Theodosiopolis
Theodosiopolis
IBERIA
VASPURAKAN
Manzikert
Martyropolis
Mosul
THEODOSIOPOLIS
CHALDIA
MESOPO-TAMIA
Tigris
Amida
[1052]
Euphrates
Trebizond
Colonea
COLONEA
Samosata
Edessa
Rabat
Harran
Teluch
SEBASTEA
Tephrice
MELITENE
Hadath
Aleppo
Sinope
Amastris
PAPHLA-GONIA
ARMENIAKON
Ancyra
Germanicea
Arabissus
Anazarbus
ANTIOCH
Raphanea
Emesa
Baalbek
Damascus
Heraclea
CHARSIANON
Adana
Tarsus
Antioch
Tripolis
Beirut
Tiberias
TZIMISCES
CELLARION
Amorium
ANATOLIKON
Seleucia
CONQUESTS
Nazarea
Caesarea
OPTIMATON
Nicomedia &
Sangarius
CAPPADOCIA
SELEUCIA
OF
Nicaea
Dorylaeum
Attalia
Cyprus
JOHN
Jerusalem
Constantinople
OPSIKION
LYCANDUS
CIBYRRAEOTS
975

BLACK SEA

Dnieper
Dniester
Theodosia (Kaffa)
CHERSON
Cherson

Adramyttium
Pergamum
Smyrna
Ephesus
Miletus
THRACE
ABYDUS
Abydus
Lesbos
CHIOS
Chios
SAMOS
Samos
Cos
Rhodes
AEGEAN SEA
Crete

Danube
Silistra
Nicopolis
PARISTRION
Vidin
Varna
Mesembria
Sozopolis
Anchialus
Develtus
Pliska
Bulgarophygon
Versinicia
Arcadiopolis
Heraclea
Didymotichus
THRACE
Singidunum
SIRMIUM
Ras
Niš
Pristina
Prizren
Scodra
Vidin
BULGARIA
Serdica
Pernik
Melnik
Strumica
Prosek
Prilep
Ochrida
Prespa
Vodena
Castoria
Servia
Berroea
Philippopol
Adrianople
Trnovo
Beroea
MACEDONIA
STRYMON
Thessalonica
Larissa
Thasos
Lemnos
SALONICA
HELLAS
Thebes
Athens
Corinth
PELOPONNESE
NICOPOLIS
Vardar
Strymon
BALKAN MTS
Morava
Margus

CARPATHIAN MTS
Danube
Sava
Drava
Sirmium
DYRRACHIUM
DALMATIA
Zara
Spalato
Ragusa
Dyrrhachium
Brindisi
Avlona
Corfu
Cephalonia
Zacynthus
Nicopolis
ADRIATIC SEA
CATEPANATE OF ITALY
Bari
Taranto
Rossano
Taormina
Syracuse
1038-43

CAUCASUS MTS

500 km
400
300
200
100
0

300 miles
200
100
0

ABYDUS   Themes shown thus
———   Extent of the Empire c.1025
- - -   Acquisitions after 1025
▒▒▒   Land over 1000 metres

heirs, from the raids of Vikings, Magyars, and Saracens, and from the violent self-help of the warrior aristocracy. Only in East Francia, under a new dynasty, did the Frankish monarchy, by successful war against the pagan Slavs and Magyars, reverse the trend sufficiently to present Byzantium with a new imperial challenge in Italy, following the imperial coronation of Otto I in 962. However, the challenge was aimed at a marriage alliance, and it was resolved in 972 by the marriage which united Otto II to Theophano, a female relative of John I. The half-Greek son of this marriage, Otto III, stood on his western imperial dignity, but in a style that clearly reflected the court of his eastern colleague, Basil II, whose niece he was preparing to marry at the time of his premature death in 1002. The crushing defeat of Otto II by Saracen forces in Calabria in 982 only confirmed what had been clear since 870: Byzantium was the only local power with the resources to organize resistance to Muslim aggression in central and southern Italy. The recapture of Crete in 961 made the reconquest of Sicily a possibility. The papacy, the city-republics of Amalfi, Naples, Gaeta, and Venice, the Lombard princes of Benevento and Capua, and the Ottonian emperors, all had to concede that an enhanced Byzantine presence in Italy, and good relations with the empire, were an unavoidable necessity.

Byzantium in the tenth century was realizing the benefits of the unglamorous strengths which it had built up in the struggle for survival in the seventh and eighth centuries, and which made it a model of cohesion and stability compared with the giants which had overshadowed it in 800. It was territorially more compact than either the Carolingian or the Abbasid state, and unlike them it was not a dynastic state; that is, it was not the creation of a dynasty and did not depend on dynastic continuity—or dynastic substitution—for its identity or its survival. Unlike most medieval empires, it was not held together by aggressive warfare to satisfy a military aristocracy's need for land and booty. It had the religious unity which was lacking in the caliphate: the iconoclast controversy, ended by the final restoration of icons in 843, had forged a strong bond between orthodoxy and political identity. At the same time, Byzantium had the apparatus of government—a bureaucracy, a standing army, a comprehensive taxation system—which was largely missing in the Carolingian realm. Its imperial capital and its holy city were the same, which was not the case in either Latin Christendom or Islam. The Abbasid capital, Baghdad, may have matched or surpassed Constantinople as a showcase of wealth, learning, and palace power. But Constantinople was older by four hundred years; its buildings and rituals were visible proof that this was still the Roman empire of Constantine, however reduced, which had existed when the Franks and Arabs were barely known to history, and Baghdad had been a vacant site up-river from the capital of the now extinct Persian empire.

Facing: Basil II receiving the submission of his enemies as he is crowned by the archangel Gabriel and handed a lance by St Michael. Miniature of a Psalter, Venice.

Within the as yet unbreached walls of the 'reigning city', Byzantium had accumulated reserves of political culture unequalled outside the Far East. It is indicative of the strength that Byzantium derived from its past that the expansion of the tenth century coincided with a major governmental effort to retrieve and codify the written tradition of antiquity up to the sixth century, as well as the record, both written and oral, of recent military, ceremonial, and diplomatic practice.

At the death of Basil II in 1025, the empire stretched from Crete to the Crimea, and from the Straits of Messina and the River Danube to the Araxes, Euphrates, and Orontes rivers. The only foreign power that seriously disputed these frontiers was the German empire under Otto III's successors, Henry II and Conrad II, who attacked Byzantine possessions in southern Italy and incited local rebels, but their base of operations was too far away for their intervention to be effective. The empire's relations with two of its northern neighbours, the Magyars and the Rus, were on the whole improved by their conversion to Christianity at the end of the tenth century. The Rus received their Christianity from Byzantium, along with Basil II's sister Anna as a bride for Prince Vladimir of Kiev, and the distance between Kiev and Constantinople precluded any recurrence of the problems that had accompanied the conversion of Bulgaria. Distance also played a part in the empire's ability to coexist with the Shiite Fatimid caliphate which after taking power in Egypt (969) emerged as the main power in the Islamic world. The main rivalry of Fatimid Cairo was with Abbasid Baghdad. Although Byzantium and the Fatimids clashed in Syria, and the mad caliph al-Hakim exacerbated relations by persecuting Christians and destroying churches, including the Holy Sepulchre in Jerusalem, coexistence became possible when Basil II, after securing the eastern frontier, halted the reconquest of the Near East which had been pursued so energetically by his predecessors Nikephoros II and John I, devoting himself instead to the liquidation of Bulgaria and, in his very last years, the reconquest of Sicily.

The forecast for Byzantium in 1025 was thus about as bright as it could have been. Twenty-five years later the empire was even slightly larger in the East through the annexation of the city of Edessa and the Armenian kingdoms of Ani and Kars. But by 1080 it was in serious trouble, rapidly losing control of its entire Asian territory, and badly shaken and eroded in the Balkans. Explanations abound for this catastrophic reversal, starting with those advanced by the Byzantine writers who narrated these events in the late eleventh century. There was clearly both a leadership failure and a system failure, although the symptoms are easier to discern than the causes: twentieth-century attempts to explain the crisis in terms of economic and military incapacity stemming from the growth of feudalism, the decline of a

free peasantry, and the conflict of civilian and military aristocracies, have worn less well than eleventh-century tales of incompetent management by irresponsible individuals. In structural terms, we may say that it was now Byzantium's turn to experience the problems of over-extension: the strengths of survival were disposable or disabling in the geographically less compact, culturally more diverse, and socially more complex organism that the empire had become as a result of profitable warfare, territorial annexation, and increased security. Yet Byzantium was still the same empire, perhaps too much so for its own good at a time when its enemies were suddenly no longer the same enemies. Byzantium had coped well with neighbours that were states, and with which it could deal from a position of superior statehood. It was less ready to deal with enemies that operated outside state structures, as was the case with the three aggressors who broke in upon it in the mid-eleventh century: the Pechenegs, the Seljuk Turks, and the Normans.

The most immediate threat, both to the imperial heartland and to the imperial achievement of Basil II, came from the Pechenegs, the tribal confederation that had dominated the western Pontic steppe since the end of the

Constantine IX Monomachos and his wife Zoe making a donation to the cathedral church of St Sophia. Constantine has been substituted for an earlier emperor, probably Romanos III, and his head accordingly changed, but it is not clear why the heads of Christ and Zoe have also been remade. Mosaic in the south gallery of St Sophia, Constantinople.

ninth century. The Pechenegs had a fearsome reputation among their neighbours, the Magyars, the Khazars, and the Bulgars, unlike whom they remained resolutely pagan and nomadic. The Byzantine conquest of Bulgaria brought them into direct contact with the empire as its principal neighbours on the lower Danube. At first the Byzantine policy was to exclude them by a heavy military presence on the border, but after a series of devastating raids in 1033–6, one of which penetrated as far as Thessalonica, the government of Michael IV (1034–42) instituted three measures to rationalize frontier defence: a reduction in the number of frontier garrisons, the creation of a depopulated, uncultivated 'waste zone' to the south of the Danube, and the financing of markets beside the border fortresses to supply the nomads with the manufactured and agricultural goods they would otherwise have sought by raiding. This policy seems to have worked until 1046 when the Pechenegs were pushed westwards by the movements of the Oghuz Turks. An attempt by the emperor Constantine IX Monomachos (1042–55) to weaken them in traditional divide and rule manner, by fomenting rivalry between two chieftains, backfired, and after Byzantium had the worst of the subsequent confrontation, a thirty-year truce was agreed in 1033, allowing the immigrant tribesmen to remain in their new habitat in the Black Sea hinterland south of the Danube—an area very close to the original nucleus of the Bulgar kingdom. The empire retained control of the Danubian towns, but the uncomfortable similarity to the seventh-century beginnings of the Bulgarian nightmare were probably not lost on the people of Constantinople. The emperor Isaac I Komnenos (1057–9) tried without great success to impose a more favourable settlement, and in the 1070s a revolt involving the Pechenegs and the local Vlachs removed the Danubian towns from imperial control. The collusion was ominous, and when hostilities resumed with the expiry of the thirty-year truce in 1083, the Pechenegs made common cause with disaffected heretical communities on the southern slopes of the Haemus mountains. The emperor Alexios I Komnenos (1081–1118) decided in 1087 to take the war north of the mountains in an attempt to repeat John I Tzimiskes' successful campaign of 971, but a confrontation at Dristra, where Tzimiskes had won his final victory over Sviatoslav, led to the complete rout of the Byzantine forces from which Alexios barely escaped. A truce establishing the frontier at the Haemus mountains soon broke down, as the Pechenegs raided deeper and deeper into Thrace, reaching the outskirts of Constantinople in 1091. The emperor's army was heavily outnumbered, and the situation was only saved by the arrival of a large host of Cumans, now the steppe people behind the Pechenegs. In the event the Cumans were persuaded to destroy the Pechenegs at the battle of Mount Levounion, but they might easily have joined the other side, and they returned as invaders three years later. They replaced the Pechenegs as a permanent menace to the north, and in 1122 either they or a remnant of the Pechenegs advanced into Thrace in great force. But the emperor John II Komnenos (1118–43) overwhelmed them at Stara Zagora in a carefully executed campaign. This confirmed the restoration of the Danube frontier which had begun in 1092. The arrangement of the mid-eleventh century—a trade zone on the Danube backed by a waste zone to the south—seems to have been reinstituted with considerable success. Until 1185, the lower Danube was the least eventful and most stable part of the imperial frontier. This may have owed something to the cooperation of the Russian princes, who had a share in the commercial wealth of the Danubian towns. But it was ultimately due to the fact that the Pechenegs and Cumans were familiar enemies: in their nomadic lifestyle, primitive religion, military performance, steppe habitat, and stateless existence, they conformed to an ethnic stereotype that the Graeco-Roman world had confronted since the beginning of history, and which learned Byzantine writers, not unrealistically, perpetuated by referring to all northern barbarians as Scyths.

The Pecheneg problem was one that could be solved because it could be contained; the Pechenegs did not have institutional backing from the rest of the 'Scythian' world. It was otherwise with the Islamicized Turks who assailed the empire from the east in the mid-eleventh century. They too were nomads in search of plunder and permanent new pastureland, both of which Asia Minor provided in abundance. At the same time, they were aggressors in a religious cause and with tribal connections to the dynastic regime which in the mid-eleventh century took over and revitalized the Abbasid caliphate. The Seljuk leader Togrul and his successors Alp Arslan and Malik Shah, who succeeded him as the power (sultan) beside the caliph, were primarily interested in reuniting Islam under the banner of strict Sunni orthodoxy, and their immediate priority was the reintegration of the Fatimid state rather than the conquest of Byzantium. However, they were happy to divert the predatory energies of the nomadic Türkmen against the Christian lands of Georgia, Armenia, and Byzantium rather than let them loose on the settled Muslim populations of Iraq, Iran, and Syria. It was the combination of nomadic free enterprise and central backing from the highest Islamic authority that made the Türkmen such a formidable threat at a time when Byzantine governments were preocccupied with their own internal security. The simultaneous incursions of multiple warbands with no fixed base made it difficult to concentrate resistance and resources, and when, finally, an emperor came to power who gave priority to the eastern front, his counter-offensive brought him into direct confrontation with the sultan Alp Arslan at the battle of Mantzikert (1071). The capture of Romanos IV Diogenes was the most humiliating defeat that a Byzantine emperor had suffered in battle since the death of Nikephoros I

260 years earlier. The defeat was actually made worse by the sultan's clemency in releasing Romanos according to a peace agreement which made minimal territorial demands; the emperor's release precipitated a civil war between him and the administrative regime in Constantinople, which rejected him in favour of his co-emperor, Michael VII Doukas. Although the government of Michael VII managed to eliminate Romanos, it failed to retain the loyalty of the army as a whole; as civil war resumed, the Turks not only advanced unopposed, but were drawn deep into Asia Minor by Byzantine generals seeking to recruit them for or against the emperor in Constantinople. The towns and villages of the interior were also totally unprepared for self-defence after more than a century of freedom from enemy raids, and local landowners looked to their interests at court rather than the preservation of their estates. Thus twenty years after the battle of Mantzikert, the Turks were established on the west coast of Asia Minor, and their occupation was progressing beyond the nomadic stage: a branch of the Seljukid family was creating the nucleus of an independent sultanate behind the massive Roman walls of Nicaea, in the Asiatic hinterland of Constantinople, while in Smyrna an emir called Tzachas, who had spent some time in Byzantine service, had built himself a fleet with which he was attempting to capture the Aegean islands.

The situation began to improve for Byzantium from 1092, when the death of Malik Shah hastened the break-up of the Seljukid realm into a number of principalities. After Alexios I saw off the Cuman threat to the Balkans in 1094, he could turn his full attention to the East. The armies of the First Crusade, which arrived in 1096–7 as a result of his appeals to Pope Urban II, helped him to retake Nicaea, and in the wake of their advance towards Antioch, his forces completed the expulsion of the Turks from the coastal plains and river valleys of western and southern Anatolia. However, Alexios did not benefit from the later conquests of the crusade, which indeed greatly complicated his attempts to recover lost territory in the East. Apart from Cilicia, in the south-eastern corner of Asia Minor, which reverted rather fitfully to imperial rule between 1137 and 1180, there was no further movement of the boundaries established at the end of the eleventh century. This failure to recover what had been the continental core of the medieval empire may seem surprising in view of the empire's recovery in other ways. Under the dynamic leadership of Alexios I Komnenos, his son John II, and his grandson Manuel I, Byzantium regained its status as a great power in the Balkans, the Aegean, and the wider Mediterranean world, capable of deploying massive armies, impressive fleets, and seemingly unlimited sums of gold.

Three reasons may be suggested. First, the empire was more often than not on the defensive against continued nomad pressure for raiding and grazing

186

in the lowlands; with one notable and disastrous exception, all the campaigns which Alexios, John, and Manuel led into Turkish Anatolia were essentially demonstrations of force or retaliatory strikes rather than systematic wars of reconquest, though the ephemeral gains were naturally given great publicity. Second, Byzantium hoped to exploit the rivalry between the two Turkish states which vied for supremacy over the Türkmen nomads: the Seljukid sultanate of Rum, which after the First Crusade relocated to south-central Asia Minor, with its capital at Ikonion (Konya); and the emirate founded by a chieftain called Danishmend in the northern and eastern areas of the plateau. Although Byzantine interests lay in preserving a balance between the two, the empire tended to side with the Seljukids against the Danishmendids, since the latter were the more committed to holy war, as is clear from the name of Ghazi (warrior for the faith) that most of them adopted. In 1161, when the Seljukid sultan Kiliç Arslan II came to Constantinople to seek support from Manuel I, the emperor formally adopted him as his son in a treaty which stipulated that in return for generous subsidies he would restore to the empire all lands which he took from the Danishmendids. But he failed to keep his side of the bargain and brought the whole of Turkish Asia Minor under his rule, which determined Manuel on a change of policy. In 1175, the emperor advanced the frontier on to the plateau by building and manning fortresses at Dorylaion and Soublaion. The next year he led a huge expedition to conquer Ikonion, but it came to grief in a classic ambush in a mountain pass at Myriokephalon. It was a humiliating end to the only serious attempt to reverse the Turkish occupation of central Asia Minor by direct military confrontation.

That such a confrontation had not been tried before is also explained by the fact that the reoccupation of Anatolia was only part of a wider strategy of political restoration in the eastern Mediterranean. This strategy focused on the areas to the east of the Seljuk sultanate, the areas which Byzantium had reconquered from the Arabs in the tenth century and resettled with a population of Armenians and Syrians. The main Turkish influx into Asia Minor had largely bypassed this region, leaving the local military command structure relatively intact in the hands of the local Armenian aristocracy, whose presence greatly facilitated the passage of the First Crusade and the establishment of crusader principalities at Edessa and Antioch. The residual infrastructure of empire in the area was a promising basis for imperial restoration, and it is thus understandable why the Byzantine government invested heavily in the effort to recover Antioch. More generally, the very existence of the crusader states, first at Antioch and Edessa, then at Jerusalem and Tripoli, was a challenge to Byzantium as the Christian empire of the East. For its credibility, as well as its security, the empire had to exercise some

Facing: Edessa (Urfa), Harran gate. Above the gate was carved an inscription naming the emperor Alexios I and commemorating the expulsion of the Turkish garrison in 1095. Only a small part of the inscription remains above the right-hand jamb.

187

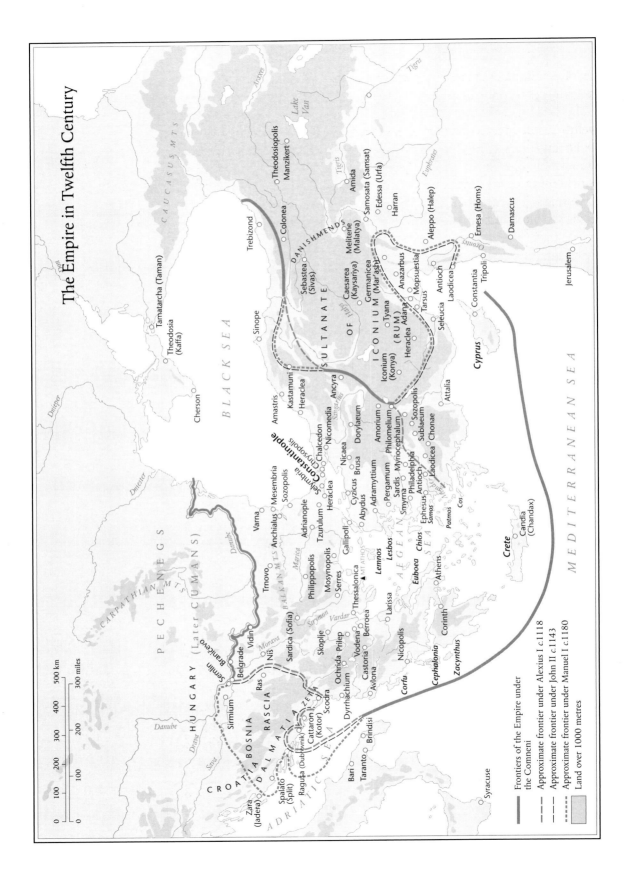

The Empire in Twelfth Century

Legend:
— Frontiers of the Empire under the Comneni
– – – Approximate frontier under Alexius I c.1118
– · – Approximate frontier under John II c.1143
····· Approximate frontier under Manuel I c.1180
░ Land over 1000 metres

Scale:
0 100 200 300 400 500 km
0 100 200 300 miles

Bodies of water and regions: BLACK SEA, MEDITERRANEAN SEA, ADRIATIC SEA, AEGEAN SEA, Dnieper, Dniester, Danube, Drava, Sava, Morava, Marica, Strymon, Vardar, Tigris, Euphrates, Orontes, Lake Van

Places and regions:
Tamatarcha (Taman), Theodosia (Kaffa), Cherson, Trebizond, Colonea, Theodosiopolis, Manzikert, Amida, Samosata (Samsat), Edessa (Urfa), Harran, Aleppo (Halep), Emesa (Homs), Damascus, CAUCASUS MTS, DANISHMENDS, Sebastea (Sivas), Caesarea (Kaysariya), Germaniceia (Marash), Melitene (Malatya), Anazarbus, Mopsuestia, Tarsus, Adana, Antioch, Constantia, Tripoli, Jerusalem, SULTANATE OF ICONIUM (RUM), Tyana, Heraclea, Seleucia, Laodicea, Iconium (Konya), Cyprus, Sinope, Amastris, Kastamuni, Heraclea, Nicomedia, Ancyra, Dorylaeum, Amorium, Philomelium, Sozopolis, Sublaeum, Chonae, Attalia, Laodicea, Constantinople, Selymbria, Chalcedon, Chrysopolis, Nicaea, Brusa, Cyzicus, Abydos, Adramyttium, Pergamum, Sardis, Philadelphia, Antioch, Smyrna, Myriocephalum, Ephesus, Laodicea, Cos, Patmos, Samos, Chios, Lesbos, Lemnos, MT ATHOS, Euboea, Athens, Corinth, Cephalonia, Zacynthus, Crete, Candia (Chandax), Corfu, Nicopolis, Larissa, Berroea, Vodena, Castoria, Ochrida, Prilep, Skoplje, Sardica (Sofia), Serres, Mosynopolis, Philippopolis, Trnovo, Vidin, Nis, Ras, Belgrade, Branicevo, Semlin, Sirmium, HUNGARY, CROATIA, BOSNIA, RASCIA, DALMATIA, ZETA, Scodra, Dyrrhachium, Avlona, Cattaron (Kotor), Ragusa (Dubrovnik), Spalato (Split), Zara (Jadera), Brindisi, Bari, Taranto, Syracuse, PECHENEGS, HUNGARY (Later CUMANS), CARPATHIAN MTS, BALKAN MTS, Varna, Mesembria, Anchialus, Sozopolis, Adrianople, Tzurulum, Gallipoli, Heraclea, Thessalonica, Amastris, Sangarius

sort of dominion over these outposts of a western Christendom which now flanked Byzantium on two sides.

The third great external challenge to Byzantium in the eleventh and twelfth centuries came from the Latin West. It came not from the revival of the Frankish empire in Germany, but from new units of aggression formed during the fragmentation of the West Frankish kingdom in the ninth and tenth centuries. The Norman adventurers who appeared on the borders of Byzantine southern Italy in the early eleventh century were the descendants of Vikings settled at the mouth of the Seine as Carolingian vassals. Their impact on Italian and Byzantine history reflected both their Viking origins and their Frankish background. On the one hand, they were predators and mercenaries of no lasting loyalties and no fixed address, who strenuously resisted commitment to any of the powers who engaged their services, whether Byzantium, the papacy, the Lombard princes of Capua and Benevento, or the Apulian rebels against Byzantine rule; it is not only Byzantine writers who refer to them as unspeakable barbarians. On the other hand, they were thoroughly rooted in the post-Carolingian culture of knightly honour and religious reform; they had strong territorial instincts, and they expressed their territoriality by reproducing the structures of lordship and vassalage which they had brought with them from 'feudal' France. As they became established, they gained the grudging respect of local religious houses and religious leaders, including, eventually, the papacy which recognized their potential value as vassals of the Church, who could defend its interests more satisfactorily than either the German or the Byzantine empire. The rise of the Normans in southern Italy coincided with growing strains in papal relationships with both powers: with Germany, because of the minority of Henry IV and then the latter's hostility to Church reform; with Byzantium, because of the age-old dispute over ecclesiastical jurisdiction in southern Italy, coupled with controversy over doctrine, papal supremacy, and liturgical usage which erupted in a dramatic exchange of excommunications in 1054 that is conventionally seen as the beginning of the schism between the eastern and western Churches. In 1059, Pope Nicholas II invested the main Norman leader, Robert Guiscard, as Duke of Apulia. With his younger brother Roger, he proceeded to occupy southern Italy and Sicily at the expense of Byzantines, Lombards, and Muslims.

In April 1071, four months before the Byzantine defeat at Mantzikert, Robert Guiscard completed his conquest of the Byzantine mainland by taking the city of Bari. Byzantium responded by proposing a marriage alliance, which Guiscard finally agreed to in 1074, two years later sending his daughter Olympias to Constantinople to await marriage with Constantine, son of Michael VII Doukas, when the couple came of age. It is a measure of how low

Facing: Manuel I Kom-
nenos, surprisingly dark
of complexion, with his
second wife, Maria of
Antioch, whom he mar-
ried in 1161. Miniature in
cod. Vaticanus gr. 1176,
which contains the acts
of the Council of 1166,
summoned by Manuel to
elucidate Christ's saying
'My Father is greater than
I' (John 14: 28).

the empire had sunk, and how far Guiscard had come from his beginnings as
a landless warlord, that he was in a position to refuse the heir to the Byzantine throne as a prospective son-in-law. The Byzantines undoubtedly feared
an invasion, but they certainly wanted Guiscard to fight the Turks for them.
Here we see a basic and perhaps fatal paradox in the Byzantine relationship
with the West: Byzantium insisted on employing the very elements in western society against which it was most powerless. Despite its bad experiences
with Guiscard and other Normans, it continued to recruit Norman and other
western knights, no doubt assuming that it could control them by its ability
to pay. The sources naturally do not highlight the many who gave loyal service, but the publicity given to those who gave trouble suggests that Byzantium seriously overlooked the extent to which westerners did not want to be
bought into accepting the Byzantine dream.

Michael VII's overthrow in 1078 provided Guiscard with a golden excuse
to launch an invasion of the Balkans in support of his ally, which he did in
1081 with the blessing of Pope Gregory VII. In the four years of fighting
which followed, Alexios I generally had the worst of his encounters with
Robert Guiscard and his son Bohemond, and only the death of Guiscard in
an epidemic which struck his invasion fleet relieved Byzantium of a major
threat to the Balkan territories that now provided the bulk of the empire's resources. Even so, Alexios did not hesitate to call upon the knights of western
Christendom, including Bohemond and other Normans from southern Italy,
to help him reconquer Asia Minor from the Turks. There is now general
agreement that Pope Urban II preached the First Crusade in 1095–6 in response to an appeal for aid from the Byzantine emperor, and that if the major
sources for the event do not mention the appeal, this is because both sides
wanted to forget it: the Latins did not want to admit the 'wretched emperor'
had anything but a negative part in their heroic, godly enterprise, and the
Byzantines were keen to portray this enterprise as an unsolicited intrusion on
imperial space and a masterpiece of imperial damage limitation. In particular,
it is now becoming clear that Bohemond's appropriation of Antioch in contravention of the oath he had taken to restore all former imperial possessions
captured by the crusade, was the result of an understanding which he had
had with Alexios, and which Alexios had put under intolerable strain by failing to join the crusader siege of Antioch when deserters, including one of the
crusading leaders, persuaded him that the situation there was hopeless.

But whatever the intentions with which the crusade was called, it resulted
for Byzantium in an eastward extension of the Norman conquest of southern
Italy, and the decisive deepening of the schism between the churches, as
Latin bishops excluded Greek clergy from Syrian dioceses that had never
come under the jurisdiction of Rome. Alexios did find other allies among the

crusaders, and he had the resources to put military pressure on Bohemond, but Bohemond took care to identify his cause with that of Latin Christendom as a whole. In 1105 he returned to Europe and, with papal blessing, recruited an army with which he crossed the Adriatic in 1107, intending to subdue Byzantium on his way to Syria. Alexios, avoiding direct confrontation with the invasion force, wore it down and trapped it in the mountains of Albania. The peace agreement which he extracted from Bohemond at the Treaty of Devol (1108) would, if implemented, have restored Antioch to the empire and established the Franks as imperial vassals on the frontier with the

Facing: Ezekiel's vision in the Valley of Dry Bones, full-page miniature in cod. Paris. gr. 510 containing the Homilies of St Gregory Nazianzen. With its pink and blue atmospheric background and its elaborate oval frame of cornucopias, this picture betrays a late antique model.

Alexios I presenting to the Fathers of the Church (shown on the opposite page of the manuscript) a refutation of the heresies by the contemporary theologian Euthymios Zigabenos.

191

Turks. But Bohemond did not return to Syria, and his successors refused to recognize the Treaty.

Alexios and his successors never really gave up on the idea that the expansionist energies of Latin Europe could be recruited to serve the empire's interests. On the whole, however, twelfth-century imperial policy towards the Latin world was defensive, and concerned with applying the security lessons that had been learned from the trauma of the Norman invasions and the crusade. One was that the Frankish colonies in Syria and Palestine could not be dealt with in detachment from the rest of Latin Europe. Another was the need for pre-emptive diplomacy to prevent the rulers of southern Italy from interfering in Syria or launching another attack on Byzantium. To this end, Alexios I and his successors cultivated good relations with the German emperors, who had their own historic reasons for refusing to recognize the Norman occupation of southern Italy and the legitimacy of the royal title which Guiscard's nephew, Roger II, received from the papacy in 1140. The Norman invasions also highlighted the need to counteract Norman diplomacy among the empire's Serbian vassals and at the court of the king of Hungary: Alexios married his son John II to a Hungarian princess in 1105, and this was the beginning of intense, if often hostile, relations between the two dynasties. Finally, the encounters with the Normans and the crusade had shown that the empire could not depend on its own war fleet, and needed to be able to call upon the navy of a dependable ally. Thus, during the war with Robert Guiscard, Alexios I made a momentous treaty with Venice, granting the Venetians unprecedented privileges in return for their aid: among other things, a trading quarter in Constantinople with a section of waterfront, and exemption from payment of the 10 per cent sales tax. The republics of Venice and Amalfi, nominally subject to the empire, had maintained a trading presence in Byzantium for some two centuries. Alexios' concessions to Venice put this presence on a new basis, which set a precedent for later, somewhat less generous concessions to Pisa and Genoa, and thus greatly increased the numbers of Italians in the empire and the amount of Byzantine trade in Italian hands.

The need for an energetic diplomatic response to the expansion of Latin Christendom was sharpened still further by the events of the Second Crusade, preached in 1145 in reaction to the first major disaster to befall the crusader states, the Muslim capture of Edessa. The crusade was led by kings Louis VII of France and Conrad III of Germany, who were anything but deferential to the young Manuel I as they led their enormous armies past Constantinople. Roger II of Sicily took advantage of the crisis to seize the island of Corfu, whence his forces systematically ravaged mainland Greece. It did not help Byzantium's reputation that the crusading armies were decimated

by the Turks in Asia Minor. The lesson was that Byzantium could not afford to be isolationist, and had to prevent a general crusade from happening again. The episode also confirmed the strategic significance of Italy, especially the south, for the empire's security in the Balkans. Manuel's primary goal was a partition of Italy with the German empire, in which Byzantium would get the Adriatic coast. However, his unilateral pursuit of this goal not only failed after some initial success, but also antagonized the new German emperor, Frederick Barbarossa, whose own plans for imperial restoration ruled out any partnership with Byzantium. Manuel was obliged to treat Frederick as his main enemy, and to form a web of relationships with other western powers, including the papacy, his old enemy the Norman kingdom, Hungary, several magnates and cities throughout Italy, and, above all, the crusader states, where he married two of his nieces to kings of Jerusalem and took a princess of Antioch as his second wife. His generous subsidies and ransoming of prisoners from the Muslims helped to maintain the defence of the Latin colonies at a time when they were under threat from a determined 'counter crusade' led by Nureddin and Saladin. The suppression of the Fatimid caliphate (1170) and the subsequent unification of Egypt with Syria under Saladin made the destruction of the kingdom of Jerusalem only a matter of time; that it did not happen sooner owed something to Manuel's support.

The internal strength of the Komnenian dynasty, and the energetic diplomacy and campaigning of Alexios, John, and Manuel, stabilized the empire's retracted frontier and surrounded it with a ring of more or less respectful neighbours, including, even, the sultan of Rum. Byzantium looked impressive when Manuel died in 1180, having just celebrated the betrothal of his son Alexios II to the daughter of the king of France. But the son was a minor, and his unpopular regency government was overthrown in a violent *coup d'état* (1182); three years later, the usurper, Andronikos I Komnenos, perished in a popular uprising, and his successor, Isaac II Angelos, survived many revolts until the conspiracy which replaced him with his brother Alexios in 1195. This troubled succession weakened the dynastic continuity and solidarity on which the strength of the Byzantine state had now come to rely. Predatory neighbours and ambitious subjects saw their chance. A Sicilian strike at the heart of the empire in 1185 was defeated and the captured cities, Dyrrachion and Thessalonica, were recovered, but at the edges Byzantium began to fall apart. The king of Hungary and the Turkish sultan seized adjoining frontier areas, the Serbian and Armenian princes threw off imperial overlordship, and the ousted imperial governor of Cilicia, Isaac Komnenos, set up as an independent ruler in Cyprus. Worst of all, the Vlachs of the Haemus mountains rose in revolt, led by the brothers Peter and Asan. With support from Cumans

north of the Danube, and with the advantage of their impregnable mountain strongholds, the rebels defeated all imperial counter-attacks and extended their operations southwards into Thrace. The hinterland of Constantinople was exposed to the ravages of an enemy who consciously recreated the Bulgarian kingdom of Symeon and Samuel, but with much less concern for recognition from Constantinople. Like his Serbian counterpart Stephen, Kalojan or Johanitza of Bulgaria, brother and successor of Peter and Asan, sought and received his royal crown from Pope Innocent III.

Byzantine rulers after Manuel added to their problems by reversing his alignment with the crusader states and the crusading movement. This may have seemed a natural consequence of the rise of Saladin and of the anti-Latin reaction which followed Manuel's death, culminating in a massacre of the Latins in Constantinople when Andronikos came to power. Both Andronikos I and Isaac II seem to have expected that an alliance with a victorious Saladin would bring substantial gains not only for the Orthodox Church, but also for the empire, in Syria and Palestine. But the expectation proved illusory, and by investing in it, Byzantium gave up the opportunity to prevent, deflect, or influence the course of the Third Crusade which was the inevitable

General view of the fortifications of Trebizond, which broke away from the empire in 1204, just before the fall of Constantinople to the Crusades.

result of the fall of Jerusalem to Saladin in 1187. Moreover, by attempting to obstruct the passage of the German crusading army under Frederick Barbarossa (1189–90), Isaac II earned a reputation as an enemy of the crusade which did Byzantium no good. It probably influenced another crusading king, Richard I of England, the Lionheart, in his decision not to return Cyprus to the empire after taking it from the rebel Isaac Komnenos. It also contributed to the antipathy with which Barbarossa's son, Henry VI, treated Byzantium on succeeding to the western empire after his father's accidental death on crusade. Henry, who added the kingdom of Sicily to his dominions in central Italy, was the most powerful ruler in the Mediterranean world. Even if he did not intend to carry out his threat to conquer Byzantium, he was certainly determined to make Byzantium pay for the new crusade which he mobilized in order to complete the unfinished business of the Third Crusade. This enterprise was abandoned after his sudden death in 1197, and the Fourth Crusade preached by Pope Innocent III was originally intended to sail from Venice against Egypt without involving the Byzantine empire at all. However, when the crusade got into financial difficulty, the idea that Byzantium was there to pay the bill proved irresistible when an imperial pretender, Alexios, son of the deposed Isaac II Angelos, turned up asking for help against the ruling Alexios III. The result was the diversion that ended in the sack of Constantinople and the election of a Latin emperor by the crusaders.

Land, Sea, and People

Between 780 and 1204, the map of the Byzantine empire changed dramatically. Not only did the empire go through extremes of territorial expansion and contraction, but its territorial centre of gravity shifted decisively from Asia Minor to the Balkans. At the same time, certain basic features did not change. The landscape remained typical of the northern Mediterranean zone, supporting an agricultural economy centred on the production of wheat, wine, and olive oil, but supplemented by extensive pastoralism and the uncultivated riches of forests and wetlands. Byzantium was self-sufficient in everything it needed apart from the spices of the Far East and the furs that came from Russia. Its economy supported a population which may have doubled in the course of the period, but followed a constant settlement pattern, and consisted of the same ethnic mix of Greeks, Armenians, Syrians, Jews, Slavs, Arabs, and Turks. Above all, the fluctuation of the empire's continental frontiers was balanced by the remarkable stability of its coastline, its capital, and the management of its territorial resources in the interests of the state.

Although stretches of coastline came and went with territorial gains and losses, the empire from 780 to 1180 dominated the shores of the north-eastern Mediterranean and the Black Sea. Its coastline was not significantly shorter than those of the Abbasid and Carolingian empires at the height of their power, and relative to its land mass was proportionally much greater than that of any other medieval state. All the most fertile agricultural regions of the empire, and most of its urban centres, lay close to the sea, and its coastal lands corresponded almost exactly to the areas of Greek settlement and colonization in the seventh and sixth centuries BC: shipping was the most efficient and least expensive means of transport and communication. From these facts, it is clear that the sea was of fundamental importance for the wealth, the existence, and the very identity of Byzantium. Perhaps surprisingly, therefore, shipping and maritime communications do not seem to have rated very highly in Byzantine politics, society, and culture. The navy was far from being the 'senior service' in the armed forces, only one of the many military leaders who attempted to seize power was the commander of the fleet, and maritime commerce was never obviously an important means to, or source of, great wealth and social status—in marked contrast to the Italian city republics of Venice, Amalfi, Pisa, and Genoa, which duly filled the gap in the empire's naval capability. This apparent disparity between the empire's dependence on the sea and the low value which was attached to maritime activity was partly a legacy of the ancient world, in particular of imperial Rome, with its large land armies and its landowning senatorial aristocracy. The primacy of the land was also decisively reinforced by the central role that the land army and the interior of Asia Minor had played in the struggle for survival against the Arabs. This is where the theme armies had been stationed; here the great noble families of medieval Byzantium had their estates, their followings, their opportunities for the spoils of war, and their heroic past. It is difficult to generalize about the economy of such a vast area as the Anatolian plateau, parts of which undoubtedly had a high agricultural yield. Yet much of it was best suited for ranching and stock-rearing, especially in the troubled conditions of the Arab invasions, and whatever it produced, the only products which could profitably be marketed at any distance were those which could move themselves, namely animals. Any other surplus had to be used for supplying the troops which were stationed there or which passed through on their way to the eastern front. Thus Byzantium in the eighth to eleventh centuries may be said to have had two economies, one of inner Asia Minor, the other of the coastal regions. The former, landlocked and geared to eastern defence and the eastern frontier, was completely lost to the empire with the Turkish occupation of the Anatolian plateau. It was not replaced in the West by the imperial recovery of the Balkan interior, where the empire was never again at home in the way it had been in Late Antiquity. Yet the priority which Anatolia had enjoyed for so long hindered the empire's total identification with, and investment in, the economy of the Aegean and Black Sea hinterland—the economy which financed the empire's expensive diplomacy and hiring of mercenary troops, paid for the conspicuous consumption of the imperial and ecclesiastical elite, and fed the growing population of Constantinople.

With a population that was probably close to 70,000 in 780 and may have risen to more than 300,000 by 1204, Constantinople was the main consumer of the foodstuffs produced in the Aegean and Black Sea rim, just as the imperial palace, which was effectively a small city within the city, took most of the silk produced in mainland Greece, the main centre of the industry in eleventh- and twelfth-century Europe. Commonly referred to as the 'reigning city' and the 'megalopolis', Constantinople did not merely house the imperial and ecclesiastical authorities and their extensive bureaucracies; it constituted the essential identity of Byzantium. It literally existed at the expense of all other towns on imperial territory. An Arab traveller of the tenth century was struck by the contrast between the rural, thinly inhabited appearance of Byzantine Asia Minor and the greater urban density of all parts of the Islamic world. Twelfth-century writers were more favourably impressed by what they and their informants saw, especially on the European side. However, with the possible exception of Thessalonica, the only provincial city which ever constituted an alternative centre to Constantinople was Antioch, during its reversion to imperial rule between 969 and 1085. And before the twelfth century, when towns in mainland Greece expanded in association with the growth of Italian commercial enterprise, the most prosperous urban centres were to be found in the frontier zone: in Italy (Amalfi, Venice, Bari), along the lower Danube and in the southern Crimea, in Armenia, and at Attaleia and Trebizond in Asia Minor, which were the main entrepôts for trade with the eastern Islamic world.

This urban prosperity at the edge of the empire was partly due to the difficulties of imposing taxation so far from the centre, but it was also the result of government concern for the stability of the frontier regions. Byzantium had neither the developed political ideology nor the repressive machinery of the modern totalitarian state, and only to a limited extent was the economy state-operated. Nevertheless, there were no human or material resources which the state did not claim the right to control and exploit, and there were few economic or social developments which did not originate in government management of resources for political purposes. The nature of this management changed by the twelfth century, as an increasing share of it was handled by lay and ecclesiastical magnates who either received exemption from the growing burden of taxes and corvées, or were granted possession of much of

the increasing amount of land which was coming under state ownership. However, the aims remained the same: to maximize fiscal exploitation and military recruitment while ensuring the protection and provisioning of Constantinople and the security of the regime. Like all medieval governments, Byzantium was constantly concerned to keep agricultural land productive by stopping the peasantry from deserting it. Perhaps more than most medieval states, it tended to solve problems of labour, recruitment, and security by large-scale transfers of population from one region to another. Byzantium was also uniquely successful in keeping its aristocracy dependent on the central government for its wealth and status. For a time, in the ninth and tenth centuries, the great families of Asia Minor who occupied the chief military commands looked set to become landed magnates like the feudal nobility of the medieval West, with a strong territorial power base of local estates and local retainers. But after two of these families, the Phokas and the Skleros, came close to seizing power from the emperor Basil II between 976 and 989, Basil made it his business to weaken the connection between the aristocracy and the land, by confiscating their estates, by closing their opportunities for land acquisition through purchase or conquest, and by posting them to short-term military commands away from their own localities. A number of important Byzantine families continued to retain strong local roots, notably at Adrianople and Trebizond, but in general Byzantine élite society in the

The move of the imperial court from the Great Palace to that of Blachernai necessitated an extension of the land walls by Manuel I. The façade of the Palaiologan Tekfur Sarayı (cf. p. 255) rises in the distance.

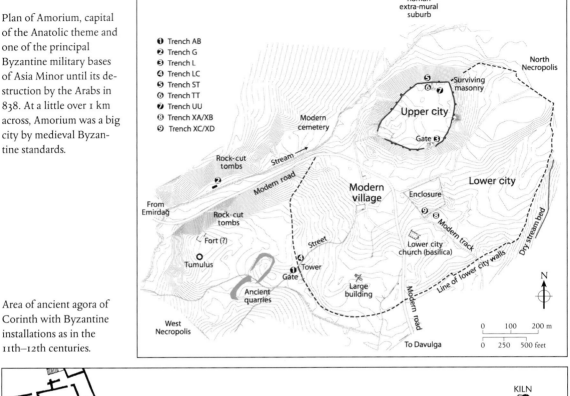

Plan of Amorium, capital of the Anatolic theme and one of the principal Byzantine military bases of Asia Minor until its destruction by the Arabs in 838. At a little over 1 km across, Amorium was a big city by medieval Byzantine standards.

❶ Trench AB
❷ Trench G
❸ Trench L
❹ Trench LC
❺ Trench ST
❻ Trench TT
❼ Trench UU
❽ Trench XA/XB
❾ Trench XC/XD

Roman extra-mural suburb

North Necropolis

Upper city

Surviving masonry

Gate **❸**

Lower city

Modern cemetery

Rock-cut tombs

Stream

Modern road

Modern village

Enclosure

❾ **❽** Modern track

Lower city church (basilica)

Dry stream bed

Line of lower city walls

From Emirdağ

Rock-cut tombs

Fort (?)

Tumulus

Street

❹ Tower

❶ Gate

Large building

Ancient quarries

West Necropolis

Modern road

To Davulga

N

0   100   200 m
0   250   500 feet

Area of ancient agora of Corinth with Byzantine installations as in the 11th–12th centuries.

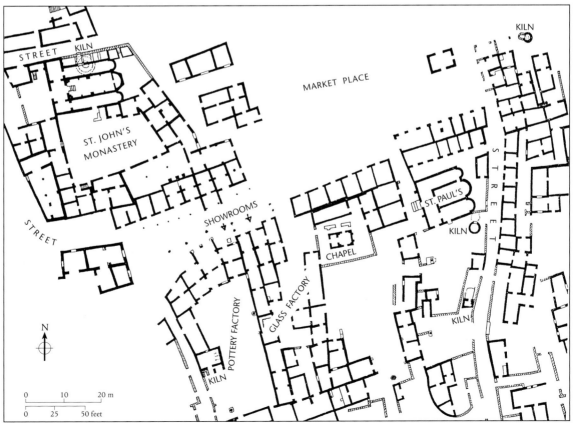

STREET

KILN

KILN

MARKET PLACE

ST. JOHN'S MONASTERY

STREET

STREET

SHOWROOMS

POTTERY FACTORY

GLASS FACTORY

CHAPEL

ST. PAUL'S

KILN

KILN

KILN

N

0   10   20 m
0   25   50 feet

eleventh and twelfth centuries was remarkable for its lack of regionalism and localism. This probably contributed to the collapse of Byzantine Asia Minor; it certainly played a part in the empire's ability to survive the loss of the homeland of so much of its high-ranking personnel.

Emperors and Dynasties

Medieval Byzantium inherited from imperial Rome a fundamental distinction between the imperial office and the person and family of the emperor. It was notoriously possible for a successful, politically astute general to seize power from a weak or unpopular ruler and then to prove that his usurpation was divinely ordained because 'nothing succeeds like success'. Of the thirty-nine emperors who ruled between 780 and 1204, nineteen were forcibly deposed, six through outright murder, with another two dying as a result of blinding, the standard method of disqualification. Foul play was suspected in at least three other imperial deaths, and of the hundreds of failed conspiracies and revolts, at least eight posed major military challenges to the incumbent regime. Yet, like ancient Rome, Byzantium recognized the special status of the imperial family and the principle that every emperor should nominate his successor in the interests of civil stability. Most successful usurpers belonged to the circle of the emperor's close associates, and nearly all attempted to consolidate their seizure of power by forming a marriage connection with the family of a former ruler.

If dynastic succession was not already the norm by the eighth century, it certainly became so in the next four hundred years. An important step in this direction appears to have been taken by the Isaurian dynasty: according to a custom which was probably instituted by Constantine V (741–75), his grandson Constantine VI (780–97) was 'born in the purple', that is, in a special palace chamber whose walls were lined with rare porphyry marble. To be 'purple-born' (*porphyrogenitus*) was to enjoy a privileged start in any competition for the throne. The Isaurian dynasty would probably have continued if Constantine VI had not been deposed by his mother Irene, who thereby invited her own deposition. If the man who dethroned her, Nikephoros I (802–11), his son Stavrakios (811), and his son-in-law Michael Rhangabe (811–13) failed to found a major dynasty, this was mainly due to their failure in war against the Bulgars. Leo V the Armenian (813–20), who deposed Michael I, was more successful, but he fell victim to one of his peers, Michael of Amorium, who envied his success, and no sooner had Michael murdered Leo than he faced a massive rebellion by another peer, Thomas the Slav. But Michael II (820–9) eventually defeated Thomas, and acquired respectability by marrying, as his second wife, Euphrosyne, the daughter of Constantine

VI. He was succeeded by his son Theophilos (829–42), who in turn left power to his young son Michael III (842–67). Michael's undoing was not his long minority, but the complete outsider whom he co-opted as junior emperor, Basil the Macedonian. The dynasty founded by Basil I (867–86) lasted for over two centuries; Michael Psellos wrote of it, 'I believe no family has been favoured by God as theirs has been.' There were certainly some wobbly moments. Leo VI, after three marriages, scandalized the Church by marrying the woman who finally bore him a male heir. The minority of the young Constantine VII (912–59) was exploited by several ambitious opportunists, starting with his uncle Alexander (912–13) and ending with the commander of the imperial fleet, Romanos Lekapenos, who not only manoeuvred himself into the role of senior emperor and married Constantine to his daughter Helen, but crowned his own sons and gave them precedence over Constantine. The ineptitude of the sons in overthrowing their father and inviting Constantine to join them (944) prevented the establishment of a Lekapenos dynasty. But the premature death of Constantine's son Romanos II (959–62) encouraged army commanders to seek supreme power at the expense of his young sons Basil and Constantine. Nikephoros II Phokas (963–9) and his murderer and successor John I Tzimiskes (969–76) relegated Basil and Constantine to figurehead roles, and although their reigns were short, they left a legacy of ambition in their relatives and associates. It took Basil II (976–1025) thirteen years to dispose of the attempted usurpations of Bardas Skleros and Bardas Phokas. Basil himself gave the dynasty a new set of problems by not marrying, so that at his death the dynastic line passed to his aged brother Constantine VIII (1025–8) and to Constantine's daughters

Greek Fire being hurled at enemy ship from a siphon, here with reference to the naval investment of Constantinople by Thomas the Slav in 821–2. Miniature of the Chronicle of John Skylitzes.

Zoe (1028–52) and Theodora (1042–56). The next four emperors all held power through association with Zoe: Romanos III Argyros (1028–34), Michael IV (1034–42), and Constantine IX Monomachos (1042–55) as her husbands; Michael V (1042) as her adopted son. The arrangement was far from satisfactory either for the empresses, who were excluded from government, apart from a short period of joint rule in 1042 which was not deemed a success, or for the emperors, who were dependent on Zoe for their authority. It was also clear by the time of her second marriage that she was not going to bear a child.

However, what is ultimately remarkable is the strength of the dynastic principle which enabled the 'Macedonian' dynasty to survive all these vicissitudes, and which prevented the intruders from eliminating the minors and the females of the dynastic succession. So great was the respect for the dynasty in its final years that after the deaths of Zoe and her last husband, Constantine IX, Theodora reigned alone and unchallenged (1055–6).

It was twenty-five years, a period of severe external crisis, before Byzan-

An emperor prostrate before an enthroned Christ, his prayer being mediated by the Virgin Mary. The emperor is usually identified as Leo VI, but Basil I is also a possible candidate. Mosaic in the narthex of St Sophia, Constantinople, late ninth or early tenth century.

203

tium filled the gap left by the 'Macedonian' dynasty. Michael VI (1056–7), the elderly bureaucrat nominated by Theodora, was only a stop-gap, and Isaac I Komnenos (1057–9), who toppled him, on abdicating passed the throne to Constantine Doukas rather than to a member of his own family. Constantine X (1059–67) and his brother, the Caesar John Doukas, did seriously attempt to start a new dynasty, but Constantine's son, Michael VII, was unpromising material at such a critical time. Although John Doukas ensured that Mantzikert put paid to the dynastic ambitions of Romanos IV Diogenes (1068–71), who married Constantine X's widow and fathered two sons by her, and Nikephoros III Botaneiates (1078–81), who overthrew Michael VII, had no progeny, it was only through association with the next successful usurper, Alexios I Komnenos (1081–1118), that the Doukai went down in history as one of the most distinguished Byzantine imperial families.

The dynastic succession started by Alexios I lasted for over a century in the male line. The Komnenoi were also the longest and the last Byzantine imperial dynasty in the sense that, almost without exception, all the emperors of Constantinople and the Byzantine successor states from 1118 to 1461 were descended from Alexios and used the name Komnenos; the very use of a surname was a significant departure from earlier dynastic precedent. This extraordinary development of the last centuries of Byzantium was due not only to the long reign of Alexios I and his success in dealing with external enemies and external conspiracies, but also to his systematic policy of building the imperial family into the central structure of the imperial constitution. The

Repeating the composition of the Constantine IX and Zoe panel (except that the Virgin and Child has been substituted for Christ), that of John II and his Hungarian wife Irene, placed in the same location, is much finer in execution. The portrait of the red-haired Irene is particularly striking. South gallery of St Sophia, Constantinople.

foundation of his dynastic succession was a dynastic regime in which impe-rial status did not just pass vertically from generation to generation, but also extended laterally to his whole kin and to the families into which they mar-ried, first and foremost the Doukai, the family of Alexios' own wife Irene. The Macedonian dynasty had not pursued, or at least not prioritized, mar-riage connections with other families, but Alexios cultivated them assidu-ously. The result was the emergence, after one generation, of a whole new aristocracy distinguished by vast wealth, princely lifestyle, high military command, kinship to the emperor, and a hierarchy of titles based on the ep-ithet *sebastos*, the Greek equivalent of 'augustus'. Alexios I and his son John II (1118–43) were thus able to pass on the succession without challenge from outside the imperial family. There was, however, a growing challenge from within the proliferating imperial family, and this challenge became destruc-tive when Manuel I (1143–80) died leaving an 11-year-old son, Alexios. In de-posing and murdering Alexios II (1180–3), Manuel's cousin Andronikos I (1183–5) made it impossible for himself or the rulers who in turn seized

The three churches of the monastery of Christ Pantokrator (now Zeyrek Kilise Camii), the prin-cipal foundation of the Komnenian dynasty, seen from the east. The biggest of the three churches, on the left, was built by the empress Irene (1118–24), the smaller one on the right a little later by John II. The middle church served as a family mausoleum.

power after him—Isaac II Angelos (1185–95), Isaac's brother Alexios III (1195–1203), Isaac's son Alexios IV, and the latter's murderer Alexios V Doukas 'Mourtzouphlos' (1204)—to command the loyalty of the imperial aristocracy and thus to prevent the conquest of Constantinople by the Fourth Crusade.

Byzantine empresses are currently receiving much attention, and it is clear that in the Middle Ages, as well as in Late Antiquity, the women's quarters (*gynaikonitis*) of the palace played an important part behind the scenes of imperial and dynastic politics. It is equally clear that empresses were important as wives or mothers, and only appeared centre-stage when their sons were minors (Irene for Constantine VI, Theodora for Michael III, Zoe for Constantine VII, Theophano for Basil II and Constantine VIII, Eudokia for Michael VII, Maria for Alexios II), or when the male succession died out, as happened with Zoe and Theodora at the end of the 'Macedonian' dynasty. However, the widowed mother of Alexios I, Anna Dalassena, was indispensable in forming the connections with other families which facilitated the rise and consolidation of the Komnenian dynasty. It was also vital for Alexios' initial success that he was able to leave her in charge of civil administration in Constantinople while he went off to fight the Empire's enemies. Later in his reign, Alexios came to rely on his wife, Irene Doukaina, for internal security. The contribution of both women to the regime was glowingly recorded by Alexios' first-born child, in her biography of her father, the *Alexiad*, which is unique not only as a piece of Byzantine women's literature, but also as an expression of frustrated ambition by a woman who felt that she had been born to imperial power.

Church and State

Byzantium is rightly described as a theocracy; that is, all Byzantines, including the emperor, considered their supreme ruler to be Christ, the King of Kings. Christ had famously said, 'My kingdom is not of this world', and he had used a Roman coin, bearing the emperor's portrait, to emphasize the very different rights of Caesar and of God. In accordance with these and other biblical statements, Byzantine Christians recognized a clear distinction between their empire and Christ's kingdom. Insofar as that kingdom was still in the future, in the Second Coming and the Last Judgement, it would supersede all earthly realms, including that of Rome, the last in the series of four world empires prophesied in the Book of Daniel. Insofar as the Kingdom of Heaven was a present reality, as a result of Christ's ministry on earth, it was represented by the Church, was populated by holy men living an angelic life of solitary or communal asceticism, and was experienced by all be-

lievers in the liturgy of the eucharist, celebrated in buildings that were decorated as microcosms of heaven, holy portrait-galleries of angels and saints
presided over by the icon of Christ who was conspicuously not attired in imperial garb. The Church had its own space, its own hierarchy, its own rules,
its own enormous wealth, its own elective procedures and deliberative assemblies; its integrity consisted in keeping these free from interference by the
secular power, and in correcting the moral excesses of rulers. On these basic
principles, Byzantium was in full agreement with western Christendom. Indeed, it was from the West that Byzantium took its paradigms of imperial
deference to priestly authority: the legend of Constantine's repentance and
baptism at the hands of Pope Silvester I, and St Ambrose's refusal to let
Theodosius I enter the sanctuary of the church after he had authorized the
massacre of a circus crowd in Thessalonica.

However, in a way unparalleled in the West, Byzantium identified the
Christian phase of the Roman empire not with the last of the four earthly
realms, but with the 'fifth monarchy' of Christ, with whom the emperor was
said to 'co-reign' in a way clearly reminiscent of the thousand-year rule of
the saints prophesied in Revelation. This idea of imperial participation in the
Kingdom of the Saints was expressed in many ways: in the canonization of
Constantine the Great as the 'thirteenth apostle'; in the designation of 'holy'
or 'saint' formally used of the reigning emperor; in the quasi-priestly role
which the emperor assumed when he entered the sanctuary at the beginning
of the liturgy, blessed the people, and delivered special sermons (*silentia*); in
the gold coinage, which after Iconoclasm reverted to the pattern, instituted
in 692, of placing the image of Christ on the obverse (i.e. the 'head' side) of
the coins and the emperor's on the reverse; in the *Nomokanon*, the considerable body of canon law which derived from imperial legislation. The fusion
of Church and State was perhaps most obvious in the magnificent chapels of
the imperial palace. These had their own clergy, who could be prevailed
upon to perform services for the emperor, such as uncanonical marriages, of
which the patriarch disapproved. The palace chapels also contained some of
the most precious of the holy relics for which Constantinople was famous;
the chapel of the Virgin of the Pharos enshrined what were believed to be the
principal objects from Christ's Passion and Crucifixion. After the Fourth
Crusade, these found their way to Paris, where they were housed in a
purpose-built chapel by Louis IX (St Louis), who incarnated the fusion between Catholic Church and national state in the French *ancien régime*.

Yet St Louis belonged to a political and religious culture defined by the
Gregorian Reform of the eleventh century, which articulated a clear institu-
tional division between a universal sacred hierarchy headed by the pope in
Rome, and the temporal regimes of national kings. Such a division was

unthinkable in Byzantium, where the emperor's palace was in the next block from the patriarch's cathedral church. Byzantium had its reform movements and its assertive religious leaders, notably the great Photios in the ninth century and Michael Keroularios in the eleventh, who promoted the active superiority of the spiritual power. Significantly, however, both men came to their ecclesiastical vocations from secular political careers. The defeat of Iconoclasm was to some extent a triumph for the Church over imperial 'tyranny', but emperors continued to impose the ecclesiastical personnel and the religious agenda they wanted, and it was only their posthumous reputations which suffered. In any case, the most interventionist emperors were also the most conscientious reformers. While the consequence of Gregorian reform in the West was to exclude rulers from ecclesiastical jurisdiction, the Byzantine Church reforms of the eleventh and twelfth centuries led to the formal designation of the emperor as the Church's *epistemonarches*, the supreme regulator of ecclesiastical discipline.

Monasticism

MARLIA MUNDELL MANGO

Monasticism started in Egypt in the late third century when some pious men retired to the wilderness for a life of solitude and prayer. Athanasios, patriarch of Alexandria introduced monasticism to a wider public with his biography of St Antony the Great, born around 250. In the early fifth century Theodoret, bishop of Cyrus, recounts in his *Religious History* the spread of monasticism from Egypt to Palestine, Mesopotamia, Syria, and Asia Minor. It also spread to points further west, as well as to the East where Christian monasticism was taken as far as China by the seventh century.

Many monasteries were founded by holy men with asceticism the most important element in their regime.

The Heavenly Ladder, written in the early seventh century by the monk John Scholastikos who lived a solitary life of forty years in the desert, sets out a programme of salvation through asceticism. Occasionally a holy man attracted attention by his strenuous feats and pilgrims flocked to see him. In the Holy Land, monasteries cared for shrines and provided lodgings for visitors at pilgrimage sites such as Mt. Nebo, where Moses viewed the Promised Land, and Mt. Sinai, where he saw the Burning Bush and received the tablets of the law.

Other monasteries were foundations of elite individuals, like the empress Eudokia retired to Jerusalem, who wished to be buried in their own establishments, with their own clergy praying for their souls. The tradition persisted in the medieval period when the foundation charter, the *typikon*, often specifies that prayers are to be said for the founder's soul. Although early monasticism is more often associated with the countryside than the city, some monasteries existed within city walls from an early date. The first monastery at Constantinople, that of Dalmatos, was founded in the late fourth century, and by 536 there were nearly thirty monasteries within the Theodosian walls of the capital. Most of the churches built in medieval Constantinople were monastic.

The monastic rule of Basil the Great, the basis of Byzantine monasticism, advocated a self-sufficient community. Hence most monasteries were land-based and engaged in agriculture much along the lines of the independent Roman villa described by Palladius in the fourth century. In his *Lives of the Oriental Saints* John

Icon illustrating the Heavenly Ladder leading from earth to heaven by way of renunciation. Its 30 steps correspond to the years of Christ's hidden as opposed to his public life. In this scheme, for example, the first step is renunciation of life, the third pilgrimage, the 27th solitude, and so forth. Sinners fall from the ladder to demons below. Eleventh century. Mount Sinai, St Catherine's Monastery.

209

of Ephesus recounts how at a monastery north of Amida monks planted 60,000 vines. The profit they generated went to the poor. The Lives of St Hilarion and Peter the Iberian in the fourth and fifth centuries in the area of Gaza, refer to monastic wine production. Egyptian documents of the sixth century attest to monasteries owning land, potteries, oil factories, and mills.

Extensive landholdings constituted the wealth of large, self-sufficient monasteries in the medieval period. These assets were amassed in a variety of ways, including imperial donation. The *typikon* of the monastery of the Theotokos Petritziotissa, was given extensive property by its founder Gregory Pakourianos, Grand Domestic of the West, in 1083. This included land in four themes which took the form of six *kastra*, twelve villages, six fields, two estates, two other monasteries, four *hesychasteria*, one dependent monastery (*metochion*), one courtyard (*aule*), other annexes, buildings, fisheries, mills, and inns. He also granted food to his rent-paying peasants and horses, oxen, asses, cows, bulls, sheep, rams, and goats for the farms. In 1152 the *sebastokrator* Isaac Komnenos provided his new Kosmosoteira monastery in Thrace with facilities for both agriculture and fishing, including twelve ships. Marshy land was improved and produced

Above: The chrysobull presented by the emperor Alexius I Komnenos to Christodoulos, the founder of the Patmos monastery in 1088. It lists imperial donations of land and tax exemptions accorded to the new foundation. Patmos, monastery of St John the Evangelist, Library.

Right: The sale of the island of Gymnopelagisia by two monks to St Athanasius, the founder of the Lavra monastery for 70 *nomismata*. The contract, dated September 993, was signed by seven witnesses. Mount Athos, Lavra Monastery.

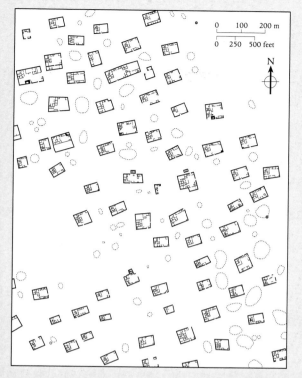

wheat, barley, pulses, wine, and oil. In addition to the endowments listed in the *typika*, landholdings are also recorded in documents preserved in monastic archives, the largest collection being those dating from the tenth century onwards in monasteries on Mt. Athos. These reveal a wide range of property transactions.

As well as prayer and agricultural or industrial production, monastic activities centred on social services. In addition to looking after pilgrimage shrines, monasteries also provided other public facilities such as inns for travellers, hospices for the poor or elderly, and hospitals. In the early period, the monasteries of St Jerome at Bethlehem (386–9) and an abbot Symeon (*c*.500) at Kalesh in Mesopotamia had schools. In the eleventh century Pakourianos set up a school for novices for his monastery in Thrace where he also provided three charitable institutions. In 1139 a large, well-equipped hospital was built in the centre of Constantinople in the Pantokrator monastery by its founder. A hospice, a hospital, and a bath for public use were built at the Kosmosoteira monastery in 1152. Some monasteries were also

Above: At the lavra monastery of Kellia in Egypt, each walled unit was composed of separate rooms for two monks, an oratory, a reception room, and a kitchen, all grouped round a courtyard and often with a well, garden, and watchtower. Sixth–eighth centuries.

Below: The coenobitic monastery of St Martyrius, founded in *c*.474, consisted of an enclosure with refectory, kitchen, cells, church, tombs, service areas, bath, and lavatory. These were all arranged round a central courtyard at one corner of which stood an external inn with stables.

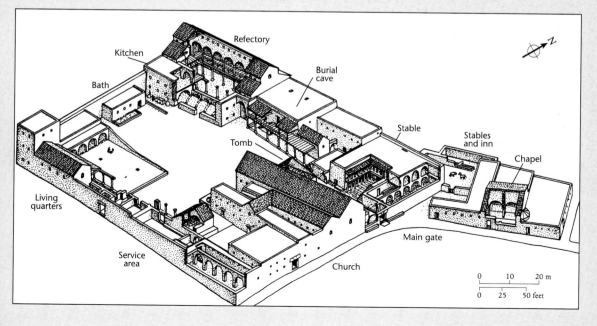

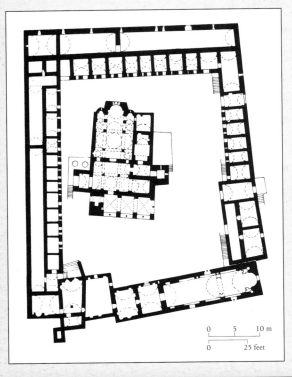

associated with the intellectual life of the early church, participating in theological debate and book production. The Studius monastery in Constantinople played an important iconophile role during Iconoclasm.

In the early period rural monastic buildings took two forms. One was that of the *lavra* where monks lived separately in cells scattered around the church and service buildings. In the other form, the coenobium, monks had communal quarters and a refectory. In Egypt, where monasticism originated, the monastery of Kellia, built in the sixth to eighth century in the Nile Delta, had about 1,600 walled units. The larger complexes at Kellia serving as community centres also have towers, refectories, and several churches. In the Judaean desert, out of sixty monastic sites studied archaeologically, about twenty were *lavra* establishments and the others coenobitic, such as that founded in *c.*474 by Martyrius, future patriarch of Jerusalem.

Left: The monastery of St Meletios on Mt. Kithairon, built in the eleventh century, has a quadrilateral enclosure ringed by cells, a refectory, kitchen, storerooms, and other buildings, with the church placed within the courtyard.

Above: Spectacularly perched on rocky outcrops, the group of monasteries known as the Meteora ('suspended in air') in Thessaly go back to the fourteenth century, but most of the standing buildings date to the Ottoman period.

Left: The Lavra monastery on Mt. Athos was founded in 963 by St Athanasios with the support of the emperor Nikephoros II Phokas. It was the most important of the 46 monasteries founded on the Holy Mountain by 1001. Some of these were foreign foundations by Georgians (Iveron), Armenians (Esphigmenou), Amalfitans, Serbs (Hilandar), Russians (Panteleemon), and Bulgarians (Zographou). Annual assemblies were held in the Protaton at Karyes.

Many features of the early monastic layout recur in the medieval period as at St Meletios on Mt. Kithairon. Although the setting of some medieval monasteries such as those of the Meteora recall the wilderness of the early Egyptian monasteries, others present a more worldly aspect. Surviving medieval monastic buildings impress us by their scale and the richness of their adornment, which is in apparent conflict with the presumed monastic ideals of asceticism, but reflects an abundant endowment. Outstanding examples are the monastery of Hosios Loukas of Stiris (see colour plate facing p. 239) and the Nea Moni on Chios, as well as that at Daphni near Athens. In Constantinople, the monasteries of Constantine Lips (907), the Pantokrator (of 1136, p. 205), the Chora, and the Pammakaristos still retain some of their original splendour.

8 The Revival of Learning

CYRIL MANGO

At the beginning of the eighth century, we are told, liberal education at Constantinople collapsed as a result of the instability of imperial rule. Whatever exactly may be meant by that statement, the fact remains that literary production in the capital ground practically to a halt. That had nothing to do with Iconoclasm as such, although it is true to say that the chronological span of the First Iconoclasm (730–80) corresponds to the most uncultivated phase of Byzantine history.

Paradoxically, the tradition of Greek letters was meanwhile kept alive in Arab-dominated Syria and Palestine. The greatest scholar and liturgical poet of this period, John Damascene, whose surname was Mansūr, was a Christian Arab (d. c.749). Another notable poet, Cosmas, bishop of Maiuma (the port of Gaza), is said to have been his contemporary. Slightly older was Andrew of Crete (so named because he ended his career as metropolitan of that island), a native of Damascus, also a liturgical poet and author of many homilies. These were followed a little later by the historian George Syncellus (d. c.811), the theologian Theodore Abu Qurra, a native of Edessa (Urfa), the 'tattooed' brothers Theophanes and Theodore, who hailed from the Moab, and the grammarian and hagiographer Michael Syncellus, an Arab from Jerusalem. We do not know the background of this literary activity, but it may be surmised that the rapid conquest of Syria and Palestine by the Arabs had caused little disruption to local intellectual life and that Umayyad rule had proved relatively tolerant towards the Christian elite. That situation was not to last very long: in the course of the ninth and tenth centuries the use of Greek virtually died out in the caliphate.

Some of the Near-Eastern intellectuals we have mentioned made their way to Constantinople and contributed to the revival of letters whose beginnings may be traced to about 780. It is surely no coincidence that the Byzantine revival was contemporaneous with a similar movement in the West, which we call the Carolingian Renaissance, as well as an upsurge of cultural activity at the Abbasid court of Baghdad under the caliphs Harūn al-Rashid (786–809) and al-Mamūn (813–33). If we confine ourselves to the two European re-vivals, we find a close parallelism: both were animated by a vision of the renovation of the Roman state, meaning not the pagan, but the Christian em-pire of Constantine and his successors; both promoted the cultivation of a correct, i.e. ancient, linguistic idiom, which entailed, on the one hand, the as-semblage of the relics of 'classical' literature for purposes of imitation and, on the other, the compilation of manuals, compendia, and other aids to learn-ing; both were accompanied by the introduction of a more compact script, the minuscule, for book production; both saw the establishment of a palace school; both extended into the visual arts, more particularly the precious arts. There were differences, too. The Carolingian Renaissance laid particular em-phasis on the reform and education of the clergy, which does not appear to have been a major concern in Byzantium. Even so, the similarities were so pronounced that some kind of mutual influence naturally suggests itself. That is not a subject, however, to which much scholarly attention has been directed.

When we look more closely at the trickle of book learning that may be dis-cerned at Constantinople in the course of the eighth century, we discover to our surprise that it was due not to ecclesiastical or monastic schools—in fact, we know nothing about schools at the time—but to the imperial civil ser-vice, especially the chancery. Among the figures prominent in the revival many originated in that milieu even if they ended up as bishops or monks. Tarasius, described as a highly cultivated man, proficient in the ancient poetic metres, served as First Secretary (chief of the chancery) before being ordained at the age of about 50 patriarch of Constantinople (784–806). Nikephoros, son of a Secretary, whom he succeeded in the same office, was patriarch from 806 until 815. While still a young man he attempted to revive the tradition of historiography in ancient Greek that had been broken since the early sev-enth century. Photios, the greatest scholar of his age, was related to Tarasius and served as First Secretary before being named patriarch in 858. Theodore the Studite (759–826) was the son of a rich treasury official and his learning was not acquired in a monastery. His uncle, St Plato (c.735–814), belonged to the same social class: he was trained as a notary for imperial service and was active as a scribe after he had become a monk. In no case do we see anything resembling an episcopal school.

The somewhat irregular advancement of three successive chancery offi-cials, who were laymen, to the patriarchal throne certainly reveals on the part of the government an awareness of the need of having an educated pri-mate of a calibre that could not be found in the ranks of the clergy. That said, however, several decades elapsed before the state took a lead in fur-thering education as a matter of policy. The first measure, which is shrouded in legend, takes us to about the year 830 and concerns Leo the Mathematician. This singular man, we are implausibly told, acquired his multifarious learning on the island of Andros by studying old books in monastic libraries. He then set up a school in his modest house at Constantinople and taught philosophy, mathematics, astronomy, and music to private pupils whose number multiplied. One of his students was captured by the Arabs and brought before the caliph al-Mamūn, whom he impressed by his superior knowledge of geometry. Mamūn invited Leo to his court, promising him vast amounts of money, but the emperor Theophilos (829–42) refused to let him go and established him as a paid public teacher at the church of the Forty Martyrs on the main street. Assuming that this romantic story is not a fabrication, all we can conclude from it is that a single public chair of secular learning was set up shortly before the end of Iconoclasm.

The next move was made by the Caesar Bardas, who acted as regent between 855 and 866 and was, incidentally, Photios' patron and kinsman. Distressed by the decline of secular science, which had allegedly sunk to almost zero through the boorishness of previous emperors (a dig at the Iconoclasts), Bardas established a palace school in a hall called Magnaura. Its head was the same Leo, who taught philosophy, and there were three other chairs, of geometry, astronomy, and grammar respectively. Of the four professors who are named only Leo and the grammarian Kometas are otherwise attested and, although we are told that the seeds sown by the school were to bear fruit for the next hundred years, we know nothing about its activity or even how long it continued functioning. Silence descends until the reign of Constantine VII, who, once again, discovered that the sciences had been neglected, and so revived the school with the same four chairs. Of the professors he named three were court officials (otherwise unknown) and one a bishop, Alexander of Nicaea, who taught rhetoric and is recorded as a scholiast of Lucian—not the most suitable author to have engaged the attention of a clergyman. Alexander does not seem to have held his post for a long time: he was exiled under circumstances that remain obscure. However that may be, we are told that the emperor took a keen interest in the students, among whom he recruited judges, administrators, and metropolitans.

That is about as much as we learn from narrative sources about imperial involvement in the reform of education. If the 'Bardas University' (as it has been rather grandly called) really functioned for a century and more, how is it that we know next to nothing about its activity, its professors, its graduates, and its impact on the world of learning? It can certainly be said that the level of literary Greek rose or rather became more recherché in the course of the ninth and tenth centuries. Genres that had been extinct for about two centuries were revived. That happened, as we have said, in the case of historiography, although it must be added that the rather mediocre attempt made by Nikephoros (in the 780s?) was not followed up until about 950. Epistolography in its late antique form reappeared in the 820s and was assiduously cultivated. The verse epigram was revived, as we shall see presently. Even hagiography, traditionally expressed in ordinary language so as to reach a wide audience, was cast in an archaically elegant mould, and the same can be said of sermons. Yet all this started happening before the 'Bardas University' had been set up and without much encouragement from the government.

The most important achievement of the Byzantine revival lay, however, not in the 'improvement' of contemporary literature, but in the preservation of a sizeable portion of the ancient Greek classics and, incidentally, of early Christian writings. From the point of view of western culture it may even be said that this act of salvage constitutes our greatest debt to Byzantium. Setting aside the bits and pieces that have been found on the rubbish tips of Egypt (precious as they sometimes are), the Greek classics as we know them have come down to us in Byzantine manuscripts. Were it not for certain obscure men who laboured anonymously in the ninth and tenth centuries, we would have neither Plato nor Aristotle (except in translation), neither Herodotus nor Thucydides, neither Aeschylus nor Sophocles, not to mention a host of other famous and less famous authors. To go one step further, all the literature in question survived because it was recopied at the time in minuscule script. What was not recopied has been lost. But here we must explain.

In antiquity books were written on rolls of papyrus. The writing, usually on one side only, was in capital letters without division between words or accentuation (which in Greek can lead to confusion). For reasons of convenience each roll could not be unduly long: in the case of the *Iliad*, for example, no 'book' exceeded about 900 verses, corresponding to some thirty printed pages, so that the entire poem took up twenty-four numbered rolls. Papyrus, produced uniquely in Egypt, was relatively cheap and durable, but the ancient system had several disadvantages: it required too much space for storage, the individual rolls contained too little text and it was difficult to look up a particular passage.

Between the first and fourth centuries AD the roll was gradually replaced by the codex, i.e. the bound book as we still know it—one of the greatest advances in the entire history of letters. A codex could contain much more text than a roll, especially if its leaves were made of parchment, which could carry writing on both sides, so that now the whole *Iliad* could comfortably fit into one volume. It saved shelf space. It also made it much easier to locate a particular passage, which is probably the reason why the codex was favoured by Christians for their sacred books. To find the prescribed reading of the day all you had to do was to insert a marker. Besides, the Bible was an

Greek majuscule book
script as exemplified by
the codex Sinaiticus
(fourth century), one of
the two oldest Greek
manuscripts of the Bible.
Here the beginning of
St John's Gospel.

exceedingly long text: the Old Testament alone would have taken up several dozen rolls. On the other hand, the codex, especially if it was made of parchment, was decidedly expensive, a consideration that was to acquire increasing importance.

The conquest of Egypt, first by the Persians, then by the Arabs, restricted, if it did not cut off entirely, the supply of papyrus, but another century and more was to elapse before steps were taken to tackle the problem of book production. At a date that cannot be determined exactly, but surely before the end of the eighth century, books began to be copied in minuscule: the earliest dated specimen that has survived, a product of the Studius scriptorium, is of the year 835. Minuscule cannot be described as an invention, since cursive writing had long been used for documents, but it had remained a specialized script, the preserve of trained notaries. It needed some adaptation for the production of books and the reading public had to get used to it. That said, minuscule offered obvious advantages. It was more compact and so required less parchment; it was also quicker to write, since the scribe did not have to lift up his pen after each letter. The process of converting to minuscule, called transliteration, was not purely mechanical, but was more akin to that of a new edition. Words had to be correctly divided and accented. Often punctuation was introduced. Besides, the model could well have been damaged or indistinct in places. In other words, the editor had to interpret the text. Down to about the middle of the tenth century minuscule and capital (uncial) scripts ran side by side. Thereafter the uncial all but disappeared, except in headings. Once transliteration had taken place, the uncial model, whether it was a scroll or a codex, tended to be discarded.

Not surprisingly, transliteration was spread over several decades, even centuries. There is some evidence to suggest that it proceeded thematically, starting with scientific and philosophical treatises, going on to orators and historians, and ending with poets. Now, if we try to imagine the total volume of Greek writing from the earliest times until Late Antiquity, there can be no doubt that it underwent progressive erosion: much more was in circulation in the fifth to sixth centuries AD than survived into the ninth, and of the latter group a good portion has since been lost. We cannot express this shrinkage

The earliest dated manuscript in Greek minuscule script is the Uspensky Gospels, St Petersburg, Public Library, cod. gr. 219 of AD 835. It was copied by the monk Nikolaos of the Studius monastery.

even in approximate figures, but some examples are suggestive. Discoveries of Egyptian papyri in locations that were not major centres of learning have given us many hitherto unknown literary texts, the most famous case being that of the playwright Menander, the foremost exponent of the New Comedy, who fell into oblivion in the Byzantine period. John Stobaeus (fifth century) in his Anthology quotes about 385 authors, most of whom are mere names to us. Photios (of whom more presently) had the complete text of Stobaeus: we have only part. Roughly the same may be said of the vast geographical gazetteer called *Ethnica* by Stephanus of Byzantium (sixth century).

Even allowing for the possibility that authors like Stobaeus and Stephanus cribbed many of their references to obscure authors from older compendia, we cannot help asking ourselves where so many books could still be consulted in the age of Justinian. At Constantinople a public library of secular authors was set up at the Basilica by Constantius II (before 357). It burnt down in 476 with the loss (so it was alleged) of 120,000 volumes—not an impossible figure if those were mostly rolls. There is no clear evidence that the collection was reconstituted, nor do we know where an obsessively pedantic antiquarian like John Lydus (also of Justinian's time) found all the books he quotes, although on one occasion he tells us that he picked up in Cyprus a copy of the 'Judaean Sibyl'. A patriarchal library did exist, but was probably limited to religious literature and (as we happen to know for the eighth century) was not too well stocked. A palace library is briefly mentioned in the ninth century as containing a book of prophecies. It was expanded by Constantine VII, but filled no more space than the mezzanine of one small building. When, in 814, the emperor Leo V ordered a bibliographic search to be made of patristic testimonia favourable to Iconoclasm, the commission he appointed for the purpose sat in the palace (perhaps for reasons of secrecy), but books had to be fetched from various monasteries and churches. The impression one gets is that old manuscripts had come to rest in a variety of places and that a diligent search had to be made for them before the process of transliteration could be undertaken. Some of them may even have been found in Arab-held territory. Hunain ibn-Ishaq (ninth century), the famous translator of scientific and philosophical texts from Greek into Arabic and Syriac, travelled to Alexandria, Damascus, and Harran in search of Greek manuscripts.

Photios, twice patriarch of Constantinople (858–67, 877–86), is our next witness. Under circumstances that remain disputed he compiled his reading notes covering 280 volumes corresponding to 386 works (since one volume may have contained several different works). Conventionally known as the *Bibliotheca*, these notes range from a few lines to several dozen pages per book and usually include a summary of its content and a stylistic judgement. The majority of the works are Christian (233) as against 147 pagan or secular ones. School textbooks are excluded as are poetry and drama. Otherwise, there is the greatest diversity. Characteristically, the great majority of books reviewed belong to Late Antiquity, with the subsequent period very sparsely represented.

A little over half the books read by Photios are either totally lost or preserved only in fragments, which suggests that he consulted them in old copies and that the works in question (or most of them) were not considered of sufficient interest to be transliterated. To our great regret, he does not inform us where he had found them. If they formed his private collection, he must have owned a far bigger library than is recorded for any other individual of the Byzantine period. To add to the mystery, not a single book bearing his ex-libris has survived, whereas in the case of his disciple Arethas of Caesarea (*c.*860–*c.*939) we still possess six manuscripts that he caused to be copied and can attribute to his library another twenty-five with greater or lesser probability.

The next stage of the Byzantine revival corresponds to the reign of Constantine VII (912–59) and has been labelled 'the age of encyclopaedism', although the age of compilation may be a more accurate description. Bookish by nature, like his father, Constantine was excluded from power by the usurper Romanos Lekapenos ('an ignorant fellow') and had plenty of leisure to devote to his studies. Once back in control, if not before, he set about instigating a series of bibliographic enterprises that were carried out by a team of collaborators. For this historians must be grateful: if we did not have the *Book of Ceremonies*, the *De administrando imperio* (a treatise on the empire's foreign relations), the *De thematibus* (a survey of the empire's provinces), we would know much less than we do about Byzantium. The above three titles, practical in intention, but largely antiquarian in content, are all concerned with the exercise of the imperial office.

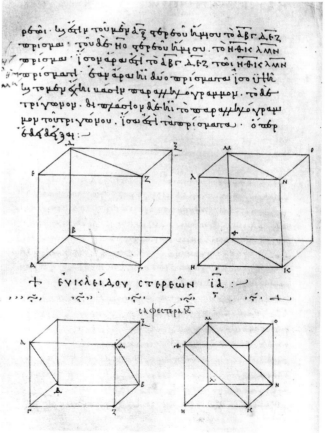

Minuscule copy of Euclid, written in AD 888 for Arethas of Patras (later archbishop of Caesarea in Cappadocia), who paid 14 gold pieces for it.

Others are of a miscellaneous character: the *Geoponica* is a collection of late antique treatises on agriculture; the *Hippiatrica* a similar compilation concerning veterinary science. Constantine also seems to have commissioned a medical encyclopaedia and another on zoology. But by far the biggest of his projects was the one conventionally called *Excerpta historica*. This was an anthology of extracts culled from a wide selection of historians ranging in date from Herodotus to George the Monk (ninth century), arranged thematically under headings such as 'The proclamation of emperors', 'Victory', 'Public speeches', 'Hunting', 'Marriages', 'Inventions', etc. Of the fifty-three named sections only one thirty-sixth has been preserved and fills six printed volumes, so that the entire work would have been the equivalent of over 200. The only possible beneficiary of such a monstrous collection would have been the emperor himself, whom we can imagine looking up precedents for this or that, be it conspiracies or embassies or deeds of valour.

Constantine's mania for systematization also extended to the religious sphere. We know for certain that he commissioned an extensive hagiographical calendar known as the *Synaxarion*, consisting of potted biographies of the saints commemorated each day, and may have been the originator (though that is far from certain) of an even vaster collection of saints' Lives *in extenso* (148 in all), paraphrased into acceptably elegant Greek by Symeon the Logothete, known as the Metaphrast in remembrance of his efforts. Finally, there is the nearest Byzantine equivalent to an encyclopaedia, mysteriously called *Souda* (literally 'ditch'), which consists of about 30,000 entries arranged alphabetically: difficult words, historical and literary notices, proverbs, mostly confined to antiquity. This appears to date from the end of the tenth century and is certainly in Constantine's spirit, although there is no evidence linking him directly to it.

What are we to make of the cultural activity that Constantine inspired? The absence of legal science is explained by the fact that an 'epuration' of the law, i.e. of Justinian's Corpus in Greek translation, had already been carried out, starting in the reign of Basil I and completed under Leo VI: this was the *Basilica* in 60 books, more of an antiquarian than a practical compendium. Military science had also been tackled by Leo VI. For the rest, one has the

Christ crowning the emperor Constantine VII Porphyrogenitus. Ivory plaque.

Facing: Moses receiving the tablets of the Law on Mount Sinai. Miniature reproducing an original of the fifth or sixth century in the Bible of the patrician Leo of the first half of the tenth century.

impression that Constantine was trying to collect and boil down all useful knowledge, most of which dated to the period of Late Antiquity. His hagiographic programme was destined for a wide diffusion, but his secular programme could not have been meant to reach much beyond the palace. It was to serve as a vast reference collection for future emperors and their courtiers.

Byzantium did not experience another dark age after Constantine Porphyrogenitus. Whilst not all the texts that were available to him have survived, the bulk of what was transliterated and excerpted in the ninth and tenth centuries continued to be copied (if only occasionally) and, therefore, to be read. The Byzantine revival not only salvaged many of the ancient classics, but also—and this needs to be stressed—determined the content of the surviving corpus, which is the product of Byzantine selection. Old texts were not copied at random; they were copied because they were considered useful either for practical ends (e.g. medicine, agriculture, military science, astrology) or as storehouses of curious knowledge or as exemplars of literary style. Besides, there was a financial factor. Arethas, who sometimes noted down the sums he expended on manuscripts he commissioned, informs us that his Euclid (now at Oxford) cost 14 gold pieces (*nomismata*), his Plato (471 folios) 13 for copying and 8 for parchment, his corpus of Christian Apologists (now in Paris) 20 for copying and 6 for parchment. These were considerable sums, beyond the reach of all but the richest individuals. By way of comparison, the yearly salary of a medium-ranking court dignitary was 72 *nomismata*. In today's prices (to the extent a comparison may be made) Arethas' Plato cost something like £5,000. Institutional sponsorship does not appear to be recorded.

Considering the constraints, it is remarkable how much was salvaged, and we can hardly complain that we would have made a different selection. Contrary to our tastes, the Byzantines had least interest in drama, more in prose than in poetry, and most of all in rhetoric: hence the endless volumes that have few readers today of Aelius Aristides (represented by

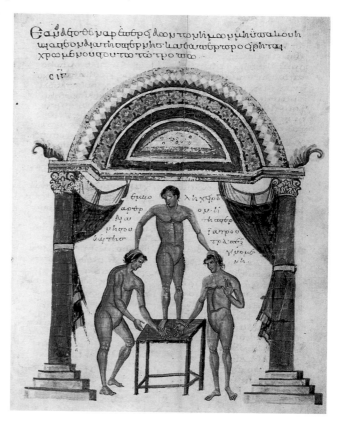

Facing: Busts of the Minor Prophets in a luxurious manuscript now at Turin, Biblioteca Nazionale, cod. B.I.2 of the latter part of the tenth century. A damaged subscription of the year 535 provides the date of the original from which the Turin manuscript was copied.

Below: Tenth-century copy of a medical treatise on the setting of bones by Apollonius of Citium (first century BC). The human figures probably reproduce an ancient original, but have been incongruously placed within ornate arches.

One of the very few secular products of the 'Macedonian Renaissance' is the illustrated copy of Nicander's *Theriaca*, a learned poem of the second century BC on snakes and other poisonous animals.

over 200 manuscripts), Lucian, Himerius, Libanius, Themistius, Choricius and many more of that ilk. Rhetoric prevailed even over religious odium, which is why we still have the Orations and Letters of Julian the Apostate, except, of course, his *Contra Galilaeos*. Surprisingly, the earliest Christian authors attracted little attention, perhaps because they were considered outdated and some were doctrinally suspect. The textual tradition of Justin Martyr, Athenagoras, Tatian, and Clement of Alexandria goes back to a single manuscript commissioned by Arethas in 914. The Epistle to Diognetus was preserved in one late manuscript, now destroyed. The *Shepherd* of Hermas, one of the oldest pieces of Christian writing, widely read in Late Antiquity and present in the famous Codex Sinaiticus of the Bible (fourth century), is found in only one other Greek manuscript as late as the fifteenth century.

The criterion of utility may be tested by a somewhat unusual example. What we call the Greek Anthology is a vast collection of about 4,000 verse epigrams ranging in date from the sixth century BC to the tenth AD. Originally an epigram was meant to be inscribed on stone, but it outgrew its inscriptional function to embrace such topics as love, drinking, and jests. It was particularly cultivated in the Hellenistic period, when the first anthologies of epigrams began to be compiled. Their production continued until the sixth century AD: the last anthology before the Dark Age, the Cycle of Agathias, published soon after 565, brought together the compositions of some twenty-five contemporary authors, most of whom were lawyers and civil servants. George of Pisidia, a notable poet, wrote epigrams in the reign of Heraclius, and then the genre died. It reappeared in the early ninth century, when a group of iconoclastic epigrams was inscribed at the entrance of the imperial palace as a kind of manifesto. Theodore the Studite took the trouble of refuting them in verse and himself composed over one hundred other epigrams on religious topics. From then on epigrams continued to be written by Byzantine litterati, very seldom in elegiacs (which is the proper metre for epigrams), usually in twelve-syllable iambics that are better attuned to the medieval pronunciation of Greek.

The Greek Anthology originated in the milieu of the palace school and was first compiled by a clergyman called Constantine Kephalas, attested in 917. His manuscript has not survived, but we are fortunate in having one that is not much later, the Palatinus 23 (at Heidelberg), usually dated 930–50. It is divided thematically into fifteen books, opening with 'Christian epigrams', perhaps to reassure the public, but going on to amatory (Book 5) and even pederastic ones (Book 12). Their imagery is predominantly pagan.

The Anthology has seldom been considered from a Byzantine viewpoint, although it is a Byzantine creation that raises some interesting questions. How is it that Kephalas and his small group of collaborators were able to lay their hands on such a mass of old epigrams? We are told that one member of the team, Gregory by name, copied verse inscriptions from stones in Greece and Asia Minor, and there are several Christian epigrams from Constantinople that were copied directly from monuments. The bulk of the poems, however, must have come from manuscripts. That means that Kephalas had access not only to the Cycle of Agathias, but to a series of earlier anthologies, going back to the Garland by Meleager of Gadara (first century BC). Furthermore, why did he go to so much trouble? The only plausible answer is that he did so to provide models for imitation. But why, we may ask, the sexual epigrams? Perhaps the good Kephalas enjoyed them or was loath to leave out any curious remnants of antiquity that came his way. In any case he deserves our gratitude even if, in the event, the elegiac epigram had a limited future in the Byzantine world.

The classicist, when he looks at the Byzantine revival, is chiefly interested in the preservation of Greek texts, but the historian of Byzantium will wish to ask a related and more difficult question: What impact did these texts have on the persons who perused them in the ninth and following centuries? Did

Marble block from the church of St Polyeuktos at Constantinople of the sixth century, bearing part of a very long epigram in honour of the princess Anicia Juliana. The epigram which was still intact in the ninth or tenth century, was copied into the Palatine Anthology.

225

the readers open themselves to the message, the values of the ancient classics? Of inspiration across the divide between Christianity and paganism there is little sign. Take the case of one of the noblest books of antiquity, the *Meditations* of Marcus Aurelius. Photios was not acquainted with it, but Arethas owned an old copy, 'not quite falling apart', as he put it. He had it transcribed and passed the original on to a bishop friend, recommending it as being 'highly beneficial'. Alas, Arethas' transcription is gone and all that survives is one manuscript of the fourteenth century. No Byzantine reader is recorded as having been particularly moved by the *Meditations*, yet when they were first published in Europe (1559), they caused a sensation.

The purpose of the Byzantine revival was to repair the gap left by the Dark Age and return to the mandarin literary culture of Late Antiquity, with its grammar, its metrics, its rhetoric, and its complement of miscellaneous erudition. In that it succeeded, except that the social basis of the recreated culture was extremely small—perhaps no more than a couple of hundred persons passing at a given time through the educational establishment, and that for the whole empire—candidates for posts in the imperial service and the higher echelons of the Church. The necessary schooling was now available only at Constantinople. We would not expect any signs of 'humanism' under such conditions. Only when something resembling a 'bourgeois' public had come into being could attitudes begin to change, but that did not happen until the middle of the eleventh century and then to a limited extent.

The revival movement, as we have said, also exerted some impact on the arts. Labelled, somewhat misleadingly, the 'Macedonian Renaissance' after the name of the dynasty established by Basil I, this phenomenon has received much more minute attention from scholars than its textual counterpart. Yet, its compass was extremely limited. Admittedly, very few works of art of the ninth/tenth century survive at Constantinople: a series of mosaics in St Sophia, admirable in themselves but not exhibiting any marked contact with antiquity, a couple of ruined churches, one of them—the monastery of Constantine Lips of 907—containing many fragments of architectural carving, practically nothing from the imperial palace, except a bit of an inlaid floor. Still, we can only form a judgement on the basis of what we have, and one thing we know well is the coinage. It shows a slight improvement in quality, but remains purely medieval, with frontal imperial and sacred images: no attempt to return to the profile head of antiquity as was done by Charlemagne. Nor do we find any trace of sculpture in the round. Even in architectural sculpture, classical elements, e.g. the Corinthian capital, are absent. The 'renaissance' ap-

Charlemagne's *denarii* with a Roman-type profile bust, struck at various mints a few years after his coronation in 800, have no equivalent in medieval Byzantine coinage.

226

Perhaps the most classical of the illuminated manuscripts of the 'Macedonian Renaissance' is the Gospel of the Stavronikita monastery, Mount Athos, cod. 43. Its evangelist portraits (here Mark) have the statuesque dignity of ancient philosophers.

pears only in the minor arts, largely in illuminated manuscripts and ivories. The manuscripts in question are fewer than a dozen in number and are largely of Christian content. The oldest in the series, the Gregory Nazianzen in Paris, is datable to about 880 and is certifiably imperial. Another, a Bible in the Vatican of the first half of the tenth century, was commissioned by a treasury official called Leo. One of the latest members of the group (c.980), reconstituted by modern scholarship as a Bible in several volumes (now divided between Turin, Florence, and Copenhagen), was copied for an imperial chamberlain named Niketas from an original of 535. The remaining manuscripts in question have no known sponsorship, but are presumed to emanate from the imperial court. The only notable example of secular

Ivory panel probably commemorating the coronation in 945 of Romanos II, who had been married to Eudokia (Bertha, daughter of Hugo of Provence, king of Italy). Romanos, who is shown as youthful, was actually six years old at the time.

Detail of the Veroli Casket depicting the sacrifice of Iphigeneia, London, Victoria and Albert Museum. The casket is decorated with an assortment of subjects drawn from classical mythology (Bellerophon with Pegasus, the rape of Europa, etc.), rendered in a somewhat humorous manner. Probably tenth century.

228

Joshua meeting the archangel Michael in front of Jericho. The city is both represented in the background and symbolized by a seated personification. Partly tinted parchment roll of the middle or second half of the tenth century, depicting the story of Joshua in a continuous frieze.

content is a copy of Nicander's poem on poisonous animals (*Theriaca*), now in Paris.

To a greater or lesser degree the miniatures of the above manuscripts exhibit antique features, such as 'atmospheric' backgrounds shading from blue to pink; personifications of cities, rivers, mountains, and abstract qualities; fantastic elements of architecture reminiscent of Pompeian painting; votive columns festooned with ribbons and topped by vases. Presumably copied from models of the fifth/sixth century, they convey a strange atmosphere of unreality.

Ivories of the same period are fairly numerous, but contain few datable pieces. A plaque depicting the marriage of Romanos II to Bertha/Eudokia in 945 (now in Paris) and a triptych probably commissioned for Constantine VII (Palazzo di Venezia, Rome) suggest that the best items belong to the middle of the tenth century. Their classicism resides largely in the draped figures of Christian personages. By contrast, a series of ivory caskets decorated with scenes from pagan mythology exhibit pudgy figures and awkward, cavorting cupids.

The fashion for the antique appears to have waned by about the year 1000. Limited to precious objects which, by definition, had little public exposure, it did not influence greatly the main lines of contemporary artistic production until it was rediscovered during the Palaiologan revival of the late thirteenth century.

9 Spreading the Word: Byzantine Missions

JONATHAN SHEPARD

The nations worship Christ. Miniature of Khludov Psalter.

The Byzantine emperor, as a successor to Constantine the Great, was acclaimed as 'equal of the apostles' in court acclamations and rhetoric. An emperor, not a patriarch or any other sort of churchman, had been chosen by God to bring about the conversion of the inhabitants of the Roman world, and proclaiming one's willingness to spread the Word was a useful political prop: it impressed the uniqueness of the emperor's relationship with God upon his own subjects as well as foreigners. The image of the emperor as carrying on the original apostles' work was projected by the ceremonial in the Great Palace at Pentecost, when the court celebrated the descent of the Holy Spirit in tongues of fire. The chanters prayed that the emperors, 'joy and pride of the Romans, may draw those who speak foreign languages into a single tongue in the Faith'. The Life of Basil I, commissioned by his grandson, Constantine VII, praises his attention to 'this apostolic work', attempting to draw various peoples into subjection to Christ. It is taken for granted that the emperor is the key to instigating missionary work not just in this imperial biography but even in the sole full-blown Lives of Byzantine-born missionaries which are known to us, those of the brothers Constantine-Cyril and Methodios. There was a certain institutional basis to the rhetoric. The emperor claimed the right to change the rank and extent of metropolitanates in certain circumstances and assumed special responsibility for regions where there were only isolated, suffraganless archbishops or no Church organization at all. Such was the state of affairs beyond the northern Black Sea. This was, from Late Antiquity onwards, the quarter from which 'barbarian' peoples were likeliest to trouble Byzantium's outposts on the Crimea and its Balkan territories. One might expect emperors to have taken a keen interest in converting the northern peoples to Christianity, if only as a means of drawing their fangs.

At first sight, reality seems to match the image of the emperor as zealous 'apostle'. The list of peoples to the north—and also west and east—of the Black Sea whom Byzantine missionaries visited is varied and long. The Bulgars under Khan Boris accepted Christianity in, most probably, 864 and although Boris switched his allegiance to the Roman pope soon afterwards, he returned to the Orthodox fold in 870, striking a deal with Basil I whose details are unfortunately obscure but which most probably gave Boris scope to approve, if not to nominate outright, his own archbishop. Missions, in the form of 'an imperial agent and priests', were sent by Basil to the Serbs and to other Slavic groupings in the western Balkans. The pious scholar and imperial aide Constantine was sent to the court of the kagan of the Khazars in 860–1, and within a couple of years he and his brother Methodios were expounding the Word and translating the Gospels into Slavic for the benefit of Rastislav, the prince of Moravia, and his subjects. Early in the tenth century the ruler of the Alans, a semi-nomadic people dominating the foothills of the Northern Caucasus, adopted Byzantine Christianity and began to impose it on his subjects with the aid of a monk and subsequently a metropolitan sent from Byzantium. From around 948 at least two parties of Hungarians headed by chieftains visited Constantinople and their leaders were baptized. After the second of the two recorded visits 'a certain monk named Hierotheos', newly consecrated as 'bishop of *Tourkia* (Hungary)', accompanied the visitors back on their return journey. Another 'state visit' took place about this time, headed by the leader of a people whose reputation for ferocity matched that of the Hungarians, the Rus. Princess Olga was, together with her entourage and other notables, treated to two receptions at the palace and at some stage in her visit she was baptized. A generation later, *c*.988, Olga's grandson Vladimir was baptized and a full-blown religious mission was sent to Kiev— 'metropolitans and bishops' according to a well-informed Arabic writer. Vladimir took as his Christian name that of the senior emperor, Basil II. Olga's godfather had been Constantine VII and she had taken the name of his wife, Helena, as her baptismal name. Likewise Khan Boris had assumed the name of Michael after that of the emperor of the day, Michael III. The Byzantines did not allow convert-peoples to forget that they had been their benefactors. The concept that each successive Bulgarian ruler was the 'spiritual son' of the Byzantine emperor of the day was aired in the protocols

Baptism of the Bulgarian king Boris in 864. The emperor Michael III, shown on the left, acts as his godfather. The bishop on the right is Photios. Miniature of the Chronicle of Manasses.

for correspondence addressed to him. A similar form of address served to remind the Alan prince of his debt to and moral dependence on the *basileus*.

Some of the missions gave rise to lasting metropolitanates and eventually to secondary expansion much further afield. However, there is no evidence of a sustained effort to spread the Word and save souls everywhere in accordance with the emperor's self-styled role as an 'apostle'. Emperors do not seem to have sponsored major missionary undertakings in any quarter between the seventh and the early ninth centuries. In 816, Leo V attempted to introduce a crowd of pagan Bulgar emissaries to Christian worship in the form of the liturgy and thereby to cement the peace treaty which he was making with them. His efforts incurred derision, as a case of pearls being cast before swine: by implication, the Bulgars were best left to their own savage ways. This state of affairs changed from the 860s onwards, but in the great majority of the cases listed above, it was foreign potentates who took the initiative, asking the emperor to send teachers capable of expounding the Christian religion or prelates and priests who might set about organizing a Church for them. According to the Life of Constantine, his journeys to Khazaria and Moravia represented the emperor's response to requests from those lands' rulers for, respectively, a bookman to counter Judaist and Muslim proselytizers and assistance in teaching the people the true Christian faith. About the same time the Rus, having failed to gain rich pickings from their raid on Constantinople in 860, sent a request for a mission. A bishop was sent and this enterprise—which proved to be unfruitful—gave Photios occasion to claim the Rus as 'subjects and affiliates' of the emperor. It is quite likely that the emperor, Michael III, was stung into a more active response to such requests than had hitherto been the norm by a particular concatenation of circumstance. The Rus assault had created panic among the citizens of Constantinople and to seize—and be seen to seize—the opportunity of averting a return visit through the dispatch of a senior churchman to the north was politic. At the same time, the Khazar leadership's decision *c.*861 to adopt Judaism in spite of the efforts of Constantine to put the case for Christianity was a humiliating rebuff. It served a warning that barbarians seemingly set in their foolish ways might abruptly turn to a monotheistic religion which owed no favours to the *basileus*. A similar turn of events seemed to be in view much closer to home. In the early 860s Khan Boris of Bulgaria was floating the prospect of his acceptance of Christianity to Louis the German, king of the East Franks. Michael III could hardly have viewed with equanimity the forging of formal links between Boris and the Franks' ecclesiastical organization or the western Church in general: this would most likely reinforce the burgeoning political alliance between Boris and Louis.

Such was the situation early in the decade which saw an unprecedented flurry of missionary activity directed by the emperor. If we follow one Byzantine version of events, the Bulgarians' acceptance of Orthodox Christianity was the result of Michael III's initiative: he threatened Boris with attack by land and sea and the Bulgars, overawed, sued for peace and offered to become Christians. The emperor is thereby credited with the Bulgars' conversion. The obvious inference to be drawn from this version is that Michael launched a pre-emptive strike, forestalling any alignment with the western Church on the part of Boris. It is, however, worth noting that other Byzantine versions ascribe the initiative to Boris. According to one, he was instructed in the faith by a captive monk and then persuaded to adopt Christianity by his sister, herself converted during a spell at the emperor's palace in Constantinople. Another has him converted by a monk who painted for him an awesome picture of the Last Judgement: Boris was scared into immediate baptism. These accounts are not necessarily totally fabulous for having an obvious hagiographical tinge. It may be that there was indeed imperial sabre-rattling over the recent closening of ties between Boris and the East Franks, but that Boris himself took the initiative, proposing to accept baptism from the Byzantine emperor's priests: he may have spent some time weighing up the advantages of abandoning paganism without committing himself to a specific replacement, mindful perhaps of the examination of monotheistic faiths which the ruler of the Khazars had recently conducted. Whichever reconstruction of events one may prefer, it is clear that the Byzantine emperor was not acting as a wholly free agent in providing a mission for the Bulgars: even if he did, in effect, force orthodoxy upon them at spear-point, he was doing so in order to thwart the advance of Latin western influence.

The evidence for Byzantine missionary enterprises beyond the frontiers before the 860s is sparse and the missions dispatched from that decade onwards were to a large extent sent in response to local rulers' requests or in competition with rival proselytizing religions. They do not seem to have been initiatives taken by the emperor unilaterally. This apparent discrepancy between propaganda and reality should not surprise us. Conversion of the heathen was only one among several duties of Christian leadership which the emperor exercised. It served, essentially, to place him on a pedestal distancing him both from his own subjects and from 'the nations' beyond. The primary function of the propaganda and court ceremonial was to highlight and celebrate the emperor's special access to God which resulted from his incomparable piety and made him a worthy successor to the first Constantine. The sublime 'apartness' of the emperor, before whom 'mighty in wisdom', all the 'nations' will 'quake' is the leitmotif of a confidential manual which Constantine VII wrote for his heir. The emperor was worried by the greed and the presumptuous demands of the barbarians of the north: they wanted to partake of the wondrous products of the palace complex, while Constantine's aim was to keep them exclusively at the disposal of his son. The cautionary tales which were to be told so as to dampen the northerners' ardour for imperial crowns, robes, and princesses assumed some acquaintance with Christian traditions. But they were to convey the moral that the exclusiveness of the 'purple-born' was at God's command. An obvious means of toning down this exclusiveness was common adherence to the Christian faith, and this caused some embarrassment for Constantine VII. He considered the possible precedent for foreign marriages which the marriage in 927 of the Christian tsar Peter of Bulgaria to a Byzantine princess could be said to have set. He insisted that even this match breached both Church law and an alleged prohibition of Constantine the Great, without however offering any substantive rejoinder to those who might cite it as a precedent. Thus while the Life of his grandfather might idealize Basil's 'apostolic' work in spreading the Word among the Bulgars almost a century earlier, Constantine himself privately recoiled from the implications of such mission work: it might open the door to 'uppity' barbarians expecting to be treated on a more or less equal footing. Constantine could hardly abandon to their fate such missionary enterprises as were already under way, and it was he who presided over the baptism of the Magyar chieftains and Princess Olga, becoming the latter's godfather. But while he sent a bishop to the Hungarians, he seems to have balked at doing the same for Olga. This would be in key with his uneasy awareness of the diplomatic repercussions when 'barbarian' peoples turned into self-confident Christians, as the Bulgars had all too evidently done.

The emperor's self-proclaimed role as 'apostle' was not, therefore, tantamount to an urge to convert entire peoples far and wide and it was to a large extent geared towards individuals or communities resident within the empire's borders, whether voluntarily or involuntarily, or directed against rival religious leaders. Thus at certain feasts in the palace Muslim prisoners-of-war attended, dressed in white beltless garments. Such was the garb worn by catechumens prior to their baptism and the choice of this outfit for the prisoners was probably meant to highlight the emperor's ability to make even Saracens change their spots. Rivalry with the Muslims, especially with the Baghdad caliphate, was one of the driving forces behind the emperor's stance as evangelist in the ninth and tenth centuries. As the world's premier Christian ruler he needed to offer a refutation of the critiques of Christianity which Muslim preachers were putting forward, and to be seen to be holding the line intellectually as well as militarily. According to a mid-ninth-century treatise entitled 'The Refutation of Muhammad', the emperor 'calls even the Arabs to piety, shooting down their preposterous and erroneous impiety by means of refutation through the truth of words'. One of the functions of scholars and churchmen sent on embassies to Baghdad was to deal with criticisms of the faith in an authoritative fashion, and to engage in disputations with Muslim sages at the Abbasid court. Their brief was to uphold the emperor's intellectual credentials as champion of Christians: they were not really in the business of converting individuals to Christianity and there can have been no serious expectation of converting the caliph or other Muslim rulers. In the mid-ninth century, young intellectuals such as Photios and Constantine took part in these embassies. It was to them that the emperor turned when he decided to respond to initiatives from Slav and other northern potentates in the 860s; he did not have at court any other pool of persons experienced in expounding the faith. This helps explain the rather cerebral tone of the surviving texts addressed to such potentates. Photios, now patriarch of Constantinople, sent a long letter to Boris of Bulgaria soon after his conversion, making no allowances for his newcomer status: doctrine as determined by the Church Councils is set out in detail and Boris' duties are spelled out in edifying terms which owed much to the classical Greek writings on rulership with which Photios was familiar. A sermon in Church Slavonic attributed to Methodius is no less stringent in the moral demands which it makes of the Moravian ruler. This suggests that the high-minded, austere tones in which the Lives of Methodios and Constantine depict their evangelizing are an accurate register of their labours. A hint of what Ihor Ševčenko has called 'the overly complicated didactic material' used for missionary work is also preserved in the *Russian Primary Chronicle*'s version of the 'speech' which a Byzantine 'philosopher' reportedly delivered before Prince Vladimir of Kiev in the late 980s. Vladimir was then making serious enquiries about various brands of monotheistic religion, Judaism and Islam among them, and his eventual choice of Byzantine-style Christianity was not inevitable. Early in the tenth century the Volga Bulgars' ruler had adopted Islam and the imperial establishment could not have contemplated the spread of Islam north of the Black Sea with equanimity. Thus missionary activity was, to a great extent, conceived of in Constantinople in terms of rivalry with the other 'Religions of the Book' and of upholding the emperor's reputation for piety and superior wisdom. To carry out these tasks, the earlier missionary leaders needed to be able to address questions of governance and justice in lofty moral tones in their written works and, probably, also by word of mouth.

In some respects the Byzantine establishment's part in the spreading of the Word is reminiscent of its stance in other spheres, such as commerce: the abiding assumption was that foreigners would come to Constantinople, rather than that it was expedient or fitting to reach out and submit all mankind to the Gospel. There is no firm evidence of a 'seminary' for missionaries in Constantinople or that specialized training in, for example, the relevant language was provided for those sent out; nor was the literary culture particularly favourable towards outward-bound ventures to save souls. The lamentations of lettered bishops upon their exile from 'the God-protected City' and its court circles to provincial sees were not mere literary stereotypes. Nonetheless, the inward-looking 'reactive' stance of the establishment contained a measure of realism and paradoxically could serve as an attraction to foreign potentates.

To have taken the initiative more overtly might have gained the Middle Byzantine Church more martyrs for the faith, but it would not necessarily have brought about a wave of conversions. In the case of any political structure enjoying a fair degree of cohesiveness, the permission of the local leadership was needed before mission work could begin. And in practice the active co-operation of those having status, influence, and resources in their communities was more or less indispensable if ordinary people were to be induced to give up their 'old ways' for good. Awareness of the key role of members of the elite is shown in a letter of the patriarch Nicholas Mystikos to the archbishop of Alania: he is urged to be lenient towards the Alans' practice of polygamy, particularly when dealing with members of the 'upper class', 'who have great power to counteract the salvation of the whole nation'. One must remember that there was often a conflict of opinions within the elite about the new religion. Boris of Bulgaria encountered violent opposition to conversion from many of the 'leading men', while Olga of Kiev's son, Sviatoslav, rejected her attempts to convert him. He maintained that, were he to agree, 'my retainers will start to laugh at this'. From the emperor's point of view, it made sense to reap such practical benefits as were to be had from the presence of Christians in the upper echelons of northern peoples, and to wait upon events—in particular, for such initiatives as might be taken by the leaders of the more stable structures. If a ruler showed interest in personally adopting Christianity from Byzantium or, more ominously, was shopping around among the various forms of monotheism, the emperor could make a move.

The so-called Assemani Gospel Lectionary (Cod. Vat. Slav. 3) was probably written in western Bulgaria in the late 10th or early 11th century. It is one of the earliest specimens of the Glagolitic script, believed to have been invented by Sts Cyril and Methodios.

Facing, above: Ivory triptych featuring the Deisis (Christ receiving the intercession of John the Baptist and the Virgin Mary), apostles, Church Fathers, and martyrs. The dedicatory inscription names an emperor Constantine, presumably Constantine VII Porphyrogenitus, as having commissioned this object.

Facing, below: Chalice in the Treasury of St Mark's, Venice. An antique sardonyx cup of the first century BC/AD, reused in a chalice by the emperor Romanos II (959–63), has cloisonné enamel plaques with busts of various saints. It was part of the booty removed from Constantinople to Venice at the time of the Fourth Crusade.

And his intellectuals could set out for the ruler elaborate ideals of governance, for which the template was the *basileus*.

Paradoxically, the very aloofness of the imperial establishment and its lack of obvious zeal to follow up every 'conversion opportunity' with teams of trained cadres may have rendered its cult more attractive to foreign potentates. This was partly a matter of scarcity value and *snobisme*, as with the palace's robes and princesses, but also of the broader scope which these very deficiencies opened up for a strong-minded ruler. He could, if a written form of the vernacular language was available, seize the chance to create not only a corps of educated nobles and potential subordinates, but also a sizeable home-grown priesthood and thus a tighter, more sophisticated culturo-religious framework over which to preside. Such an option was available to the Slavs, in the form of an alphabet catering for the particular sounds of the Slavic tongue and also of a lucid, flexible literary language into which the Greek Scriptures, the liturgical offices, and also the Church Fathers' guidelines on the Faith could be translated. The alphabet was the invention of Constantine-Cyril, and his brother Methodios joined him in the task of translation, carrying this on and composing or commissioning a number of new works after the death of Constantine-Cyril in 867; among them was a Life of Constantine-Cyril himself. There is no firm evidence that the Byzantine establishment had envisaged translation-work on such a scale when the mission was dispatched to Moravia. The initiative seems to have been taken by the brothers in Central Europe, far from the glare of the imperial court whose denizens might reasonably doubt the desirability of giving mere Slav

Right: An early example of the Cyrillic script, this inscription, carved in 1016, commemorates the refurbishment of the fortress of Bitolja (Macedonia) by John Vladislav, brother of the Bulgarian king Samuel, after the latter had been decisively defeated by Basil II. The inscription was discovered in 1956 in the ruins of a mosque at Bitolja.

archontes tools for creating a distinctive political culture. A few gifted pupils of Methodius and also, apparently, some translated texts became available to Boris of Bulgaria soon after Methodios' death in 885. Boris appreciated the potential of the newly translated pious literature for furthering pastoral work and raising his own status, but it was his son Symeon who developed it fully, encouraging the translation of Church Fathers' treatises on doctrine and sermons and setting himself up as a direct educator of his nobility and as the enlightener of his subjects in general. He proved himself ready from the start of his reign to use *force majeure* to back up his insistence on self-determination and respectful treatment by the emperor. This and his subsequent demand to be recognized as an emperor made him the *bête noire* of the imperial establishment and his incursions and devastation of the empire's European provinces from 918 made him a 'man guilty of the shedding of much Christian blood' in the eyes of ordinary Byzantines. The spectre of Symeon and the substance of the self-confident Christian polity which he had helped form may well have hardened the reservations which emperors such as Constantine VII harboured as to missionary initiatives towards the rulers of entire peoples.

It is tempting to conclude that the Byzantines' missionary 'Commonwealth' was gained in an absence of mind. But to do so would be to overlook the scale of the problems faced by anyone attempting to change by peaceful means social and cultural mores in the early medieval Balkans and Eurasia as well as to ignore the role of monks and churches on the empire's outer fringes. The importance of such outriders did not go unrecognized by statesmen at the centre of things in Constantinople, who sometimes tried to harness or liaise with them. Appreciation of the desirability of instructors in the faith being able to communicate directly with their hearers was shown by Michael III when he chose Constantine-Cyril and Methodius in response to Rastislav of Moravia's request. According to the Life of Methodius, he said to them: 'You are Thessalonicans and all Thessalonicans speak excellent Slavic.' The brothers were probably exceptional in being highly educated members of the metropolitan establishment who nonetheless retained traces of their origins in an 'ethnic' borderland, and who had language skills of specific use to Michael's project. But other imperial decision-makers showed general awareness of the value to mission work of persons from outside the metropolitan scene. The Life of Basil I commissioned by his grandson praised his dispatch to the Bulgarians not only of prelates but also of 'the pious monks, summoned from the mountains and from the caves of the earth'. Self-reliance, asceticism, and the graphic embodiment of other Christian virtues were presumably their credentials for mission work, rather than any ability to preach or teach in Slavic.

Much of the work of spreading the word about Christianity was done

Facing: The scene of Pentecost symbolized the preaching of the Gospel to all the nations. Mosaic in the pilgrimage church of Hosios Loukas in Phokis (Greece) showing the descent of the Holy Spirit on the assembled apostles and, in the pendentives, groups of 'Nations' and 'Tongues'. Early eleventh century.

unofficially, even unwittingly, by communities of monks established on or far beyond the empire's periphery. The evidence for the monasteries' existence is mainly archaeological and the dating of the sites and interpretation of the occupants' precise origins and activities are often highly speculative. But there is little doubt that eastern Orthodox monasteries and nunneries were functioning in Bulgaria before Boris' conversion. They may mostly have lain in former Byzantine territory which Bulgar khans had brought beneath their sway earlier in the ninth century. But there is some evidence of foundations farther north, notably the small cave-chapels at Murfatlar, in the Dobroudja. Some monks possessed spectacular skills which were not usually available even at the higher echelons of barbarian society: the monk who so alarmed Boris with a painting of the Last Judgement had been commissioned by him to come up with an awesome and arresting composition to decorate a hunting lodge. This tale cannot be taken literally, but there is significance in its assumption that monks could be at large and valued for their technical services in a pagan-led society. A type of small church similar to the Murfatlar chapels, although above-ground, is to be found in various areas on the fringes of the Byzantine world and it has been plausibly suggested that these churches have some connection with Byzantine missions. Several examples of these simple, single-nave buildings with elongated semicircular apses and a measuring scheme which made them easy and cheap enough to construct occur in Moravia. Others have been found at Cherson on the Crimea and in the northern Caucasus, where monks played an important role in the 'official' mission to the Alans of the tenth century and beyond. It may be that these small churches often register the presence of monks, whether spontaneous or on assignment from the central authorities. That teams of monks were sent on missions for finite periods is suggested by a letter of Nicholas Mysticus addressed to 'our spiritual sons' labouring to strengthen the faith in a 'desolate' land which may be identifiable with Alania.

With the easing of Bulgaro-Byzantine tensions after 927 and in particular the foundation of the Great Lavra on Mount Athos in 962/3, the journeys to the Balkans and other northern lands of Byzantine-trained monks, as individuals or organized groups, became more common. The rulers of the Poles, the Hungarians, and the Rus all accepted baptism in the final third of the tenth century, but their powers of propaganda and coercion were not such as to instil the new faith and its concomitant rites and normative values into their subjects at a stroke. Nor did the allegiance of the Polish and Hungarian rulers to the Roman papacy necessarily close the door to Orthodox monks and ministers. An Athonite monk who was also a priest was at large in Poland in the 1020s. Furthermore, monastic houses containing 'Greeks' and allowing for Orthodox styles of asceticism were founded by King Andrew I near

Višegrad and on an Athos-like peninsula jutting into Lake Balaton. These sites lay beyond the lands in southern Hungary where Orthodox priests and churches were particularly prominent in the eleventh and twelfth centuries. The visibility of Orthodox rites in the south is most probably due to the labours of the monk Hierotheos and his successors, whose status was raised to that of 'metropolitan of *Tourkia*'. Within a generation of Prince Vladimir of Kiev's conversion, there were Rus monks residing on Mount Athos. One of them, named Anthony, came under pressure from his spiritual father—presumably a Byzantine—to return to the north: 'Go back to Rus and let the blessing of the Holy Mount be upon you, for from you there shall come to be many monks.' The prime objective of the spiritual father, as interpreted by Anthony, seems to have been the practice of rigorous monasticism rather than the preaching of the Word and, upon returning to Kiev, Anthony occupied a hollow in a bluff overlooking the Dnieper, living as a recluse. But 'good people' learnt of his way of life quite soon and brought him food. Brethren 'to the number of twelve' gathered round him and in practice the monks (whose numbers rose further still) performed a pastoral role for the inhabitants of Kiev nearby. Their abbots acted as counsellors and consciences to the princes and new houses in the distant north-east were founded by alumni of the Cave Monastery. One of them, Kuksha, suffered martyrdom while preaching the Word to a pagan people, the Viatichi. The Cave Monastery was of unique importance in fostering Christian observance and a sense of manifest destiny among the Rus. The Athonite monks' aim may have been the narrow one of disseminating ascetic values and the number of returnees was probably small, but their effect on Christian life in the north was much more immediate than that of the mostly monoglot metropolitans sent out from Constantinople.

Athos was, like Thessalonica, perched on the edge of the predominantly Slav-speaking Balkan hinterland, and yet its monasteries enjoyed very close connections with the emperor. A rather different mode of linking a peripheral area with both evangelization and the earthly centre of things was to be found at Cherson. This Crimean port was in one sense a provincial backwater while the towns and small settlements strung along the southern Crimean coastline were even more secluded, and only loosely under the authority of the emperor. For that very reason, iconodule monks sought refuge in the region in the late eighth and earlier ninth centuries, adding to what seems already to have been a sizeable number of cells and monastic communities reaching well into the mountainous interior of the southern part of the peninsula. Chapels and cells were cut out of the cliff-rock at such places as Inkerman (not far from Cherson) and Tepe Kermen, further inland. There are hints that the monks had some impact on the local inhabitants; for example,

The deep-water harbour at Cherson, near modern Sebastopol. Having massive land walls and rapid maritime communications with Constantinople and the south coast of the Black Sea, Cherson was the chief stronghold of the empire in the Crimea. Chersonite clergy played an important part in missionary activity among the steppe nomads, Khazars, and Rus.

at the Bakla fortress has been found a burial-vault which seems to have belonged to persons of rank and substance bearing Turkic as well as Christian names, which are inscribed on its side in Greek. Cherson itself contains probable traces of conversion work, in the form of finds of shallow cups of white clay with black crosses on their base. They are datable to the ninth to tenth centuries and the other examples of this type have mostly been found on or far beyond the empire's territorial frontiers: on the Lower Danube, at Preslav, Thessalonica, the Straits of Kerch, and at Novgorod in a stratum datable, significantly, to 972–89, the era of the Rus' conversion to Christianity. They have been interpreted as 'liturgical bowls' from which newly converted adults would drink milk and honey symbolizing the fact that they had been born again and now had access to paradise.

The find of several examples of these 'liturgical bowls' at Cherson suggests that conversion work was occurring there on a substantial scale. In fact the letters of Nicholas Mysticus suggest a very active interest in evangelization on the part of at least one of the archbishops of Cherson; in themselves they attest the imperial authorities' awareness of Cherson's value as a sort of 'devolved' mission station. Communications by sea were quite frequent, at least in summer, since emperors looked to governors and other agents there to brief them on activities in the steppe.

These ties were sometimes put to the use of missionary enterprises: the archbishop of Cherson was directed to take charge of mission work in Khazaria and he seems to have spent some time there. Patriarch Nicholas Mystikos expressed deep appreciation of his 'zeal on behalf of that deluded nation' and left it to him to choose a person to be made archbishop of Khazaria. It is likely that the Chersonite clergy were more accustomed than Constantinopolitans to everyday dealings with barbarians, Khazars and Rus among them. There are indications from graffiti of the presence of Alans in the town and it was there that Constantine-Cyril gave himself a crash course in Hebrew, while on his way to the court of the Khazar kagan. Rus traders were visiting Cherson by the second half of the ninth century and before long Chersonites were paying fairly regular visits to the Middle Dnieper region. It is significant that Prince Vladimir, after being baptized in Cherson, brought the town's priests back to Kiev, where they helped officiate at the mass baptism of the citizens in the Dnieper. A priest from Cherson, Anastasios, became a close associate of Vladimir, who put him in charge of the show church built for him by Byzantine 'masters', assigning Chersonite priests to work as his subordinates. According to the Rus *Primary Chronicle*, Anastasios had betrayed the town to Vladimir by revealing to him the location of its water pipes. This allegation cannot be dismissed out of hand, but there may be a simpler explanation for the prominence of Chersonite priests in the newly converted Kiev: their experience of dealing with the Rus, if not personal links with individuals, and very possibly a smattering of Slavic, the *lingua franca* employed by the Rus in their trading operations.

The importation of the Chersonites into Kiev *c.*988 was a result of initiatives taken by Vladimir and not the emperor, but the imperial authorities were prepared to co-operate by way of the full-blown mission from Constantinople mentioned by Yahya of Antioch. In a sense, then, the emperor's role was that of a cog, not a pivot, in the intricate process of disseminating the Word. The mainspring of action lay among the northerners who, for a variety of reasons, sought out baptism or simply more information about the Byzantine brand of Christianity. In some areas, such as the Black Sea steppe, Christianity never took root and the imperial government usually regarded a nomadic way of life as incompatible with the practice of Christianity. And much of the groundwork, before a ruler opted to become a Christian and imposed the new religion on his people, is likely to have been done by individual monks or clergymen living on the periphery of the Byzantine world. Nonetheless, the propaganda representing the emperor as a living Apostle leading people to salvation was not without substance; the emperor did see to the baptism of eminent as well as captive visitors at his court and his palace's combination of piety, marvels, and power exerted a fascination on members of many different foreign elites. This left its mark on the literary culture and the 'mentality' of some. Constantine VII is given the leading role in the baptism of Olga in the Rus *Primary Chronicle*'s version of her visit to Constantinople. The story's casting of him in this role is all the more suggestive in that it is almost pure fiction.

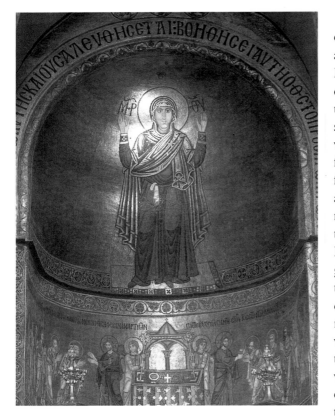

The cathedral of St Sophia, Kiev, begun in 1037, was the biggest church built in Russia until the end of the fifteenth century. It is crowned by thirteen domes in pyramidal formation. The exterior has been greatly altered in the baroque style and the frescoes of the interior extensively re-painted, but the core of the structure is original as are its Byzantine mosaics.

Such a notion of the ruler as presiding over an established-looking cult appealed to a number of ambitious potentates in the Balkans and to the north of the steppe. They could herd the inhabitants of the lands under their sway into at least outward observance of Christian forms of worship while priests and choirs offered up prayers for their own personal salvation. The very functioning of an ecclesiastical organization across scattered settlements and broken terrain brought definition as well as legitimacy to a regime. The churchmen, whether of Byzantine or (far more frequently) local origin were beholden to the princes for most of their possessions and income. Sprawling dominions such as those of the Rus long remained, in effect, missionary churches, whose clergy had to look to the princely authorities for their physical protection. They were seldom in a position to offer sustained opposition to the princes' policies or actions, except in matters of doctrine or Church discipline. In any case, the Orthodox Church within the Byzantine lands did not set much of a lead, either for the taking over of responsibility for administration or for developing an ideology to justify such a move. Even in the later years of the empire, when senior churchmen had the ear of ordinary people more than emperors did and when bishoprics and monasteries grew rich from their extensive landholdings and trading networks, the tendency was to prize above all withdrawal from earthly power struggles. Issues of 'public policy' (such as resistance against the Turks) were not seen as a major concern of the patriarch. The preservation of doctrine and ritual free from innovation or alien influences was the Byzantine Church's principal duty, and little value was put upon education or book-learning which led beyond those ends.

In eastern Europe the Church's priorities were much the same. When the Mongols subjugated the Rus principalities in the mid-thirteenth century, churchmen acquiesced in the new order as being the will of God, even referring to the *khan* as their legitimate overlord, *tsar* (the Russian word for 'emperor'). In return they gained properties and wide-ranging rights of jurisdiction. After the Mongols' power waned and, in the mid-fifteenth century, the prince of Moscow found himself predominant in the ensuing vacuum, churchmen drew on Byzantine ceremonial and early Byzantine writers such as Agapetus to bolster the concept of the ruler as appointed by God and answerable to him alone. So long as the autocrat remained pure in doctrine and broadly respectful of the Church as an institution, he could get away with much—and even, literally, with murder in the case of Ivan the Terrible. The Church would sometimes take a stand when 'Latins' or other heretics tried to impose false doctrine on the faithful. Attempts by the tsar and the

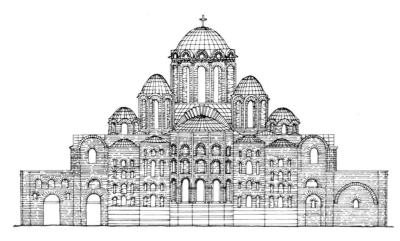

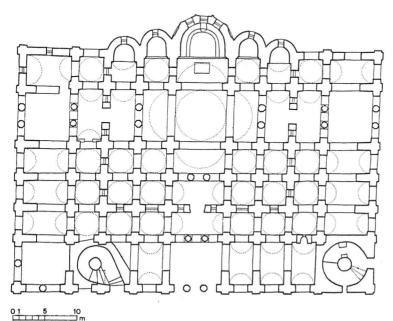

Reconstructed elevation and plan of St Sophia, Kiev.

patriarch in the mid-seventeenth century to correct the text of the Scriptures and service-books and to bring aspects of ritual into line with the practices of the Greeks evoked furious protests that the age of Antichrist was at hand. Many monks and parish clergy chose to end their earthly lives rather than jeopardize their souls through breaking with tradition, and the 'Old Believers' (as they were called) numbered hundreds of thousands. Their descendants, mostly living in the outer reaches of the Russian empire, saw out the Soviet Union and at the end of the twentieth century their numbers were swollen by neophytes who saw in their imperviousness to change an expression of Russian 'nationhood'.

The Old Believers' position encapsulates, in an extreme form, the strengths and weaknesses of the Byzantine bequest to the Slavic-speaking peoples. On the one hand, the creation of a sizeable body of sacred writings and service-books in Slavic translation facilitated regular worship and individual devotion on the part of the many and enabled a pious handful to lead ascetic lifestyles modelled on those of the Desert Fathers. The development of a literary language not far removed from spoken Slavonic also allowed for original compositions to serve local purposes. Outstanding among these works is the *Primary Chronicle*, where extracts from translated Byzantine works, exegeses of doctrine and pious excursuses are interspersed with tales of Rus princes' exploits and internecine quarrels. The birch-bark letters found in Novgorod and other towns are, in themselves, testimony to fairly widespread functional literacy in the urban centres along the major riverways. The letter writers took for granted their readers' familiarity with Christian prayers, saints, and feast days, and their veneration for oaths taken 'on the Cross'. Attachment to these rites and the belief systems and lore which underlay them enhanced order and social cohesion across wide spans of territory, encouraging the making of long-distance loans and contracts, and thus fostering the trade and prosperity of pre-Mongol Rus. However, the Church's reverence for tradition reinforced existing peasant suspiciousness of the unfamiliar and gave it a broad ideological justification, discouraging any individuals who might have wanted to explore the intellectual contents of books and to enquire further. As the case of the Old Believers shows, veneration for books could have a primarily symbolic significance, the inviolability of the text prevailing over all attempts at rectification of errors and inconsistencies. Gradually, from the time of Vladimir's conversion onwards, countless small worlds, inward-looking and variegated but with common Christian bearings, emerged across the expanses between the Black Sea steppe and the Arctic Circle and from the southern Balkans to the Ural mountains and beyond. Whatever their particular institutional arrangements, they owed their existence ultimately to the missionary efforts of the

Orthodox, and a certain awareness of their shared rites, doctrines, and traditions persisted through all the rivalries of their hierarchs and the power struggles between their political overlords. It was compounded rather than weakened by the lengthy periods of unbelievers' rule, the Turks in the Balkans, the Mongols in Rus. A sense that the Orthodox had a common cause transcending their linguistic and cultural differences was evident even at the end of the twentieth century, when the peoples of Russia, Bulgaria, and Greece showed sympathy and active support for their fellow Orthodox Serbs in the face of Kosovar separatism and 'Western' intervention. Material and diplomatic considerations specific to the twentieth century played some part in shaping the alignments, but underlying these was the distinctive line of development upon which the Byzantine emperors, churchmen, and monks had set them.

10 Fragmentation (1204–1453)

STEPHEN W. REINERT

From the perspective of political history, the final 250 years of the Byzantine experience frequently impress the reader as little more than a pathetic spectacle of accelerating fragmentation, disintegration, and decay. The trajectory begins in April 1204, with European crusaders dismembering and occupying much of the empire, and ends in irrevocable defeat on 29 May 1453, when an Ottoman army storms Constantinople and brings the Byzantine imperial tradition to a close. Much of what transpires in between appears to be a tiny cauldron boiling with endless inner and external conflicts, some of them unfathomably petty, but nonetheless earnestly waged with alarmingly limited economic resources. Throughout these centuries, in short, the once magnificent Byzantine empire seemingly devolves into little more than caricature, a disordered and dysfunctional polity—overall, a biosphere of impoverishment, absurd pretensions, and generalized *Angst*. Seen against this wider backdrop, its rarefied cultural flowering in art, architecture, and classical scholarship seems to provide the only convincing rationale for exploring the final chapters in the history of the Byzantine state.

The reader's weariness is understandable, and certain of his summary impressions may indeed be correct. But the historian is engaged as much with the study of catastrophes, decline, and decay as of their opposites, and the narrative of late Byzantine history is in fact more complexly textured than the novice may suppose. Our aim, therefore, shall be to sketch the fate of late Byzantium with sympathy for its component episodes, rejecting a teleological obsession with 1453. To that end, we shall describe the political evolution in six phases, none coinciding with the dates of particular emperors' reigns, and all of varying thematic consequence. In general, notwithstanding its melancholy tone, we contemplate here a story of persistent struggle against relentless and often overwhelming adversity, punctuated with instances of genuine valour and patriotism. And despite numerous examples of mediocre leadership, at least one of the

A re-creation of the conquest of Constantinople in 1204. Painting by Domenico Tintoretto (1598–1605) in the Ducal Palace, Venice.

Palaiologan emperors, Manuel II (1391–1425), justly ranks among the greatest Byzantine statesmen, and as a brilliant figure in the fourteenth-century revival of letters.

1204–1261: Dismemberment, Survivals, and Competition for Constantinople

The structure of the Byzantine empire had in fact begun to fracture before the Fourth Crusade arrived in Constantinople, as evidenced by the secession of Bulgaria and Serbia in the mid-1180s, the rise of independent lordships in

Cyprus, the Peloponnese, and western Anatolia from the 1180s through the early 1200s, and the establishment of the 'Empire of Trebizond' in the Pontus in April 1204. This incipient fragmentation, however, was peripheral, whereas the assault inflicted by the crusaders in the storming and sack of Constantinople (12–15 April 1204) and the ensuing expeditions of conquest in that and the following years dismembered Byzantium at its very core. By 1210, from this calculated orgy of violence—prosecuted 'in the name of God' against 'Greeks' conceived as 'the enemies of God'—there had emerged on formerly Byzantine soil some six new Frankish states, dozens of minor dependent lordships, and a vast scattering of Venetian and Genoese colonies.

Four of the new Frankish states deserve mention. The immediate heir to the Byzantine order in Constantinople was the so-called 'Latin Empire of Constantinople', the first emperor of which was Baldwin, count of Flanders (1204–5). This Latin empire endured fifty-seven years, but its last truly vigorous ruler was Baldwin's successor, Henry (1206–16). It was created with territorial claims to Constantinople, parts of coastal Thrace, Anatolia, and the islands of Samos, Chios, and Lesbos—but by 1225 was reduced to little more than the capital. The second-ranking Frankish state to emerge in the wake of 1204 was the 'Kingdom of Thessalonica', founded by Boniface, marquis of Montferrat (d. 1207). Its original territorial base was in Macedonia and Thessaly, but its fortunes quickly dissipated after 1207, when Boniface was killed in a war with the Bulgarians. The lands of this kingdom soon returned to Greek control in 1224, leaving little trace of the intervening Frankish presence. A more long-lived Latin polity was the 'Principality of Achaia', the conquest of William of Champlitte and Geoffrey Villehardouin, the former being viscount of Dijon, and the latter hailing from Champagne. Originally centred at Andravida, in the north-west Peloponnese, it continued to exist, in increasingly emaciated form, down to 1430, when the Greeks of Mistra absorbed its final remnants. Finally, the 'Duchy of Athens and Thebes' was established, again through conquest, by Boniface of Montferrat, who quickly transferred its territory to a Burgundian knight, Otho de la Roche (d. 1225). Of its two centres, Thebes was the more flourishing, with workshops producing silk and other fine fabrics, and colonies of Jewish and Genoese merchants. In 1311, the duchy was conquered by a rampaging army of Catalan mercenaries; in 1388, it was purchased by a Florentine family, the Acciajuoli, who controlled it down to the Ottoman conquest in 1450. Such, then, were the chief Frankish principalities taking shape after 1204, and theoretically forming a feudal hierarchy, with the Latin emperor of Constantinople at the top. Alongside this, the Republic of Venice obtained a number of prime maritime territories, which rapidly expanded her Mediterranean commercial empire. Venice's key acquisitions in these years included three-eighths of Constantinople, Dyrrachium, the Ionian Islands, most of the Aegean Islands, the key ports of the southern Peloponnese (Modon and Coron), Crete, and other important harbours on the Black Sea coast of Thrace.

Surprisingly, this Latin appropriation of core Byzantine territories did not entail a concomitant liquidation of the Byzantine political tradition. While much of the Hellenophone element of the former Byzantine state was indeed absorbed within the new Frankish and Italian entities, some of the Rhomaioi regrouped in three peripheral areas which now assume the character of Byzantine successor states—Epiros, Nicaea, and Trebizond. As noted above, the empire of Trebizond actually took shape in April 1204, before the fall of Constantinople to the Latins. Its founders, Alexios and David, were scions of the Komnenoi dynasty, and it lasted down to 1461, when the Ottomans took the capital city of Trebizond. Economically, this Pontic outpost enjoyed considerable prosperity owing to the trade in luxuries, especially spices, coming from western Asia and points further east. More central to our narrative, however, was the emergence of Epiros and Nicaea as new Hellenophone centres, potentially poised to confront the Franks, above all the Latin regime in Constantinople.

Roughly half the population in the area of Constantinople that managed to flee before the Latin conquest migrated to north-western Greece—the highland area of Epiros, Acarnania, and Aetolia. Here a small principality took shape under the leadership of Michael Komnenos Doukas, a cousin of the former Byzantine emperors Isaac II and Alexios III. The entity he founded is customarily called the 'Despotate of Epiros', although Michael himself never held the title *despotes*. In essence, Michael established himself as the accepted leader and rallying force of Greeks in the vicinity of Arta, and under his rule (1204–15) Epiros became the European centre for preserving Byzantine culture, as well as formulating plans and military agendas for curbing further Latin expansion in the region. Michael's descendants were to have a long history. In fact their polity may be traced, albeit with discontinuities, down to 1461, when it was finally conquered by the Ottomans.

Facing: Detail of one of the two 'pilastri Acritani', erected outside St Mark's basilica, Venice. Part of the loot of the Fourth Crusade, they were removed from the sixth-century church of St Polyeuktos at Constantinople.

In Asia Minor, the chief Hellenophone successor state was the so-called 'Empire of Nicaea'. This was situated in north-western Anatolia, and was founded by Theodore I Laskaris, son-in-law of Alexios III Angelos Komnenos. Laskaris clearly aimed at rebuilding the Byzantine imperial establishment—i.e. at translating to Bithynia the core institutions of emperor, court, patriarch, bureaucracy, and army. He was not actually crowned emperor until 1208, by the newly elected patriarch Michael Autoreianos, but by that act he officially proclaimed the existence of a Byzantine 'empire in exile'. His successors ruled Nicaea down to 1261, and it was nominally on behalf of the ruling Laskarid dynasty that Constantinople was recovered in that seminal year. Since the empire of Nicaea eventually controlled the western flank and rim of the Anatolian plateau, its economy became a prosperous mix of grain production in the rich riverine valleys, and craft production and trade in roughly a dozen key cities. The capital, Nicaea, was blessed with powerful walls, and was situated with rapid access to Constantinople.

We cannot explore here the evolution of these new entities—Frankish, Italian, and Greek—over the period 1204–61 in any detail. A salient theme for future Byzantine history, however, was the parallel ambition of Epiros and Nicaea to recover Constantinople, and the eventual emergence of Nicaea as the stronger of the two, ultimately winning the prize. The expansion of Nicaea was the collective achievement of three rulers—Theodore I, the founder; his successor John III Doukas Vatatzes; and ultimately Michael Palaiologos, who usurped the throne of Vatatzes' grandson, John IV, and returned to Constantinople to found the last dynasty that ruled the imperial city.

Theodore Laskaris rose to power in Nicaea as a resistance leader, organizing refugees and native Bithynian Greeks into a fighting force to block the Franks from expanding in Anatolia, and likewise maintain the realm intact vis-à-vis the Seljuks to the east. In the latter endeavour he scored major successes, but by 1214, when he concluded a détente with the Latins, the latter were still ensconced in the Nicomedian peninsula. By this treaty, however, he established a *modus vivendi* with the Franks, and in 1219 he similarly made peace with the Venetians of Constantinople on generous terms. At no point in these rapprochements, however, did Theodore make major theological or ecclesiastical concessions; his concern was to stabilize relations with the new European powers, and establish the fledgling Nicaean state on secure foundations. The administrative apparatus that evolved in his reign was largely court-centred, and evidently a simplification of the preceding Constantinopolitan pattern. In sum, his was a credible, if frequently precarious, beginning.

It was especially in the reign of Theodore's son-in-law and successor, John III Doukas Vatatzes, that the rivalry between Epiros and Nicaea

Facing, above: The city of Nicaea, which is only 1.5 km across, remained protected by its Late Roman walls, repaired in the eighth, ninth, and thirteenth centuries. Here the eastern (Lefke) gate.

Facing, below: The box-like, three-storey palace of Nymphaeum (Kemalpaşa) near Smyrna was one of the favourite residences of the Nicaean emperors. First half of the thirteenth century.

Facing: The great Deisis in the south gallery of St Sophia, of which the central figure of Christ is shown here, is perhaps the most delicate and accomplished of all Byzantine mosaics. There is no evidence as to the circumstances of its execution, but current opinion places it soon after the Byzantine re-occupation of the city in 1261.

emerged in full form. During the 1220s it seemed as if Epiros would attain the goal, particularly after Michael I's successor, Theodore Komnenos Doukas (c.1215–30), recovered Thessalonica (1224) and Adrianople (1225), and was crowned emperor a few years later. The Epirote *essor* was cut short, however, when Theodore was defeated and captured by the Bulgarians at the Battle of Klokotnitsa, following which a significant chunk of Epirote territory was provisionally annexed to the Bulgarian empire. While the star of Epiros was waning, however, John III Doukas was steadily consolidating his strength in Anatolia—expelling the Franks in 1224 (Battle of Poimanenon) and driving the Seljuks from the Maeander Valley some time before 1231. His subsequent endeavours down to his death in 1254 were targeted at expanding in Europe, in hopes of reconquering Constantinople. His campaign of 1246 was particularly successful, in the course of which much of Macedonia was seized from the Bulgarians, Thessalonica was captured, and the imperial ambitions of Epiros were scotched.

The honour of restoring Greek rule to Constantinople would fall neither to John III's son, Theodore II (1254–8), nor his grandson, John IV (1258–61). The former was more of a philosopher king—a scholar who gathered at his court a glittering coterie of literati, whose achievements constitute the prehistory to the Palaiologan revival of letters. The latter ascended the throne at the age of 7, but effective control of affairs quickly passed to Michael Palaiologos, scion of one of the great military families of Asia Minor, initially as regent and soon thereafter as co-emperor. Michael quickly proved his worth by organizing victory over a coalition of resurgent Epiros, Achaia, and Sicily (1259)—safeguarding the Nicaean position in Europe, and moreover establishing, via the subsequent acquisitions of Mistra, Monemvasia, and Maina, a springboard for future recovery of the Morea. His most famous accomplishment as co-emperor, namely the reconquest of Constantinople from the Latins in July 1261, was merely a stroke of good fortune, effected by his general Alexios Strategopoulos with minimal military exertion. Nonetheless, when Michael solemnly entered 'the city' a month later and was recrowned by Patriarch Arsenios, he celebrated the triumph of decades of Laskarid strategic planning, and effectively his rise to sole rule. The following December, he ordered John IV to be blinded.

1261–1341: The Early Palaiologan Attempt at Reconstruction

With an Orthodox, Hellenophone imperial regime restored to Constantinople, the challenge that Michael VIII and his immediate successors faced was that of maintaining the Laskarid legacy in Anatolia and Europe, and recovering and reintegrating the remaining array of territories lost since the

Right: Purple silk banner representing a suppliant in court costume at the feet of the archangel Michael. The owner has been identified, rightly or wrongly, with Manuel, illegitimate son of John V Palaiologos, who, as commander of the Byzantine fleet, inflicted a minor defeat on the Turks in 1411.

Below: The colossal composition of the Dormition of the Virgin Mary occupies the west wall of the monastery church of the Holy Trinity at Sopoćani, Serbia, founded by King Stephen Uroš I in *c.*1260. Inscribed in Slavonic, not Greek, the paintings of Sopoćani foreshadow many traits of the Palaiologan style.

cataclysm of 1204. It was a formidable and ultimately impossible challenge, but one of which the early Palaiologan emperors were acutely aware. Throughout the interval from 1261 to 1341, the challenge was most successfully met by the founder of the dynasty, Michael VIII (1261–82). In the reigns of his son Andronikos II (1282–1328) and great-grandson Andronikos III (1328– 41), the fortunes of the state markedly deteriorated, yet even in 1341, decades after the Anatolian component of the empire had been lost, Byzantium still had the resources and possibilities of enduring as a fairly compact Balkan state.

Having attained the throne of Constantinople at the age of 36, Michael VIII found himself confronted with a plethora of agonizing problems, a situation that would persist to his death in 1282. His blinding of John IV immediately unleashed critiques of the legitimacy of his rule—in the capital, Patriarch Arsenios responded with excommunication (for which he was deposed in 1265, and replaced by Joseph I); in Bithynia, Michael came to be viewed, particularly by the soldiers, as a usurper trampling upon the glorious

Façade of the palace known by its Turkish name Tekfur Sarayı (late thirteenth century) before restoration. Built against the Theodosian land walls and preceded by a large courtyard, this was probably the main imperial residence during the Palaiologan period.

The miraculous icon of the Virgin Hodegetria being carried in procession through the streets of Constantinople, followed by a crowd of worshippers. In the foreground is a group of itinerant vendors, peddling fruit, vegetables, and caviar. Tracing of wall painting in the monastery of Vlacherna near Arta, end of the thirteenth century.

Laskarid legacy. After nearly six decades of Latin rule, Constantinople's infrastructure was close to ruin, testimony to the ineptness and profound impoverishment of the successors of Baldwin and Henry. Michael fully anticipated, finally, that those recently dispossessed of Constantinople—notably the Latin emperor Baldwin II, and the Venetians—would surely embark on agendas of reconquista, which would entail a costly military and diplomatic response. To his credit, Michael established his rule and dealt with these challenges with remarkable success. The attendant costs were indeed enormous, and it would fall to his infinitely less talented son and successor, Andronikos II, to digest their realities. But for this 'new Constantine', his very *raison d'être* was to preserve his throne, restore Constantinople with its traditional imperial and orthodox complexion, and defend it from retaliatory western assault—no matter what the price.

Michael's renovation programme included a major restoration of the Blachernai Palace; an Orthodox refurbishing of Hagia Sophia; reconstruction of defence works (e.g. the walls, the Kontoskelion harbour) and public buildings (e.g. markets, streets, baths, harbours, hospices); and a rebuilding of several major monasteries. At the same time, private patronage was responsible for the building or renovation of various other churches throughout the city. The emperor himself even subsidized the construction of a new mosque, replacing that burnt by the crusaders in 1203, with an eye to cultivating political, military, and economic links especially with the Mamlukes.

On the military and diplomatic front, Michael VIII's most serious challenge came from the Catholic West. The deposed Latin emperor, Baldwin II, was resolved to recover what he deemed his legacy, and initially placed his hopes on his relative, the Sicilian king Manfred, for aid to that end. Before Manfred could act, however, he fell victim to the continuing papal–Hohenstaufen rivalry, when Pope Clement IV reiterated his predecessor Urban IV's invitation to Count Charles of Anjou, brother of the French king Louis IX, to take possession of the kingdom of Sicily—i.e., with full ecclesiastical sanction. At length Charles invaded and crushed Manfred in a battle at Benevento (1266), whereupon Sicily and southern Italy now came under French rule, with Charles as their first Angevin king.

With a papal client now on the Sicilian throne, Clement IV readily espoused Baldwin II's cause. In May 1267, at Viterbo, the pope mediated a pact whereby Charles would provide military aid to recover Constantinople, Baldwin would reciprocally provide territorial concessions, and a marriage alliance between the former's daughter and latter's son would be formed. Charles was unable to deliver immediately on his campaign promise, and Michael VIII meanwhile manoeuvred adroitly to negotiate a way to neutralize the enemy. In a protracted series of negotiations with the papacy and Louis IX, Michael succeeded in staving off an Angevin invasion by proffering the possibility of ecclesiastical union between Rome and Constantinople, which eventually was achieved, in July 1274, at the Second Council of Lyons. In essence this was a treaty between the emperor and the reigning pope, Gregory X, the key terms of which entailed recognition of papal primacy, and the Catholic doctrines on purgatory and the *filioque*.

View of the former Genoese town of Galata or Pera in the second half of the sixteenth century.

Facing: Monastery of Chora (Kariye Camii), Constantinople, mosaic of the Deisis, *c*.1315. The two little figures of donors are those (*left*) of Isaac Komnenos, son of Alexios I, who had actually died shortly after 1152, and (*right*) of the nun Melane, former 'Lady of the Mongols', i.e. Maria Palaiologina, illegitimate daughter of Michael VIII, who married the Mongol khan Abaga. She lived on until after 1307.

The aftermath of the Union of Lyons was a mixed and short-lived blessing for Michael. While it temporarily stalled Charles of Anjou's aggression (and as of 1273, when Baldwin II died, he was still pursuing the project of recovering Constantinople on behalf of his son-in-law, Philip of Courtenay), it simultaneously destroyed Michael's credibility with his own people—the vast majority of whom now regarded him as an odious traitor who had surrendered to the Latins on the most sensitive of issues, the truths of the Orthodox faith. Moreover, its military value was nullified in 1281, when, through Charles's influence, his friend Simon de Brie was elected as pope Martin IV. In July of that year, convinced that Michael's adherence to the Union was hypocritical and politically motivated, Martin endorsed Charles and Philip's plans for an expedition to recover Constantinople. The following November he excommunicated Michael, denouncing him as 'patron of the Greeks who are inveterate schismatics and fixed in the ancient schism'. For Charles, of course, this was effectively an ecclesiastical green light to launch an invasion to reconquer Constantinople for the Latins.

Such an undertaking could easily have spelled disaster for Byzantium, but Michael VIII cleverly manoeuvred to undermine Charles from within his own realm. Apprised that Manfred's son-in-law Peter III of Aragon aspired to recover the Hohenstaufen legacy for his wife, Michael allied with him and dispatched generous subsidies for an invasion of Sicily. It is likely, moreover, that monies found their way from Byzantium into the hands of Sicilians chafing under the oppressions (chiefly fiscal) of Angevin rule, who were coordinating with Peter to stage a rebellion. The upshot was the famed Sicilian Vespers revolt, commencing 30/31 March 1281, which completely sidetracked Charles from his projected campaign to Constantinople, and paved the way for Peter's installation as the first of the Aragonese kings of Sicily.

Michael VIII's role in undermining Charles and saving Constantinople from a Latin revanche is rightly regarded as one of his greatest diplomatic triumphs—and this in a career replete with such exploits. Tellingly, it was barely appreciated by his subjects, who all but rejoiced in his death a few months later, and registered no concern that he was denied a decent Orthodox burial. From the Byzantines' perspective, Michael's policies had alienated the imperial regime from society at large, and the crushing burden of taxation imposed to support them, particularly in Anatolia, was intolerable. It was now left to his son and successor Andronikos to realign the imperial government with the Orthodox populace, and attempt a mode of government that would be financially sustainable.

In the judgement of many historians, Andronikos II (1282–1328), who came to the throne at 24, was a sadly incompetent ruler, severely lacking in strategic vision and incapable of effectively addressing the most critical

Constantine Komnenos Raoul Palaiologos and his wife Euphrosyne Doukaina Palaiologina. Typikon (charter) of the nunnery of Our Lady of Good Hope at Constantinople, founded in the second quarter of the fourteenth century by Theodora, niece of Michael VIII.

military challenges of his time. His ecclesiastical policy was a pragmatic and welcome healing measure—his first official act was to repudiate the Union of Lyons, and to conciliate those who felt themselves victims of Michael's manhandling of ecclesiastical affairs—yet it only alienated the papacy further. The economies he instituted early in his reign (e.g. reductions in naval and armed forces, extraordinary taxes on pronoiars for campaign financing, debasement of the *hyperpyron*) were short-sighted and destructive. His inability, finally, to avert major territorial losses in the Balkans and Anatolia, and control the dynastic strife that erupted in the closing phase of his reign, were egregious failures foreshadowing the irrevocable ravaging of the state in the period 1341–71.

Andronikos' chief difficulty in the Balkans arose with the vigorous expansion of Nemanjid Serbia under King Stephen Uroš II Milutin (1282–1321), the highlights of which were the conquest of Skopje (1282), and a continuing guerrilla-style assault along the Macedonian frontier into the late 1290s. When Byzantine counter-attacks proved futile, Andronikos attempted to stabilize relations in 1299 by a pact of appeasement—marrying his 5-year-old daughter Simonis to Milutin, and conceding 'as dowry' Serbian conquests north of the arc of castles running from Ochrid to Štip to Strumica. This Serb penetration deep into Byzantine territory would continue and climax in the reign of his grandson Stephen Uroš IV Dušan (1331–55). Reciprocally, the treaty inaugurated a significant flow of Byzantine cultural influences into the Serbian court, which would reach their apogee in Dušan's reign.

The contraction of Byzantine territory in Anatolia under Andronikos II was particularly tragic in that he, unlike Michael VIII, was seriously concerned by the Turkish expansion towards the coasts that had accelerated throughout the 1270s, as the Seljuk state was disintegrating at the centre, eventually to be replaced, by the early fourteenth century, by a series of smaller principalities or lordships (beyliks). Two years before his father's death, Andronikos had personally seen the devastation and depopulation wrought by Turkish raids in the Maeander Valley, in the early stages of the rise of the Menteshe beylik. As sole emperor, Andronikos was resolved to establish a more regular and vigorous military presence in Anatolia, although his preoccupation with Balkan affairs prevented him from doing so until the 1290s. By this time, the Ottoman beylik had crystallized under Osman south of the Sangarios River around Söğüt, and booty raids, with mixed Muslim and Christian participants, were regularly operative in the nominally Byzantine territory across the river.

Between 1290 and 1307, Andronikos pursued a variety of measures for stemming the Turkish tide, none of which had lasting effects. In 1290–3, the emperor moved his court to Anatolia, where he personally oversaw the rebuilding of fortifications, and generally attempted to boost morale. In 1294–5, his general Alexios Philanthropenos campaigned quite successfully in the Maeander Valley, but these gains were summarily lost when Philanthropenos staged an abortive coup and was blinded. In the spring of 1302, Andronikos' son, Michael IX, and the general Mouzalon led expeditions respectively to recover control of the Maeander defences, and expel the Ottomans from the vicinity of Nicomedia, which they were harrying. Both were futile, the defeat Mouzalon experienced at Bapheus (July 1302) counting as Osman Beg's first major victory over the Byzantines. Later that same summer a desperate Andronikos contracted the services of the Catalan Grand Company. For exorbitantly high pay, the latter—some 6,500 strong, and led by the mercurial Roger de Flor—duly campaigned in Anatolia in the spring and summer of 1303, driving back the Turks in a swathe from Cyzicus to Philadelphia, and simultaneously pillaging and plundering at will. But again these gains were ephemeral. No sooner did the Catalans vacate these territories than the Turks resumed raiding and besieging key fortresses. At this juncture, however, the Catalans themselves became a scourge to Byzantium, when Roger was assassinated whilst visiting Michael IX in Adrianople. They now undertook a two-year war of revenge, the main theatre of which was Thrace, whose cities and villages were mercilessly raided and pillaged. In summer 1307 the Company began moving west for new spoils, eventually establishing themselves as the masters of the Duchy of Athens and Thebes, after defeating Walter of Brienne in 1311. Thus, instead of enabling a solid Byzantine recovery in Asia Minor, the Catalans reduced much of Thrace and Macedonia to scorched earth, and likewise left Anatolia in chaos.

Thereafter Andronikos II sent few troops to Anatolia. Instead, he intensified negotiations for an alliance with the Mongol Ilkhanids of Persia, hoping thereby to attain troops to attack the Turks, in particular the Ottomans, who by now had begun a regular siege of Nicaea. Evidently these, too, were fruitless, and throughout the closing decades of his reign the Ottoman and Karasi beyliks rapidly consolidated as the major Turkish successors to Byzantium in north-west Anatolia, as did Saruhan, Aydın, and Menteshe to the south. Meanwhile, the Rhomaioi who opted not to live under Turkish rule fled into Byzantine territory across the Marmara, or to the few unconquered strongholds—which in Bithynia amounted to Nicaea, Nicomedia, and Prousa until 1326, when it capitulated to Osman's son Orhan. South of these, the only significant quasi-autonomous centre remaining at the end of Andronikos II's reign was Philadelphia (finally lost in 1390), and for that privilege its citizens paid tribute to the neighbouring begs of Germiyan.

The dynastic strife marring the final eight years of Andronikos II's reign was a simmering conflict between a profoundly bewildered old man (in 1320, Andronikos was 60) whose policies were bankrupt, and a somewhat reckless and flamboyant grandson in his 20s—namely Andronikos III, who anticipated inheriting the throne in direct succession to his father, Michael IX. However, the elder Andronikos disinherited his grandson in 1320, following a tragic incident wherein the latter's brother was murdered and their father subsequently died of shock and sorrow. The younger Andronikos promptly organized armed opposition, drumming up popular support with promises of generous tax cuts. In all, the tensions between the two Andronikoi were played out from 1320 through 1328 in three stages of open warfare. In the first round (1321), the younger Andronikos marched on Constantinople and eventually negotiated receipt of Thrace as an appanage. The second (1322) resulted in Andronikos III's formal investment as co-emperor, along with a stipend, state-supplied troops, and residence in Didymoteichon. The third and final round of open warfare (1327–8) was something of a miniature Balkan war, with Andronikos III backed by the Bulgarians, and Andronikos II supported by the Serbs. The action culminated with the younger Andronikos taking Constantinople on 23 May 1328, following which his grandfather abdicated. He would die as the monk Antonios, in 1332. This lengthy period of transition clearly fragmented and enfeebled government, and acutely damaged the economy, particularly agriculture. Still, its negative effects do not appear to have been permanent.

Andronikos III's accession at 31 brought a new circle of advisers to the helm, most prominent of whom was the aristocratic and immensely wealthy John Kantakouzenos, who served as Grand Domestic (army commander-in-chief). They collectively faced the challenge of recovery and likewise retrenchment—of digesting the reduction of Byzantium to the dimensions of a small European state in the face of increasingly powerful neighbours to the north (primarily Serbia) and south (the rising beyliks in north-west Anatolia). Andronikos III's objectives in Anatolia appear to have been twofold—

to retain control over the remaining Bithynian outposts (Nicaea, Nicomedia), and likewise of the key eastern Aegean islands next to the nascent maritime beyliks. A final attempt to relieve besieged Nicaea was mounted in summer 1329, but imperial troops were defeated by Orhan at Pelekanos (10 June), and within two years the city capitulated. Andronikos endeavoured to spare Nicomedia the same fate by negotiating a tributary arrangement with Orhan in August 1333, the first of its kind with the Ottomans, but its value was shortlived, and Nicomedia likewise surrendered in 1337. By that date, then, Byzantine Bithynia had become substantially incorporated into the Ottoman beylik, the prosperity and vitality of which at this time deeply impressed the contemporary Arab traveller, Ibn Battuta. On the west coast, the Byzantines scored a significant victory in recovering Chios in 1329, in which context Andronikos III personally met with the beg of Saruhan and an envoy from Umur, the beg of Aydın. Six years later Andronikos would form a close tie with the latter, also involving financial indemnities, that enabled him to recover Lesbos.

In Europe, Andronikos and Kantakouzenos exhibited military and diplomatic finesse in reincorporating Thessaly (1333) and Epiros (1340–1), which brought together a considerable block of territory that had not been under imperial rule since 1204. The tragedy, however, was that this region would soon be targeted for attack and settlement by the Serbs, when Stephen Dušan created his little Balkan 'empire' in the 1340s and 1350s, partly at Byzantium's expense. Stephen came to power in 1331, and quickly resumed Serbia's southward expansionism in a series of campaigns extending to 1334. In a peace negotiated that year, Andronikos surrendered five key fortresses, including Ochrid and Prilep, and formally recognized Serbian conquests of Byzantine territory effected since the days of king Milutin. It was an attempt at stabilization, and likewise at obtaining in Serbia an ally and, as with Aydın, a future supplier of mercenary soldiers.

All in all, Andronikos III's foreign policy showed considerable signs of vigour. It was a sustained effort to take a difficult and deteriorated situation in hand, and make something new of it; it constitutes the last important example of its kind in Palaiologan history.

1341–1371/2: The Irreparable Ravaging of the State

The interval 1341–71/2 was an agonizing time of troubles from which Byzantium never recovered. The state was again torn to shreds by civil wars, notably in 1341–7 (the so-called 'Second [Palaiologan] Civil War') and again in 1352–7, with new episodes of dynastic strife brewing again in the early 1370s. These civil wars were accompanied and succeeded by foreign invasion

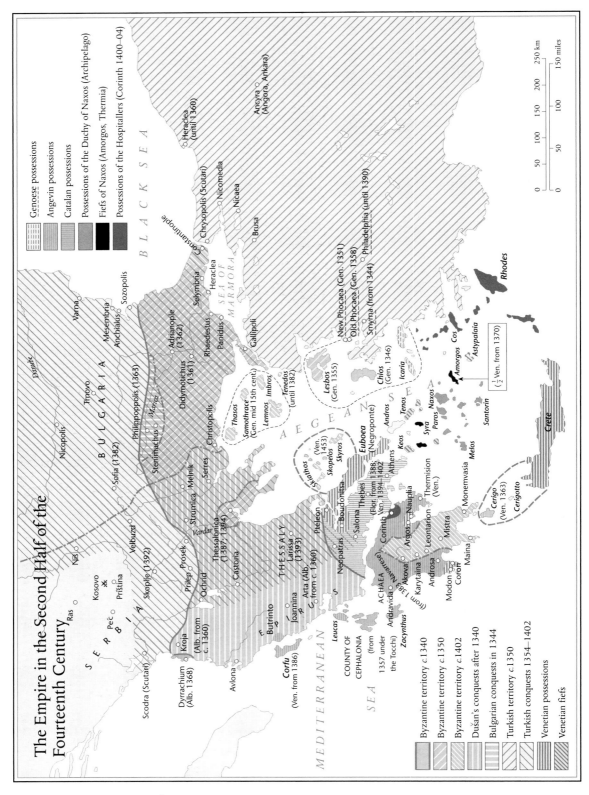

The Empire in the Second Half of the Fourteenth Century

Legend (top):
- Genoese possessions
- Angevin possessions
- Catalan possessions
- Possessions of the Duchy of Naxos (Archipelago)
- Fiefs of Naxos (Amorgos, Thermia)
- Possessions of the Hospitallers (Corinth 1400–04)

Legend (bottom):
- Byzantine territory c.1340
- Byzantine territory c.1350
- Byzantine territory c.1402
- Dušan's conquests after 1340
- Bulgarian conquests in 1344
- Turkish territory c.1350
- Turkish conquests 1354–1402
- Venetian possessions
- Venetian fiefs

Scale: 0 50 100 150 200 250 km / 0 50 100 150 miles

BLACK SEA

SEA OF MARMORA

AEGEAN SEA

MEDITERRANEAN SEA

Ancyra (Angora, Ankara)

Heraclea (until 1360)
Chrysopolis (Scutari)
Nicomedia
Nicaea
Brusa

Constantinople
Selymbria
Heraclea
Rhaedestus
Panidus
Gallipoli

New Phocaea (Gen. 1351)
Old Phocaea (Gen. 1358)
Smyrna (from 1344)
Philadelphia (until 1390)

Rhodes
Cos
Astypalaia
Amorgos ($\frac{1}{2}$ Ven. from 1370)
Naxos
Paros
Syra
Santorin

Crete

Lesbos (Gen. 1355)
Chios (Gen. 1346)
Icaria

Tenedos (until 1382)
Lemnos
Imbros
Thasos
Samothrace (Gen. mid 15th cent.)

Andros
Tenos
Keos
Melos

Euboea (Negroponte)
Skyros
Skiathos (Ven. 1453)
Skopelos

Athens
Thebes (Ven. 1394–1402)
Boudonitsa (Flor. from 1388)
Salona
Corinth
Thermision (Ven.)
Leontarion
Mistra
Monemvasia
Maina
Argos (Ven.)
Naupli a
Karytaina
Androsa
Modon
Coron
Akova
ACHAEA (from 1383)
Andravida (N. N. Nerantza)
Neopatras
Pteleon
Christopolis
Serres
Melnik
Strumica
Thessalonica (1387; 1394)
Larissa (1393)
THESSALY
Castoria
Prosek
Prilep
Ochrid
Arta (Alb. from c. 1360)
Ioannina
Butrinto
Kroja (Alb. from c. 1360)
Avlona
Dyrrachium (Alb. 1368)
Scodra (Scutari)

Cerigo (Ven. 1363)
Cerigotto

Corfu (Ven. from 1386)
Leucas
Zacynthus
COUNTY OF CEPHALONIA (from 1357 under the Tocchi)

SERBIA
Ras
Peć
Kosovo
Priština
Niš
Skopje (1392)
Velbužd
Stenimachus
Didymotichus (1361)
Adrianople (1362)
Philippopolis (1363)

BULGARIA
Danube
Varna
Mesembria
Anchialus
Sozopolis
Trnovo
Sofia (1382)
Nicopolis
Vardar
Maritza

264

and settlement, notably Serbian and Ottoman, on a serious and devastating scale. Throughout the 'Second Civil War' and after, Byzantine cities were simmering with social unrest, with instances of bloody collision between rich and poor. At the same time, society became divided by Byzantium's last major religious controversy, Hesychasm, the outcome of which had a decisive impact on future directions of philosophical and theological speculation. Finally, nature herself seemed to conspire against the Byzantines in those years, with several major earthquakes of devastating impact. The general misery was compounded from 1347 on by the appearance of bubonic plague. The interplay of all these factors makes the interval 1341–71/2 a transition into serious decay. Indeed, that the state even survived the 1340s and 1350s is amazing. As the fourteenth century progressed, the main objective of its leaders became more and more the preservation of Constantinople, Thessalonica, and its territories in the Morea.

The Grand Duke Alexios Apokaukos (killed in 1345). On a lectern in front of him is a manuscript of the Hippocratic corpus open on the aphorism 'Life is short, art is long', etc. The manuscript in question, at one time in the library of the Sultans' Seraglio at Istanbul, is the present Paris gr. 2144.

The core problem throughout this time of troubles was a chronic power struggle within the leadership, which fractured government and facilitated foreign encroachments. In essence this would evolve as a protracted conflict between the Palaiologoi and the Kantakouzenoi, in three major phases: 1341–7, 1347–54, and 1354–7.

The downward spiral was triggered in 1341 by the fact that Andronikos III's son and successor, John V, was barely 10 years old at his father's death. Thus a regency council was established, its members being John's mother Anna of Savoy, Kantakouzenos, and the patriarch John XIV Kalekas. Difficulties arose in the summer of 1341, when the ambitious Kalekas, in alliance with the High Admiral Alexios Apokaukos, convinced the empress that Kantakouzenos' secret agenda was to overthrow Anna and John, and establish his own dynastic rule. In September, while Kantakouzenos was in Thrace, Kalekas proclaimed himself regent, and a violent assault on Kantakouzenos'

family and supporters was unleashed; in October, Anna ordered Kantakouzenos to resign his command. Ostensibly to protect and secure the rights of young John V, Kantakouzenos replied by accepting acclamation as emperor at Didymoteichon. This opened the 'Second Civil War' that would last down to 2 February 1347. It was especially devastating because both sides made extensive use of foreign mercenary soldiers—Kantakouzenos engaging Serbs and Turks, and the regency relying mainly on Turks. Throughout much of the struggle, Kantakouzenos' Turkish mercenaries came from Umur, beg of Aydın. In 1345, however, he formed close ties with the Ottoman sultan Orhan—to whom he gave his daughter Theodora in marriage the following year. The five years of violence this war entailed profoundly ravaged the Thracian and Macedonian countryside, with war bands pillaging and looting at will, often in lieu of pay. The continuous intervention of foreign mercenaries finally worked to their own expansionary advantage. Throughout this crisis, down to his death in 1355, Stephen Dušan in particular exploited the chaos within Byzantium to expand the Serbian state into a tiny empire, including much of Macedonia and large chunks of northern Greece. Eventually Kantakouzenos triumphed, entering Constantinople in early February 1347, and forming an accord with Anna whereby he and John V would rule as co-emperors, the latter as the junior partner throughout the next decade. The liaison was sealed later that May, when Kantakouzenos' daughter, Helena, was married to Anna's son, now aged 15.

At this juncture Byzantium was truly in delapidated shape, with its agricultural and commercial foundations severely battered, an empty central treasury, and its populace impoverished and demoralized. Against this background we can only assume that the impact of bubonic plague, beginning in late summer 1347, must have been considerable—as indeed it was in neighbouring areas like Cairo, where its horrors are well documented. Moreover, eight subsequent outbreaks are recorded between the 1360s and 1420s.

While John VI's 'dual rule' with his son-in-law between 1347 and 1354 is interesting for his efforts, albeit futile, to impose a favourable balance of power and interests vis-à-vis the re-established Italian colonies in Constantinople (Genoese and Venetian), and for the support he gave to the triumph of Hesychasm[1] as championed by Gregory Palamas in 1351, ultimately it was a politically unstable arrangement that quickly unravelled. On the one hand, Kantakouzenos' own supporters felt that he should establish a dynasty in his own right, elevating his son Matthew (b. 1325) as co-emperor and heir apparent. John V Palaiologos, on the other hand, growing into his late teens and early twenties, began scheming to attain full power, and be rid of Kantakouzenos' tutelage. Down to 1353 Kantakouzenos attempted to conciliate the ambitions of both his son-in-law and son, but finally, after John V had unleashed a

Facing: John VI Kantakouzenos presiding over the council of 1351, which condemned the opponents of Gregory Palamas. Miniature of a manuscript containing the deposed emperor's theological works, 1370–5.

[1] A method of attaining divine illumination through meditation and the constant recitation of 'the prayer of the heart', championed in the 14th century by St Gregory Palamos, but going back to earlier ascetic practices.

military attack upon Matthew, he relegated John V to exile on the island of Tenedos, and in 1354 had Matthew crowned, with an appanage in Thrace. In effect, Kantakouzenos had finally proclaimed what his antagonists had feared all along—the usurpation of Palaiologan rule. The Palaiologoi, however, would not be displaced since popular and ecclesiastical opinion supported the claims of John V, and the foundations of Kantakouzenos' regime quickly disintegrated. In 1354 the Ottoman Turks led by Orhan's eldest son Süleyman Pasha occupied the key fortress of Kallipolis. With this the Ottomans obtained an important crossing point from Asia Minor to Thrace. In the ensuing months, Süleyman not only refused to surrender Kallipolis, but began fostering Ottoman settlements throughout the Gallipoli peninsula, which would form a spearhead for the Ottoman invasion of Thrace. This development created panic in Constantinople, upon which John V and the Genoese capitalized to stage a coup that returned him to the throne, in November 1354, now as sole occupant. Kantakouzenos abdicated and became a monk, occupying himself with writing his memoirs and theological treatises until his death in 1383.

John V's final duel with Matthew Kantakouzenos in 1354–7 constituted the closing stage of the protracted Palaiologan–Kantakouzenid rivalry. Throughout Matthew obtained troops from Orhan, his brother-in-law, and Süleyman at Kallipolis may likewise have been supportive. It climaxed in summer 1356 with Matthew's capture, which derailed his planned attack on Constantinople, and ended when he renounced his title (1357) and later withdrew to the Morea (1361–83 or 1391). Thus, at the age of 25 John V finally established himself as the rightful successor to Andronikos III.

As mentioned above, Süleyman Pasha's movements into Thrace after spring 1354 represented the first steps in the Turkish expansion into southeastern Europe. By the time he died, in 1357, it was apparent to all that the Turks were well on the way to encircling Constantinople from behind. The upper and middle stretches of the Maritsa River were under Turkish control, and the key northern fortresses of Didymoteichon and Adrianople were within striking distance. In occupied territory villages were being assigned as fiefs to various commanders, some in fact being Turkified, as colonists from Anatolia moved into this new 'land of opportunity'. The extent to which Orhan, the reigning Ottoman sultan, supported this incipient expansion into Europe is not known, though he seemingly endorsed it without actively participating himself. After a lull between 1357 and 1359, the Turkish commanders in Rumili continued their raids, taking Didymoteichon in November 1361. These accelerated throughout the 1360s, but without any central direction from Orhan's successor, Murad I (1362–89), who was fully occupied in Anatolia the first decade of his reign. Philippopolis, then Bulgarian and a major fortification on the Belgrade-to-Constantinople highway, was captured in 1363 or 1364. It seems, finally, that Adrianople was taken in 1369.

John V's reaction to these setbacks cannot be plotted in detail, although he clearly realized their gravity. At the outset of his sole rule, however, he concluded that the only viable hope was aid from the West—judging from his appeal to Pope Innocent VI in 1355 for ships and troops, proffering in return ecclesiastical union, and his son Manuel as papal ward and guarantee of compliance. Innocent was unmoved. A decade later John placed his hopes on his cousin Amadeo VI of Savoy, who envisioned a crusade in the classic style, prefacing recovery of the Holy Land with succour for Byzantium. Amadeo indeed sailed from Venice in June 1366 and seized Kallipolis from the Ottomans. Between April and early June 1367, John and Amadeo explored a variety of possible stratagems in Constantinople, including an ecumenical council to secure the union of the two churches, and John personally journeying to Rome to formally confess the Catholic faith. When Amadeo returned to Italy with Byzantine envoys the proposals were presented to Urban V, who rejected a council as useless, but would welcome an imperial visit. Perhaps moved by the fall of Adrianople, John V relented, and on 17 October 1369 professed the Catholic faith in the Hospital of the Holy Spirit in Rome. Three days later he endured a public spectacle of submission on the steps of St Peter's basilica.

No other Byzantine emperor had abased himself so profoundly to the papacy, which *ipso facto* reveals the extent of John V's despair over the future of his realm. After a further five months' stay in Rome, and another year in Venice, he returned to Constantinople in autumn 1371. In the interim no help had materialized from the West, and the situation in the Balkans had deteriorated even further. At this juncture, the epigonoi of Stephen Dušan's empire—principally King Vukašin, in the vicinity of Prilep, Skopje, and Ochrid, and his brother Jovan Uglеša, based further south at Serres—attempted to organize a counter-offensive against the Turks in the vicinity of Adrianople. On 26 September 1371, roughly a month before John V's return, the Serbian forces confronted a Turkish army near the Maritsa River at Černomen and were annihilated. For the Serbs, the consequences of this defeat were momentous, since Turkish absorption of the southern Slavic lands seemed virtually assured. Several of the surviving lords now submitted to the Ottomans as tributary vassals, including the legendary Marko Kraljevič, the son of King Vukašin, who had died in the battle.

Byzantium's reaction to this disaster was mixed. On the one hand, John V's most gifted son, Manuel, then governor of Thessalonica, exploited the Serbs' defeat to recover Serres. John V, conversely, drew the melancholy conclusion that he, too, must construct a *modus vivendi* with the Ottomans on terms of vassalage. This was arranged with Sultan Murad by treaty, according to which Byzantium was henceforth obliged to convey regular tribute (*kharadj*), and contribute troops to the Ottoman army on demand. In return, John hoped that Murad would restrain the Turks in Europe from attacking what remained of Byzantine territory. In any event, the consequence of this pact was a new type of coexistence between Constantinople and Bursa, one which drew the ruling elite on both sides into close contact and collaboration.

1371/2–1394: The First Period of Vassalage to the Ottomans

After the initial treaty of vassalage between John V and Murad I was concluded in 1371/2, Constantinople remained tributary to the Porte for a quarter of a century. On the Byzantine side this encompassed the remainder of John V's reign (he died in 1391), the usurpation of his eldest son Andronikos IV (1376–9), the usurpation of the latter's son John VII (summer 1390), and the early years of Manuel II, John V's second born. Murad I's rule continued until he was assassinated at the Battle of Kosovo Polje in 1389, when he was succeeded by his remarkable son 'Thunderbolt' Bayezid, whom Tamerlane captured at the Battle of Ankara in July 1402. The significance of this interval is twofold. First, resurgent and persistent power struggles within the Palaiologan clan intensified the entanglement between Byzantium and the Ottomans, as ambitious competitors for the throne bargained with the sultans—and likewise with the Italians, variously Venetians or Genoese—for support against the incumbent emperor. In the process, the prestige of the imperial regime increasingly came to be questioned at home and abroad. Parallel to this Byzantine political decay, the Ottomans continued their steady advance into the central Balkans, establishing control largely through suzerainty over a patchwork of Christian vassals. Under Murad, the highlights after c.1371/2 included the conquests of Sofia (1385) and Niš (1386), followed three years later by his fateful victory over a large Serb and Bosnian coalition at Kosovo, which sealed the fate of the various Serbian lordships. In 1393, Bayezid definitively annexed the core of Bulgaria to the empire. Against the backdrop of this expansionary dynamic, let us sketch, now, the Palaiologan–Ottoman interface in this first period of vassalage.

The ruinous 'dependency relationships' engendered by dynastic strife emerged when John V became engulfed in a savage conflict with his son, Andronikos IV, who at that time was the designated heir to the throne. In spring 1373 the latter staged a joint rebellion with Murad I's son, Savci Çelebi, their objective being to depose their respective fathers and rule in their place. John V and Murad summarily co-ordinated strategies and forces (in the course of which Murad probably made his first crossing into Rumili), and by late September Andronikos had been captured and partially blinded (as was his 3-year-old son John [VII]), and Savci Çelebi most probably had been executed.

In punishment, Andronikos and his son were now imprisoned; John V elevated his second son, Manuel, as co-emperor; and the seeds of a long vendetta were sown. In the next episode, in July 1376, Andronikos and his son escaped, obtained Genoese and Turkish help, and returned to Constantinople to wreak vengeance. John V and Manuel were captured and put in prison, where they languished for the next three years, while Andronikos established his rule, crowning his own son John as his co-emperor. Murad evidently shifted his support from John V to Andronikos IV because the latter promised, in compensation for troops, the return of Kallipolis (which Amadeo of Savoy had captured in 1366)—and this indeed transpired by 1377. Beyond the dynamics of dynastic strife, the motives for Andronikos' usurpation are difficult to fathom, although he may have represented a faction that rejected John V's submission to the papacy as a humiliating return to the errors of Michael VIII.

The pattern of Andronikos' coup in 1376 was repeated in June 1379, when John V and Manuel escaped, predictably with Venetian help, and promptly journeyed to Bursa, offering the sultan larger tribute if he would abandon Andronikos, and back the restoration of John V. Again Murad nodded to the highest bidder, and thus in late June of that year, assisted by Venetian ships and Turkish troops, John V and Manuel attacked Constantinople, managed an entry, and re-established their regime. On this occasion, however, Andronikos evaded capture and retreated with his family and hostages to Galata, where he fought on with Genoese support until 1381. Finally, in May 1381, a family compact was reached whereby Andronikos would be forgiven and reinstated as John V's heir, and thereafter the succession would pass to Andronikos' son John, the future John VII.

This arrangement, however, failed to restore peace and harmony among the Palaiologoi. Since Manuel had effectively been excluded from the succession, he angrily returned to Thessalonica in 1382, and thereafter pursued a rebellious course, embarrassing to John V's policy of compliance with Murad. By 1383 Manuel had established suzerainty over Thessaly and Epiros, a wayward 'expansionism' that so alarmed the sultan that he dispatched troops to obtain the surrender of Thessalonica. This Manuel refused, and consequently, down to 1387, he was occupied defending the city from an Ottoman siege. Meanwhile, Andronikos IV and his son John had retired to their appanage centred on Selymbria, but were still embroiled in territorial disputes with John V when Andronikos died in 1385.

The tragedy of Palaiologan political history in this decade and the next was that Andronikos IV's conflict with his kinsmen was not buried at his death. Instead, it persisted as a legacy to his son, John [VII], who in 1385 was 15, and keenly ambitious to preserve the provisions of the 1381 succession pact. His fears that his claims might be overturned were exacerbated in spring 1387, when Thessalonica capitulated to Hayreddin Pasha, and Manuel began manoeuvring for reconciliation with his father—and likewise the sultan. Eventually in the autumn of that year John V permitted his son to return to Constantinople at Murad's behest, whereupon Manuel's ambition henceforth was to recover his status as John V's co-emperor and designated successor. While the elder emperor was not unsympathetic (in 1387 he was aged 55), he resisted taking action that would push his grandson to rebellion, and thus left Manuel's political status undetermined, relegating him to provisional exile on the island of Lemnos, where he would remain through late summer or early autumn 1389.

For John [VII], Manuel's progress from Thessalonica to Constantinople was sufficient cause to begin preparations for a coup against his grandfather, which he intended to accomplish with Genoese and Ottoman support. By May 1389 he was in Genoa, where he was recognized as emperor and received loans. He returned east to approach the sultan early in 1390—by now Bayezid had replaced Murad—after rumours had reached him that John V had died. In point of fact the latter had fallen seriously ill, which apparently prompted Manuel to rush from Lemnos to his father's side—strategically positioned, as it were, for immediate succession. But John V miraculously recovered, and likewise seems to have sanctioned Manuel's return, anticipating that war with his grandson would shortly commence. Indeed, when the younger John met Bayezid, the latter agreed to provide him with troops, though it is again unclear precisely what was promised in compensation. In any event, John's bid for power as John VII was successful, sympathizers inside Constantinople facilitating his entry the night of 13/14 April 1390. His reign lasted only five months, however, throughout which his grandfather remained blockaded in a little fortress near the Golden Gate, and his uncle Manuel scurried for military assistance from other quarters to topple his nephew's regime.

John VII's grasp on power in Constantinople was undermined by Manuel's success in obtaining help from the Knights Hospitallers of Rhodes, for which he pawned a large stash of ecclesiastical treasures. Once he and his father had re-established themselves on the throne, their key problem was reconstructing a *modus vivendi* with Bayezid, and finding stratagems to keep John VII from again subverting their rule. The latter challenge would occupy Manuel, off and on, down to John VII's death in 1408. An accommodation was reached with Bayezid, part of which involved the dismantling of the

Golden Gate fortification, and documentary evidence suggests that the sultan did not oppose Manuel's succession to John V, when he at length died in February 1391. Thereafter down to 1394, Manuel behaved himself towards Bayezid as a loyal vassal, however much psychological and ideological turmoil it caused him (as is evident from his writings). Conversely, whatever reconciliation he achieved with his nephew was transitory and superficial.

More than anything else, the political tergiversations that unfolded between 1373 and 1394 underscore how very much the fate of the Palaiologoi depended on the will of foreigners, principally Italians and Turks, and how profoundly incapable that clan was in articulating power amicably within its ranks for the general welfare of its subjects. It exhibits, furthermore, how skilfully Murad and Bayezid manipulated the family rivalries of their Christian vassals to maximize their advantage.

1394–1424: Rebellion and Precariously Recovered Autonomy

Manuel II's rationale for breaking with his father's long-standing policy of subordination to the Ottomans is profoundly mysterious, particularly since his material and military resources at the time were as slender as ever. It is evident, however, that in 1393/4 Manuel had been negotiating with John VII for a formal reconciliation, the crux of which entailed a redefinition of the succession order, and that John betrayed this to Bayezid, who was furious. Indeed, during the assembly of vassals Bayezid convened at Serres in 1393/4, after the reduction of Trnovo, he reportedly ordered Manuel's execution, but then relented. Manuel himself asserts that this episode destroyed his 'friendship' with the sultan, and a further provocation may have arisen when Bayezid demanded the construction of a new mosque, installation of a kadi, and establishment of a large Turkish colony in Constantinople. Whatever the background, Manuel broke his ties with the Ottomans in about spring 1394—in essence, refusing to pay the *kharadj*, provide troops, or simply answer the sultan's summons. From the Ottoman perspective this was an act of rebellion, the first of its type by a *tekfur* (tributary prince) of Constantinople.

Bayezid's response was necessarily military, and he now launched an attack on Constantinople that was to last, off and on, for about eight years. As is evident from Manuel's own writings, Bayezid's initial objectives, or at least professed objectives, were not to displace Palaiologan rule, but rather to re-install John VII as the sultan's loyal lieutenant. Whatever the case, his assault on Constantinople certainly played a role (though hardly a decisive one) in stimulating Philip the Bold of Burgundy and Sigismund of Hungary to organize one of the last great international crusades. From spring 1394 to autumn 1396, the Ottoman action at Constantinople was more a blockade than a determined siege. However, following Bayezid's spectacular victory over the aforementioned crusaders at Nicopolis on 25 September 1396, a major contingent of Ottoman forces was positioned at the walls, and a full-scale siege unfolded. The situation quickly became desperate, but Manuel persevered in organizing defences through late 1399, at which time he was persuaded by Marshal Boucicaut, who had earlier arrived with minor relief, that he should journey to France and appeal for more serious help from the West. Through Boucicaut's good services, John VII and Manuel were reconciled, and John, incredibly, was left in command of Constantinople while his uncle sailed west.

Manuel's subsequent travels in Europe (from 10 December 1399 to 9 June 1403) involved fascinating state visits to Venice, Padua, Milan, Paris, and London. Throughout he was generously entertained, and he regarded King Henry IV as a particularly charming and likeable host. Even so, his negotiations with the western princes resulted in no appreciable aid or military commitments. Indeed, during the year and a half he resided in the Louvre as guest of Charles VI, perhaps his most significant accomplishment was writing a lengthy treatise on the Orthodox view of the procession of the Holy Spirit.

In the Byzantines' own view, Constantinople was saved by the timely intervention of the Virgin Mary, and indeed it was a kind of *deus ex machina*, in the person of Timur (Tamerlane), that averted its surrender in 1402. In late July of that year, while Manuel was still in Paris, the great khan's decisive clash with Bayezid took place at the legendary battle of Ankara, in which the Ottoman army was disastrously routed, and Bayezid himself was captured. It appears, moreover, that John VII had negotiated with Timur in summer 1401, offering Byzantine solidarity against the Ottomans. In the aftermath of Bayezid's defeat, the Ottoman assault on Constantinople evaporated, and early in 1403 a peace treaty was drawn up between John VII and other local Christian powers, on the one side, and Bayezid's successor in Rumili, Süleyman Çelebi, which was favourable to Byzantium. The emperors were formally absolved of tributary obligations and moreover recovered Thessalonica, Mount Athos, a stretch of the Black Sea coast from Constantinople to Mesembria or Varna, and a few Aegean islands. When Manuel himself returned to Constantinople, the treaty was reconfirmed, and he additionally gave his illegitimate niece, Theodora, in marriage to Süleyman.

The mood in Byzantium after 1402 was one of renewed, albeit qualified, optimism about future chances for survival. Not only had the threat of Bayezid been eliminated, his empire was now in ruins—deconstructed to its earlier dimensions by Timur, and reduced to chaos by protracted wars of succession among Bayezid's sons, played out between 1403 and 1413. By the latter date Mehmed I had triumphed, with generous Byzantine support.

Bird's-eye view of Constantinople in Cristoforo Buondelmonti's *Liber insularum*, *c.*1422. This is the only delineation of the city before the Turkish conquest that bears any relation to reality. It survives in many different versions, none of which is the original.

Mehmed's sole, undisputed reign continued down to May 1421, and throughout these years a stable coexistence prevailed between Constantinople and the Ottomans. Much of this was due to the even hand of Manuel II, as well as the willingness of Mehmed to refrain from resurgent expansionism.

This period of peace quickly disintegrated in late 1421, largely owing to a change of leadership in Constantinople. By 1420 Manuel II was an exhausted man of 70, and had resolved to withdraw from public life. In 1421 he surrendered the helm to his eldest son, John VIII, whose attitude to the Turks was less restrained and diplomatic than his father's. Simultaneously there was

275

a change of leadership on the Ottoman side, when Mehmed I died in May 1421 and was succeeded by his son Murad II. The latter's attitude towards the Byzantines was hardly accommodating and the stage was set for confrontations that ultimately would restore the *status quo ante* 1403.

When John VIII and his advisers learned of Mehmed's death, they stupidly resolved to incite an internal rebellion against the new sultan. To that end, in August 1421, they backed the pretensions of a certain Mustafa, who claimed to be a long-lost son of Bayezid, and indeed gathered some support in Europe. Murad II's reply, however, was swift and decisive. In January 1422 his army smashed Mustafa's troops, and Mustafa was captured and hanged. The following June he dispatched an army to attack Constantinople, and another to besiege Thessalonica. In the face of these disasters Manuel counselled yet another trouble-making stratagem to divert Murad—namely, supporting the claims of his brother in Anatolia, Küçük Mustafa. After a general assault on Constantinople failed on 24 August, Murad withdrew in early September to deal with Mustafa, who by now was besieging Bursa. Eventually, in February 1424, Manuel and Murad negotiated a settlement whereby Constantinople was again reduced to tributary status—the price for survival, according to the historian Doukas, now being 300,000 silver coins per year.

In essence, the entire interval from 1394 through 1424 was shaped by Manuel II's vision of liberation from 'servitude' to the Ottomans, and its genuine successes, aside from the accidents of fortune or divine intervention, rested on his *savoir-faire* as a statesman tempering the headiness of rebellion and recovered autonomy with the practicalities of coexistence and accommodation. His epigones were, unfortunately, made of lesser stuff.

The Muradiye Camii (1424–7) at the hot springs of Bursa was built by Sultan Murad II. It has an Italianate arcaded façade incorporating many Byzantine marble elements.

Far left: Portrait medal of John VIII Palaiologos by Pisanello made from sketches executed at the time the emperor attended the Council of Ferrara–Florence (1438–9). Pisanello was much taken by the exotic costumes and accoutrements of the Greek delegation.

Left: Portrait medal of Mehmed II by Costanzo da Ferrara, who was sent to Constantinople at the sultan's invitation by King Ferrante of Naples. The medal is dated 1481, the year of Mehmed's death at the age of 49.

1424–1453: Restored Vassalage and Final Defeats

Given the nastiness of the conflict that had unfolded between 1421 and 1424, the Ottomans could hardly help but regard Palaiologan Constantinople as a liability, the direct absorption of which was by now, if not before, a prime desideratum. Nonetheless, throughout the remainder of Manuel II's reign (he died in 1425), the sole rule of John VIII (1425–48) and the early years of Constantine XI (1449–51) Murad II left Constantinople in peace, and the terms of the 1424 treaty were observed. The critical shift in attitude came with the accession of Mehmed II, in February 1451, for whom the conquest of the city was a driving ambition.

John VIII's reign was suffused with a mood of profound apprehension and repeated disappointments. While Constantinople enjoyed a measure of peace and security after 1424, what remained of Byzantium elsewhere was in a state of chronic threat. As a punitive gesture, the Morea (which, under despot Theodore II (1407–43) had begun to expand at the expense of the Latins) was ravaged by the troops of Turahan Beg in late May 1423. In Macedonia, the siege of Thessalonica that Murad had launched in 1422 continued with such intensity the following year that famine was endemic. Under these dire circumstances, the Byzantines surrendered the city to the Venetians (September 1423), who were quickly overwhelmed by the costs of its defence. Finally in spring 1430 Murad II resolved to take Thessalonica once and for all, and personally led an enormous army into Macedonia, which achieved its objective. Since its leaders had refused to surrender peacefully, Thessalonica was now subjected to a fearful three days of destruction and plunder; the captives unable to secure ransom were sent to the slave markets of Rumili and Anatolia. When the canonical three days of license had passed, Murad immediately enacted measures to reconstruct the city. At that time,

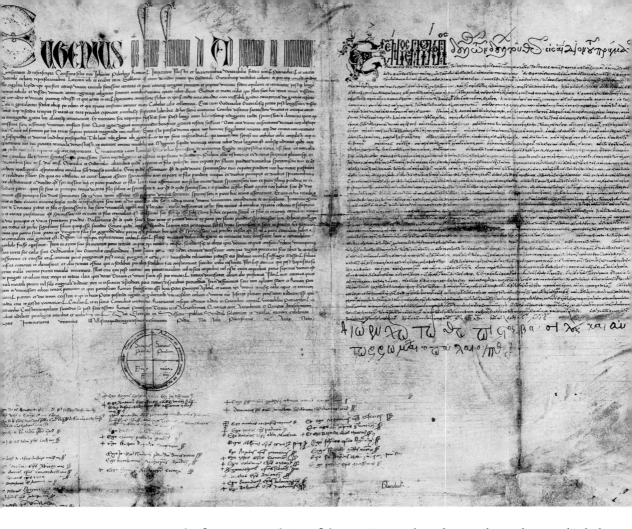

Bull of the union of the Roman and Greek churches (Florence 1439). Text in Latin and Greek, signed by Pope Eugenius IV and the emperor John VIII. The signatures of the Greek ecclesiastics are missing from this copy, one of 18 that are preserved.

the former second city of the empire numbered around two thousand inhabitants.

Although the fall of Thessalonica in 1430 was certainly considered a powerful portent of doom, the Rhomaioi and their leaders still nurtured hopes over the next decade and a half that their fortunes might again change for the better. Some still believed that the West might rally to a vigorous defence, especially if the Churches of Constantinople and Rome could be brought into a sincere union. There was also the parallel hope that the central European powers, especially the Hungarian kings, might finally sense a lethal danger across the Danube and mount serious expeditions against the Ottomans in Europe. Indeed, in the late 1430s and 1440s, there was a bustle of anti-Ottoman activity, although the results were again transitory.

On the Byzantine side, John VIII renewed efforts to attain union with Rome in the late 1430s, negotiating for a resolution of dogmatic differences at a council to be held in Europe. It was agreed that the locale would be Italy, and that the emperor and his retinue would participate. This council was eventually held in two places, and hence is termed the Council of Ferrara–Florence (1438–9). John VII, the patriarch Joseph, and other high dignitaries duly arrived in Ferrara early in 1438, and after lengthy discussions a basis for agreement was found. The Orthodox substantially accepted the doctrine of papal primacy, and conceded that the *filioque* dispute was based on a semantic confusion. This solution failed to satisfy everyone in the imperial party, and indeed some objected and left. Nonetheless, a formal union was celebrated on 6 July 1439, in the recently built cathedral of Florence.

As in the past, the benefits of union turned out to be negligible for Byzantium. Most importantly, it did not evoke much western sympathy for the plight of Constantinople. At the same time, it again alienated the imperial regime from the Orthodox community. At home and elsewhere in the 'Orthodox Commonwealth', John VIII's behaviour was branded as betrayal, on a par with that of Michael VIII. In Constantinople, the division over union was particularly serious, since it now fractioned a populace facing the inevitability of a renewed Ottoman effort to conquer the city. Already, in the aftermath of Ferrara–Florence, there were those wondering if the 'mufti's turban' would be preferable to the 'papal tiara'.

Pen and ink portrait of the patriarch Joseph II, who attended the Council of Ferrara–Florence. Joseph, who was in his eighties, died in 1439 and was buried in the church of Santa Maria Novella at Florence where his tomb still survives.

A Christian military revival in the 1440s initially showed some promise of success, but ultimately failed to reverse the situation. At that time several powerful antagonists to the Ottomans emerged in the western and northern Balkans. In Transylvania, the *voivoda* Janosh Corvinus Hunyadi mounted a series of successful campaigns against the Turks in Serbia and Wallachia. The same spirit was to be seen in the young Hungarian king, Vladislav III, and the Serbian despot George Brankovič. In Albania, a colourful resistance leader appeared in the person of Georgios Kastriotes or 'Scanderbeg' (a corruption of 'Iskender Beg'). This spirit of regionalized resistance eventually crystallized into another international crusade. In the autumn of 1443, a combined force of some 25,000 warriors crossed the Danube under the leadership of Vladislav, Hunyadi, and Brankovič, defeating the Ottoman regional commander at Niš, temporarily occupying Sofia, and then wintering back in the northern Balkans. Overwhelmed with problems in Anatolia, Murad II

279

Above: Detail of wall painting purporting to represent the siege of Constantinople by the Avars in 626, but clearly inspired by the Turkish siege of 1453. Here the sultan Mehmed II followed by a contingent of Janissaries. Romania, Monastery of Moldoviţa (1537).

Facing: Prophetic literature, notably the Oracles of Leo the Wise, concerning the liberation of Constantinople from the Turks, enjoyed wide diffusion until the seventeenth century. In this richly illustrated copy of 1577 made in Crete by Francesco Barozzi we see the Turks being driven out of Constantinople by a coalition of Christian princes.

negotiated an armistice (June 1444), which the Hungarians promptly broke the following autumn. Inspired by his recent successes, Vladislav believed the opportunity had come to drive the Ottomans from the Balkans, and hence in September he organized another expedition, though without Serbian participation. When this army clashed with Murad II at Varna (10 November 1444), it was annihilated, and the revived hopes of the 1430s and 1440s perished with it.

With the end of the 1440s and early 1450s came the last change of rulership, on both the Palaiologan and Ottoman sides, before the fall of Byzantium. In Constantinople, John VIII died childless in 1448, to be succeeded by his brother Constantine, despot of the Morea, and since 1447 likewise tributary to the Porte. In 1451, Murad II died and was succeeded by one of the most fascinating figures of the entire fifteenth century—Fātih Mehmed, or 'Mehmed the Conqueror', in whose hands the fate of Constantinople now rested.

If the 19-year-old Mehmed ascended the Ottoman throne with vague plans of taking the city, Constantine XI quickly supplied him with a pretext to act when, in autumn 1451, he threatened to foment a rebellion against the new sultan unless certain subsidies were provided. Within six months Mehmed signalled the tenor of his reply, when he began building an

enormous fortification up the Bosporos (the 'Boghaz-Kesen' or 'Channel Cutter'), intended to control traffic plying those waters, and as a preliminary to his assault on Constantinople. Constantine, in turn, was firmly convinced that the survival of the city rested securely on close relations with the West. When the papal legate, Cardinal Isidore, arrived he was greeted with the utmost courtesy, and a celebration of the union was held in Hagia Sophia (12 December 1452), something which John VIII had at least deferred. In point of fact, the Union proved worthless in defending Constantinople from Mehmed's soldiers, who commenced their attack on 6 April 1453, and penetrated the walls on 29 May. The fate of Thessalonica in 1430 was repeated, and again the conquering sultan would quickly turn his attention to the more difficult task of rebuilding, repopulating, and revitalizing the city.

With Constantine XI's death in battle that mournful day, and Fātih Mehmed's triumphal journey to Hagia Sophia—henceforth the premier mosque in Constantinople—the core of the Byzantine state was extinguished forever. The subsequent acquisitions of Mistra (1460) and Trebizond (1461) were but aftershocks. Yet by this victory Mehmed had not destroyed a culture, a faith, or a people. The essential rhythms of Byzantine life would endure within the framework of the Ottoman order, and beyond.

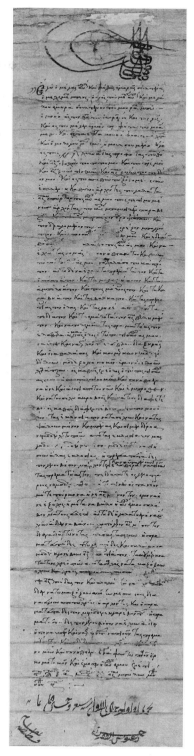

Left: Miniature of the same manuscript of Leo's Oracles showing the resurrection of the saviour emperor, who lay buried in the western part of Constantinople. In the background the column of Arcadius whose reliefs were believed to foretell these events.

Right: Grant of religious and commercial liberties to the Genoese of Galata, who had surrendered to the Turks. Text in Greek, headed by the *tughra* (monogram) of Mehmed II and signed by the third vizier Zaganos Pasha, 1 June 1453.

11 Palaiologan Learning

IHOR ŠEVČENKO

Despite its small extent, political weakness, and growing impoverishment, the late Byzantine state, along with its Greek satellite principalities, produced a remarkable cultural efflorescence. To call it a renaissance, as many scholars have done, tends to blur its fundamental difference from the one, true Renaissance which occurred in western Europe in the fifteenth century. It is also confusing to speak of Byzantine humanism for this or any other period. The cultural revival of the Palaiologan age (1261–1453) should rather be seen in the perspective of previous Byzantine revivals, notably those of the ninth–tenth centuries (see Chapter 8) and of the eleventh–twelfth, although it went some distance further than its predecessors. Indeed, conditions had changed. For one thing, the diminished Byzantine world was no longer the vast polyethnic entity it had been earlier: it was now almost exclusively Greek, a fact that redefined to some extent its attitude towards Greek antiquity. For another, close, if not always friendly, contact with the West meant that Latin literary and philosophical culture (whether of Latin, Arabic, or even Hebrew origins) could no longer be ignored to the extent to which it had been by a Photios in the ninth century or a Psellos in the eleventh.

An indicator of changing perspectives is provided by the word 'Hellene', which, before the thirteenth century, had predominantly meant 'pagan'—a pejorative term whose origin goes back to the books, apocryphal and genuine, of the Old and the New Testaments. There 'Hellene' simply denotes a non-Jew, i.e. a gentile. The negative meaning of 'Hellene' was absorbed by ecclesiastical and secular elites in Byzantium's early centuries, almost completely eliminating its neutral use. By the thirteenth century, however, intellectuals started proudly affirming that they were members of the 'Hellenic nation'. Under the new conditions of relative ethnic homogeneity and even some xenophobia, their search for roots led them back to the glorious Hellenic past. So with many intellectuals, but not all: when Demetrius Kydones translated into Greek the *Summa contra gentiles* of Thomas Aquinas (in 1354), he still called it *Book against the Hellenes*.

284

The literary product of the Palaiologan period is abundant and falls for the most part within established Byzantine categories, setting aside writings in the vernacular, such as the romances of chivalry, which are relatively few. It is represented by three lengthy historical works, which treat contemporary events, but draw on ancient models, especially Thucydides; a vast body of epistolography, usually very complicated and obscure in its style; rhetorical addresses of remarkable verbosity; a great deal of iambic poetry and rather less in hexameter; a relatively large body of hagiography in high style; two encyclopaedic works, one on medicine, the other ranging from rhetoric to the disciplines of the *quadrivium*; and a vast array of theological polemic against the Latins, the Orthodox of the adverse camp (Palamite or anti-Palamite as the case may be), and Islam. The two last categories continued to attract the greatest degree of passionate commitment.

Thanks to this extensive body of writing—and little of what was penned at the time is lost—it is possible to gain a pretty full picture of the intellectual milieu that produced it. For the two centuries between 1261 and 1453 we can identify about 150 literati, both laymen and ecclesiastics, who were active mostly at Constantinople, but also at Nicaea, Arta, Thessalonica, Trebizond, and Mistra. The correspondence of these authors reveals so much crisscrossing of names that it seems everybody knew and wrote to everybody else. In this restricted society subgroups gravitated round the centres of power that were able to provide them with substantial patronage. In descending order of importance, that patronage came from the imperial court, especially before the civil wars of the 1320s; from peripheral courts; from individual aristocrats and rich bureaucrats who kept their own 'salons'; from the patriarchate, and, finally, from metropolitan archbishops. To take one example, the scholarly career of the polymath Nikephoros Gregoras (*c*.1290–*c*.1360) was largely predicated on patronage. As a

Manuscript of Hesiod's *Works and Days* in the hand of the scholar Demetrius Triklinios, dated 20 August 1316.

285

young man he was supported by his uncle, the metropolitan of his native town Heraclea Pontica (now Karadeniz Ereğlisi). When he arrived at Constantinople, he received encouragement from the patriarch John XIII Glykys and the emperor Andronikos II, but especially crucial was the continuous protection afforded to him by the prime minister Theodore Metochites, who declared Gregoras his spiritual heir and granted him a sinecure in his restored monastery of Chora.

Books and libraries were the main prerequisites of intellectual activity. It is a moot question how much of the earlier bibliographic accumulation had been destroyed as a result of the Latin conquest, but it is certainly true that the Palaiologan age was marked by an intense quest for ancient texts, their copying and annotation. Present-day classicists are vastly indebted to the efforts of their Palaiologan predecessors, such as Demetrius Triklinios, Manuel

Manuscript of the Greek Anthology in the hand of the scholar Maximos Planudes, dated 1301. The Planudean Anthology was printed in 1494 and remained *the* Greek Anthology until the earlier Palatine version became known in the early nineteenth century.

Moschopoulos, Thomas Magister, and Maximos Planudes. These men wrote dictionaries of Attic words. They made new editions of poets such as Hesiod and Pindar, whose metric system they reconstructed with competence, and of the tragedians Sophocles and Euripides. They wrote scholia to Pindar, the tragedians, and Aristophanes; and a number of their readings, e.g. of Sophocles and Theocritus, are still accepted as felicitous conjectures. They rediscovered authors about whom tradition had been silent for hundreds of years, as Maximos Planudes rediscovered Ptolemy's *Geography* and the *Dionysiaca* by Nonnus of Panopolis. Their complete editions of various authors remain the basis of our own knowledge: Planudes, again, edited (and partly rediscovered) Plutarch and the Greek Anthology of epigrams, the latter in a version that we call 'Planudean'. 'Indecent' antique epigrams, especially those of homosexual content, were expurgated from this version; in return, Planudes gave us almost 400 epigrams not found elsewhere. Scholars and aristocratic bluestockings searched for ancient texts, borrowed manuscripts from each other and, when they could afford to, created libraries of both secular and religious works. The collection that Theodore Metochites assembled in the monastery of Chora in the first quarter of the fourteenth century remained the largest library in Constantinople until 1453. Some of Chora's volumes or parts thereof survive today in the libraries of Istanbul, Oxford, the Vatican, Vienna, and Paris.

Philological activity was not new in Byzantium, even if we grant that in the Palaiologan period it attained a particularly high level of intensity and excellence; neither was the cultivation of a recherché atticizing style at the expense of clarity and simplicity. The question we have to ask is whether the Palaiologan revival broke new ground in its relation to the classical heritage, in enlarging the field of its interests and, finally, in breaking out of the traditional Byzantine mould. On all three counts we can give a somewhat qualified affirmative answer.

It has been repeatedly stressed in the course of this book that Byzantine literary culture was largely based on that of Late Antiquity and what we call the Second Sophistic. The most widely imitated authors were not those that are studied in departments of classics today, but rhetoricians like Lucian, Aelius Aristides, Libanius, Synesius, and their Christian analogues, the Cappadocian Fathers, such as Gregory of Nazianzus and St Basil. Preoccupation with style rather than with ideologically suspect content meant that these authors were removed from their historical habitat and, as it were, lined up on a pedestal as timeless exemplars of literary excellence. This influence of the rhetoricians did not diminish in the Palaiologan period, but now for the first time antiquity came to be viewed in three rather than two dimensions. Metochites, in his critical essay on Demosthenes and Aelius Aristides, attributed

Facing: Initial B (*Beatus vir*) from the Psalter, Biblioteca Riccardiana, Florence, cod. 323. It has been argued that this splendid Psalter was commissioned by the emperor Frederick II and produced at Jerusalem in *c*.1235. It shows a creative blending of a western tradition with Byzantine figure style and iconography.

the difference between their kinds of oratory to the different periods in which they had lived. Demosthenes orated in the heyday of democracy, when one had to speak to the point and answer questions on the spot, whereas Aristides lived under a monarchy, a condition that favoured panegyric and encouraged verbosity. That may strike us as a truism, but it does imply a degree of historical understanding.

With regard to our second criterion, we may note an increased interest in the sciences, like mathematics (where, again, the versatile Planudes was at work) and medicine, but especially in astronomy. The relevant ancient texts (notably Ptolemy and the Handy Tables by Theon) had been recopied in the ninth century, but no original work on them appears to have been done at the time. It fell to Metochites to produce without recourse to direct observation a new *Introduction to Astronomy* based on Ptolemy's *Almagest* and recalculate the old parameters for a starting point in 1283 (the first regnal year of An-

First page of Theodore Metochites' *Introduction to Astronomy* with a notation in the hand of his disciple Nikephoros Gregoras.

dronikos II). He was followed, amongst others, by Nikephoros Gregoras, who annotated our most luxurious surviving manuscript of Ptolemy and who is praised for proposing a revision of the calendar that anticipated the Gregorian reform.

Gregoras was made aware of Arabic astronomy, but made no explicit use of it. Actually, exclusive adherence to Ptolemy proved a dead end. The real progress that had been achieved in the tables and treatises compiled by Arab and Persian astronomers reached the Greek world about 1300, at first through lowlier social channels, namely through translations made from Persian and Arabic by men moving between the capital and Trebizond in the east, like George-Gregory Chioniades, who had to go to Persian Tabriz to acquaint himself with oriental science, and, later on, by his follower George Chrysokokkes. By the middle of the fourteenth century, Ptolemaic data were criticized as inadequate by professionals, and either 'Persian' tables were substituted for Ptolemy, or both Ptolemaic and 'Persian' tables were used in different books of the same work. The latter was the case of the *Three Books* by Theodore Meliteniotes, published about 1352. Already by about 1309, however, a treatise on the use of the astrolabe was translated in Constantinople from a Latin version of the Arabic original. In the second quarter of the fifteenth century, another astronomical work, the *Six Wings*, dating from the fourteenth century, was translated into Greek, this time from the Hebrew. Here we may be dealing with western influences: the *Six Wings*'s Jewish author hailed from southern France, and the work itself may have reached Byzantium through Venice or one of its possessions. In spite of its non-Hellenic and non-Christian origin, the new astronomy was predominantly cultivated by Greek Orthodox ecclesiastics. Thus George Chioniades ended up as bishop of Tabriz and Theodore Meliteniotes was head of the Patriarchal School. Here practical needs were victorious over cultural pride and ideology.

Another area of enlargement concerned translations from the Latin (mostly by Planudes) which, however, reflected a typically medieval range of interests: Ovid, Cicero's *Dream of Scipio* with Macrobius' commentary on it, the *Disticha Catonis*, the *Grammar* of Donatus, Boethius' *Consolation of Philosophy*, and St Augustine. More ambitious and influential in terms of contemporary religious concerns was the translation of parts of the *Summa* and other works of Thomas Aquinas by the brothers Demetrius and Prochoros Kydones in the second half of the fourteenth century.

Originality of thought can only be demonstrated in a few cases. Once again, Metochites comes to the fore. Keenly aware of the decadence of his times and the precariousness of his own literary fame (by which he set great store), he was the first to question one of the axiomatic doctrines of Byzan-

tinism, namely that the empire played a central role in the cosmic drama and was destined to survive to the end of days. For Metochites the empire was just another political entity, and its impending collapse, another manifestation of the universal law of creation and decay. Unlike his predecessors, Metochites saw Byzantine civilization as neither unique nor superior to all others. A historical relativist, he even considered the infidel Tatars noble, more so in some respects, especially in moral behaviour, than his Byzantine fellow Christians.

The other Palaiologan maverick was the Neoplatonist George Gemistos, who renamed himself Plethon (c.1360–1452). He, too, composed an astronomical work in which he used 'Persian' and perhaps Hebrew tables, but his claim as original thinker lay elsewhere. Although his astronomical computations were useful for establishing the dates of Easter, and although he had defended the cause of Orthodoxy at the Council of Ferrara–Florence (1438–9), Plethon in his old age fell into neo-paganism, perhaps under the influence of Italian humanists. In a treatise called, like Plato's, *The Laws*, he advocated a somewhat modified 'Hellenic' pantheon, headed by Zeus, who was assisted by Poseidon (married to Hera!) and four types of other gods of descending power. Plethon professed a belief in both the message of Zoroaster and that of the Seven Wise Men, and posited the immortality of the soul *before* its descent into the body. He also believed in fatalism, probably under the influence of Islam. No wonder that when, some time after his death, the master copy of the *Laws* was handed to the patriarch of Constantinople, Gennadios Scholarios, the latter ordered it to be burnt. As a result, we know of Plethon's religious system mainly from refutations by the same patriarch, from numerous fragments copied by Plethon's adherents, and from a page or so in Plethon's own handwriting. He may have exerted some influence on his Italian admirers, but had only a few followers among his fellow countrymen. Fittingly, his ashes repose in the Tempio Malatestiano of Rimini, the most pagan of Renaissance churches.

By the middle of the fourteenth century the sources of patronage that had supplied Byzantine intellectuals with their bread and butter began to dwindle. It was a lucky coincidence that their expertise, namely their mastery of the Greek language, their knowledge of ancient texts and access to manuscripts, came to be increasingly valued in Italy. Emigration was a hard choice that often entailed conversion to Roman Catholicism, but some were ready to leave the sinking ship. At first, as in the case of Demetrios Kydones, they would go to Venice for a few years, then return home or stop half-way in Venetian-held Crete, but from the end of the century onwards they began emigrating permanently. The story of these scholars is a well-known part of that of Renaissance humanism, but two of the most important émigrés deserve a brief mention here. Between them, Manuel Chrysoloras, who died at

Facing: Theodore Metochites, who refounded the monastery of Chora at Constantinople, was both a politician and a scholar. He created an extensive library and distinguished himself as an astronomer. Dressed in turban and caftan, he is here offering his monastery to Christ. Mosaic of Kariye Museum, Istanbul.

Constance in 1415, and John Argyropoulos, who died in Rome in 1487, taught in Padua, Rome, Milan, Pavia, and, above all, Florence. They introduced Byzantine didactic practices, possibly the curricula and certainly the techniques of philology to Italy, translated Aristotle's works and Plato's *Republic* word by word into Latin, and taught or influenced such prominent humanists as Leonardo Bruni, Guarino of Verona, Marsilio Ficino, the Florentine Poggio Bracciolini, Filelfo, and John Reuchlin. They did well in their new homes, none better than Bessarion of Trebizond, who was made cardinal and titular patriarch of Constantinople, narrowly missing being made pope.

It is tempting to imagine the aged Plethon, who died one year before the fall of Constantinople, sitting on the hill of Mistra within sight of ancient Sparta as he devised his 'Hellenic theology', complete with its rites and prescribed prayers to the gods. Perhaps he was getting senile, but it is just possible that he did come to understand what had been evident to Julian the Apostate eleven centuries earlier, namely that Christianity, much as it came to be indebted to Hellenism, in the end was incompatible with it.

Facing: John Argyropoulos teaching medicine at the hospital of the Kral (a foundation of the Serbian king Stephen Uroš II Milutin, attached to the Petra Monastery at Constantinople) in *c.*1448. At the top of the page is a list of his students.

12 Towards a Franco-Greek Culture

ELIZABETH JEFFREYS AND CYRIL MANGO

The fall of Constantinople was followed in a few years by the conquest of the Despotate of the Morea (1460) and the bloodless absorption by the Turks of the kingdom of Trebizond (1461). When Mehmed the Conqueror died in 1481, the greater part of Greek-speaking lands were under Ottoman rule, excluding the islands which were gradually mopped up: Rhodes in 1522, Chios in 1566, Cyprus in 1570–1, the Cyclades in 1579, finally Crete between 1645 and 1669. Only the Ionian Islands were never subjected to Turkish occupation.

While the great majority of Greek populations that had once belonged to Byzantium experienced a longer or shorter period of *Tourkokratia*, their previous fate had varied greatly from region to region. We may set aside those, notably in Cappadocia, that had been conquered by the Seljuk Turks at the end of the eleventh century and to all intents and purposes disappeared from history. Among more visible areas, the Black Sea coast passed directly from Greek autonomy to Ottoman domination. Constantinople, the kingdom of Thessalonica, Epiros, and the Despotate of the Morea underwent a relatively short period of Latin occupation before reverting to Greek rule. The Aegean islands, on the other hand, along with Cyprus and Crete remained in Latin hands for several centuries before submitting to the Turks. The diversity of political status led to different cultural results, which may still be felt today.

The imposition of Ottoman rule meant the preservation of Byzantinism. The subject Orthodox population, both Greek and Slav, remained for the most part segregated from its Muslim neighbours and was constituted into a single 'nation' (*millet*), placed under the authority of the patriarch of Constantinople. In effect, the patriarch and the metropolitan bishops under him gained enormously by this arrangement. They received a further priceless boon when the Ottomans absorbed Syria, Palestine, and Egypt (1516–17), so bringing the patriarchates of Alexandria, Jerusalem and Antioch, and the dependent pilgrimage sites of the Holy Land and Sinai into the Greek network. If the Greek hierarchs did not prosper more than they did, that was because of their continual squabbles and the ever-increasing bribes they paid to their Muslim overlords. The one proviso, which the patriarchs had no trouble in observing, was that the Church should remain loyal to the sultan, now commonly referred to as 'Basileus'. Being loyal meant, above all, being anti-western, and that, too, came naturally. While the pope remained the chief enemy, Constantinople also learnt by bitter experience to keep its distance from the new Protestant powers which were up to no good. To preserve Orthodoxy uncontaminated, education had to be restricted to its medieval curriculum of grammar, rhetoric, theology, and a modicum of Aristotelian philosophy. At the same time the Church and its monasteries provided a means of employment and often opportunities of rapid advancement in the hierarchy to Greek men of letters. They have left a literary heritage in the Byzantine tradition, a heritage now covered by a thick layer of dust.

Conditions were very different in the lands that came under Latin domination. It cannot, of course, be claimed that the colonists were welcomed by the natives, even if, in the case of Cyprus, it is admitted (by a rabidly anti-western author) that Richard Lionheart was received with open arms (1191). For the peasant population it made little difference who was on top, although they certainly resented the restrictions and humiliations imposed on the Orthodox clergy by their new masters. In Crete several rebellions erupted against the Venetians. As time went on, however, there was a steady rapprochement between 'Franks' and the better-off Greeks. Western fashions in dress, ideals of chivalry, entertainments spread to the natives, while third- and fourth-generation Franks spoke more Greek than Italian or French and came to venerate local saints.

Here we must cast a glance backwards. Cultural contacts between Byzantium and the West had never, of course, been entirely interrupted, but remained weak until the age of the Crusades. The one exception was Italy, where Byzantium maintained a presence until the fall of Bari in 1071. Italian merchants, at first mainly from Pisa and Amalfi, started trading at Constantinople in the tenth century. Venice, nominally a vassal of the empire, built and decorated its cathedral of St Mark's in the Byzantine style. The basilica of Monte Cassino, reconstructed in 1066–71, owed its decoration (but not its architecture) to Byzantine artists. But while Byzantine influences flowed to Italy, they seldom extended north of the Alps, and very little flowed in the opposite direction. In the domain of letters practically no Latin writings, except a few works of hagiography, were translated into Greek since Late Antiquity until c.1300. The thinning of the cultural divide between the eastern and western areas of the Mediterranean is particularly clear in literary developments that took place from the thirteenth century onwards. From this period, for example, come the romances which are the works of

A western family that has gone native. Dedicatory panel of a village chapel at Galata, Cyprus, AD 1514. The donors are identified as 'miser' Stefano Zacharia, his son Paolo and their respective wives Louise and Madelena. The Zacharia family was originally Venetian.

Byzantine literature with the most immediate appeal to readers today, and which are the forerunners of the literature of modern Greece.

Most of the literature produced in Byzantium was written in a manner that is not easy for someone from outside that culture to appreciate: much of it was theological and much was written following linguistic rules which required years of study and were increasingly remote from the spoken language. In the period after the Fourth Crusade, however, the linguistic conventions of previous generations were increasingly ignored, especially in the areas on the fringes of the empire, and new topics attracted writers' attention.

The new topics include the romances just mentioned. Although there had been a brief interest in love stories, written in a highly erudite language, in the middle years of the twelfth century, fiction of this sort had never been as prominent in Byzantine literary culture as it had become in the Latin East. Now there appears a significant series of narratives that deal with the fortunes of star-crossed lovers, who have names like Velthandros and Chrysantza or Livistros and Rodamni. They frequently retreat to castles; they also encounter ogres and witches, hazards drawn from folk tales, as well as the pirates and furious parents that come from the classical Greek tradition. The indebtedness of these texts to a culturally mixed environment can be deduced from several characteristics. Some, most notably the *War of Troy* and *Phlorios and Platzia-Phlora* are close translations, the one of a French and the other of an Italian original. Others, like the *Achilleis*, refer casually to features of Frankish culture such as hairstyles or fashions in clothing. Less tangibly there is in all of them an assumption of a court culture that owes more to the feudal customs of the West than to Byzantine hierarchies, and there is a vocabulary to cover these items with many words taken over from French, Italian, and Latin. Furthermore the relationship between the lovers is depicted in a manner which arguably owes much to the conventions of the western *amour courtois*.

Perhaps connected to the focus on personal relations implicit in the romances, there is also apparent a renewed interest in an individual's own feelings and his (never her) reactions to his surroundings. And so we find Stephanos Sachlikis in hot pursuit of the ladies of the night of Rethymnon, Leonardo Dellaportas musing from prison on the inadvertent wrong turnings his life had taken, Marino Falieri reporting his dreams. All these writers come from the Venetian–Greek cities of Crete in the early years of the

Carved slab from Athens showing a soldier in Frankish accoutrement, a snake twined round a palm tree, and a crowned siren holding a flower (thirteenth century). The meaning of the composition remains unexplained.

297

fifteenth century. Here the imported Venetian aristocracy had combined sufficiently with the native Greek *archontes* to develop a culture with its own characteristic blend of Italian and Greek elements. From this came the dramas, such as those of Chortatsis, that were performed in the literary 'academies' (the Stravaganti, the Sterili, and the Vivi) of Rethymno and Chania in the last years of the sixteenth century.

Though certainly not a new topic, since the writing of history is one of the salient features of the Byzantine literary tradition, we now find narratives focusing on regional history, rather than the Constantinopolitan-based deeds of emperors. These narratives record the history of areas where communities of Franks were established. Thus from the late fourteenth century there is the *Chronicle of the Morea*, which recounts how William of Champlitte and Geoffrey Villehardouin took over the Peloponnese in 1205 with a handful of knights, and carries the story—in the surviving versions—through the next hundred years. The multiple versions in which this account survives (Italian, Catalan, and Aragonese as well as French and Greek) also testifies to the multicultural nature of the society that was then developing, as does the continuing debate over whether the first form of the *Chronicle* was written in French or in Greek. Much clearer is the case of the *Chronicle of Tocco*, which despite dealing with the fortunes of the Italo-Greek dynasty ruling in Kephallonia, was never written in anything other than Greek. As was the lively account of the Lusignan rulers written by Leontios Makhairas (*c.*1380–1432), though it is strongly marked with Cypriot orthography and vocabulary. Its vignettes of court life carry a vivid impression of the tensions endemic in a hybrid community.

All the works mentioned so far share one striking characteristic. They are all written in a register of Greek which is very far from the formal atticizing language that was normally expected when pen was put to paper, and which was described in the grammatical exercises of, say, Manuel Moschopoulos (1265–1316) or Thomas Magister (1270–1347/8). The texts from the areas of the Byzantine world settled by Franks use a form of the spoken Greek of the period; in the case of Makhairas this is particularly clear since he uses the Cypriot dialect. In the others there are no signs of regional dialect but there are syntactical and morphological constructions which foreshadow features of Modern Greek. The most reasonable explanation for this phenomenon is that these works were produced in a multilingual environment where Byzantine linguistic conventions were blurred. The audience was one whose oral comprehension of Greek would have been good but who would have been oblivious to, or had no means of discovering, the complexities of formal Greek. The censorship and education which in Constantinople would have removed neologisms from written forms of Greek were not in place in these

areas. Undoubtedly, too, the mingling of cultures would have brought an awareness of literary fashions in other areas of Europe, as the translated texts demonstrate. It should be remembered that one of the most obvious features of the literatures of Frankish Europe in the thirteenth and fourteenth centuries is the dominant role taken by the vernaculars, with French and the regional dialects of Italy being especially innovative.

This acceptance of the vernacular must also be a factor behind the other feature shared by all the works mentioned so far, with the exception of Makhairas, and that is that they are written in verse. The metre used is a rhythmic fifteen-syllable line that first appeared in the tenth century, with no clear classical and learned antecedents. The lack of classical models meant that there were no established rules for its use. It would thus have been accessible to writers and audiences used to the patterns of everyday speech to whose rhythms and forms it was well suited. So well suited was the fifteen-syllable line to the rhythms of speech that it became in effect the national metre of modern Greek literature. It was given a subtlety that the earlier examples lacked in the flexible patterns of the *Erotokritos* (1590–1610), Cornaros' romantic epic that, as much as Chortatsis' dramas, epitomizes the social and literary fusions of Venetian Crete. In subsequent centuries the

Monastery church of St Sophia at Trebizond, founded by the emperor Manuel I (1238–63). Exterior from the south. While basically Byzantine both in its architecture and painted decoration, St Sophia shows a curious intrusion of Caucasian, Italian, and even Seljuk elements.

299

The Palace of the Despots at Mistra, more western than Byzantine in style, is a three-storey rectangular building with a spacious throne room at the top. It is similar in disposition to the palace of Nymphaeum and Tekfur Sarayı at Constantinople.

conscious compositions in the fifteen-syllable line of writers as diverse as Solomos (1798–1857), Palamas (1859–1943), Ritsos (1909–90), or even Elytis (1911–96) draw on an epic and ballad tradition of uncertain antiquity but with roots in an oral tradition which received a great impulse in the period of the Franco-Greek societies.

In many cases the areas which saw the creation of these texts are apparent from the texts themselves: this is so for Cyprus (Makhairas), Crete (Sachlikis, Dellaportas), the Peloponnese (the *Chronicle of the Morea*). In other cases, like the *War of Troy*, there are no clear statements in the text so one has to fall back on arguments that a work of such length and so closely connected to a French original must have been due to a patron operating in an area where there was close French and Greek contact, in this instance perhaps the Morea in the fourteenth century under the later Angevins. In other cases again it is very likely that the author was resident in Constantinople itself, since that city was also not immune to the pressures of a multicultural world. For many years there had been substantial communities of Italian traders, most notably the Genoese in Galata, while the imperial house had continued the practice, begun in the twelfth century, of marriages into western families. Theodore Palaiologos, the Marquis of Montferrat, for example, son of Andonikos II, eventually became virtually indistinguishable from any other Italian nobleman, and himself made a Latin version of the treatise on government that he wrote in Constantinople in 1327.

The probable literary activity of a cousin of Theodore's, Andronikos Palaiologos, highlights a number of the issues raised by the texts from this period. This Andronikos is generally taken to be the author of the romance *Kallimachos and Chrysorrhoi*, on the basis of a not particularly close paraphrase in which a romance is attributed to him. *Kallimachos* is on the fringes of the texts we have been considering—it is in verse, it is linguistically at the lower end of an acceptable register of Greek and is full of folk-tale elements,

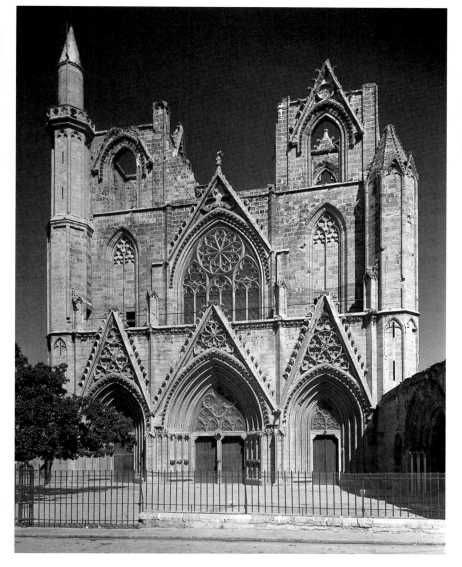

Built in French Gothic style, the cathedral of St Nicholas at Famagusta (first half of the fourteenth century) has served as a mosque since 1571. It was here that the Lusignan kings of Cyprus were crowned kings of Jerusalem.

though the Frankish features are minimal. But this is the only romance for which we can even begin to think we can identify the author.

A surprising amount of the Franco-Greek writing is anonymous: in effect all the romances and all the history apart from Machairas, though none of the Cretan personal poetry. Here perhaps the role of the verse medium comes into play again for there are many stereotypical lines whose presence can perhaps be best explained as a reference to a traditional oral style which demanded anonymity, however elevated the writer's social status.

In the domain of the visual arts we also find from the twelfth–thirteenth century onwards a fusion of Byzantine and Latin elements. Most visibly, buildings in the western style were put up in Latin principalities and colonies, not only castles, but also churches, abbeys, and mansions. At Constantinople the Italian trading colonies, it seems, started erecting their own churches before 1204, and there was certainly some building activity in the period of the Latin Kingdom. The Genoese colony of Pera, established in 1303 on the opposite shore of the Golden Horn, was built in the Italian style. Mistra, capital of the Despotate of the Morea, was initially a Frankish foundation, and its multi-storey Palace of the Despots was more western than Byzantine. In Cyprus the splendid cathedrals of Nicosia and Famagusta, not to mention a great number of other important foundations, were erected by French architects in the Gothic style. Greeks, therefore, came into daily contact with a tradition of architecture to which they had not been previously exposed and which was technologically more advanced than their own. The selective borrowings they made—the belfry, the pointed arch, decorative machicolations, possibly the stained glass window—show their willingness to learn. Figural sculpture, except for rather flat relief icons, had been underdeveloped in the Byzantine tradition and now assumed greater prominence under Frankish influence, e.g. in funerary monuments, although full-scale statues were avoided.

In painting, the foremost medium of Byzantine art and, theologically, the most

David playing the harp from the
Psalter, Paris, Bibliothèque
Nationale, gr. 139 of the second
half of the tenth century. This
miniature was directly inspired
by a late antique original, which
in turn reproduced the pagan iconography of Orpheus charming
the beasts.

David playing the harp from the
Psalter, Vatican Palatinus gr. 381B
of the late thirteenth century. This
is a direct copy of the Paris miniature, except for the elongation of
the format and of the figures as
well as the omission of some animals. We have here a clue to the
kind of model that was used by
artists of the Palaiologan period.

This small triptych of the Pietà flanked by St Francis and St Mary Magdalen, used for personal devotion, is attributed to Nikolaos Tzafouris, a Cretan painter known in 1489–1500. This type of icon executed in the *maniera italiana* or *greca* by post-Byzantine artists, is mentioned in contracts preserved in archives in Venice.

Domenico Theotokopoulos (El Greco), Dormition and Assumption of the Virgin Mary, *c.*1567. Church of the Dormition, Hermoupolis, Syros. His signature appears on the base of the Renaissance candlestick, centre foreground.

sensitive, influences appear to have flowed mainly in the opposite direction. When, fifty years ago, Hugo Buchthal was able to reconstruct a school of manuscript illuminators who were active in Jerusalem and Acre in the twelfth and thirteenth centuries, he found that these French and Italian artists copied or adapted Byzantine iconographic models, while at the same time retaining typically western features such as full-page decorated initials. It seems, therefore, that they recognized the prestige or superiority of Byzantine figure style. More recently a large group of 'Crusader icons', also painted by westerners according to the conventions of Byzantine iconography, has been identified in the monastery of St Catherine on Mount Sinai, a pilgrimage centre that had at the time closer links with the West than with Constantinople. Most strikingly, a fragmentary cycle of the life of St Francis of the 1240s or 1250s has come to light in a church of Constantinople that must have been converted to the Latin rite.

The age of the Palaiologoi, in spite of its political and economic decadence, saw a remarkable flowering of religious painting in a distinctive style that came to the attention of European scholars about a hundred years ago. The frescoes of Mistra and the mosaics of the monastery of Chora (Kariye Camii) at Constantinople were seen to bear an uncanny resemblance to the art of the Italian primitives like Pietro Cavallini, Cimabue, and Duccio. What came to be called the 'Byzantine question', i.e. who came first, has long been debated without being brought to a complete resolution. We now know that the Palaiologan style crystallized in c.1260: we first meet it in the monastery of the Holy Trinity at Sopoćani in Serbia, and something not unlike it in the church of St Sophia at Trebizond of about the same date. We assume without hard proof that these two monuments, standing as they do at opposite ends of the Byzantine periphery, were decorated by artists from the 'centre'—but where exactly was the centre in the 1260s? The prevalent view is that the Palaiologan style, in spite of some iconographic borrowings from the West (e.g. the Tree of Jesse), was of Byzantine origin, going back to very old models, in particular illuminated manuscripts of the tenth century. If that is so, one may see it as a conscious effort to create a school of Orthodox religious painting grounded in ancient precedent, yet satisfying a new taste for a fuller and more picturesque narrative style. It certainly emerged in a context of interaction between eastern and western artistic traditions.

While losing some of its initial freshness, the Palaiologan style remained to the end the dominant form of Byzantine painting. It did not lead to the

Detail of a highly damaged St Francis cycle in the church of the Virgin Kyriotissa (Kalenderhane Camii) at Constantinople. Painted no later than the 1250s, this is one of the earliest known cycles of the life of St Francis of Assisi, canonized in 1228.

303

rapid development we witness in Italy. By the time Giotto painted the Arena Chapel (*c.*1306)—some ten years before the mosaics of Chora—Italy was well ahead and had nothing further to learn from Byzantium. By the middle of the fourteenth century, in any case, commissions must have been drying up at Constantinople, thus forcing artists to seek their livelihood elsewhere. The most famous of them, Theophanes the Greek, emigrated to Moscow, where he trained many disciples including Andrei Rublev. Others moved to Crete, which became the most active centre of Byzantine painting until its conquest by the Turks. Recent research in Venetian archives has revealed the activity of a large group (over a hundred) of named painters, who produced mostly icons, but occasionally did murals as well. They worked in a quasi-industrial manner both for export and home consumption, using stencils, which were handed down from generation to generation. What is particularly interesting is that they were able to switch from a Byzantine to a late Gothic manner depending on their clientele. In other words, their Orthodox customers eschewed western icons and vice versa. On the plane of individual religiosity the two traditions remained distinct.

Italian painting was, however, bound to prevail in the end. In the sixteenth century western infiltration, mostly through the medium of engravings, was still sporadic. The painter Theophanes the Cretan, who executed several large cycles on the Meteora and Mount Athos in the years 1527–46, followed in the main Byzantine tradition, but copied the Massacre of the Innocents from an engraving, after Raphael, by Marcantonio Raimondi. Also on Mount Athos the Apocalypse cycles in the monasteries of Lavra and Dionysiou were inspired by Dürer's woodcuts. By 1600 the Byzantine style was in terminal decline. The most famous Greek painter hailing from Crete, Domenico Theotokopoulos (El Greco), started his career with some rather Italianate icons, but was then completely won over by contemporary Mannerism. Despite claims to the contrary, the only Byzantine element of his famous paintings was his signature in Greek lettering.

Facing: The Journey to Bethlehem in the monastery of Chora invites comparison with Giotto's nearly contemporary Flight into Egypt in the Arena Chapel, Padua. While the composition and rocky landscape are broadly similar, the Italian painting has figures that are more statuesque and step on real ground instead of tiptoeing on a stage set.

Chronology

Nikephoros I (802–11)

805	Byzantine control of Peloponnese restored
806	Arabs advance to Ancyra
809	Death of Caliph Hārūn al-Rashid
811	Nikephoros defeated and killed by Bulgarians

Michael I Rhangabe (811–13)

812	Bulgarians capture Develtos and Mesembria
813	Bulgarian victory near Adrianople

Leo V the Armenian (813–20)

814	Death of Bulgarian Khan Krum
815	Iconoclasm reimposed

Michael II the Stammerer (820–9)

821–3	Revolt of Thomas the Slav
827	Arab occupation of Sicily begins
c.827	Conquest of Crete by Arabs begins

Theophilos (829–42)

838	Arabs destroy Amorion and Ancyra

Michael III the Drunkard (842–67)

843	Final restoration of Images
856	Deposition of Empress Theodora
858–67	First patriarchate of Photios
860	Russian attack on Constantinople
863	Arabs defeated at Poson
c.864	Conversion of Bulgaria
866	Basil murders Caesar Bardas

Basil I (867–86)

872	Defeat of Paulicians in Asia Minor
873	Victories over Arabs
877–86	Second patriarchate of Photios
878	Arabs take Syracuse

Leo VI (886–912)

894–6	War with Bulgaria
902	Fall of Taormina
904	Sack of Thessalonica
911–12	Attempt to recover Crete fails

Alexander (912–13)

Constantine VII Porphyrogenitus (913–59)

913	Symeon of Bulgaria appears before Constantinople
917	Symeon's victory at Anchialos
920–44	Romanos I Lekapenos co-emperor
923–44	Successful campaigns against the Arabs by John Kourkouas
941	Russian expedition against Constantinople

946	Princess Olga of Russia converted

Romanos II (959–63)

961	Crete conquered by Nikephoros Phokas
962	Otto I crowned emperor

Nikephoros II Phokas (963–9)

965	Conquest of Tarsus; annexation of Cyprus
969	Conquest of Antioch and Aleppo

John I Tzimiskes (969–76)

971	John annexes eastern Bulgaria; defeats Sviatoslav
975	John invades Palestine

Basil II Boulgaroktonos (976–1025)

989	Baptism of Vladimir
997	Samuel of Bulgaria devastates Greece; conversion of the Magyars
1000	Annexation of Georgian principality of Tao
1001–18	Conquest of Bulgaria
1022	Annexation of Armenian kingdom of Vaspurakan

Constantine VIII (1025–8)

Romanos III Argyros (1028–34)

1031	Byzantium gains Edessa

Michael IV Paphlagonian (1034–41)

1038	Reconquest of Sicily by George Maniakes begins
1040	Bulgarian revolt

Michael V Kalaphates (1041–2)

Zoe and Theodora (1042)

Constantine IX Monomachos (1042–55)

1043	Russian attack on Constantinople
1043–4	Rebellion of Maniakes fails
1044–5	Annexation of Kingdom of Ani
1054	Schism with papacy

Theodora (1055–6)

Michael VI Stratiotikos (1056–7)

Isaac I Komnenos (1057–9)

1058	Patriarch Michael Keroularios deposed

Constantine X Doukas (1059–67)

1061–91	Norman conquest of Sicily
1064	Seljuk Turks conquer Greater Armenia

Romanos IV Diogenes (1067–71)

1071   Bari falls to Normans; Byzantine defeat at Manzikert

Michael VII Parapinakes/Doukas (1071–8)

1071–81   Seljuk Turks occupy Anatolian highlands and Jerusalem

Nikephoros III Botaniates (1078–81)

1078   Civil war with Nikephoros Bryennios and others

Alexios I Komnenos (1081–1118)

1082   Normans take north-west Greece; grant of trading concessions to Venice
1091   Defeat of Pechenegs
1097   Passage of First Crusade
1099   Franks establish the kingdom of Jerusalem
1108   Alexios defeats Bohemond

John II Komnenos (1118–43)

1122–6   Byzantium at war with Venice
1127   War with Hungary
1137   John annexes Antioch

Manuel I Komnenos (1143–80)

1147–9   Second Crusade
1152–4   Byzantium at war with Hungary
1159   Manuel enters Antioch
1171   Venetians at Constantinople arrested
1176   Manuel defeated by Turks at Myriokephalon
1180   Foundation of Serbian monarchy by Stephen Nemanja

Alexios II Komnenos (1180–3)

1182   Massacre of Latins in Constantinople

Andronikos I Komnenos (1183–5)

1184   Isaac Komnenos makes himself ruler of Cyprus
1185   Thessalonica captured by Normans

Isaac II Angelos (1185–95)

1186   Bulgaria becomes independent
1187   Saladin captures Jerusalem
1189–92   Third Crusade
1191   Richard I of England occupies Cyprus

Alexios III Angelos (1195–1203)

1201–4   Fourth Crusade

Isaac II Angelos again (1203–4)

Alexios IV co-emperor
1204   Alexios Komnenos founds Kingdom of Trebizond

Alexios V Doukas Mourtzouphlos (1204)

1204   Constantinople falls to Crusaders

LATIN EMPERORS OF CONSTANTINOPLE

Baldwin of Flanders (1204–5)

Henry of Flanders (1206–16)

Peter of Courtenay (1217)

Yolande (1217–19)

Robert II of Courtenay (1221–8)

Baldwin II (1228–61)
John of Brienne, regent (1229–37)

GREEK EMPERORS OF NICAEA

Theodore I Laskaris (1208–21)

1219   Creation of separate Serbian church; Theodore makes peace with Venetians

John III Doukas Vatatzes (1221–54)

1222   Mongols appear in Europe
1235   Patriarch Germanos II makes head of Bulgarian Church a patriarch
1240   Mongols destroy Kiev
1246   John III takes Thessalonica

Theodore II Laskaris (1254–8)

1254   Mamluk Turkish Sultans established in Egypt
1258   Mongols destroy Baghdad

John IV Doukas (1258–61)

Michael VIII Palaiologos (1259–61)

1259   Battle of Pelagonia
1261   End of Latin Empire at Constantinople

Select Bibliography

⟨⟨⟩

INTRODUCTION

Reference

A. P. Kazhdan (ed.), *The Oxford Dictionary of Byzantium*, 3 vols. (New York and Oxford, 1991).

General Histories

G. Ostrogorsky, *History of the Byzantine State*, tr. J. Hussey (Oxford, 1968).
W. Treadgold, *A History of the Byzantine State and Society* (Stanford, 1997).
The nearest to an economic history is M. Hendy, *Studies in the Byzantine Monetary Economy* (Cambridge, 1985).

Ethnic Groups

P. Charanis, *Studies in the Demography of the Byzantine Empire* (London, 1972).

Civilization

N. H. Baynes and H. St. L. B. Moss (eds.), *Byzantium. An Introduction to East Roman Civilization* (Oxford, 1948).
A. Guillou, *La Civilisation byzantine* (Paris, 1974).
C. Mango, *Byzantium: The Empire of New Rome* (London, 1980).

Ideology

H. Ahrweiler, *L' Idéologie politique de l'Empire byzantin* (Paris, 1975).
G. Dagron, *Empereur et prêtre* (Paris, 1996).
F. Dvornik, *Early Christian and Byzantine Political Philosophy*, 2 vols. (Washington, DC, 1966).

Historiography

There is as yet no monograph on this subject. The relevant facts may be extracted from Gy. Moravcsik, *Byzantinoturcica*, 2nd edn., i (Berlin, 1958) and H. Hunger, *Die hochsprachliche profane Literatur der Byzantiner*, i (Munich, 1978).

CHAPTER I

G. Bowersock, *Julian the Apostate* (London, 1978).
P. R. L. Brown, *The World of Late Antiquity* (London, 1971).
A. Cameron, *The Later Roman Empire* (London, 1993).
—— and P. Garnsey (eds.), *The Cambridge Ancient History*, xiii; *The Late Empire, AD 337–425* (Cambridge, 1998).
—— B. Ward-Perkins, and M. Whitby (eds.), *The Cambridge Ancient History*, xiv: *Late Antiquity: Empire and Successors, AD 425–600* (Cambridge, 2000).
R. Collins, *Early Medieval Europe* (London, 1991).
J. A. S. Evans, *The Age of Justinian: The Circumstances of Imperial Power* (London, 1996).

A. H. M. Jones, *Constantine and the Conversion of Europe* (London, 1948).
—— *The Later Roman Empire*, 3 vols. (Oxford, 1964).
P. Magdalino (ed.), *New Constantines* (Aldershot, 1994).
M. Whittow, *The Making of Orthodox Byzantium* (London, 1996).

CHAPTER 2

J. Balty, *Guide d'Apamée* (Brussels, 1981).
D. Claude, *Die byzantinische Stadt im 6. Jahrhundert* (Munich, 1969).
A.-J. Festugière (ed. and tr.), *La Vie de Théodore de Sykéôn*, 2 vols. (Brussels, 1970).
—— and L. Rydén, *Vie de Syméon le fou et Vie de Jean de Chypre* (Paris, 1974).
C. Foss, *Byzantine and Turkish Sardis* (Cambridge, Mass, 1976).
—— *Ephesus after Antiquity* (Cambridge, 1979).
—— *Cities, Fortresses and Villages of Byzantine Asia Minor* (Aldershot, 1996).
A. H. M. Jones, *Cities of the Eastern Roman Empire*, 2nd edn. (Oxford, 1971).
J. H. W. G. Liebeschuetz, *The Decline and Fall of the Roman City* (Oxford, 2001).
C. Roueché, *Aphrodisias in Late Antiquity* (London, 1989).
I. and N. Ševčenko, *The Life of Nicholas of Sion* (Brookline, Mass, 1984).
J. Shereshevski, *Byzantine Urban Settlements in the Negev Desert* (Beer-Sheva, 1991).
G. Tate, *Les Campagnes de la Syrie du nord* (Paris, 1992).
G. Tchalenko, *Villages antiques de la Syrie du nord,* 3 vols. (Paris, 1953–8).

CHAPTER 3

P. R. L. Brown, *Society and the Holy in Late Antiquity* (London, 1982).
D. J. Chitty, *The Desert a City* (Oxford, 1966).
J. Howard-Johnston and P. Hayward (eds.), *The Cult of Saints in Late Antiquity and the Early Middle Ages* (Oxford, 1999).
G. A. Kennedy, *Greek Rhetoric under Christian Emperors* (Princeton, 1983).
R. Lane Fox, *Pagans and Christians* (London, 1986).
J. H. W. G. Liebeschuetz, *Continuity and Change in Roman Religion* (Oxford, 1979).
R. MacMullen, *Christianizing the Roman Empire* (New Haven, 1984).
H.-I. Marrou, *Histoire de l'éducation dans l'antiquité*, 6th edn. (Paris, 1965).
A. Momigliano (ed.), *The Conflict between Paganism and Christianity in the Fourth Century* (Oxford, 1963).
A. D. Nock, 'Early Gentile Christianity', in Z. Stewart (ed.), *Essays on Religion and the Ancient World*, i (Oxford, 1972), 49–133.
N. G. Wilson (ed.), *Saint Basil on Greek Literature* (London, 1975).

CHAPTER 4

M. Cook, *Muhammad* (Oxford, 1983).
—— and P. Crone, *Hagarism: The Making of the Islamic World* (Cambridge, 1977).
P. Crone, *Meccan Trade and the Rise of Islam* (Oxford, 1987).
A. Ducellier, *Le Miroir de l'Islam: Musulmans et chrétiens d'Orient au Moyen Âge, VIIe–XIe siècles*, 2nd edn. (Paris, 1996).
G. Hawting, *The First Dynasty of Islam: The Umayyad Caliphate, AD 661–750* (London, 1986).
R. Hoyland, *Arabia and the Arabs from the Bronze Age to the Coming of Islam* (London, 2001).
Ibn Ishaq, *Sîrat al-nabî/ The Life of Muhammad*, tr. A. Guillaume (Oxford, 1955).
E. M. Jeffreys, 'The Image of the Arabs in Byzantine Literature', *The 17th International Byzantine Congress* (New Rochelle, 1986), 305–21.
F. E. Peters, 'The Quest for the Historical Muhammad', *International Journal of Middle East Studies* 23 (1991), 291–315.
A. Rippin, *Muslims, their Religious Beliefs and Practices,* i: *The Formative Period* (London, 1990).

I. Shahîd, *Byzantium and the Arabs in the Sixth Century* (Washington, DC, 1995).
For reference see *Encyclopaedia of Islam*, ed. H. A. R. Gibb et al. (Leiden, 1960–2001).

CHAPTER 5

J. Fine, *The Early Medieval Balkans* (Ann Arbor, 1983).
J. Haldon, *Byzantium in the Seventh Century* (Cambridge, 1990).
C. Head, *Justinian II of Byzantium* (Madison, Wis., 1972).
W. Kaegi, *Byzantine Military Unrest, 471–843: An Interpretation* (Amsterdam, 1981).
R.-J. Lilie, *Die byzantinische Reaktion auf die Ausbreitung der Araber* (Munich, 1976).
P. Speck, *Artabasdos* (Bonn, 1981).
A. Stratos, *Byzantium in the Seventh Century*, 5 vols. (Amsterdam, 1968–80).

Social Structures

W. Brandes, *Die Städte Kleinasiens im 7. und 8. Jahrhundert* (Berlin, 1989).
M. Kaplan, *Les Hommes et la terre à Byzance du VIe au XIe siècle* (Paris, 1992).
A. Kazhdan and A. Cutler, 'Continuity and Discontinuity in Byzantine History', *Byzantion* 52 (1982), 429–78.
P. Lemerle, *The Agrarian History of Byzantium* (Galway, 1979).
W. Treadgold, 'The Break in Byzantium and the Gap in Byzantine Studies', *Byzantinische Forschungen* 15 (1990), 289–316.
—— *Byzantium and its Army, 284–1081* (Stanford, 1995).

CHAPTER 6

P. J. Alexander, *The Patriarch Nicephorus of Constantinople* (Oxford, 1958).
M.-F. Auzépy, *La Vie d'Étienne le Jeune par Étienne le Diacre* (Birmingham, 1997).
—— *L'Hagiographie et l'iconoclasme byzantin* (Birmingham, 1999).
A. Bryer and J. Herrin (eds.), *Iconoclasm* (Birmingham, 1977).
Averil Cameron, 'Images of Authority: Elites and Icons in late Sixth-Century Byzantium', *Past and Present* 84 (1979), 3–35; repr. in *Continuity and Change in Sixth-Century Byzantium* (London, 1978), study XVIII.
G. Dagron, 'Le christianisme byzantin du VIIe au milieu du XIe siècle', in *Histoire du Christianisme*, iv (Paris, 1993), 9–348.
S. Gero, *Byzantine Iconoclasm during the Reign of Leo III with Particular Attention to the Oriental Sources* (Louvain, 1973).
—— *Byzantine Iconoclasm during the Reign of Constantine V with Particular Attention to the Oriental Sources* (Louvain, 1977).
P. Karlin-Hayter, 'A Byzantine Politician Monk: St. Theodore Stoudite', *Jahrb. d. Österr. Byzantinistik* 44 (1994), 217–32.
Nikephoros (Patriarch), *Discours contre les Iconoclastes*, tr. M.-J. Mondzain-Baudinet (Paris, 1989).
—— *Short History*, ed. and tr. C. Mango (Washington, DC, 1990).
Theophanes Confessor, *Chronicle*, tr. C. Mango and R. Scott (Oxford, 1997).

CHAPTER 7

M. Angold, *The Byzantine Empire, 1025–1204: A Political History*, 2nd edn. (London, 1997).
J.-C. Cheynet, *Pouvoir et contestations à Byzance, 963–1210* (Paris, 1990).
J. F. Haldon, *Warfare, State and Society in the Byzantine World, 565–1204* (London, 1999).
A. Harvey, *Economic Expansion in the Byzantine Empire, 900–1200* (Cambridge, 1989).
B. Hill, *Imperial Women in Byzantium, 1025–1204: Power, Patronage and Ideology* (London, 1999).
M. McCormick, *Origins of the European Economy: Communications and Commerce, AD 300–900* (Cambridge, 2001).

P. Magdalino, *The Empire of Manuel I Komnenos, 1143–1180* (Cambridge, 1993).

M. Mullett and D. Smythe (eds.), *Alexios I Komnenos* (Belfast, 1996).

N. Oikonomides, *Fiscalité et exemption à Byzance (IXe-XIe siècles)* (Athens, 1996).

P. Stephenson, *Byzantium's Balkan Frontier. A Political Sudy of the Northern Balkans, 900–1204* (Cambridge, 2000).

S. Tougher, *The Reign of Leo VI (886–912): Politics and People* (Leiden, 1997).

W. Treadgold, *The Byzantine Revival, 780–842* (Stanford, 1988).

M. Whittow, *The Making of Orthodox Byzantium, 600–1025* (London, 1996).

CHAPTER 8

Alan Cameron, *The Greek Anthology from Meleager to Planudes* (Oxford, 1993).

A. Cutler, *The Hand of the Master: Craftsmanship, Ivory and Society in Byzantium (9th–11th Centuries)* (Princeton, 1994).

R. Devreesse, *Introduction à l'étude des manuscrits grecs* (Paris, 1954).

R. J. H. Jenkins, 'The Classical Background of the Scriptores post Theophanem', *Dumbarton Oaks Papers* 8 (1954), 11–30; repr. in *Studies on Byzantine History of the 9th and 10th Centuries* (London, 1970), Study IV.

P. Lemerle, *Le Premier humanisme byzantin* (Paris, 1971).

R. McKitterick (ed.), *Carolingian Culture: Emulation and Innovation* (Cambridge, 1994).

K. Weitzmann, *Die byzantinische Buchmalerei des 9. und 10. Jahrhunderts* (Berlin, 1935).

—— *The Joshua Roll. A Work of the Macedonian Renaissance* (Princeton, 1948).

—— *Studies in Classical and Byzantine Manuscript Illumination*, ed. H. L. Kessler (Chicago and London, 1971).

N. G. Wilson, *Scholars of Byzantium*, 2nd edn. (London, 1996).

CHAPTER 9

A. Avenarius, *Die byzantinische Kultur und die Slawen. Zum Problem der Rezeption und Transformation (6. bis 12. Jahrhundert)* (Vienna and Munich, 2000).

F. Dvornik, *Byzantine Missions among the Slavs: Saints Constantine-Cyril and Methodius* (New Brunswick, NJ, 1970).

J. V. A. Fine, Jr., *The Early Medieval Balkans: A Critical Survey from the Late Sixth to the Late Twelfth Century* (Ann Arbor, 1983).

S. Franklin and J. Shepard, *The Emergence of Rus, 750–1200* (London, 1996).

C. Hannick, 'Les nouvelles chrétientés du monde byzantin: Russes, Bulgares et Serbes', in *Histoire du Christianisme*, iv (Paris, 1993), 909–39.

D. Obolensky, *The Byzantine Commonwealth: Eastern Europe, 500–1453* (London, 1971).

—— *Six Byzantine Portraits* (Oxford, 1988).

—— *Byzantium and the Slavs* (New York, 1994).

I. Ševčenko, 'Three Paradoxes of the Cyrillo-Methodian Mission', *Slavic Review* 23 (1964), 220–36; repr. in *Ideology, Letters and Culture in the Byzantine World* (London, 1982), Study IV.

J. Shepard, 'Slavs and Bulgars', in R. McKitterick (ed.), *The New Cambridge Medieval History*, ii (Cambridge, 1995), 228–48.

—— 'Bulgaria: The Other Balkan Empire', in T. Reuter (ed.), *The New Cambridge Medieval History*, iii (Cambridge, 1999), 567–85.

L. Simeonova, *Diplomacy of the Letter and the Cross: Photios, Bulgaria and the Papacy, 860's–880's* (Amsterdam, 1998).

P. Stephenson, *Byzantium's Balkan Frontier. A Political Study of the Northern Balkans, 900–1204* (Cambridge, 2000).

V. Vavřínek, 'The Introduction of the Slavonic Liturgy and the Byzantine Missionary Policy', in V. Vavřínek (ed.), *Beiträge zur byzantinischen Geschichte im 9.–11. Jahrhundert* (Prague,1978), 255–81.

—— and B. Zástěrová, 'Byzantium's Role in the Formation of Great Moravian Culture', *Byzantinoslavica* 43 (1982), 161–88.

A. P. Vlasto, *The Entry of the Slavs into Christendom: An Introduction to the Medieval History of the Slavs* (Cambridge, 1970).

CHAPTER 10

M. Angold, *A Byzantine Government in Exile: Government and Society under the Laskarids of Nicaea (1204–1261)* (Oxford, 1975).

F. Babinger, *Mehmed the Conqueror and his Time*, tr. R. Manheim (Princeton, 1978).

J. Barker, *Manuel II Palaeologus (1391–1425): A Study in Late Byzantine Statesmanship* (New Brunswick, NJ, 1969).

M. Bartusis, *The Late Byzantine Army: Arms and Society, 1204–1453* (Philadelphia, 1992).

C. Cahen, *The Formation of Turkey: The Seljukid Sultanate of Rūm, Eleventh to Fourteenth Century*, tr. and ed. P. M. Holt (Harlow, 2001).

G. Dennis, *The Reign of Manuel II Palaeologus in Thessalonica, 1382–1387*, Orientalia Christiana Analecta 159 (Rome, 1960).

D. Geanakoplos, *Emperor Michael Palaeologus and the West, 1258–1281: A Study in Byzantine–Latin Relations* (Cambridge, Mass, 1959).

J. Gill, *Byzantium and the Papacy, 1198–1400* (New Brunswick, NJ, 1979).

P. Grierson, *Catalogue of the Byzantine Coins in the Dumbarton Oaks Collection and in the Whittemore Collection*, v: *Michael VIII to Constantine XI, 1258–1453*, in 2 parts (Washington, DC, 1999).

M. Hendy, *Catalogue of the Byzantine Coins in the Dumbarton Oaks Collection and in the Whittemore Collection*: iv, *Alexius I to Michael VIII, 1081–1261*, in 2 parts (Washington, DC, 1999).

C. Imber, *The Ottoman Empire, 1300–1481* (Istanbul, 1990).

A. Laiou, *Constantinople and the Latins: The Foreign Policy of Andronikos II, 1282–1328* (Cambridge, Mass, 1972).

P. Lock, *The Franks in the Aegean, 1204–1500* (London and New York, 1995).

D. Nicol, *Byzantium and Venice: A Study in Diplomatic and Cultural Relations* (Cambridge, 1988).

—— *The Despotate of Epiros, 1267–1479* (Cambridge, 1984).

—— *The Immortal Emperor: The Life and Legend of Constantine Palaiologos, Last Emperor of the Romans* (Cambridge, 1992).

—— *The Last Centuries of Byzantium, 1261–1453*, 2nd edn. (Cambridge, 1993).

—— *The Reluctant Emperor: A Biography of John Cantacuzene, Byzantine Emperor and Monk, c.1295–1383* (Cambridge, 1996).

S. Reinert, 'The Palaiologoi, Yildirim Bayezid and Constantinople: June 1389–March 1391', in S. Langdon et al. (eds.), *To Ellenikon: Studies in Honor of Speros Vryonis Jr.*, i (New Rochelle, 1993), 289–365.

S. Runciman, *The Fall of Constantinople 1453* (Cambridge, 1965).

G. Soulis, *The Serbs and Byzantium during the Reigns of Tsar Stephen Dušan (1331–1355) and his Successors* (Washington, DC, 1984).

S. Vryonis, *The Decline of Hellenism in Asia Minor and the Process of Islamization from the Eleventh through the Fifteenth Century* (Berkeley and Los Angeles, 1971).

CHAPTER 11

B. L. Fonkitch, *Manuscrits grecs dans les collections européennes* (Moscow, 1999).

E. Fryde, *The Early Palaeologan Renaissance (1261–c.1360)* (Leiden, 2000).

J. Irigoin, *Tradition et critique des textes grecs* (Paris, 1997).

I. P. Medvedev, *Vizantijskij gumanism XIV–XV vv.*, 2nd edn. (St Petersburg, 1997).

S. Mergiali, *L'Enseignement et les lettrés pendant l'époque des Paléologues (1261–1453)* (Athens, 1996).

D. M. Nicol, *Church and Society in the Last Centuries of Byzantium* (Cambridge, 1993).

D. Pingree, 'Gregory Chioniades and Palaeologan Astronomy', *Dumbarton Oaks Papers* 18 (1964), 135–60.

L. D. Reynolds and N. G. Wilson, *Scribes and Scholars: A Guide to the Transmission of Greek and Latin Literature*, 3rd edn. (Oxford, 1991).

S. Runciman, *The Last Byzantine Renaissance* (Cambridge, 1970).

J. Scarborough (ed.), *Symposium on Byzantine Medicine* = *Dumbarton Oaks Papers* 38 (1984). Cf. esp. A. Hohlweg on John Aktouarios, pp. 121–34.

I. Ševčenko, 'Theodore Metochites, the Chora and the Intellectual Trends of his Time', in P. A. Underwood (ed.), *The Kariye Djami*, iv (Princeton, 1975), 19–91.

—— *Society and Intellectual Life in Late Byzantium* (London, 1981).

A. Tihon, *Études d'astronomie byzantine* (Aldershot, 1994).

—— 'L'astronomie byzantine à l'aube de la Renaissance', *Byzantion* 66 (1996), 244–80.

—— and R. Mercier, *Georges Gémiste Pléthon: Manuel d'astronomie* (Louvain-la-Neuve, 1998).

—— et al., *Une version byzantine du Traité sur l'astrolabe du Pseudo-Messahalla* (Louvain-la-Neuve, 2001).

W. Treadgold (ed.), *Renaissances before the Renaissance* (Stanford, 1984), esp. ch. 7 by I. Ševčenko.

N. G. Wilson, *Scholars of Byzantium*, 2nd edn. (London, 1996), chs. 12, 13.

C. M. Woodhouse, *George Gemistos Plethon: The Last of the Hellenes* (Oxford, 1986).

CHAPTER 12

Literature

H.-G. Beck, *Geschichte der byzantinischen Volksliteratur* (Munich, 1971).

D. Holton (ed.), *Literature and Society in Renaissance Crete* (Cambridge, 1991).

B. Knös, *Histoire de la littérature néogrecque: La période jusqu'en 1821* (Uppsala, 1962).

L. Politis, *A History of Modern Greek Literature* (Oxford, 1973).

Neograeca medii aevi: New work on the literature of the late Byzantine and early Modern Greek period is being presented in a series of international congresses which are published under this heading (Cologne, 1991; Venice, 1993; Vittoria, Spain, 1995; Cyprus, 1997; Hamburg, 1999; Oxford, 2000).

Art and Architecture

Ch. Bouras, 'The Impact of Frankish Architecture on Thirteenth-Century Byzantine Architecture', in A. Laiou and R. P. Mottahedeh (eds.), *The Crusades from the Perspective of Byzantium and the Muslim World* (Washington, DC, 2001), 247–62.

H. Buchthal, *Miniature Painting in the Latin Kingdom of Jerusalem* (Oxford, 1957).

M. Chatzidakis, *Études sur la peinture postbyzantine* (London, 1976).

O. Demus, *Byzantine Art and the West* (New York, 1970).

—— 'Die Entstehung des Paläologenstils in der Malerei', *Berichte zum XI. Internationalen Byzantinisten-Kongress, München 1958*, iv.2.

—— 'The Style of the Kariye Djami and its Place in the Development of Palaeologan Art', in P. A. Underwood (ed.), *The Kariye Djami*, iv (Princeton, 1975), 107–60.

J. Folda, 'Art in the Latin East, 1098–1291', in J. Riley-Smith (ed.), *The Oxford Illustrated History of the Crusades* (Oxford, 1995), 141–59.

—— *The Art of the Crusades in the Holy Land, 1098–1187* (Cambridge, 1995).

J. H. Stubblebine, 'Byzantine Influence in Thirteenth-Century Italian Panel Painting', *Dumbarton Oaks Papers* 20 (1966), 85–101.

K. Weitzmann, 'Icon Painting in the Crusader Kingdom', *Dumbarton Oaks Papers* 20 (1966), 49–83.

Illustration Sources

The editor and publishers wish to thank the following for their kind permission to reproduce the illustrations as listed below:

Key:
BN = Bibliothèque nationale de France
DO = Dumbarton Oaks, Washington, DC
l = left   *r* = right   *t* = top   *b* = bottom

All chapter openings show a detail from the Justinian mosaic, San Vitale, Ravenna, Archivi Alinari, Florence

ii-iii Girol Kara, Istanbul
4 Archivi Alinari, Florence
17 *l* Erich Lessing/AKG London
17 *r* BN
18 *l* and *r* DO
20 Archivi Alinari, Florence
21 BN Gr. 510 f 440r
25 New York University Excavations at Aphrodisias
26 ©British Museum
29 BN Gr. 510 f 374v
31 Cyril Mango
34 Cyril Mango
35 *l* The Master and Fellows of Trinity College Cambridge MS O.17.2
35 *r* Archaeological Museum Istanbul/Erich Lessing/AKG London
37 Archivi Alinari, Florence
39 Cyril Mango
43 Girol Kara, Istanbul
44 DO
45 Museo d'Arte Antica del Castello Sforzesco/Index, Florence
47 Cyril Mango
48 A. F. Kersting
49 ©British Museum
50 *t* Cyril Mango
50 *b* Cyril Mango
54 reproduced through the courtesy of the Michigan-Princeton-Alexandria Expedition to Mount Sinai
56 The Metropolitan Museum of Art: Gift of J. Pierpont Morgan, 1917 (17.190.396). All rights reserved, The Metropolitan Museum of Art
60 Archivi Alinari, Florence
61 *t* Bodleian Library, University of Oxford MS Canon Misc 378 f 5
61 *b* Egypt Exploration Society, P. Oxy XVI 1928
62 Ashmolean Museum, Oxford
63 after G.Schlumberger 'Un boullotirion byzantin ou appareil à fabriquer les sceaux à l'époque byzantine', *Comptes rendus de l'Académie des Inscriptions et Belles Lettres*, 1911
64 *tl* Cyril Mango
64 *bl* Judith McKenzie
64 *r* *DO Papers* 51, 1997 Clive Foss, 'Syria in Transition, AD 550-750: An Archaeological Approach'
65 Cyril Mango
66 *bl* The Master and Fellows of Trinity College Cambridge Ms O.17.2
66 *br* DO
67 *t* Cyril Mango
67 *b* Girol Kara, Istanbul
68 *t* Cyril Mango
68 *b* DO
69 Girol Kara, Istanbul
74 Cyril Mango
75 S. Gibson and J. McKenzie based on material by W. Kolataj
77 Clive Foss *Ephesus after Antiquity: A late antique, Byzantine and Turkish City* Cambridge University Press 1980

80   Cyril Mango
81   Cyril Mango
82   ©Archaeological Exploration of Sardis/ Harvard University: from J. Stephens Crawford *The Byzantine Shops at Sardis* 1990
84   *t* W Müller-Wiener 'Von der Polis zum Kastron' *Gymnasium* 93, 1986
84   *b* *DO Papers* 51, 1997 Clive Foss 'Syria in Transition, AD 550–750: An Archaeological Approach'
85   Cyril Mango
86   ©IRPA-KIK, Brussels
88   Archaeological Institute, Belgrade
90   *The Cambridge Ancient History* Vol XIV, Cambridge University Press 2000. After H. C. Butler, *Architecture, Section B. Northern Syria.* Publications of the Princeton Archaeological Expeditions to Syria in 1904–5 and 1909, Leiden 1920
91   Cyril Mango
92   Cyril Mango
93   Cyril Mango
94   *t* Richard C. Anderson
94   *b* Cyril Mango
97   Jean Charles Balty
98   The J. Paul Getty Museum, Malibu, California
100 Cyril Mango
104 Biblioteca Capitolare, Vercelli, Cod 165
107 Hirmer Fotoarchiv, Munich
108 *l* Scala, Florence
108 *r* Marlia Mango
109 Ashmolean Museum, Oxford
112 *t* M. Piccirillo, Studium Biblicum Franciscanum
112 *b* University of St Andrews
113 The State Hermitage Museum, St Petersburg
114 Museum für Spätantike und Byzantinische Kunst, Berlin/©BPK 2002, photo by Steinkopf
115 *t* John Wilkinson 'Christian Pilgrims in Jerusalem during the Byzantine Period' *Palestine Exploration Quarterly* 1976-7
115 *b* Jane Taylor/Sonia Halliday Photographs
116 *t* Balage Balogh/The Israel Museum, Jerusalem
116 *bl* ©Archivio Fotografico, Musei Vaticani
116 *br* Museo del Duomo, Monza
117 Cyril Mango
118 *tl* ©Photo RMN-Hervé Lewandowski/ Louvre
118 *tr* ©British Museum
118 *b* reproduced through the courtesy of the Michigan-Princeton-Alexandria Expedition to Mount Sinai
119 *l* Diözesanmuseum, Limburg, photo: Edizioni Fotografiche Alberto Luisa
119 *r* ©British Museum
122 *t* Richard C. Anderson
122 *b* Cyril Mango
123 Studium Biblicum Franciscanum Archive
124 Cyril Mango
125 Princeton Theological Seminary/DO
127 *t* Cyril Mango
127 *b* Ashmolean Museum, Oxford
132 *t* André Guillou
132 *b* Cyril Mango
133 ©British Museum
135 Cyril Mango
139 Cyril Mango
143 *b* W Müller-Wiener 'Von der Polis zum Kastron' *Gymnasium* 93, 1986
144 J.-M. Spieser *Thessalonique et ses monuments du IV au VI siècle, contribution a l'étude d'une ville paléochréti-enne* École Française d'Athènes 1984
145 Cyril Mango
146 Cyril Mango
147 *top two* Klaus Randsborg *The First Millennium AD in Europe and the Mediterranean* Cambridge University Press 1991
147 *bottom three* *Le Grand Atlas d'Archéologie* Encyclopaedia Universalis
151 *l* ©British Museum
151 *r* reproduced through the courtesy of the Michigan-Princeton-Alexandria Expedition to Mount Sinai
152 *l* Studio Kontos/Photostock
152 *r* reproduced through the courtesy of the Michigan-Princeton-Alexandria Expedition to Mount Sinai
154 Marlia Mango
155 Cyril Mango
156 Collection Chrétienne et Byzantine/École Pratique des Hautes Études,Paris
157 DO
158 Nicole Thierry
159 Archive of Theodore Schmidt, Library of the State Hermitage Museum, St Petersburg
160 Cyril Mango
161 ©British Museum
162 DO
163 *t* photoarchive of the 11th Ephorate of Byzantine Antiquities, Veroia
163 *b* ©The Petrie Museum of Egyptian Archaeology, University College, London/ Science Museum/ Science & Society Picture Library
164 *t* Cyril Mango
164 *c* J. A. Riley in *Excavations at Carthage 1977 conducted by the University of Michigan*, VI, ed. J. H. Humphrey, Ann Arbor 1981
164 *b* Dr Charalambos Bakirtzis, 9th Ephorate of Byzantine Antiquities, Salonica

290 DO
292 Bodleian Library, University of Oxford, MS
Barocci 87 f 33v
296 Cyril Mango
297 Byzantine & Christian Museum, Athens
299 Cyril Mango
300 Cyril Mango
301 A. F. Kersting
302 British Library, Egerton MS 1139 f 12v
303 Cecil L. Striker
304 *t* DO
304 *b* Archivi Alinari, Florence

In a few instances we have been unable to trace the copy-right holder prior to publication. If notified, the publishers will be pleased to amend the acknowledgements in any future edition.

Picture research by Sandra Assersohn and Index, Florence

Index